SPORT

LIBRARY OF WALES

SPORT

EDITED BY

GARETH WILLIAMS

PARTHIAN
LIBRARY OF WALES

Parthian
The Old Surgery
Napier Street
Cardigan SA43 1ED
www.parthianbooks.co.uk

The Library of Wales is a Welsh Assembly Government initiative which highlights and celebrates Wales' literary heritage in the English language.

The publisher acknowledges the financial support of the Welsh Books Council.

The Library of Wales publishing project is based at Trinity College, Carmarthen, SA31 3EP.
www.libraryofwales.org

Series Editor: Dai Smith

First published in 2007
© The Authors

Foreword © Rhodri Morgan
Afterword © Gareth Williams
All Rights Reserved

ISBN 1-902638-89-1
ISBN 978-1-902638-89-8

Cover design by Marc Jennings
Cover photo by Kiran Ridley
Typeset by logodædaly

Printed and bound by Gwasg Gomer, Llandysul, Wales

British Library Cataloguing in Publication Data

A cataloguing record for this book is available from the British Library.

FOREWORD

Are we Welsh obsessed with Sport? Are we too obsessed with sport? Well – dip into this book and you will find out. Our relationship with sport is different from most countries. It is an example of a very special relationship. So what is so special?

In all societies, sport started as practice for hunting and then as practice for war, or later as a substitute for war. In Wales, what is special is small country psychology – a special kind of need for heroes that could reassure us of our existence as a country. We might not have the conventional signs of life, or the institutional trappings of nationhood, but boy, could we produce runners and footballers and swimmers and fighters we could all look up to.

Provided we had those heroes, we could do without our own royal family, our own parliament, national cathedral or supreme court. Our heroes reassured us that we were not going to disappear as a nation, that we could not be discarded into the dustbin of history.

Our national anthem makes this strange transition from its words of praise for the loss of blood of slain heroes of the battlefield into encouragement of heroic effort on the sports field. It is sung, not to the marching rhythms of most national anthems but to a waltz tune composed in the backroom of a pub in Pontypridd by the local pub harpist. That's Wales for you in a nutshell.

What comes clearly through Gareth Williams' anthology is

not just Wales' hunger as a small nation for sporting heroes, but that modern Wales emerged more than two hundred years ago as a tough proletarian industrial society of a kind the world had never seen before. What kind of sports would take your mind off the back-breaking, dirty, dangerous work you did six days a week in coal mines and steelworks? How would the individual obsessions with whippets, pigeons, horses, billiards and darts compete with boxing and wrestling? How would they compete with the spectator sports like football, rugby and cricket? How much extra meaning did those team sports derive, if they involved wearing the red jersey as well? Read this book and find out.

As a September 1939 baby, I grew up in a world with no sport and no sporting heroes. By 1946, when I was seven, sport emerged from the long, dark tunnel of war into a Wales that was incredibly thirsty for sport.

Cardiff City would draw crowds of more than 40,000 in the Third Division South. Cardiff–Newport rugby matches would draw huge crowds as well. When Ronnie James of Pontardawe fought Ike Williams for his world lightweight title, it drew an all-time record crowd to Ninian Park in 1946.

But my most vivid memory of the psychology of the Welsh obsession with sport came from closer to home, to my upbringing in the village of Radyr. Every week in the summer, I would ride my bike down to a small-holding with greenhouses to pick up my mother's order of tomatoes, cucumbers, lettuce etc from the farmer, Steve Edwards. Every week he would regale me with fascinating hair-raising stories of his career as a professional sprinter in the Valleys in the 1930s and his occasional forays to Scotland for the

Powderhall Professional Sprinting Championships. It's hard to think back now to the era when amateur athletics followed the road that led to the Commonwealth Games and Olympics and the professional sprinters who accepted prize money were debarred from all that.

Steve was a class sprinter with a 9.8 seconds 100 yards time to his name but I will always remember as though it was yesterday, his huge and powerful frame looming over me and saying, with tears welling up in his eyes 'I wish I had remained an amateur because then I would have represented my country.' Understand that emotion, that sense of loss, that sense of an unfulfilled ambition and you can understand the Welsh obsession with sport, and why this collection of the best writing on sport in Wales can be your lifelong companion.

Rhodri Morgan

SPORT

CONTENTS

vii

Four Legs and Feathers

Cricket

Speed and Strength

Climbing

Tee Breaks

Golf

Final Whistle

WARMING UP

'Draig Glas'

The Welshman as Sportsman

The Welshman has no national sport or pastime, unless it is playing dominoes, or 'rings,' for beer, in the pot-house. Cricket is, comparatively speaking, unknown, not a single county having a team composed of Welshmen that could hold its own anywhere outside the Principality. Golf is entirely in the hands of English or Scottish people, and most other pastimes are non-existent. It is easy to understand this when one is reminded how the Nonconformist ministers and deacons are never tired of denouncing games of every description, how they crush any inclination on the part of the children to indulge even in such innocent recreations as 'roundabouts' and 'swing-boats' at village fêtes, and how they terrorise the adults with threats of excommunication if they dare to spend their leisure in amusement while the week-day chapel meeting is there for their entertainment and deliverance! Yet these pseudo-religionists, when once they get away to London, having changed their clothes for holiday wear, are the first to patronise – to an excess – the music-halls and other entertainments which at home they denounce as being dens of perdition and vice.

In football, Wales rather prides itself upon having the most successful combination in the Rugby Union. But if we grant that, let us never forget that Rugby football in Wales is

1

confined to a very small area, namely, that part of the South or other industrial centres which owes its success entirely to English or other foreign enterprise. Nine-tenths of the Welsh people outside those comparatively small areas have never seen Rugby football at all. In the North, and a great part of the West and Mid-Wales, it is unknown, and there Association only, of a distinctly feeble and third-rate class, is played. Therefore I say that Wales as a whole cannot lay claim to any distinction in Rugby football, whatever the few thickly populated and distinctly Anglicised portions of the country may do.

On the whole, the Welshman as a sportsman and drinker – for both pastimes are inextricably connected – cuts a very sorry figure. He is too mean-spirited to attack his game with fair weapons, and, being so hopelessly devoid of humour, pluck, and enterprise, and so wrapped up with self-conceit, he is incapable of understanding – much less appreciating – any kind of reasonable recreation. For all-round bodily exercise he has no appreciation, and will never indulge in it unless obliged to; but he is never tired of exercising his lungs, for he sings his lugubrious chants on all and every occasion, inflicting upon his hearers, uninvited, the most meaningless and unrestrained vocal efforts that ever ear of man suffered. So utterly wanting is he in discretion in matters of this sort, and so inflated with his own opinion of himself, that he never stops to consider whether you appreciate his company when thrust upon you in that way. It may be, for example, that you are staying at a sporting inn and would like to smoke a pipe with the natives of the district, from whom – so you imagine – some useful and interesting hints in matters pertaining to woodcraft may be learned. But nothing but disappointment awaits such a move on your part. In the first place, the Taffies assembled will be silent. Full of a cunning suspicion as to who you are, what you want, and whether you understand their language, they cast shy, uneasy glances at you. And not until they have absorbed all you have said to the landlord, not until you have proved your good faith, so to speak, by supplying them generously with beer, will they relax and become communicative. But alas! just when you think that some entertaining topics relating to sport, or to the wild life of the neighbourhood, are about to be discussed, someone begins to sing, when all hope for further peace or conversation is at an end. But that is not the worst of it, for, unless your discretion suggests an immediate retirement to your own room, the beer-soaked singer may approach too near for comfort, and, in that familiar manner of his, bellow his blatant rhymes direct into your very face. I add this as a warning, so that any fellow-sportsman who happens to visit Wales will not be unwise enough to give Taffy credit for ordinary decency in behaviour, for he does not possess it. He is either uncomfortably suspicious in your presence, or intimate beyond the bounds of reason. It is safer to keep him at arm's length. I have never yet met, neither have I heard of, any one who, as a sportsman in Wales, has had a good word to say for the Taffies. The very incarnation of deceitfulness, they make any hope of ensuring one's sporting prospects impossible. They have been taught from their youth up, for so many generations that it has become engrafted with their blood, that poaching is no sin. The preacher, both in the chapel pulpit and in his capacity as political agent, drives it home to his hearers that the landowners and game preservers who 'prey upon the poor' should be robbed without fear. But the fact that those few Welshmen who, inspired by English precept, have fought against the crushing tyranny of the chapel and shaken off the shackles of religious bigotry and their own self-importance, have proved themselves to be capable of displaying the true spirit of sport would appear to indicate that Taffy, in this respect, is not altogether beyond hope. But unless he makes a more strenuous effort than he has ever yet dreamed of to throttle that viper, whose coils have strangled his liberty and all opportunities of advancement – even in the comparatively obscure realm of sport – for so long, his chances of proving his prowess in the field are indeed remote.

from *The Perfidious Welshman* (1910)

EARLY FOOTBALL

George Owen (1603)

Cnapan

I cannot overpass a game used in one part of this shire among the Welshmen both rare to hear, troublesome to describe, and painful to practise... This game is called cnapan and not unfitly, as shall be shown. The game is thought to be of great antiquity and is as followeth.

The ancient Britons being naturally a warlike nation did, no doubt for the exercise of their youth in time of peace and to avoid idleness, devise games of activity where each man might show his natural prowess and agility, as some for strength of the body by wrestling [and] lifting of heavy burdens, others for the arm as in casting the bar sledge, stone or hurling the bowl or running, and surely for the exercise of the part aforesaid this cnapan was prudently invented had the same continued without abuse thereof. For in it, besides the exercise of bodily strength, it is not without a resemblance of warlike providence, as shall be here after declared.

Plays would oftentimes be by making of match between two gentlemen, and that at such holiday or Sunday as pleased them to appoint the time and place, which most commonly fall out to be the greatest plays, for in these matches the gentlemen would divide the parishes, hundreds or shires between them, and then would each labour to

5

bring the greatest number and would therein entreat all his friends and kinsmen in every parish to come and bring his parish wholly with him, by which means great number would most usually meet. And therefore against these matches there would also resort to the place divers victuallers with meat, drink and wine of all sorts, also merchants, mercers and pedlars would provide stalls and booths to show and utter their wares. And for these causes, some to play, some to eat and drink, some to buy, and some to sell, others to see and others to be seen (you know what kind I mean) great multitudes of people would resort besides the players. They contend not for any wager or valuable thing, but for glory and renown – first for the fame of their country in general, next every particular to win praise for his activity and prowess, which two considerations ardently inflameth the minds of the youthful people to strive to the death for glory and fame, which they esteem dearer unto them than worldly wealth.

The companies, being come together about one or two of the clock after noon, beginneth the play in this sort. After a cry made, both parties draw together into some plain, all stripped bare saving a light pair of breeches – bare headed, bare bodied, bare legs, and feet, their clothing being laid together in great heaps under the charge of certain keepers appointed for the purpose, for if he leave but his shirt on his back in the fury of the game it is most commonly torn to pieces. And I have also seen some long-locked gallants trimmed at this game, not by polling but by pulling their hair and beards... This kind of trimming they all do bestow freely without asking anything for their pains.

The foot company thus meeting, there is a round ball prepared of a reasonable quantity so as a man may hold it in his hand and no more. This ball is of some massy wood as box, yew, crab or holly tree, and should be boiled in tallow for to make it slippery and hard to be held. This ball is called cnapan and is by one of the company hurled bolt upright into the air, and at the fall he that catcheth it hurleth it towards the country he playeth for. For goal or appointed place there is none, neither needeth any, for the play is not given over until the cnapan be so far carried that there is no hope to return it back that night, for the carrying of it a mile or two miles from the first place is no losing of the honour so be it still followed by the company and, the play still maintained, it is oftentimes seen the chase to follow two miles or more in the heat of course both by the horse and foot.

The cnapan being once cast forth you shall see the same tossed backward and forward by hurling throws in strange sort, for in three or four throws you shall see the whole body of the game removed half a mile and more, and in this sort it is a strange sight to see a thousand or fifteen hundred naked men to concur together in a cluster in following the cnapan as the same is hurled backwards and forwards.

If the cnapan happen to come to the hands of a lusty hurler he throweth the same in a wonderful sort towards his country, further than any man would judge the strength of the arm were able. If it happen to the hands of a good footman he presently singleth himself and runneth and breaketh out of the body of the game into some plain ground in the swiftest sort he can which, being perceived, all the company followeth, where the good footmanship of all the company is plainly discerned, being a comfortable sight to see five or six hundred good footmen to follow in chase a mile or two as greyhounds after a hare, where shall see some gain in running upon his precedents, some forced to come behind those that were once foremost, which greatly delighteth the beholders and forceth them to follow likewise to see the pleasure of the chase. And thus the one seeketh to win honour by his footmanship until he be overtaken by a better runner or encountered by one of the scouts which will not fail to meet with him, and when he seeth himself near surprised or that his breath or legs fail him, he hurleth the ball forward towards his country, with a great violence, and perchance it lighteth to some of his fellows, who carry the same as far again which, notwith-standing, is not given over as long as the main body is anything near at hand: and when the ball happeneth to one of the contrary party it cometh back again as fast.

It is strange to behold with what eagerness this play is followed, for in the fury of the chase they respect neither hedge, ditch, pale or wall, hill, dale, bushes, river or rock or any other passable impediment, but all seemeth plain unto them wherein also they show such agility in running, such activity in leaping, such strength and skilful deliverance in hurling, such boldness in assaulting, such stoutness in resisting, such policy in inventing, such skill in preventing, as taking them out of their game they are not able to perform or invent half the prowess or devices shown in the same, a thing much noted of men of judgement...

You shall see gamesters return home from this play with broken heads, black faces, bruised bodies and lame legs, yet laughing and merrily jesting at their harms, telling their adversaries how he broke his head, to another that he struck him on the face and how he repaid the same to him again, and all this in good mirth, without grudge or hatred. And if any be in arrearages to the other they store it up till the next play and in the meantime will continue loving friends.

This play of cnapan seemeth to be an ancient exercise described to us Welshmen from our first progenitors the Trojans...

from *The Description of Penbrokeshire* (1603)

Anon.

Football in the Olden Time

On making enquiry of aged people in two or three Cardiganshire towns, I have failed to obtain evidence respecting the playing of football on Shrove Tuesday... All agreed in stating that the great football contest occurred on Dydd Nadolig – Christmas Day. Football, it appears, was football in those days; and as I put the question to men and women over whose heads eighty summers had passed, it seemed to have a magical effect on them. 'Remember playing football?' and they, with bright faces and unusual sprightliness of voice 'Remember playing football on Christmas Day? Well, aye, to be sure; and I've kicked the ball hundreds of times.' The question evidently recalled to them 'the good old times when George the Fourth was King,' times of simple fare and simple manners, when no railways invaded the solitude of their villages, when almost all the villagers were related to one another by blood or marriage, and when the school-master and the newspaper were as unknown as differences of opinion in politics or even in religion. But though dozens could be found who had 'kicked the ball on Dydd Nadolig' in their youth, and to whom the remembrance was a pleasure, few could describe the modus operandi of the game or give any incidents.

In South Cardiganshire it seems that about eighty years ago the population, rich, and poor, male and female, of opposing parishes, turned out on Christmas Day and indulged in the game of football with such vigour that it became little short of a serious fight. The parishioners of Cellan and Pencarreg were particularly bitter in their conflicts. Men threw off their coats and waistcoats and women their gowns, and sometimes their petticoats; and one of my informants said that at a football match on Christmas Day, in the parish of Llandyssul, a damsel whose attire was as scanty as the 'cutty sark,' seen by Tam O'Shanter in Alloway Kirk, secured victory for her parish by a magnificent kick that sent the ball across the river Teify, which at Llandyssul has no mean width.

At Llanwenog, an extensive parish below Lampeter, the inhabitants for football purposes were divided into the Bros and the Blaenaus. My informant, a man over eighty, now an inmate of Lampeter Workhouse, gives the following particulars:– In North Wales the ball is called the Bêl Droed, and was made with a bladder covered with the Cŵd

Tarw. In South Wales it is called Bêl Ddu, and was usually made by the shoemaker of the parish, who appeared on the ground on Christmas Day with the ball under his arm, and, said my informant, he took good care not to give it up until he got his money for making it. The Bros, it should be stated, occupied, as their name signifies, the high ground of the parish. They were nick-named 'Paddy Bros,' from a tradition that they were descendants from Irish people who settled on the hills in days long gone by. The Blaenaus occupied the lowlands, and, it may be presumed, were pure-bred Brythons. The more devout of the Bros and Blaenaus joined in the service at the parish church on Christmas morning. At any rate, the match did not begin until about mid-day, when the service was finished. Then the whole of the Bros and Blaenaus, rich and poor, male and female, assembled on the turnpike road which, divided the highlands from the lowlands. The ball, having been redeemed from the crydd [cobbler], it was thrown high in the air by a strong man, and when it fell Bros and Blaenaus scrambled for its possession, and a quarter of an hour frequently elapsed before the ball was got out from among the struggling heap of human beings. Then if the Bros, by hook or by crook, could succeed in taking the ball up the mountain to their hamlet of Rhyddlan they won the day while the Blaenaus were successful if they got the ball to their end of the parish at New Court. The whole parish was the field of operations, and sometimes it would be dark before either party scored a victory. In the meantime many kicks would he given and taken, so that on the following day some of the competitors would be unable to walk, and

11

sometimes a kick on the shins would lead the two men concerned to abandon the game until they had decided which was the better pugilist. On one occasion when the Bros were winning, a Blaenau attempted to rob them of their victory by stabbing the ball with a knife. There do not appear to have been any rules for the regulation of the game. 'The art of fencing,' said one of Macaulay's subjects, 'was to hit,' and the art of football playing in the olden time seems to have been to reach the goal. There seems, however, to have been some sort of understanding that the ball was not to be carried too long. My informant said he once carried it the width of two large fields pursued by his opponents, and then kicked it, as he thought he had carried it as far as he honourably could carry it without kicking. When once the goal was reached, the victory was celebrated by loud hurrahs and the firing of guns, and was not disturbed until the following Christmas Day. At the conclusion of the play, 'the quiet ones,' as the old man termed them, went home, but a large number went to the public house, where not a few made a night of it. This custom continued to be observed until about fifty years ago, when a venerable Nonconformist minister preached against it, and the people listened to him. Victory on Christmas Day, added the old man, was so highly esteemed by the whole countryside, that a Bro or a Blaenau would as soon lose a cow from the cow-house, as the football from his portion of the parish.

from *Bye-Gones*, 2nd March 1887

BANDO

Charles Redwood

The Bandy Match 1839

Bandy is the prime game here, and in the opinion of our rustics leads to the highest of all distinctions. Prodigious are the jealousy and heartburning which a rivalry in it produces between two parishes; and then, to decide their pretensions, they repair to the seashore sands, where twenty or thirty players engage on each side, and multitudes of spectators and partisans, too often mingle in the contest.

The famous parish of Lantwit had long tossed its head exceeding hoity-toitily among the neighbouring villages, and carried everything with a high hand. At all fairs and mabsants the Lantwit roisterers swaggered it proudly, as who should say, 'Who but they?' until at length another parish, that could ill brook all this hectoring, challenged them to a match at Bandy. To be sure, with what vapouring the Lantwit folks deigned to accept the challenge! They talked as though no parish was fit to contend with them, but all ought to submit in quiet to their huffing.

However, as the day of the contest approached, they set about in good earnest to prepare for it; and the players practised daily in the most spacious fields. Interest deepened, and talk swelled throughout the country, and all was suspense, until the day arrived.

13

All the Vale now flocked down to the seashore, looking and talking great things by the way, each for his party. It is surprising how fiercely some of the more violent bragged and flourished as they strode with huge strides before their companions. The women too kept a prodigious clapper-clawing.

When the goals had been set, and all necessary arrangements made, the concourse separated into two parties, out of which, the players presently issued.

On the side of the challengers came a dapper, thickset man, who stepped forward with a confident air, and was followed by a troop of fellows, who, now that they were stripped and on their mettle, the looks of all confessed to be 'exceeding proper young men.' The first on the other side was one who had been a wild youngster and a noted player, but having been lately converted at a Methodist Revival, had not been without some difficulty persuaded to take a part in this match. His eye was now bent to the ground, and his lips moved in silence, as he led a band by no means inferior to their competitors. A loud shout was raised by the partisans of each side, as the players came forward with distinguishing favours on their left arms, and flourishing their bandies with their right.

Long and doubtful was the contest, and various were the chances of the game. Many of the younger men soon exhausted their wind and strength; some were disabled by luckless falls, and at length the weight of the contest fell on the challenger and the Methodist. Great now became the exertions of these rivals in fame. The beetling cliffs were deafened with the shouts of their partisans. The Methodist

14

was the fleeter of foot, the challenger the more sturdy. The mob of partisans closed upon them, and the ball was driven into the throng. Loud were the shouts of the men and the yells of the women, as the contending players clove their way through. The fleet Methodist was foremost, but searched in vain for the ball; for the virago wife of the challenger straddled over and concealed it with her petticoat until her dapper spouse came panting up. But the Methodist's mother, an outrageous termagant, saw the fraud, and fell, with loud execrations, upon the sturdy wife. However, the ball was carried off by the challenger, pursued by his fleet opponent. Dire is the contest between them. The challenger strives to secure the game, the Methodist to rescue it. They are again straining to reach the ball – the fleet Methodist close after and striving to pass his opponent. And he does pass: but the challenger stretches and trips up his heel, and the impetuous Methodist plows the sand with a headlong fall, amid shouts that peel from one tall cliff to another far along the shore.

from *The Vale of Glamorgan* (1839)

Sally Roberts Jones

Song of the Margam Bando Boys

Before rugby there was bando – a sort of combined hockey and football. The best team in the whole of Wales came from Margam, and this is a true story.

Wil was the very best they had,
The fulcrum of their team;
A golden man – he jinked, he swerved,
His passing was a dream.

With him they won the league, the cup,
The crown – each new award
Fell to the magic of his touch,
He was their shield, their sword.

Until one day he chanced to hear
A passing preacher's word
And fell a prey to doctrines some
Would say were quite absurd.

'I can no longer join you, friends,'
He told them. They, aghast,
Could not believe he'd changed so much,
So cruelly, so fast!

'My mind is fixed on higher things,'
He added, and they wept
To think of all the glory lost,
The promises unkept.

They tempted him with beer and girls,
They even offered gold.
But nothing worked, each crafty plan
They tried just left him cold.

Till finally they took a shirt
In the colours of their team
And placed it where he'd surely see
Its rich, seductive gleam.

He saw; he trembled; stretched his hand
To touch the scarlet cloth –
Then stopped, in anguish, torn between
Love and high Heaven's wrath.

Love... lost. The fallen hero held
To his ungentle creed;
His team-mates mourned their championship,
Their day was done indeed.

And so his three-score years and ten
Passed by in holiness;
Till he'd forgotten that wild gift
He'd struggled to repress.

Until the summons came; he rose
To realms celestial –
To find, with some astonishment,
His team-mates, stick and ball.

And there God stood, and Peter too,
In a hopeful sort of way:
'You see,' said God, 'I've one regret –
I never saw you play.

'If you could just – I hardly like –
One game, that's all we ask...'
Wil looked around him, saw his friends,
Knew he'd accept the task.

'We've found a team for you to play,'
St. Peter said, 'the best,
With Henry Eight and Edward One
At Lucifer's request.'

And so if you should chance to hear
Thunder from skies of blue
Or catch a glimpse of red at dusk,
Well now, I'll tell you true,

It's not some scientific law
Behind that mighty noise,
But God and St. Peter cheering on
The Margam Bando Boys!

from *Roundyhouse* (1999)

SOCCER

Dannie Abse

The Game

Follow the crowds to where the turnstiles click.
The terraces fill. Hoompa, blares the brassy band.
Saturday afternoon has come to Ninian Park
and, beyond the goal posts, in the Canton Stand
between black spaces, a hundred matches spark.

Waiting, we recall records, legendary scores:
Fred Keenor, Hardy, in a royal blue shirt.
The very names, sad as the old songs, open doors
before our time where someone else was hurt.
Now, like an injured beast, the great crowd roars.

The coin is spun. Here all is simplified,
and we are partisan who cheer the Good,
hiss at passing Evil. Was Lucifer offside?
A wing falls down when cherubs howl for blood.
Demons have agents: the Referee is bribed.

The white ball smacked the crossbar. Satan rose
higher than the others in the smoked brown gloom
to sink on grass in a ballet dancer's pose.
Again it seems we hear a familiar tune
not quite identifiable. A distant whistle blows.

Memory of faded games, the discarded years;
talk of Aston Villa, Orient, and the Swans.
Half-time, the band played the same military airs
as when the Bluebirds once were champions.
Round touchlines the same cripples in their chairs.

Mephistopheles had his joke. The honest team
dribbles ineffectively, no one can be blamed.
Infernal backs tackle, inside forwards scheme,
and if they foul us need we be ashamed?
Heads up! Oh for a Ted Drake, a Dixie Dean.

'Saved' or else, discontents, we are transferred
long decades back, like Faust must pay that fee.
The night is early. Great phantoms in us stir
as coloured jerseys hover, move diagonally
on the damp turf, and our eidetic visions blur.

God sign our souls! Because the obscure staff
of Hell rule this world, jugular fans guessed
the result halfway through the second half,
and those who know the score just seem depressed.
Small boys swarm the field for an autograph.

Silent the stadium. The crowds have all filed out.
Only the pigeons beneath the roofs remain.
The clean programmes are trampled underfoot,
and natural the dark, appropriate the rain,
whilst, under lamp-posts, threatening newsboys shout.

from *Tenants of the House* (1957)

Geraint H. Jenkins

Leigh Richmond Roose

It is one of the commonplaces of sport that a goalkeeper is rather different from the rest of mankind and certainly from his fellow footballers. From the days of William ('Fatty') Foulke, the gargantuan Shropshire-born international custodian who used to get his retaliation in first by waddling naked into visiting dressing-rooms to intimidate opponents and referees, to Rene Higuita (El Loco), the eccentric Colombian keeper whose surges upfield and scorpion kicks passed into folklore, goalkeepers have taken pride in being deemed a breed apart. Arguably the most gifted superman of them all was Leigh Richmond Roose, the 'Prince of Goalkeepers' in Edwardian Wales, whose *curriculum vitae* was a thing of wonder. No other member of the Welsh Hall of Footballing Fame can claim to have sat at the feet of the father of modern science fiction H. G. Wells, won nineteen of twenty-four international caps playing alongside the incomparable 'Welsh Wizard' Billy Meredith, represented clubs as diverse as Stoke, Everton, Sunderland, Huddersfield, Aston Villa, Woolwich Arsenal and Celtic, entertained the music-hall star Marie Lloyd, and prompted the dry-as-dust Welsh historian Thomas Richards to refer to him in awe as 'this wondrous Hercules' ('Yr Ercwlff synfawr hwn').

Born on 27 November 1877, Roose was a native of Holt, near Wrexham. His Anglesey-born father, Richmond Leigh Roose, was a Presbyterian minister and the author of *The*

Five Senses of the Body (1875). He sent his son to Holt Academy, whose prospectus offered 'a sound English Education, together with Greek and Latin, or German and French'. Under its principal, James Oliver Jones, discipline at the academy left much to be desired, and when the young H. G. Wells was appointed master in 1887 the menacing attitude of some of the older pupils unnerved him. While refereeing a football match on a wet Saturday afternoon, Wells fell on the muddy field and was severely kicked in the back by Edward Roose, Leigh's brother, and spent several weeks incapacitated with a ruptured kidney. Wells left shortly afterwards, but it may well be that his provocative independence and obsession with the bizarre fruits of science left their mark on Leigh Richmond Roose and that this prompted him to read science when he arrived at the University College of Wales, Aberystwyth, in 1895.

Although the 'College by the Sea' was not, as the embittered Goronwy Rees liked to claim, 'a theocratic society, ruled by priests and elders', the Nonconformist way of life was a powerful influence on staff and students alike. When R. Williams Parry, later to become one of Wales's most celebrated poets, confessed to Principal T. Francis Roberts that he smoked cigarettes and played billiards, he was asked: 'What other sins have you, Mr Parry?' Most students worshipped regularly and the historian R. T. Jenkins recalled seeing Roose many times in his sober dark blue suit in the English Presbyterian chapel. However, since his father had failed to pass on the native language, Roose never darkened the meetings of the Celtic Society (Y Geltaidd), and wild horses would not have dragged him to the coy soirées and at-homes which figured so prominently in the social round of staff and students. He had the reputation of being a self-possessed, rather aloof loner. From time to time, however, he figured in tempestuous student debates, interjecting on one occasion 'at a speed of some 300 words per minute' in order to demolish the argument of a priggish Liberal, and, on another occasion, winning thunderous applause by vigorously opposing a motion that athletics was 'detrimental to the best interests of the nation'. In February 1899 he was persuaded to take part in a mock trial, 'The Ass and the Ass's Shadow: The Great Case of John Jones v. John Jones in the Shadow of the Ass'. Cast as a policeman, his sole contribution was to roar 'Silence in Court!', which he did with such panache and authority that many believed it was the highlight of the evening. Roose was also one of the few students who dared to twit the head porter, Sergeant Wakeling, a tragicomic Falstaffian figure who ruled the quad with a rod of iron and whose malapropisms provoked much private hilarity.

As a result, although 'Mond' Roose kept his distance from fellow students, he became an iconic figure. Women students adored him and flocked to sporting events in order to cheer on and flirt with their hero. Puerile rules and regulations designed to restrict the mingling of the sexes were ignored or circumvented at the Vicarage Fields where, summer and winter alike, Roose was the principal focus of attention. At cricket his superlative fielding more than compensated for his Tufnell-like batting (his average was

3.83 in 1898) and his bowling was brisk and lively. During the annual Sports' Day he basked in the adulation of his admirers, proving invincible at throwing a cricket ball and winning the shot putt, high jump and piggy-back events in May 1899. Only when other mortals fell below his high standards did he lose his composure. At a gymnastic display held in the examination hall, a dishevelled Roose failed to rally the Science team in a tug-of-war competition and was reported to have been 'uncertain whether to stand on his head or his feet'.

But it was as a brave, unorthodox, idiosyncratic and marvellously athletic goalkeeper that Roose gained his reputation as a genius. While playing for the College, he particularly savoured the bruising contests against the students of Bangor, and such was his prowess that Aberystwyth Town FC also captured his signature. Roose represented the 'Old Black and Green' on eighty-five occasions, and on 16 April 1900 he was carried shoulder-high from the field when Aberystwyth trounced the Druids 3–0 in the Welsh Cup Final. By the time of his departure from the College, the *Cambrian News* had exhausted its fund of superlatives in recounting the exploits of this extraordinary figure. Roose moved to London to train as a doctor at King's College Hospital, but although James A. H. Catton, who wrote under the pseudonym 'Tityrus', referred to Roose in the *Athletic News* as 'this eminent bacteri-ologist' he never qualified as a doctor and thus earned a living as an extremely expensive 'amateur' player for a host of illustrious clubs in the First Division of the Football

League. He made 144 League appearances for Stoke in 1901–4 and 1905–8, helped Everton to reach the runners-up position in the League and the semi-final of the FA Cup in 1904/5, and during four seasons at Roker Park helped Sunderland to finish in third place in the League on two occasions. When the *Daily Mail* invited nominations for a World XI to challenge another planet, Roose was the undisputed choice as goalkeeper. His League career ended with Woolwich Arsenal in 1911.

... Like wicketkeepers, goalkeepers are born rather than made, and Roose certainly possessed all the necessary physical attributes. Standing 6ft 1in. tall and weighing 13st 6lbs, he cut an impressive figure and could both physically and literally look down on most of his fellow players. Roose's jutting browline, small intense eyes, well-groomed moustache (at least in his student days) and wide, powerful shoulders oozed authority and defiance. His phenomenal reach and huge hands – Thomas Richards referred to his 'prehensile grip' – enabled him to make saves which lived long in the memory. Moreover, his sharp eyesight, startling reflexes, competitive instinct and reckless bravery made him an extraordinarily daunting opponent. Goalkeeping is a demanding position and Roose's flamboyance should not blind us to his athletic and technical prowess.

Yet throughout his career (and even unto death) there remained an air of surprise and mystery about Roose. A repertoire of well-rehearsed, though sometimes impromptu, eccentricities were an integral part of the Roose legend. The fact that he was a middle-class amateur in a largely professional game did not mean that he played purely for pleasure, for his 'amateurism' was a token of his social exclusivity as well as a passport to financial gain as a roving 'guest' player. He expected, indeed demanded, extravagant expenses and lavish hospitality for his services. Often he would awaken public interest by arriving at the ground in a horse and carriage, which was followed through the streets by entranced young supporters. On one occasion he hired a special locomotive to transport him from London to Stoke, and charged the costs of the journey to the club. A born self-publicist, Roose knew how to add thousands to the gate. When Wales were due to play Ireland in March 1909, he arrived at Liverpool for the journey to Belfast with his hand heavily bandaged. He claimed that although two fingers were broken he would be fit to play the following day. His two closest friends, Billy Meredith and Charlie Morris (both from Chirk), were too streetwise to be taken in and, peeping through the keyhole of Roose's room in their Belfast hotel, they saw the great man remove the bandage and wiggle his fingers without any sign of discomfort. News of Roose's 'disability' spread like wildfire and on the following day, before a huge crowd, the Welsh goalkeeper played a blinder and Wales won 3–2.

Like many (perhaps all) goalkeepers, Roose was highly superstitious. His attire was strikingly different: he wore white sweaters, twin-peak caps and padded knee-bandages. Although he carried white gloves onto the field, he seldom wore them, preferring to catch and fist the ball with his bare hands. Like Neville Southall, his dishevelled appearance at the beginning of a game gave the impression that he had just completed another. He preferred to play in unwashed shorts and during his season at Everton it was noticed more than once that his pants 'carried about them the marks of many a thrilling contest'. He insisted on wearing another shirt (some claim it was the old black and green shirt of Aberystwyth Town FC) under his international jersey and he never allowed charwomen to wash it.

Whereas most goalkeepers in the Edwardian era walked on to the field of play, Roose used to run briskly, acknowledging the applause before pacing the goalmouth like a restless tiger.

... Even though the heavy brown footballs used in Edwardian days virtually became medicine balls in wet conditions, Roose could kick and throw them prodigious distances. On dry days he sent thumping kicks the length of the field and punched the ball well beyond the half-way line. According to James Ashcroft, an intelligent goalkeeper with Woolwich Arsenal, nothing gave a goalkeeper greater satisfaction than fisting the ball long distances: 'It is more than a sensation. It is an ecstasy.' But one suspects that Roose derived even greater pleasure from plunging headlong among flying feet and bruising bodies. 'Rushing the goalkeeper', particularly from corners, and heavy shoulder-charges were part and parcel of the game. But aggressive forwards held no terror for Roose and when, for instance, a scrimmage developed when Stoke met Arsenal it was 'all Lombard Street to a halfpenny orange that the Reds would score', only for Roose to emerge from the ruck with the ball clasped to his chest. Roose deliberately intimidated opponents with his fists and during his spell at Aberystwyth liberal quantities of Robert Ellis's celebrated embrocation for sprains, stiffness and bruises were required by chastened forwards.

Roose's physical presence was a powerful psychological advantage for his teams. Like Peter Schmeichel, he oozed confidence, filling the goal with his mighty frame and 'psyching' opposing forwards. He exercised a strangely hypnotic influence over hesitant strikers, forcing them to scuff their shots or blast them wide of the goal. He enjoyed taunting experienced international forwards, some of whom felt the full force of his fist in goalmouth mêlées. On his day, he was an extraordinary shot-saver. In his first international he saved a point-blank drive from six yards by trapping the ball between his knees. Crowds marvelled at his spectacular leaps across goal and his mysterious ability to change his body posture in mid-air. If contemporary accounts are reliable, the save which Roose made while representing Aberystwyth against Builth in the Leominster Cup in April 1897 was at least the equal of that made by Gordon Banks against Pelé at Guadalajara in the 1970 World Cup. Some of his most breathtaking mid-air saves were from penalties. When Thomas Richards, the son of a Cardiganshire cottager who became Wales's foremost authority on seventeenth-century Puritanism and Dissent, was persuaded by a fellow student to attend a memorable encounter between Aberystwyth Town and Glossop North End, a professional team from the Midland League, he was so intoxicated by Roose's performance that, many decades later, he was able to describe the match as if it had occurred the previous day.

In a Cardus-like portrait, written in Welsh and entitled 'Gŵr o Athrylith' ('Man of Genius'), Richards depicted with subtle scriptural nuances an astonishing penalty save by Roose:

> ...one of the full backs committed an unforgivable foul in the penalty box; the harsh blast of the referee's whistle, his finger pointing to one of the most calamitous places in the purgatory of this life – the penalty spot. The heavy odour of death hung over this fateful spot: did you not hear a crowd of thousands suddenly become dumb mutes, did you not see the players standing in a half circle as if they were at the graveside... Everyone holding his breath. I have always believed that Roose grew to his full height as a man in the purgatorial crisis of a penalty, drying off the clay around his feet, washing away the dross which entered his character with the gold... Arthur's sword against the bare fist. Then came the signal; the ball travelled like a bolt from the foot of the penalty-taking forward, and in the blink of an eyelid, revolution, a thump, and the ball landed in the heather and gorse of the Buarth.

from *For Club and Country* (2000)

Peter Corrigan

Billy Meredith

Whether L. R. Roose would have continued playing had he survived the war is hard to say. Possibly Meredith's example would have encouraged him for Billy's career stretched well into the 1920s. He played his last game for Wales in March 1920, against England in London, when he was 46 years old and he was but a few months short of his 50th birthday when he played for Manchester City in an F.A. Cup replay at Cardiff in 1924.

His career was prodigious which ever way it is looked at. Some estimate he played as many as 2,000 games. More likely was the figure that he claimed of 1,568 of which 857 were League matches played in the 31 years between making his League debut in 1894 and when he eventually retired in 1925. Before he died in 1958 at the age of 83, Meredith was asked what he thought of Stanley Matthews, that other evergreen right winger whose brilliance challenged Meredith's. The reply was most complimentary until the famous Welshman concluded: 'But I do wish Stan could have scored a few more goals.'

And there was the great difference. Meredith scored 470 goals in his career and many were match-winners. But his record was unassailable from so many directions. He became the oldest player to play in the International Championship in that 1920 game against England which was his 48th appearance in the Championship.

Ivor Allchurch and Cliff Jones have amassed higher totals

for Wales, while Billy Wright, Bobby Charlton and Bobby Moore have all passed the 100 mark for England – but no-one throughout the four home countries has played in as many Championship matches as Meredith. There were no official fixtures against foreign opposition in his day so the Championship was the only source of caps and even then he missed many games for Wales because of club duty.

He played for both Manchester clubs, he was with United between 1906 and 1915, and played for both in a F.A. Cup Final. As well as those two medals, he had two League Championship medals, two Second Division Championship medals and two Welsh Cup medals.

Later, when he kept a pub in Manchester and his customers drank thirstily at his stories about the game, he could be persuaded to lay out his medals and caps along the counter and, as he pointed out, the caps were all the same size – 6 and 7/8ths.

But there was frequent controversy over the number of caps Billy Meredith gained. Even he thought he had won over 50, but he was entitled to that confusion because the Football Association of Wales made a presentation to him in February 1920 in recognition of his 50th cap and he played for Wales once more after that.

The F. A.W., however, were misled. Although Meredith was selected to play against Ireland in 1899 his club refused to release him at the last minute and somehow his name stayed in the records as having played. His official total was 48, made up of 20 matches against England, 12 against Scotland and 16 against Ireland, and he also played in two 'victory' internationals against England in 1918 which are not recognised as official games.

By 1900 he was established both in the Football League and internationally as a winger of exceptional class. He had made his Welsh debut at the age of 20 in Ireland in 1895 where, despite being seasick on the voyage to Belfast, he played well in a 2–2 draw. On the following Monday they had to play England at West Kensington where, he said, 'I saw more top hats than I had ever seen in my life.'

England had an all-amateur team out that day and Billy met the famous C. B. Fry and W. J. Oakley, the latter giving him a hard time of it. 'He made me gallop that day. Once he kept shoulder to shoulder with me for half the pitch which was 150 yards long.'

The following year Meredith was included in the Welsh team which met England in the first soccer international ever played in Cardiff, and which as a missionary project was a disaster for England won 9-1, the legendary Steve Bloomer scoring five of the goals.

The South Walians who looked askance upon that performance probably didn't even notice the young right winger because Billy Meredith was not the sort of player to excite interest at first glance. His sparse, erect body was perched on legs so spindly they did not look capable of supporting a piano stool. His face was drawn and unremarkable apart from the eyes that were direct and challenging. Overall the impression he gave to the stranger was more likely to attract sympathy than admiration.

But once he started playing the transformation must have been staggering. He didn't have great speed but he had that vital quickness over the first few yards and those legs provided so much balance and manoeuvrability that he could take the ball past you in a telephone kiosk. Once in flight and free of immediate challenge he had hair splitting accuracy, whether placing a cross with great precision or letting fly with a shot that had surprise as its first ally and force as its second.

And all the time his teeth were champing on a tooth pick, deftly transferring it from one side of his mouth to the other as his feet and brain worked their miracles. Some thought the toothpick served some mystical, calming purpose but the reason was more basic.

When he worked down the mines he chewed tobacco constantly and carried on the habit when he went to play for Manchester City. But his dribbling must have been fairly fluent all round for soon the laundry were complaining at the state of his jersey front and he was kindly asked would he chew something else. He chose a toothpick.

By the time the Welsh F.A. bucked up enough courage to play in Cardiff again, which was in March 1900, Meredith was far better known. 'The finest right winger living' said the *Western Mail* in passing.

Wales borrowed Cardiff Arms Park for the occasion, which meant they had to play on a Monday because Cardiff R.F.C. were playing Newport there on the Saturday and even though the rugby hero of the day Gwyn Nicholls was not playing because of injury, there was a crowd of 10,000 for the game.

The F.A.W. were expecting 20,000 for the soccer international with excursions coming from all over the country. The *South Wales Echo* reported, somewhat haughtily, 'the kick-off has been arranged for 4 p.m. to allow the artisan classes to see the game without undue sacrifice of working time'.

Wales, dressed as they were in those days in shirts of white and green halves, took the field to a slight sprinkling of snow and within three minutes were a goal down. According to the reports they would have stayed that way had it not been for Meredith. He had gone very close with a shot from the touchline in the first half, but in the second half the following happened:– 'Morgan Owen gave Meredith a beautiful long pass and he dribbled prettily past Oakley and getting close to Robinson put in a drive which no man on earth could have stopped. The ball hit the crossbar and bounced off into the net amid immense cheering'.

The score remained at 1–1 and the crowd went away happy at having Meredith's greatness confirmed before their eyes. Had Roose been able to play they might have had a second hero to discuss, but one was enough to prove that here was a man, and here was a game, worth some attention.

from *100 Years of Welsh Soccer (1976)*

Martin Johnes

Fred Keenor

The 1920s saw Cardiff City establish itself as one of Britain's leading clubs. With the help of a vast support across the Valleys, the club attracted large attendances and purchased quality players. The team rose rapidly from the

Southern League to the First Division of the Football League, missing out on the Championship in 1923/4, under the system then used, on a goal average of 0.024. But it was in the FA Cup that the club achieved its greatest glories. After being beaten semi-finalists twice and runners-up in 1925, Cardiff City finally won the trophy in 1927. It was to be the pinnacle of their success, as the depression that had engulfed south Wales took its toll on the belligerent soccer club. Gate receipts had already begun to tumble and the income from the successful years was invested in the ground not the ageing team. After 1927, the club's decline was rapid. Four years after lifting the FA Cup, Keenor found himself captain of a team relegated to the Third Division South.

Keenor played an integral role in Cardiff's successes during these years. He became the inspiration and captain of both club and country and a favourite amongst supporters. Yet Keenor was not the type of player who normally attracted adoration. He was neither a skilful dribbler nor a prolific goal-scorer. Instead, he was one of soccer's hard men, a rugged and uncompromising performer, playing usually at centre-half or half-back. Skill on the ball was not his forte and, at 5ft 7in, neither was size, but he more than made up for it with his resolve, strength, fitness and energy. A team-mate said of him,

> '... he was one of the hardest tacklers in the game, some said he was dirty but he was just hard. Nobody took liberties with old Fred ... [He] could run all night, he couldn't run with the ball mind you, but he could run all day.'

In 1928, it was said that 'He might not be a stylish player but his doggedness and determination makes him one of the most effective centre-halves in the country.' Such levels of fitness required hard training, particularly when, liking a drink and being a heavy smoker, the rest of your life was not always dedicated to staying in peak condition. While the other Cardiff players were doing ball practice, he was lapping the pitch in old army boots. He would often turn up late for training and, ignoring the trainer and other players, just begin running around the ground to build up his stamina and work off the previous night's beer. His robust style may have won him friends in Cardiff but he was not always so kindly treated by supporters of the teams which had to oppose him. While at Crewe, Keenor was assaulted at the end of a match, then followed to the train station and had to be given a police escort. Alongside his strength and stamina, Keenor was renowned for his courage. In 1929, he injured his neck on the morning of a match between Wales and Scotland. With Wales unable to call a reserve in time, Keenor played with his neck strapped and under orders not to head the ball, enduring the pain in order not to let the side down.

Keenor's ability to inspire others made him a natural choice as captain of both club and country. Although he did not become captain of Cardiff City until 1925/6, his influence and length of time at the club made it later seem as if he had always led the team. He was said to have 'marshalled his men magnificently' in the 1927 FA Cup Final, and in 1928 was described as 'a leader in every sense of the word, he commands respect of colleagues and sets an inspiring example by his whole hearted enthusiasm'. No doubt such leadership skills were also instrumental in pushing him towards management as his playing days drew to a close. Yet he could also be a domineering leader, angrily shouting and swearing at his team-mates. He was nearly sent off playing for Wales against Scotland in 1930 for swearing at the rest of the Welsh team, but the referee accepted that Keenor was so involved in motivating the others that he did not realize what he was saying. When Cardiff City's goalkeeper was chipped from the half-way line in a match against Blackpool, Keenor ran back and began shaking him roughly while the crowd shouted at them to get on with the game. Such a belligerent temperament did not always endear him to the Cardiff City management, and the end of his career at the club was marked by arguments with staff and other players. He even had a transfer request granted during the FA Cup winning season after being unhappy about being dropped for several matches. Keenor had his opinions and standards, and he expected fellow players and club officials to conform to them. Thus he was very much the quintessential 'British' player: physical, committed and determined, making up in strength for what he lacked in skill. And he expected the same from those around him.

It was in this style of play that Keenor's popularity originated. He embodied the working-class masculine ideal; strong and brave, an individual yet part of a team. He displayed all the virtues that the supporters on Ninian Park's Bob Bank valued. The agile deftness of a rugby fly-half may have been admired and even revered in south Wales, but it was the more down-to-earth but directed brute strength of a prop-forward, a boxer or a soccer centre-half that was in touch with what working men experienced in their daily lives. They valued and celebrated the artists of the game, but it was to the skilled artisans whom they related most closely. There are obvious parallels between the characteristics that Keenor embodied and those of the coal industry that dominated the lives of so many Cardiff supporters, Keenor may not have been a master of ball-control, but he still had a degree of skill that enabled him to become a professional player in the first place. There was a talented player beneath the rough veneer. Much as miners were proud of the physical side of their work, they were also quick to point out the technique involved. Strength and courage were admirable, but one still had to know how to apply them.

There was nothing particularly Welsh about the attributes and values that contributed to Keenor's popularity. They were characteristics shared by working-class communities across Britain. Yet Keenor's popularity also owed much to his roots. Although the professional nature of soccer created teams made up of players from across Britain, this did not prevent players from becoming representatives of the towns they played for. It was the team that was important not the individual. But when a local player did stand out it was something to celebrate. Keenor was a true 'Cardiff boy', and the local press repeatedly proclaimed how the city could be proud that one of its sons was an integral part of its multinational, star-studded soccer team. Reporters used Keenor to deflect the accusations of the rugby fraternity that soccer's success was imported into Cardiff and, in so doing, they helped mould him into a local hero.

Keenor's pride in playing for Wales ensured that his popularity extended beyond Cardiff. Like all good Welshmen, he saw England as the primary enemy. As he once said, 'We Welshmen do not mind much if we have to bow the knee to Scotland or Ireland but we do take a special delight in whacking England'. He also acknowledged the importance of Cardiff City to Wales at large and when the club was elevated to the Football League he said, 'We had made up our minds that, come what may, we'd do our best to shine and show England that Wales could run a big club successfully'. Before the 1927 Cup Final, he talked of bringing the trophy to Wales not Cardiff. Keenor was not alone in such rhetoric but, none the less, he was telling people what they wanted to hear and this helped ensure that it was not just Cardiff who appreciated him.

from *For Club and Country* (2000)

'A Special Correspondent'

Stirring Moments at Wembley, 1927

'Nineteen-twenty-seven – the year Cardiff City first won the Cup' That is how Welsh football history and, perhaps, some other history too, will come to be dated in the future. And no one who was present at Wembley on Saturday can easily forget the scenes or the singing, the tense anxiety of the closing minutes of the game, the great Welsh shout of triumph when the referee shrilled out the final and Keenor, captain of Cardiff City, followed by his men, went up to the King to receive the FA Cup, which, for the first time in its half-century of history, has been taken out of England.

The winning goal came when many of us had almost resigned ourselves to a replay. Neither side seemed to be playing sufficiently good, clever and finished football to win, or to deserve to win. Then the unexpected happened. Ferguson shot into the goal-mouth. The Arsenal goalkeeper caught it. Len Davies was not far off, but still far enough away to be no cause of anxiety. Lewis, the goalkeeper, had plenty of time apparently to clear. He bent to his knees to gather the ball, and in bending he turned away from Davies, who was racing up. Everybody expected to see him rise and get the ball away. Nobody really expected a score. The silence was tense all the same. Then Lewis fumbled – that is how it seemed to spectators in the stands: Cup-tie nerves, perhaps. It is said that the ball was spinning and was difficult to hold, and that may be, of course, the explanation. At any rate, we saw the ball slip out of his hands and roll, all too slowly, it seemed, towards the net. There were Arsenal shouts of dismay and Cardiff shouts of joy. Lewis tried to grab the ball. Too late: it had crossed the line. Len Davies was leaping high in the air; a leap of triumph. Lewis, a rather pathetic figure, went slowly into the net to get the ball. It was destined to be the winning goal, and Lewis, who had played so well, had seemingly let his side down.

When the great crowd, close upon a hundred thousand, realised what had happened, such a shout went up as Wembley had never heard before. The crowded tiers of the vast amphitheatre became a stormy sea of tossing, waving hats and blue and white favours. Everywhere people were standing up, shouting themselves hoarse. In the Royal Box the King was smiling. Behind his Majesty the face of Mr Lloyd George was wreathed in patriotic smiles. Behind him again Mr Winston Churchill was smiling over to his old colleague of Coalition days little messages of national congratulation.

The Lord Mayor of Cardiff, excusably forgetful in the circumstances of the decorum of the Royal Box, joined the throng in a demonstration of enthusiasm that has rarely been equalled on a football field.

When the shouting had ceased and the game was re-started, there were many who, on reflection, qualified their enthusiasm with sympathy for the Welshman who was keeping goal for the Arsenal. And let it be said at once that a misfortune which might have unnerved most players seemed only to stimulate the Arsenal to greater efforts and to make Lewis himself rise to great heights again and again to avert further disaster. Cardiff City's supporters lived through anxious moments in the last fifteen minutes of the game. There were keen, desperate attacks and thrilling saves. Experts may call the quality of the football poor, but there was no denying the tremendous pace, the eager attack, the stern defence...

At the start it seemed as if both sides were suffering from nerves. Arsenal were playing the better football – their passing was infinitely superior. Buchan was always in the picture leading attacks, and Hardy was always in the picture, too, breaking them up and making magnificent clearances. As the game proceeded the pace increased, and when Cardiff scored it gave them just the tonic and the confidence they seemed hitherto to lack. Desperately anxious and thrilling though the close was, Cardiff City were now clearly the winners and they played a sporting open game to the end. There was none of that futile, unsportsmanlike waste of time that has spoiled many a good match after the first score. Up to the very call of the whistle, both sides were striving hard, one to equalise, the other to increase its lead. And so, whatever the experts may say of the quality of the football and the nature of the goal, Cardiff City's victorious Cup Final will be remembered as amongst the most sportsmanlike and the cleanest on record.

It will be remembered, too, for many other things. Some will call it the singing Cup Final. If this community singing is persevered in, it will not be necessary soon to come to Wales to hear singing. For many hours before the game began the crowds waiting in the Stadium were singing, and as the people surged into the great amphitheatre the volume of sound increased until, when the King came in, the National Anthem went up with a fervour that recalled the heroic, loyal days of 1914. It was a great crowd of sportsmen, more than half red, perhaps a third blue and white, judged by the favours that were shown about, and a very large section neutral, but whether the warp and woof were red or blue the result was a web of happy, loyal sportsmen gathered to witness a great contest. Instinctively they all turned to the King after the National Anthem, and spontaneously they sang the old song of democratic greeting and good-fellowship, 'For he's a jolly good fellow'.

Then, as the crowds continued to pour in, favourite old hymns and songs were sung. As Welshmen we longed for 'Cwm Rhondda', with its thrilling, almost barbaric, beauty of swelling harmony, but 'Hen Wlad' satisfied our national pride; and most beautiful and wonderful of all was 'Abide with me', sung with all its pleading tenderness by ninety thousand people. Not even the thrills of the game, nor the shouts of triumph, can efface the memory of that great hymn sung by so many, and yet sung so tenderly. Let it not be said that the English are not an emotional race. The Welsh men and women in the crowd were moved as one expected them to be; but so were the English; and many an eye was dimmed with tears, the memory carried back, perhaps, to heroic days of peril and sacrifice and unfaltering trust.

The memory of this deep emotion stands out against a background of joyous festival. For the English Cup Final is much more than a great football contest – much more than the climax of the football year, the conflict between the two teams that survive the ordeal of the rounds. It is a tremendous festival, and this year to an occasion hitherto – with one exception, and that again Cardiff City – exclusively English was added the flavour of an international: something of the flavour of an England v Wales Rugby contest at Cardiff or at Twickenham.

From Wales the men and women went up to London in legions. All through the Friday night and the early hours of Saturday morning the streets of London were musical with Welsh hymns and songs. The leek and the daffodil were almost as abundant, worn as favours, as the City's colours. It was not merely a Cardiff City occasion. It was an all Wales occasion.

from the *Western Mail* 25 April 1927

43

Harri Webb

The Bluebirds

It was in 1927, all on an April day,
The Bluebirds flew from Ninian Park, at Wembley for to play,
'Twas there they won the English Cup and humbled
England's pride,
And none of us will ever forget the City's winning side.

There was Nelson and Watson, Farquharson and Ferguson
Curtis and Davies and Irving,
Hardy and Maclachlan
Beat the Arsenal man for man,
Never was a team more deserving.
Sloan, he played the game
But Fred Keenor's the great name,
And all will live for ever in the City's Hall of Fame.

The crowds they packed the stadium tight and loudly they
did sing,
Lloyd George was in the Royal Box (and so too was the King):
The Arsenal heroes all in red then bravely took the field,
But when the final whistle went, to Cardiff had to yield.

'Twas fifteen minutes from the end, and after a close game,
Maclachlan passed to Ferguson, and Fergy's big chance came.
He swerved and then shot straight for goal, there was magic
in his feet,
The ball it travelled fast and low, and the goalie he was beat.

It was the solitary goal of that immortal day,
When the Bluebirds won the English Cup and flew with it away.
When they came back to Cardiff, the City all went mad,
And even down in Swansea Town they said that they were
glad.

The hooters hooted from the mines, from railway engines too,
The bells of Wales in triumph rang to hail the men in blue,
And everybody danced and sang as if they were in heaven,
When Cardiff City won the English Cup in 1927.

There was Nelson and Watson, Farquharson and Ferguson
Curtis and Davies and Irving,
Hardy and Maclachlan
Beat the Arsenal man for man,
Never was a team more deserving.
Sloan, he played the game
But Fred Keenor's the great name,
And all will live for ever in the City's Hall of Fame.

from *Rampage and Revel* (1977)

Huw Bowen

Jack Fowler

During the 1920s, the spectators who stood on the rough
stone-and-ash banks that formed three sides of Swansea
Town's 'rubble heap' of a Vetch Field ground often indulged
in enthusiastic bouts of community singing. The songs they

sang echoed the Welsh hymns and arias usually associated with the crowds that gathered in rather smaller numbers at the nation's rugby football venues. Indeed, followers of the 'dribbling code' gave as good as their rugby counterparts, and observers were often moved by the strength and passion of their impromptu renditions of 'Cwm Rhondda', 'Hen Wlad Fy Nhadau', 'Sospan Fach' and other favourites. It was reported that the volume of noise generated by the Vetch Field crowd could be heard 'ordinarily' as far away as Fforestfach, and the effects of massed Welsh voices on opposition players and supporters could at times be quite overwhelming. One Stoke City supporter was taken aback when he heard a section of the Swansea crowd launching wholeheartedly into 'Yn y Dyfroedd Mawr a'r Tonnau' and, on finding that he was listening to a funeral hymn, he was moved to suggest that the visiting contingent from the Potteries should perhaps starts humming 'Show me the way to go home'. These choral outpourings allowed many spectators to give vocal expression to their identity and celebrate their Welshness, if only for ninety minutes on a Saturday afternoon, and visiting English teams often felt that they were playing in an unfamiliar foreign land.

The Vetch Field, however, was not an exclusively Welsh sporting theatre. The changing and expanding nature of Swansea, the 'dirty witch' of a town evoked by Edward Thomas, was such that many immigrant working men of English, Irish and Italian descent also took their place in a cosmopolitan crucible. Alongside the deep-rooted influences of chapel and choir was also to be found a liking for choruses of a quite different type, and this enabled

Swansea supporters to find a place for themselves within mainstream popular British culture. 'I'm for ever blowing Bubbles' was taken up with gusto during the early 1920s, and the crowd swayed vigorously, and often dangerously, from side to side in time with the chorus. Only later did 'Bubbles' become more exclusively associated with the followers of West Ham United. Swansea supporters, who before 1914 had sung their own 'war song', also adapted a favourite contemporary ditty by supplying appropriate words of their own which served to elevate one player, Jack Fowler, to the status of popular hero. To the tune of 'Chick, chick, chick, chick, chicken, lay a little egg for me', the Vetch Field crowd often sang 'Fow, Fow, Fow, Fow, Fowler, score a little goal for me. We haven't had a goal since the last match, and now it's half past three.' On the North Bank terraces of modern times it often has been loudly proclaimed that there is only one Alan Waddle, or one Alan Curtis, but during the mid-1920s there was, in both song and deed, most definitely only one Jack Fowler. He was Swansea Town's first footballing hero of the professional era, a talismanic figure who became the idol of thousands.

... The excitement of supporters knew no bounds. They gathered at newspaper offices to hear first news of Cup draws; they cheered visiting teams at High Street station; they flocked to Swansea on match days to queue for hours to gain entry to the ground; they sang their hearts out; and at the Vetch Field they let their emotions run wild. Against the Arsenal, the crowd was 'packed' onto the banks by a megaphone-wielding police force that would shortly be dealing with crowds of a different type during the General

Strike. This 'packing' strategy, based on the notion that 'The closer the crowd, the less danger there is', was undoubtedly distressing and dangerous for those crushed at the front of the bank, but it had the effect of greatly enhancing the atmosphere as the crowd swayed, surged and sang together. The success of the team, the drama of the occasion, and the vigour of the action all combined to create a rich brew of heady excitement that at times was translated into extraordinary scenes of rejoicing. At the Stoke match, it was reported that 'as the clever Fowler piled up a continuous succession of goals, the enthusiasm passed all limits. The frantic fervour of the crowd was a wonderful thing. It must have left thousands of people hoarse and voiceless long before the end.' But this was surpassed by the scenes following the victory against the Arsenal, a game that ended with Swansea pressed back and resorting, rather shame-facedly, to booting the ball as far as possible up the field. The match report in the *South Wales Daily Post* declared that 'The final whistle at the Vetch Field on Saturday was the signal for the most amazing outburst of enthusiasm that Welsh soccer has ever known. It was roar of relief as well as joy. A dense mass of almost hysterical supporters – shouting, cheering, brandishing flags, rattles, sticks, and even leeks – yelled in unison for the heroes of the afternoon. Several women were in tears of joy.' Not surprisingly, Fowler was mobbed as he left the field.

The Swans were representing the town and its industrial hinterland, and the enthusiastic celebrations of victory can be seen as expressions of local pride, but the team was also taken up and supported by large numbers of people drawn from across south, west and mid Wales. As such, it can be said that Swansea carried the hopes of a significant part of the nation, including those in Cardiff. This much can be inferred from the elaborate transport arrangements that were put in place on match days. With a precision and timing of the type associated with military manoeuvres, the GWR and LMS provided trains to carry supporters into Swansea and out of Wales. For home ties, football excursions arrived in the town from all points near and far, with services running from Craven Arms, Gowerton, Llandovery, Llandrindod, Llanelli, Loughor, Pontarddulais and Pembroke. Trains from Cardiff and Newport brought in large numbers from the east and the Valleys. As groups of supporters from Caernarfon and Colwyn Bay mingled with those from Ireland and the north of England, the cosmopolitan nature of the crowds was a matter for comment.

The number of supporters travelling away was also increasingly substantial and they were carried on excursions which offered discounted prices, guaranteed match tickets, and all the 'steam-heated comforts' of fast modern 'corridor expresses'. On the day of the Millwall match five day-excursion trains were booked from Swansea and a half-day trip ran from Cardiff to London. With the game being for the Swans 'an event calculated to be the biggest moment in their history', supporters went to great lengths to get to the match. These were reported in the local press as 'astonishing stories', especially the tale of the '200 South Wales men who left their pits on Friday night without bothering to change, went straight to their reserve carriages, and arrived in London in their 'Yorks'. It was thought by some that this story was 'scarcely credible', but it was reported on good authority that the miners had in fact been seen driving in a specially hired charabanc to the game in New Cross. Popular folklore in Swansea still suggests that the Millwall game was marred by punch-ups with South London dockers, but reports of violence did not make their way into the local press.

In the event, Swansea's Fowler-inspired Cup run ended at the semi-final stage of the competition, although by that point many confident supporters were already planning their trips to 'Wembley and worrying about the size of ticket allocations for the finalists. Indeed, it was reported in the press that some people remained at home in Swansea over the semi-final weekend because they were saving their money for the excursion to the final. Others were no doubt offended by the fact that the price of tickets was more than double the amount they were used to paying. Those who did travel to London formed part of an 'early morning invasion' and a 'human avalanche at Paddington'. More than 2,300 football supporters travelled by train from Swansea, and more than 700 from Cardiff, to take their place in a 25,000 crowd. As the Swans' followers poured onto the platforms at Paddington, they held aloft a replica of the FA Cup with Fowler's picture on it. They carried daffodils, flags, leeks, miniature swans, and rosettes decked out in blue, a choice dictated by the fact that Swansea had been obliged to change their playing colours because of a clash with the white of Bolton. Rugby supporters and players from Llanelli – soccer converts for the day – carried 'sospans' with them. As they spilled out onto the streets of London, groups of supporters struck up the Fowler song.

Local residents were taken aback by the sudden arrival of this seething mass of humanity and were baffled by the unfamiliar Welsh accents they could hear. 'Who are the Swans?' asked one old woman, to which a supporter in an 'Ystalyfera muffler' replied, 'Wales!' Two Londoners listened intently to the words of the Fowler song. Not surprisingly, they could not understand them, one declaring to the other 'It is Welsh they are singing, Bill'. Logic dictated to one bystander, a 'precocious youth', that the many blue favours in evidence belonged to those who had come to watch the university boat race, also taking place that day. He was put firmly in his place by three 'women of Wales' wearing large blue hats who 'promptly reminded him that they were members of the proletariat'.

from *For Club and Country* (2000)

Raymond Williams

Parry, R.

Mr Stanton walked briskly down the steps of the Brynarw Arms, chewing the ends of his ginger moustache. Mr Stanton was a sportsman. From the pocket of his Norfolk jacket a copy of *Sporting Life* protruded artlessly. In his inside wallet pocket was a sheaf of betting slips. In his swinging left hand was a leash. But these public acknowledgments of sport were not Mr Stanton's claim to be a sportsman. His connection with the great morality was much more intimate. Mr Stanton, as well as being one of those on the inside, was an impresario. He was a valued man in Brynarw.

When called upon to register his occupation in some governmental inquiry, Mr Stanton was accustomed to enter 'Miscellaneous'. It was the most accurate description he could offer. On one occasion a bad-tempered clerk had objected to its vagueness, and Mr Stanton had eventually gone into the files as 'businessman'. But business is not thought much of in Brynarw; on all other occasions Mr Stanton retained his 'miscellaneous'. No reliable list of Mr Stanton's occupations has ever been compiled, but it is at least known that he is an agent for a large insurance company, an agent for the Christmas clubs of two well-known multiple firms, an agent for a Birmingham firm with a household name for household products, such as brushes and aluminium pans, an agent for a noted firm of football pool promoters, the manager of a boxer who trains in the room above the statics of the Greyhound Inn in the local town, the treasurer of the Brynarw United Choir, the groundsman of the Brynarw Bowling Club and of the Brynarw Tennis Club, an occasional dealer in horses, antique furniture, pictures and books, and one half of that thriving enterprise known as Border Bookies Ltd, which has its registered office in the sitting-room of Mr Stanton's lodgings above the Brynarw Post Office. This list would perhaps seem miscellaneity enough, but what is perhaps Mr Stanton's most important job (his occasional work of gravedigging at the chapel he sets little store by) is his management, secretaryship, and training of the Brynarw F. C.

The Brynarw F. C. plays in the First Division of the North

Monmouthshire League. For as long as could be remembered its play had been mediocre, but two seasons before the present date, in the first season of the club's contact with Mr Stanton, who had arrived casually in the village one hot August day, it had swept all before it, and had won the League Championship and the coveted Martineau Cup. Lady Martineau, who was a resident of Brynarw, was so delighted that the cup which she had presented should reside for a whole season in a glass case in the Martineau Memorial Hall, that she felt (although she did not wish to interfere, and of course she was a vice-president and accustomed to subscribe but she was after all only a lady and it was notorious that ladies knew nothing of football), in all goodwill, oughtn't Mr Stanton to be given permanent control of the club? There had been voices raised in extra-mural protest, for some held the view that the improvement in the club's form had nothing whatever to do with Mr Stanton, but was due rather to the excellent play of a young boy who had just come into the team as centre-forward, Reg Parry. But in the committee the matter was soon settled, and so it had remained. The club's fortunes had continued to prosper. If they did equally well in the present season, which seemed highly likely, they would win the Martineau Cup outright. Mr Stanton was proud indeed of his lads, who were a credit to him.

As he walked now towards the ground for this afternoon's important game Mr Stanton swung his shoulders in a manner that in a lesser man might be called swaggering. Ahead of him he saw the chapel, and leaning over the wall, apparently staring at the serried headstones, was a man who was a stranger to Mr Stanton. Mr Stanton hummed a tune.

53

'Hullo Mr Parry.'

Mr Stanton looked sharply over his shoulder and as sharply continued his walk.

'I said Hullo Mr Parry.'

The voice of the man who had been leaning over the chapel wall had become aggressive. Mr Stanton went on his way.

'Parry', shouted the man, Mr Stanton stopped. Tapping the leash smartly against his calf, he turned. He stared at the man by the chapel, who was short, fat, bald, and dressed in a gleaming white mackintosh.

'You Parry?' said the man. 'The name's Hargreaves.' Mr Stanton looked at his boot.

'Are you trying to be smart?' he asked, quietly. The fat man drew himself up.

'I'm telling you who I am,' he said.

'Why?' Mr Stanton asked, spitting carefully.

'Because I want to know you,' said the other. 'Is your name Parry?'

'Stanton,' said Mr Stanton.

'Ho Christ, Ho Jesus, thanks for the relief,' Hargreaves could barely control his laughter. He moved back to the chapel wall and leaned against it, shading and covering his face. Mr Stanton looked perplexed, but waited politely for the other to recover himself.

'Sorry old boy. Must seem cracked laughing my head off like that. Only Christ...'

Some new recollection convulsed the stranger again and he turned to the wall, holding his face in his hands. Mr Stanton watched the fat body shaking under the gleaming mackintosh.

'Look' said Hargreaves, turning towards him and crooking his little finger. 'Come over here and look'. Mr Stanton moved to the chapel wall and looked obediently. Following the direction of the pudgy finger his eye fell on the headstones which marked the graves of many generations of Brynarw Baptists.

'Well?', he asked.

'Don't you see?' said the other.

'See what?'

'There, the gravestones.'

'What about them?'

'Don't they strike you as odd?'

'Nothing odd about gravestones', said Mr Stanton.

Hargreaves turned and looked up into Stanton's face, seeming perplexed. Then he reached to the other's pocket and tapped the protruding copy of the *Sporting Life*.

'You're a sensible fellow, aren't you?', he asked. Mr Stanton nodded.

'You can read I suppose?'

Mr Stanton clenched his fist for the only sensible reply, but restrained himself.

'Yes', he replied, simply.

'Then go on', said the fat man. 'Read'.

'This?' Mr Stanton asked, extracting his *Sporting Life*.

'No, no. Not the paper, the gravestones'.

'Oh!'

Mr Stanton did as he was told. The little man looked up into his face expectantly as he read.

'Don't you see?' he burst out at last. 'They're all called Parry'.

Mr Stanton started. He peered at the stones. Quickly he realised that Hargreaves was right. Thomas Parry, David Parry, Peter Parry, Mary Ann Parry, Jane Parry, Blodwen Parry, Kate Parry, William Parry, John Parry, Evan Parry, Ruth Parry, May Parry, Job Parry, Parry, Parry, Parry. Every gravestone within his sight bore the same surname. Certain of the stones were crumbling with age, and most were overgrown with ivy and had shifted to oblique angles in the loose soil near the river. Perhaps away from the road were other names and other families. But here were the bones of generations of Parrys, who seemed all to have died either in early infancy or in advanced old age. Many names were coupled, Job Parry and Kate Parry, Evan and Ruth, David and Blodwen. Certain of the women lay in single graves. On all were marked dates of death and birth, and ages. All bore phrases of propitiation.

'That's odd indeed', said Mr Stanton. 'Parry. Well of course there's no shortage of living Parrys. Only to think I've never noticed... '

'You live here?' Mr Stanton gazed at the fat man reflectively.

'Yes. Not a native though.'

'I'm just here for the day', said Hargreaves, smiling. Stanton looked back at the gravestones.

'Why did you call me Parry?' he asked intently.

'Well, think. You're sensible. I come to this place to see a Parry. I look at the graves and everywhere I see Parrys. You come along, the first man I see. What do I naturally think? Parry.'

'Yes. Of course its really Stanton.'

'Of course. Stanton.'

'And now I must get along.' Mr Stanton kicked his leg up behind him nervously and swished with the leash. 'Got my lads to get ready. For the match.'

'You mean football?'

'I'm manager,' said Mr Stanton, pulling importantly at his nose, 'manager and trainer of the Brynarw F.C.'

'Well there,' said Hargreaves. 'Imagine. I'm talent-scout – you know, spotter – for Cardiff. Got a tip about a young centre-forward. Parry. R. Parry. Reginald Parry. Ho Christ. Ho Christ... '

Hargreaves turned back to the wall. His fat neck reddened and rolled. He gasped. 'Parry.'

Mr Stanton took his fellow-sportsman to the scene of the match. Hargreaves commented that the field was a bit rough, and Mr Stanton affected not to hear. He led the way into the dressing-room, which was the back-kitchen of The Half Moon. A group of men were in varied states of undress; one or two were already equipped in the amber and black colours of the Brynarw F.C. At the door lounged a company of elder boys, smoking. There was a heavy smell of embrocation, for all the players seemed to be massaging their legs, rubbing the heavy liquid along hair and bone. There were several nods at Mr Stanton.

'That's young Reg Parry,' Mr Stanton said quietly to Hargreaves, indicating a heavily-built, freckled boy, with a mop of ginger hair. Hargreaves rubbed his stomach and made appreciative noises as he silently surveyed Parry. He grunted with great amiability.

'Looks all right,' he remarked to Mr Stanton behind his

57

white palm. 'All right.' He dropped his hand. 'So far,' he added, with a crescent tone of aggression. Several players stopped rubbing themselves and looked up at him with some surprise. He turned his back and walked away.

The opponents in the match – Llanfair F. C. – were changing in the bus which had brought them to Brynarw. As Hargreaves emerged from The Half Moon and walked slowly towards the pitch the Llanfair players came running out, kicking an old ball between them. Hargreaves looked at them for a moment and then turned definitely away. He took a mannikin cigar from his waistcoat and lit it thoroughly. When Mr Stanton joined him, having followed out the Brynarw players who converged on the far goalmouth, Hargreaves spoke with the cigar rolling along his lips.

'Course this class of football...,' he said.

'Young lad go on in it too long, hold him back, never reach the top...'

Mr Stanton spat, and then wiping his lips mentioned a plan that he had expounded to his players before they left the dressing-room. Hargreaves removed his hat.

The field was good pasture between the river and the main road. The grass was quite long, and the sawdust-marked lines were difficult to see at any distance. A footpath ran diagonally across the pitch to the stile by The Half Moon. The herd which normally occupied the field had moved back to the river. Groups of people stood on the touchlines, and one or two spectators joined with the players in their practice.

Hargreaves and Mr Stanton were each reckoned, in their respective circles, good judges of the game. When the whistle had blown however, and the game had begun at a huge pace and with much hefty kicking, they fell mainly silent. Even when young Reg Parry had scored two quick goals, and the whole team were around him, stretching out arms at his back, Hargreaves and Mr Stanton exchanged no real comment, and showed little emotion or excitement. Hargreaves was heard to repeat an occasional remark about 'this class of football'; Mr Stanton was once heard to say that 'individual importance was all very well but what struck him today was the cohesion of the team'. Towards the end of the game, however, Hargreaves took Mr Stanton's arm.

'What's he do?'

'Who?'

'Parry.'

'Oh, Parry. Now yes, Parry. Farmhand.'

'I shall offer him...' Hargreaves said expansively, '... a good offer. Professional terms.' Mr Stanton ground his heel into the earth.

'Is that wise?' he asked sharply.

'He's good' said Hargreaves, casually. 'Promising, that is to say. Most promising. Given proper training and so on...'

'Get back you fool,' Mr Stanton shouted suddenly, gesticulating with his leash at a full-back who had strayed into attack. But it was too late. Brynarw's defence had been beaten, and the visitors scored.

'Professionalism,' said Mr Stanton, as the final whistle blew, 'professionalism is the curse of sport. It is a corruption of our youth. I shall warn Parry against your offer.' Hargreaves smiled, and buckled the wide belt of his gleaming mackintosh.

Four days later with his fare paid by Hargreaves, Reg Parry travelled to Cardiff. There, after a further trial, he signed professional forms, and settled to a sporting career.

Mr Stanton left Brynarw some six weeks later. Few were told of his departure, although it was reported by a housemaid that he had told Lady Martineau – in strict confidence, ma'am but a very substantial offer, indeed a quite exceptional opportunity, a post involving the training of young lads, on strictly sporting and amateur lines, during their service with the militia.

The Brynarw F.C., regrettably, has lapsed into its old mediocrity. At first some interest was taken in the career of Reg Parry, who soon got into Cardiff's reserve team and began scoring goals. There was indeed at one time much talk of a cup-winning medal being brought back to Brynarw to be displayed among the other trophies of the village, but for some reason or another this had never materialised. For a while the printed Parry, R., was read out carefully from the list of the reserve team which appeared in the Sporting Echo; but now it is only rarely seen, and the dreams of headlines have been quite definitely discarded and replaced.

It is not exactly known why Parry failed to do well. He was after all a very promising local boy and had the advantage of a fine start. Perhaps it is that he pays insufficient attention to his game, and has developed other interests which are less sporting, interests which places like Cardiff know well enough to provide. It is all rather a shame, as you might say, for the boy might have done well and reflected much credit on his village. Mr Stanton also, that man who is now so greatly missed, he who did so much for the boy, must feel himself let down and altogether grieved. Parry, R. indeed!

(*previously unpublished*, c. 1939)

Kenneth O. Morgan

The Arsenal Welsh

The most notorious of the Arsenal Welshmen was surely Dan Lewis, the temperamental goalkeeper from Maerdy, who played for Arsenal from 1924 to 1930, and won three Welsh caps. His moment of disaster came in the 1927 Cup Final against Cardiff City, no less. Arsenal easily dominated the play but somehow failed to score. Near the end, a simple shot by Cardiff's Ferguson was allowed by Lewis to slip under his body and over the line. It was said that a smooth unwashed jersey caused this disaster: ever since, Arsenal goalkeepers (Bob Wilson, for instance) have supposedly worn recently washed jerseys. At the time, dark rumours abounded that Lewis had missed the ball deliberately to allow his countrymen to take the Cup to Wales for the first (and only) time. When presented with the runners-up medal he hurled it to the turf in anger, but Bob John picked it up for him. Lewis might have found solace in 1930 when Arsenal won the Cup for the first time, beating Huddersfield Town 2-0, but he was injured and Arsenal's goal was defended, after a fashion, by their third-choice keeper, Charlie Preedy. He was reckless, straying far beyond his goal area: by trade he was a taxi driver – the joke was that Charlie was never around when you needed him. But it was all more bad luck for Dan Lewis who never played again.

In my years after the war, Arsenal featured several eminent Welshmen. The saddest was Bryn Jones, born in Merthyr, transferred from Wolves to Arsenal in 1938 for a record fee of £14,000 which was said to weigh on him. Jones, an inside-left, was undoubtedly one of the finest players Wales ever produced: he was uncle to the later Spurs winger, Cliff Jones. But the truth was that he lost his best years to the war. When I saw him in 1946–8 he was a marginal figure in the team, outshone by Logie, replaced by Lishman. His career simply petered out. There was, however, another Welshman rising through the ranks – Walley Barnes, born in Brecon, and a full-back, either on the left or right, of great authority. He became a fixture in the team from the end of 1946, playing for long in tandem with the English right-back Laurie Scott. He won a League medal in 1948 and a Cup medal in 1950. He also played in the 1952 final when his serious injury caused him to miss a whole season. However he played on for three more seasons. He won many caps for Wales, for whom he was captain and later manager, before becoming a BBC commentator. He was an orthodox defender who played in the full-back's accepted style, that is he seldom ventured far from his own penalty area. But Barnes could pass stylishly as well as hoof the ball upfield. He was out-standing in the 1950 Cup Final. He also became Arsenal's penalty-taker. He took penalties in the way that I always feel they should be taken, simply kicking the ball as hard as he could. He took a twenty-yard run-up and aimed for the goalkeeper's left ear. This makes it harder for the goal-keeper to make a save, in my view, than having to dive to one side. At any rate, Barnes never missed when I saw him. A fine, whole-hearted player was Walley Barnes, whose worried brow and receding hair gave him a sympathetic professorial look, or so I thought.

Another great Welsh player who came into the team in 1949 was Jack Kelsey, the famous goalkeeper from Llansamlet, signed by Arsenal from humble Winch Wen. He succeeded George Swindin in goal and played for Arsenal until 1962, appearing in 327 League games. He also won forty-one Welsh caps and played stirringly for his country, notably in the 1958 World Cup finals in Sweden. Kelsey was a courageous performer whose confidence inspired the whole defence. It was certainly not his fault that his time at Arsenal coincided with a period of steady decline. Another very skilful Welshman who appeared for the Gunners between 1949 and 1953 was Ray Daniel of Swansea, later to play both for Cardiff City and Swansea Town. His opportunities were restricted for years since he was long-term understudy to Leslie Compton. When he did become a regular in 1951–3 he proved to be a somewhat untypical Arsenal centre-half, not a robust stopper but a graceful, almost languid defender whose casual approach in the penalty area could terrify his colleagues. He played for Wales against England in 1950, when still in the reserves, outshining his opposite number, no less than Leslie Compton. It is somewhat mysterious that Daniel left Arsenal for Sunderland in 1953 when at the peak of his powers, perhaps persuaded to move by Trevor Ford. He was never perhaps quite the same player again after he left Highbury.

Another stalwart was David Bowen from Maesteg, signed from Northampton Town, a team which he later managed with some success. He was a left-half and thus had to spend many seasons in the Combination side, since Arsenal with Joe Mercer and Alex Forbes in their team were well equipped in that area. When Mercer broke his leg, colliding with a colleague in a game I saw, Bowen, a cultured, calm player, took over, playing 146 League games. He also won eighteen caps, and captained Wales with distinction in the 1958 World Cup in Sweden; later he was an excellent manager of the national team. There were two other notable Welshmen whom I saw play for the Gunners – but in the mid and later 1950s when my attendances at Highbury were becoming infrequent. Derek Tapscott from Barry and Barry Town, was a nippy goal-scoring centre-forward. He played in 111 games between 1954 and 1958, scoring the remarkably high tally of sixty-two goals. He later played for many seasons for Cardiff City and Newport County. For a time he appeared to be the centre-forward Arsenal had been looking for since the heyday of Reg Lewis (not a Welshman). Finally, I caught brief sight of Mel Charles of Swansea and brother of the great John, of course. He was a utility defender of great strength. But his time at Arsenal in 1959–62 was much disrupted by injury, and his best years were with Swansea Town, On balance, a record of sheer bad luck. After that, Arsenal's Welsh brigade seemed to peter out: John Roberts of Swansea played some games in the 'double'-winning side of 1970/71, Peter Nicholas of Newport played in the early 1980s. Swansea's distinctly limited John Hartson is the only recent player I can recall.

These Welsh players were part of a distinctive, memorable team. The fact that Arsenal played a defensive style of game, massing around the stopper centre-half, gave matches at Highbury a kind of Rorke's Drift quality which made them more exciting. But they scored plenty of goals in counter-attacks all the same. Matches at Highbury give a structure to my childhood memories. A home game offered a complete day, if not weekend. In the morning's *News Chronicle*, I would peruse the views of Charles Buchan, a famous Arsenal player of the 1920s. As we wended our way from Finsbury Park station, you might get a glimpse of Alex James, who ran a tobacconist and newsagent's nearby. After the match, you could read a report on the early play by Bernard Joy (uniquely, an amateur centre-half with Arsenal), in a late-night edition of the *Star*. Then, back home, to a ritual of listening to the wireless to hear Buchan's monotone report on the day's matches. He would invariably end with words like the Toffees beat lowly Rotherham 3-0 and this is Charlie Buchan saying cheerio and good luck. The following morning meant a walk to Wood Green to buy our Sunday papers, *The Observer* and the left-wing *Reynolds News*, to read accounts of events at Highbury. Then I forgot all about it until the next home game. Football was not discussed at school. It was thought a proletarian game and our masters tried, totally in vain, to interest us in the exploits of Blackheath and Rosslyn Park, wherever they were.

65

I do not associate my schoolboy visits to Highbury with any of the adolescent angst so memorably described in Nick Hornby's *Fever Pitch*. His account of divorce and difficulties with girls does not relate to my own, no doubt duller, experiences at all. Anyhow, the timing of my rites of passage rather parallels that of Philip Larkin (1963). For me, a rare defeat for Arsenal brought disappointment but not disaster. Highbury just meant an evanescent private world of heroism and delight.

Francis Thompson's cricket poem 'At Lords' ends as follows:

For the field is full of shades as I near the shadowy coast
And a ghostly batsman plays to the bowling of a ghost,
And I look through my tears at a soundless-clapping host,
As the run-stealers flicker to and fro, to and fro,
O my Hornby and my Barlow long ago!

I do not know what my bundle of sensations will be when (or, indeed, if) I reach that stage of life. My miasma of recollection may well feature academic activities, books or lectures, perhaps blurring into each other. But part of me will always be clinging excitedly to a barrier at the Laundry End on a misty autumn day, cheering Barnes's tackle or Kelsey's save, a time when life was innocent and it all seemed right, and mind, heart and soul could unite in celebrating the greatest team on earth.

from *For Club and Country* (2000)

Peter Corrigan

The Jones Boys

Bryn Jones came from a Merthyr family with a unique record in soccer. There were few ways out from the poverty and indignity of the Merthyr Valley and soccer was one of them. The Jones family found it and for them it became an avenue.

For 50 years, starting with Ivor Jones in 1918 and ending with Cliff Jones in 1968, the family had at least one member playing professional football.

The story began in the family home at 13 Baden Terrace, Penyard, just one of a jostle of expressionless houses perched on the hill above Merthyr and from where William Daniel Jones went to his work as a collier. Each of his five sons in turn followed him to work down the pit and, to his great joy, they each in turn escaped to the green grass and fresh air of football.

The natural skill they had was sharpened in street football when to gain possession of the rag ball was to have the world at your feet. Will John 'Shoni' was the oldest brother and he played for Aberdare and Merthyr when they were in the Football League but he didn't catch the eye as much as Ivor, the second son.

Ivor was just about old enough to be called up in 1917 and he ran away home after a week. His father walloped him and sent him back. When Ivor returned, legitimately and unscathed, from France he signed for Caerphilly. Swansea had bought him within weeks, Wales had capped him within months and West Bromwich Albion eventually claimed him for the delight of English crowds.

Like all the Joneses, Ivor was a forward, nimble, quick and skilled with the ball. The third son Emlyn had all those abilities as well as a quiet, gentle nature. He was signed straight from the pit by Merthyr's shrewd manager Albert Lyndon and weighed only eight and a half stone when he made his debut in the Third Division.

Emlyn remembered the signing well. His father had taken him down to Penydarren Park and the offer was £3 a week. Jones senior said he was sorry but it would have to be £3.10s and there were shaking of heads and shrugging and the Joneses walked silently back up the hill to Penyard.

Emlyn cried that night. The thought of having to go down the pit again next day suddenly became too much. But he didn't have to go, for Merthyr sent for him first thing and £3.10s it was.

'I signed the same day as Dai Astley who was six foot tall but as thin as a broom handle,' Emlyn recalled. 'He had been working up to his waist in water underground. They used to tell us both to stand on the terraces and just breathe the air.'

After three months at Merthyr, Emlyn was transferred to Bournemouth and for a boy who had previously only been as far as Cardiff to run in handicap sprints the transformation in environment must have been tremendous. He was only at Dean Court for six weeks before Everton signed him and he was mixing with Dixie Dean and the giant Welshman Tommy Griffiths. After that whirlwind start it was small wonder that he couldn't settle and he moved on to Southend where he played for seven years before ending his career at Barrow.

By then the fourth son, Bryn, was the most expensive player in Britain and certainly one of the finest inside forwards in the game. His entry into the game, however, was slightly confusing. Bryn played with Emlyn at Southend, and then with Glenavon in the Irish League before returning to Wales to play for Aberaman. Wolves suddenly swooped to pay £1,500 for him and he was an overnight sensation at Molineux, winning his first Welsh cap in 1935. Bryn was bigger and stronger than his brothers and scored goals far more frequently.

When he was sold to Arsenal in 1938 for that staggering £14,000 record fee Bryn undoubtedly suffered from the publicity and, although playing well for Wales, did not hit it off in his first season for Arsenal. But he recovered his form in Arsenal's Scandinavian tour in 1939 and played brilliantly until the war interrupted.

Without question the war cost Bryn Jones his best years as a footballer – it cost the youngest brother Bert his life. Bert had been good enough to join Aston Villa just before the war but he was killed in Burma.

Bryn came back to rejoin Arsenal but not to recover from those lost years. He finished his career as player-coach to Norwich City by which time the next Jones generation had started to follow the first. Ken Jones, son of Emlyn, signed for Southend in 1949 and subsequently played for Swansea and Hereford. While at Swansea he linked up with his cousins, Brin and Cliff, sons of Ivor...

The Jones family of Merthyr had still a lot left to provide

and generations still to come may yet improve on their record of providing eight Football League professionals.

from *100 Years of Welsh Soccer* (1976)

Hywel Teifi Edwards

Ninian Park, the first time

Soccer won my allegiance when I was a boy in the 1940s and the memory of the post-war years when our communal fears were exuberantly volleyed to oblivion in town and village will never fade. For three intoxicating years my village, Llanddewi Aberarth, its 'boys' having returned from active service, actually fielded a side in the second division of the North Cardiganshire League. Our first game was a 'friendly' against a team of PoWs in nearby Llannon who had been kicking a ball around for the better part of five years. We lost 13-1 and my mam-gu developed an immediate interest in the Nuremberg Trials. It did not help that my father had been a prisoner near Bremen for the better part of three years.

On 21 October 1950, Aberarth AFC went to Cardiff to see Wales play Scotland at Ninian Park. It was a trip worthy of Dylan Thomas's word-spinning. I had only once before been to Cardiff and that had been a Sunday school outing. The trip to Ninian Park would be a venture of a different kind. Perched on the parapet of the bridge we listened like so many ravenous nestlings to one of our stalwart merchant mariners as he warned us in unbiblical

Welsh about the predators who preyed upon innocents abroad in big cities:

'Bloody hell, watch out for the women in Cardiff! Hell's bells, be prepared!'

'What do you mean, Rhys?'

'What do I mean? Listen boi bach, there are women in Cardiff who can play with your cock and take your ticket at the same time!'

Dear God! In the darker recesses of one's anticipation something stirred only to be instantly neutered by the terror of a lost ticket.

'Don't tell your lies, Rhys.'

'Lies, be damned! Listen boi bach, the last time I went to a match one old sow tried it out on me, but nothing doing, boi bach. This one of mine has been round the world!'

On our way home to an early bed we debated the veracity of our counsellor's anatomical evidence and decided that we would be well advised to disembark in Cardiff wearing a bathing costume over our underpants. And we made it to Ninian Park, giving females of all ages a wide berth and attracting compassionate looks as we crabbed along pavements, left hand thrust deep in trouser pocket, right hand clamped to right breast. There was a crowd of 50,000 to see the match and it was my first palpitating experience of being part of a nation exhorting its team to victory. I will never forget it. We lost, 3-1, but the boys from Aberarth had actually seen their heroes for the first time – Barnes, Sherwood, Tommy Jones, Burgess, Paul and Ford – Trevor Ford! We would re-enact their roles on the village schoolyard until the following October.

I did not see the inside of the Arms Park until 26 January 1952 when I took another bus trip with my schoolfellows to watch Hennie Muller's fearsome Springboks reduce the Barbarians to kindergarten stature as they defeated them, 17-3. A heavy snowfall in west Wales saw a few of us make the journey to Cardiff in Wellington boots, only to be met with bright city sunshine without a snowflake in sight. We trudged, ruefully rustic, to the stadium but quickly felt at ease as the Barbarians, with the exception of Bleddyn Williams, played as if they, too, were wearing Wellingtons. I relished it as another initiative experience but to my mind it could not begin to compare with the fervour of Ninian Park. In the years ahead I would be disabused of that idea.

from *Heart and Soul* (1998)

Leslie Norris

The Night Before the Game˙

When night comes early and darkness
fills the streets, all the way
from the cold road past roofs and chimneys
to the colder stars, he takes
his tennis ball to the circle of light
beneath the street lamp. And begins. He taps
the ball from one foot to the other, walks
it about the iron standard, patting it
with deft little directives of his shoes,

never letting it out of his easy reach,
as Con Holland had taught him.

Now he is trotting, the ball
two smooth inches from his toes,
never getting away, never breaking
the rhythm of the circle
around the lamp-post. And he
dances after it, swaying from side
to side, feinting with hips and shoulders
so that imaginary tacklers sprawl
behind him, and the little
grey ball veers minutely
in its steady circling as he steers
and strokes it.

       'Be in control,'
Con Holland had said, 'Keep the ball
with you, protect it, push it and pat it,
left foot and right foot'.

         So he runs around
in the ring of light, a small thin boy,
until his running is automatic and the ball's
response is to something other than his feet,
something different, a sudden unity,
a harmony, like happiness.

Knowing he can do anything,
he pounces two-footed, traps
the ball between his feet, throws it

73

a yard in front of him, and lofts
its bounce head high, holds it a moment
on his forehead, allows it to drop
to his lifted thigh, pause, and fall,
soft as a mouse, to the ground.
He repeats this again and again, until
it is perfect beyond anticipation.

And goes home.

      Although it is dark
he can almost see his white shorts
folded on the bedside chair, with
his new stockings. His shirt, red
with gold sleeves, is on a hanger
behind the door. He is straight
and calm in his sheets. His bed
is flat as a field.

'Be aware', Con Holland had warned,
'of every man on the field. Protect
the ball, move it safely. Know
where everybody is. And best of all,
know the spaces between them.
Keep the ball until you know those spaces.
Push the ball at exact speeds
into spaces your men can run to fill.'

Almost asleep, he imagines the green game
in the morning, how the ball will roll
into the spaces between his friends,

intricately connecting them,
a web, a moving thread of playing.

And on the touchline fathers and brothers
and people who leave their cars
to watch boys play soccer, they too
have their spaces, move into them,
shouting their support.

And behind them are the spaces of their homes,
the places they work, the places of travelling,
all to be filled, people moving at exact speeds,
all intricately connected.

    Arthur Ferguson,
who's gone to Australia, there's a huge space.

  We are connected,
he thinks, turning into the warm darkness,
we are all the same.

       from *Collected Poems (1996)*

Ron Berry

A Rhondda Derby

Betty had her eight-pound baby that particular Saturday
morning, somewhere around two o'clock, consequently
Gee-Gee lost a night's kip, but he galloped on to the Galed

75

Blues' field like a Corinthian stalwart. We were a man short and Morley'd puffed around the fistful of spectators begging for a volunteer.

'What's it feel like being a father?' I asked Gee-Gee.

'She's a good kid,' he approved. 'Forgot about that cyst entirely when the time came. Doctor told her all along it was nothing to worry about.' He breasted down a volley from our goalkeeper, chipped it out to Nebo's son, and high pranced from the knees for a few moments. 'We can beat this bloody shower,' he said vindictively.

I said, 'Any idea what you're going to name the baby yet?'

'Aye, Elizabeth Ceinwen, Ceinwen after Betty's old lady. There's the whistle. Now listen, watch out for the through balls, Hughie. I'll be sending 'em on to you.'

'Did you hear about Tegwyn Thomas?' I said.

'Yeah, Betty mentioned something about her. In the pudding club, isn't she?'

'Joe Hart, he's the...'

'Burquish bastard he is,' Gee-Gee said. 'Gerrup in front, mun, the ref's waiting for you.'

On the whistle I pushed the ball to our inside left, who jinked like a drunken buzz-fly, banging himself into Galed Blue's inside right. Straight off they had the ball, and I heard Morley Latham wailing at us to pass square. He was very nigh double rupturing himself over passing the ball square; he'd experienced this Continental type football via the telly box. But Albion All-Stars were eleven highly individual players with no genuine regard for team play. You take the average big-minded South Walian, he believes he can lick the world, he's better than George Bernard Shaw, or he could

76

become richer than Clore if he really set his mind to it. Any brand of power or genius, the chopsy, industrialised South Walian knows it all. He'll work in the same pit or factory throughout his life, but he knows the lot. Irrepressible entertainers are the lowest of the low, and we come next.

Galed Blues sneaked a goal inside five minutes. They had the awkwardest right winger you'll ever see; he ran like a man with a stalk on, or as if he had a bunch of grapes between his legs. Gee-Gee tackled him and slid full weight over the touch-line, then this winger let our goalie crash into him, but he rose, climbing up space like a spider and all he had to do was tap the ball into the net. Our goalie bawled at Gee-Gee, accusing him of failing to mark his man.

'Man each, boys! Mark a man each!' appealed Morley.

Gee-Gee told the winger, 'You won't bloody-well do that again, butty.'

He didn't either, until the second half.

The game settled down to ding-dong from end to end, with the full-backs booting the ball anywhere off the twenty-five yard line. Our boys were marking all right, never a thought of trying something constructive, just mark, stop, slam into touch. And Galed Blues clung to their lead with the same tactics. At half-time I asked Gee-Gee about the through balls he was going to chip on for my benefit.

'This next half,' he said. 'We've got the bastards weighed up now. See that bloke on the wing? He's had his lot.'

'Oh aye, well done, boy,' I said.

But directly from the kick-off that awkward winger did another solo run. Leaving Gee-Gee grass-cutting on his knees, he worked the ball into the top left-hand corner. We were two down and Morley came waddling on to the field as if he meant to book the ref. They were all packed around him, demanding a foul on Gee-Gee, but clearly enough Gee-Gee and the winger tangled legs and Gee-Gee lost the use of his. Our side pulled together then, we had to because there were a few under-couraged ones in the Galed team, I mean obvious preeners who loved themselves in their football togs.

The ground was hard, and I still wore those Johnny Haynes boots, but I had to do a lot of chasing. My first offer came from a long high lob which deceived the Galed centre-half. We went up for it side by side, nothing resembling the leaping salmon or red deer you read about from John Arlott in *The Observer*, and I just managed to nod it back to our inside-right, Esger Rogers, who couldn't lose his first team place, not while his mother laundered our jerseys and shorts. A neat footballer, Esger, anyway. He worked the ball on a few yards, their left-back coming at him Zulu-wise, then Esger ran over the ball, blocking the full-back, and all I had to do was shove it past the goalie, Esger's goal as much as mine; he took a spew-maker in the taters from the full-back.

Right then, 2–1, Morley hurrahing up and down the touch-line like a co-ed's daddy. The game developed rough and boring afterwards. I shan't bother any more with it – we won 3–2. Esger scored, Gee-Gee got one off the spot, and Nebo's son Dilwyn, he headed the false teeth of Galed's centre-forward. His upper dentures fell into his cupped hands like broken dominoes.

from *The Full Time Amateur* (1966)

Dannie Abse

City Supporter

In the authorised silence of the house, upstairs in my bedroom, long past the fidgety tick of midnight, I lie horizontal under the sheets, my head on the pillow. The curtains are drawn. My wife, inert, asleep beside me. I stare at the back of my eyelids. This is the Waiting Room of Sleep. Before I am called to the other side of the adjoining door's frosted window, something needs to inhabit the restless mind.

I confess that during those last wakeful moments which stretch and elongate with advancing age like shadows moving away from a night lamppost, I frequently summon eleven blue-shirted Cardiff City football players, along with three substitutes, into the now crowded Waiting Room to autograph Sleep's Visitors' Book. I have done so intermittently over many decades. Different players file in, one by one. All wear the Bluebird shirt. Some announce their famous names: Trevor Ford, John Charles, Mel Charles, Ivor Allchurch, all of whom played for Cardiff City in their declining football years.

What a pathetic confession! What a ridiculous obsession! Am I a baby needing a sort of dummy before I can fall asleep?

Here I am, a grown-up man, indeed an old man, still dreamily involved with a relatively down-and-out Division Three soccer team. More than that, I'm hungry for Cardiff City news: who's asked for a transfer? Who's injured? Who's in, who's out? What happened to X and will Ryan Giggs really sign for Cardiff?

In recent years I have become friendly with Leslie Hamilton, the Cardiff City doctor. Sometimes, when the Bluebirds play in or near London where I spend three-quarters of my life, he invites me to join him in the directors' box and enjoy the backstage pre-match and half-time hospitality of the home side. Always first, though, a sighing admonition: 'You can't come like that, Dannie. You have to be suitably dressed.' The short-haired businessmen who populate the boardrooms of football are stuffily rank conscious. Some Saturdays I wear a tie.

I must irritate my friend, Dr Hamilton, not only sartorially. Because I want to hear the latest Cardiff City gossip, the behind-the-scenes misdoings and machinations, the comings and goings, the resignations and aspirations, the betrayals of the last manager, the style of the new one, I sometimes clutch Dr Hamilton's lapels and cross-examine him. He, alas, remains, as a doctor should, invincibly discreet. Or I display my own swanking medical knowledge and query the constituents of the team's pre-match diet or propose, 'Given the absence of joint changes on clinical and X-ray examination; given normal laboratory findings, maybe it's just a psychogenic arthralgia?' How often he diverts my penetrative suggestions or diagnoses by telling me that he met someone who writes poetry. 'One of the players?' I ask hopefully, remembering the forgettable verses of ex-Cardiff City centre-forward, John Toshack.

I learn more about happenings at Ninian Park by reading the *South Wales Football Echo* which I have sent to me at my London home all season. Even when I worked as Writer-in-Residence at Princeton University, New Jersey 08540, USA for the 1973-74 academic year, I ensured that the pink newspaper regularly reached our rented home in Pine Street. I did not subscribe to the *Times Literary Supplement*, the *New Statesman*, the *Listener*, or the *Spectator*. I needed to keep in touch only with vital news.

More important, of course, than football chatter is watching the actual games. This I did and this I do for I am a season-ticket holder. I arrange my frequent sojourns in South Wales to coincide with Cardiff's home fixtures. If invited to give a poetry reading at Hereford or Hartlepool or Scunthorpe or any other sad Division Three town I scan the Bluebirds' fixture list to suggest a particular Saturday evening date so that I can be rewarded by watching my team play on that same away-day afternoon.

Once upon a youthful time I often shared a platform or stage at a provincial town hall, theatre, library or pub, with Laurie Lee. When we were offered a tandem gig somewhere in the United Kingdom it used to worry me that Laurie would consult his address book to see if he had a friend, for all I know a girl friend, in this or that town whereas I merely fumbled yet again for the City fixture list. Dummy. Dummy. Cider only with the Bluebirds and not a Rosie in sight. Were, and are, my priorities wrong?

'If you want to go, you're on your own,' insisted my seventeen-year-old brother, Leo.

'The *Echo* reckons they'll do better than last season,' I said, trying to persuade my big brother to take me to Ninian Park.

'They couldn't do worse.'

81

'They've eight new players,' I mumbled.

Almost a year earlier I had seen my first game. Leo had allowed me to accompany him to watch the Bluebirds play Torquay United. We had joined 18,000 jugular critics for that Division Three (South) match. City had lost only 0-1, so I was hooked!

That 1933-34 season when I first became a fan, Cardiff City's ponderous and awkward defence leaked 105 goals. If they, surprisingly, scored first then the headlines in the *South Wales Echo* would inevitably read BLUEBIRDS FLATTER TO DECEIVE. They finished bottom of Division Three and, pleadingly, had to seek re-election – their worst season in their history. Only a few years earlier, in the previous decade, the Bluebirds had been Division One League Championship runners-up, FA Cup finalists and FA Cup winners. But since 1929 they'd slid down the league tables as if greased. How are the mighty fallen! Tell it not at the Kop, publish it not in the streets of Highbury, lest the daughters of Swansea Town rejoice.

Though I had never seen them in their prime, they were still my heroes. When I kicked a football in Roath Park or a tennis ball in the back lane with villain Phillip Griffiths, I underwent a wondrous metamorphosis. I wore an invisible royal blue shirt and I responded to the name of speedy Reg Keating, the City centre-forward, a blur of blue, who was known to have once scored a goal. So I was very disappointed that on Saturday, 25 August 1934, Leo would not take me to Ninian Park because, as he said, they lost all the time.

So what? We always seemed to back losers in our house.

We sided with the workers but the capitalists continued to water the workers' beer. Hadn't he, himself, taught me an alternative rhyming alphabet which began – A stands for Armaments, the capitalists pride, B stands for Bolshie, the thorn in their side? We voted Labour, didn't we? But around our patch they always lost the elections. Leo drummed into me that the Red Indians were the good guys not the imperialist cowboys. It was true too: Saturday mornings at the Globe cinema, the cowboys, led by Tom Mix, always won. And hadn't I heard my mother muttering, shaking her head, 'Your Dad's a loser'? Was she, I wonder, only talking about horses and greyhounds?

It was my gentle and beloved father, though, who one Saturday of late August sunlight financed me – pennies for the tramcar journey, sixpence for the game – so that I could go ON MY OWN, for the first time, to Ninian Park. Still only ten years high, I set out on this daring expedition from our semi-detached house in Albany Road. I don't remember my farewell in the hallway but I bet my mother fussed and kissed me goodbye as if I were going on a trek to the North Pole.

An hour or so later I stood outside the Ninian Park stadium disconsolate. I searched through my pockets once more only to find the used tram ticket, pennies for my return journey and the handkerchief that my mother had pushed into my pocket before I left the house. The sixpence had vanished, the little silver sixpenny bit, so generously given to me despite business being so bad and Australia winning the final Test match by 562 runs, had become invisible.

All around me people filed through the turnstiles. Someone was shouting, 'Programmes, getcher programme,' and another fellow with a strange Schnozzle Durante croak attempted to sell the converging crowds this or that differently coloured rosette. There were policemen on foot and policemen on horses and amid all the whirl of movement a few stood lazily in front of an unhygienic-looking van whose owner in a white coat purveyed sizzling sausages and onions.

I listened glumly to the conversations of those standing at the van. I don't recall what they were saying. Perhaps they spoke fondly of the old days, of the great players who wore the royal blue shirt – Fred Keenor, Hardy, Ferguson and Farquharson, legendary figures before my time. I did not know what they were saying and soon, in any case, they moved off. No one loitered near the sausage van. Gradually the crowds in Sloper Road thinned out, to join the flat-capped masses swaying in the swearing terraces. I could hear the military band playing within the ground. I stood there, close to tears, knowing the misery of the world and that. Outside is a lonely place.

How did I lose that sixpence? On the way maybe, upstairs in the smoke-filled tram? Had I pulled the handkerchief out of my pocket and inadvertently sent the sixpenny bit rolling beneath one of the varnished wooden seats? Surely the pipe-smoking pensioner sitting next to me wasn't an evil, clever pickpocket? What would I tell them all when I returned home? Mama, I sat next to Bill Sykes.

A sudden, barbaric roar from the crowd within the stadium signalled that the teams had appeared from the tunnel. The game would soon begin. Still some stragglers hurried towards the turnstiles as I waited there, unwilling to retrace my steps down Sloper Road. Soon there were no longer any late-comers. I stood in solitary vigil listening to the crowd's oohs and resonant aahs, coming and fading now that the game had begun. I must have been crying for suddenly a gruff voice said, 'Whassermara, sonny?' He bent down, he was a policeman so he sided with the oppressors of the workers – Leo had told me. But when I confessed that I had lost my sixpence he advised, 'They let the unemployed in near the end of the game. They open the gates at the Grangetown end. You could slip in then, sonny.' He began to walk away. Then he changed his mind. He came back and gave me sixpence.

I joined the 20,000 spectators in Ninian Park who attended the first Division Three (South) game of the 1934-35 season. In the crowded Grangetown area between the goalposts I, umbilicus-high, tried to struggle through the massed supporters so that I could see my heroes. Suddenly, as was the custom with small boys, I was elevated by benign hands and passed down good-naturedly over capped heads to join other pygmies near the front. We beat Charlton Athletic 2-1 and Keating scored one of the goals. I thought you'd like to know that. Though we won those late summer matches we ended that season 19th in the league. As so often City 'flattered only to deceive'.

*   *   *

I am trying to recall in more detail how it used to be at Ninian Park before and after the old wooden Grand Stand, one evening in 1937, lit up with incandescent fury as it burned on and on and to the ground. The Canton Stand had not then been surgically abbreviated to render it safe to sit in. The Grangetown end, now open to the frequently raining Welsh skies, used to be steeper and higher and owned a long oblique roof. The Division Three crowds averaged 20,000 not the current 3,000.

Before the match a brass band, a uniformed platoon, would march around the touchlines, hoompa hoompa, as they played rhythmic military airs. Bollocks. And the same to you. Bollocks. A man pregnant with a huge drum would trail behind the platoon, while leading them an ostentatious conjurer would, at intervals, throw a somersaulting pole high into the air before catching it in his croupier-white gloves. How the crowd would have loved to observe that Clever Dick lose and drop it.

Just before kick-off the brass band would assemble outside the players' tunnel. When the team spurted on to the turf the band would strike up Cardiff's inappropriate, inanely optimistic, signature tune: HAPPY DAYS ARE HERE AGAIN. The crowd's welcoming shout to the emerging players would zenith to such decibels that the pigeons which, at one time, thrived under the roofs of the stands would fountain up and out and away.

In those sepia days before the war, season after season I, alone or with school friends, used to observe this pre-match ritual from behind the goalposts at the Grangetown end. Opposite, the length of the green pitch away, loomed the slanting roof of the Canton Stand on which was painted an advertisement for Franklyn's Tobacco. Beneath it, in the depths of the posterior darkness, small sparks of light would transiently appear here and there, above and below, to the left and to the right - evidence that the advertisement had been effective for the spectators were lighting up their pipes or cigarettes.

Before the commencement of the game, a flotilla of motorised wheelchairs carrying cripples of the First World War would settle below the wings of the Grand Stand behind the touchlines near the corner flags. By 1939 these odd, closed, ugly vehicles had become scarce but after the Second World War, out of the smoke as it were, in an unhappy reincarnation, new wheelchair vehicles appeared. Years passed before they vanished from the scene.

So often have I visited Ninian Park in fine, wet, or wind blown weather, have stood on the terraces, sat in the stands, been comfortable or bloody cold as I observed football fashions changing: the prolegomenon and the tactics on the pitch. Everything so different and so much the same. I see the brown ball become white, see it passed back to the goalkeeper who picks it up, though directed from his own teammate. I hear a referee's long whistle blow from a bygone year. How does the song go? I remember it well. And 1952 was a very good year: City returned (briefly, alas) to Division One and over 50,000 attended the final Second Division game against Leeds.

Memory of faded games, the discarded years,
talk of Aston Villa, Orient, and the Swans.
Half-time, the band played the same military airs
as when the Bluebirds once were champions.
Round touchlines the same cripples in their chairs.

In those lean, utility, post-war years, before the introduction of floodlighting, fixtures began at 2.30 p.m. and
the kick-off was even earlier mid-winter. Often, late in the
game, the players in the smoke-brown, thickening gloom,
would become, at the distant Canton end, anonymous
astigmatic figures drifting this way or that without evident
purpose. At the confusion of the final whistle, whatever the
score – win, lose or draw – hordes of youngsters would
invade the pitch. Some would bring on a ball and
incompetently kick it into the empty Grangetown end goal
with amazing delight, others would seek the players'
autographs. They were hardly chased off. They had become
part of the Saturday afternoon ritual.

Nor did one experience feelings of incipient threat as the
crowds dispersed into and through the dusk of Sloper Road.
Because money was scarcer, trains slower, motorways not
yet built, away fans did not usually attend the game in
numbers. The home crowd, being more homogeneous,
shared the same gods (who failed them), chanted the same
chorus. They belonged to the same defeated tribe.

Like many of the youngsters near the barrier behind the
goalposts I held back at the end of the match in order to
avoid the crush of the crowds converging through the big
gates of the Grangetown end. How quickly Ninian Park
became empty, forlorn, abandoned, as the unaccompanied
small boys patiently waited there. Outside the lampposts
jerked into luminous activity and somehow emphasised the
oncoming darkness of a December night.

How many occasions did I see City lose; how often the
thin, damp, Welsh rain descended in melancholy sympathy

at lighting-up time as I quit the ground into Sloper Road to progress under the hoardings, to re-enter real life. 'South Wales Echo, sir. Last edition. NAZIS ENTER RHINELAND. Echo. Echo. Echo.'

Silent the stadium. The crowds have all filed out.
Only the pigeons beneath the roofs remain.
The clean programmes are trampled underfoot
and natural the dark, appropriate the rain
while under lampposts threatening newsboys shout.

from *Perfect Pitch* (1997)

Trevor Ford

The Centre Forward

...All this confirmed my great faith in my style of play. It is fair, it produces goals and it pulls the crowds. Yes, I am fully conscious of the fact that many people roll up to the game just to jeer and hoot at Ford, but at least my style has the virtue of being positive; it is something strong and definite, not the milk-and-water stuff that is causing attendances to drop all over the country. To pull in the crowds and be a Soccer personality a centre-forward must have a lot. He must be able to let fly with both feet and from any angle. If he can't then he will never survive because a leader perpetually crowded by the stopper centre-half with little space in which to manoeuvre and no time to spare must have that something extra that notches the goals.

So let's give him equal facility with both feet. What else does he need? Speed – speed off the mark and the ability to put on a terrific burst; he must know no fear, he must have a powerful shot, and a high mobility with the Houdini flair for wriggling out of tight corners.

Anything else? – in my opinion, yes! He must be a worrier of the most pestilential sort, a bustler with utter disregard for the size of the full-back and the opinions of the hotheads on the bob bank, and a trier of the absolutely impossible. If, like me, he believes that there is a future in British Soccer, then he will have this fact burned into his brain; the thrills in Soccer are all there in the penalty box ready to be produced in all their noisy glory by the centre-forward who has all the qualities that I have spoken about. The mid-field moves, the clever approach work, the wing-to-wing passes are all very entertaining, but it is when that ball skids into the penalty area that the crowds begin to pant. That is when I go on the rampage hunting for a thrill for the crowd. They are goal-hungry, every man jack of them. They have come to see goals scored and it is my job to score them. If that includes charging the goalkeeper, either to get the ball from him or to bundle him and the ball over the goal line, then I am within my rights – and I am giving the public what it wants. Shoulder-charging is part of Soccer just as crash-tackling is part of rugby; take it away and we lose for ever that all-in action which the public demands – and has every right to expect from professional footballers. They pay the piper and I for one don't blame them calling the tune.

But so many men on the bob bank do not realize that if

the shoulder-charge is banned from Soccer, then Soccer will die. Just as well take the hops from beer or the salt and vinegar from the late-night bag of fish-and-chips! Ban the shoulder-charge and this great game of ours would degenerate into a milk-and-water 'after you, my dear!' affair more like a leisurely, polite Sunday croquet engagement than a Saturday afternoon blood-warming trial of masculine strength and skill.

And another thing! A ban on shoulder-charging would allow considerably more scope to the snakes of Soccer – the really dirty players.

Who do I mean? – the crafty ankle-tappers who put men out of the game for a month, and openly boast of it in the dressing-room; the completely unprincipled players who hack blindly at a man's shins when the referee turns his back; the roughs who lunge deliberately with their knees into a player's thigh muscle or groin; the back-slashers – players who kick up – backwards at a man coming from behind and rip his legs with a set of football studs. These are the snakes of Soccer; these are the men for whose blood the fans on the terraces should scream – but don't. And why? Because the snakes of Soccer are like the reptiles after whom I name them – they are cunning and vicious; they strike incredibly swiftly and at the right moment – when the referee is unsighted. So crafty are these rotten characters that their underhand tactics go unseen in the hurly-burly of the match.

It has always struck me as peculiar that most of the football snakes I have run up against are small weasel-like men. They have insufficient weight to use a shoulder-charge effectively, so they call on all the mean, dirty tricks they know – and get away with it.

Yet, because I am playing centre-forward and am right there in the glare of the goalmouth limelight, I am reviled and barracked when I go crashing and bashing my way through legitimately. Strange, isn't it? And how some of these snakes love to put me off my game! A few minutes after the starting whistle one of them will crack me on the ankle and grate, 'Take that, you Welsh – !' A couple of minutes later he'll give me another wallop and I know then that the stirring-up treatment is coming. The idea is to give me such a hammering early in the game that I progressively get angrier and angrier and go for someone a bit too fiercely. Then, because the Ford name is all too well known, an irate referee bounces over and snarls, 'Any more of that, Ford, and off you go!' I used to be a sucker for the stirring-up technique but I'm wise to it now. And I'm glad to say that there are a good many English League referees who are wise to it, too. Several have told me at various times, 'Just play within the rules as you have been doing, you have nothing to fear from us.'

I've tried all along the line to play within the rules and have run foul of referees on remarkably few occasions. Nevertheless, the bitter heartbreaking barracking and cat-calling I received from the fans when I was with Aston Villa and Sunderland forced me to the conclusion – sadly, I admit – that part of it at least was motivated by something that had nothing to do with football or any lack of skill on my part. Up there in the crowd were bigoted, prejudiced men and women who hurled vile abuse at me – merely because I am Welsh. I heard what they shouted and often my heart sank.

If these pig-headed people call themselves sports lovers then they do the name of sport a grave injustice. No real sportsman would allow his judgment to be warped by the fact that a player was born in Swansea and not Southsea. I am Welsh and proud of it; those who insult me because of my nationality merely betray themselves as intolerant, besotted followers of a game that is supposed to encourage all that is fine in man. Football deserves better supporters than that. And in the main – thank goodness – it has.

from *I Lead the attack* (1957)

John Toshack

The Gentle Giant

The greatest player I've ever seen,
I'm sure you know the one I mean.
From watching him I learned so much,
A Gentle Giant with a subtle touch.

A Big Man with a secret gift,
He gave his colleagues such a lift.
In defence or in attack,
Nobody could hold him back.

It really was a marvellous sight,
To see him moving in full flight.
And when the ball was in the air,
Opponents used to stand and stare.

There wasn't a thing he couldn't do,
King John could score goals, stop them too!

Welshmen worshipped the ground he trod,
Italians treated him like a God.
But in spite of his undoubted fame,
His character remains the same.
Though all his goals are in the past,
The memories will always last.

from *Gosh it's Tosh* (1976)

David Farmer and Peter Stead

Ivor

Across the land people knew of Ivor and for many years his name was largely synonymous with Swansea. 'Where are you from?' one would be asked, or more usually, 'Who do you support?' and the mere mention of 'Swansea' would be enough to elicit the immediate response: 'Ivor Allchurch'. Fans read about him in match programmes although, as had been implied, they hardly needed them as far as team line-ups were concerned. If Swansea Town were named on the cover then sure enough Ivor would be at inside-left wearing No. 10. But, as Sir Matt Busby once commented in a marvellous and entirely appropriate tribute, Ivor 'never needed a number on his back' for his polish and class were unmistakable. In fact almost everything about him was unmistakable. In those days footballers came in a far greater variety of physical shape and size and, indeed, one reason for the game's popularity in urban Britain was the way it catered for all the types to be found in the average terraced row, village or school class. Michael Parkinson once provided a useful guide for readers who could not remember those days when horribly ugly gnarled legs determined full-backs and wing-halves, frailty wingers, madness goalies, robustness centre-forwards, ranginess and thick skulls centre-halves and vision inside-forwards, with the distinct probability that the inside-left would be a consumptive intellectual. That final tag could never have been applied to Ivor but, even if he had appeared without a number, a crowd to whom he was a stranger would have spotted him immediately as the side's thinker, the ideas man, the passer, the genius, the player who would make things happen, and all that would have been obvious even as he ran out for the warm-up. Already he stood out, for there was a studied and yet natural elegance about the man, a refinement that was clinched by his unnaturally blond and wavy hair. Most fans saw him first wearing the white of Swansea, and that too invested him with a slightly unnatural and perhaps even priestly aura: there was, even before the kick-off, a presence and potential about this No. 10 which promised a new dimension – and a challenging one if he was in the opposing team.

In the game itself all that class and polish to which Sir Matt referred soon became evident. There was a rhythm and flow to Ivor's play that will become very familiar as his playing career is recalled. He was usually to be found just inside his opponent's half, either in or adjacent to the centre circle. On receiving the ball he would instinctively turn to shield it from any opponent before looking up and passing the ball immaculately either to a nearby colleague or, more usually to a waiting winger some thirty yards distant. Now this was prettily done and suitably applauded, but it was par for the course and almost every team in the land had a visionary who instinctively passed the ball in such a way as to convince the crowd that he could 'do it with his eyes closed'. But Ivor was more than a slide-rule passer. There was his control, his balance, his grace, his ability to dictate the pace of the game and to unlock midfield stalemates, but even more there was the way in which his whole body would suddenly be capable of changing the general rhythm of the game with just a sudden surge of energy that for him seemed utterly natural. That surge might involve a body swerve; that was one of his hallmarks and John Crooks once memorably referred to the way in which Ivor was capable of sending 10,000 people behind the goal 'the wrong way'. There could be quick one-twos with other forwards and then a short sprint followed by a surprisingly powerful and direct shot or a cruelly effective chipped shot, for he was a genuine finisher to a far greater extent that most mere 'passers'. If a goal had been scored he would turn quickly to get on with the game but there was always just a hint of a smile that conveyed real pleasure. If the shot hit the bar or narrowly missed he would simply shrug, gently flicking out his lower arms as the crowd shared his sense not so much of the game's frustrations as of its exhilarating tension. Every game was like this with no dissent, no anger, just a recital of skills within the shape and form of the team game that had its own course to run. Some games were won, others were drawn or lost but always there was the rhythm, the expectation, the moments of sheer delight, the poetry. Watching Ivor play was a confirmation of how life, however humdrum, allowed instances of utterly natural grace and excellence.

from *Ivor Allchurch, MBE* (1998)

Huw Richards

Inter-City Rivalry

It is a truth universally acknowledged, at least if one's universe starts west of Bridgend, that the single good thing to have come out of Cardiff is the road to Swansea. Our capital city was recently branded by Swansea's *South Wales Evening Post*, in a headline making up in pungent expression of local opinion what it lacked in linguistic elegance, as 'a greedy city with a big mouth'. Amid the immense range of fissures characterizing modern Wales and exposed most graphically in the referendum on the creation of the National Assembly for Wales – north v. south, east v. west, Welsh-speaking v. Anglophone, Objective One v. Not Quite So Poor – none is more ferocious than that conducted, ever since the two communities emerged out of industrialization as the pole-stars of south-east and south-west Wales, between Swansea and Cardiff. Part of this rivalry is rooted in differences in character. Swansea's fortunes were built on metal-bashing, its cosmopolitanism as a seaport leavened by the influence of a hinterland which is consciously Welsh and not infrequently Welsh speaking. Cardiff's raison d'être was its location as entrepôt to the Rhondda coalfields, its character informed by rapid late-nineteenth-century immigration which brought it not only West Countrymen but the black and Irish populations who have made such an immense contribution to its sporting culture. But the real roots of dislike are common to anywhere two cities of roughly comparable size jostle for leadership, and the prizes that it brings – Manchester v. Liverpool, Newcastle v. Sunderland and Southampton v. Portsmouth come to mind. This battle has been won conclusively by Cardiff, taking not only newly created baubles such as capital status and the series of government agencies that go with it, but also prizes which were once shared – international rugby in 1954 and county cricket in the later 1990s. If no one in Swansea ever truly believed that the city would get the National Assembly, the irony that Cardiff was this time awarded a prize against which it had voted added a further edge to the bitterness of rejection.

That rivalry is seen at its most visceral in sport, an outlet providing a notionally objective test of superiority. One reason why Glamorgan cricket did not fix a county headquarters at the time of its foundation in the 1880s was that matches between Swansea and Cardiff were noted for skullduggery and contested results, and the club had no desire to import the quarrel. Wilfred Wooller, an adopted Cardiffian, wrote of the utter fury of a Swansea crowd when he stole victory at St Helen's with a late drop-goal some time in the 1930s. In football, a tangible air of fear and loathing hangs like malignant ectoplasm over derby matches at Ninian Park and Vetch Field, with the day's battles liable to be worked out ad nauseam in the letter columns of the local press by the one-eyed and the brain-dead of both sides. The match also has an inexplicable charm for satellite television's match-schedulers who fail to recognize that the quality of the football, however good or bad the teams in their other matches, is almost invariably lamentable. Like certain sexual practices, Swansea City v. Cardiff City matches should be performed in private with participation confined to consenting adults. And the rivalry also spreads into other matches. If some apparently inoffensive opponent is singled out for non-stop hostility at the Vetch Field, the likeliest explanation is that he is a former inmate of Ninian Park.

Yet there has been considerable interchange between the clubs over the years. This was underlined, perhaps unconsciously, in 'Only Sixty-Four Years', the poet Dannie Abse's beautiful essay on his lifetime as a Cardiff fan, in *Perfect Pitch*. Abse described how he would while away hours of sleeplessness by summoning up the images of great Cardiff players: 'All wear the Bluebird shirt. Some announce their famous names: Trevor Ford, John Charles, Mel Charles, Ivor Allchurch, all of whom played for Cardiff City in their declining football years.' Cardiff fans will have reacted to that sentence by considering the counter-claims of such as Fred Keenor, Alf Sherwood and Phil Dwyer. No Swansea City fan can read it without instantly remarking that the four names Abse conjures from Cardiff memories dating back to the 1930s all came from Swansea and all, but John Charles, first played for the Swans.

from *For Club and Country* (2000)

David Eastwood

Ryan Giggs

On 14 April 1999 Manchester United faced Arsenal in a FA Cup semi-final replay at Villa Park. United's season was on a knife edge: they were still in the UEFA Champions' League and chasing the Premiership, but now were reduced to ten men and fighting to stay in the FA Cup. In extra time a pulsating game seemed to be heading towards the synthetic climax of a penalty shootout, when suddenly the match reached its apotheosis with a goal of transcendent quality. Ryan Giggs picked up the ball fifteen yards inside the United half. In a mesmerizing run he beat defender after defender and then scored with a thunderous shot into the roof of the net. Football is sometimes a game devalued by hyperbole, but when Alex Ferguson described this as a 'historic' goal, no one demurred. When he hailed it as 'one of the best goals ever scored in major football', few disagreed. Many footballers can score fine goals, only the greatest score goals as such as this.

This one goal symbolized Giggs's career and footballing greatness: mesmeric ball control, the ability to float past defenders, pace and balance, courage and commitment, and sheer exuberance in scoring. His goal opened the road to Manchester United's unique treble of winning the Premiership, FA Cup, and European Champions' League.

... Although Manchester United is a club that inspires enthusiasm and hatred in a uniquely passionate way – although rival supporters constantly urge one another to 'stand up if you hate Man. U.' – Giggs's goal, like Giggs's talent, stood outside this passionate antipathy. Everyone applauded; everyone who loved the game hailed this as a moment of consummate beauty in the beautiful game, Ryan Giggs was a player who compelled admiration and escaped the polarizing mixture of envy and criticism that defined the popular reputation of so many stars.

His semi-final goal also recalled a former United number 11, George Best. That comparison had been made early in Giggs's career and continued to be made thereafter. They both had the same close control, the same cruel ability to devastate defenders by their pace or turn them with an almost balletic sense of balance. They both had the same eye for goal. They also had similarly striking looks, and both had complex and rich ethnic identities: Best as a Northern Irish Protestant, Giggs as a Welshman with mixed ancestry. These parallels could be and were overplayed. Best was an even more complete player: genuinely two-footed, and a wonderful header of the ball. Indeed to many who saw him Best lingers in the memory as a unique talent. He was also, notoriously, a victim of his talent, and his ended as a career corroded rather than crowned by stardom. By contrast Giggs's personality managed to comprehend his talent. He lived life to the full, but not to overflowing. He carefully policed the borderlines between his public career and his private life and, long after fame beckoned, he retained strong commitments to family and friends. His manager, Alex Ferguson, relates one incident where he was informed that the young Ryan Giggs, Lee Sharpe, and other young professionals were partying loudly between two important games. Ferguson arrived and ordered them home, cuffing each errant player on the back of the head. Giggs, according to Ferguson, never transgressed again. He was, Ferguson believed, 'a fine young man' and 'a credit to his mother'. Many careers were destroyed by excess. Giggs saw and rejected such excess, and in so doing gave his talent full rein and earned respect throughout his sport.

Ryan Giggs was born Ryan Wilson, in Cardiff, on 29 November 1973. He lived in the Welsh capital until he was seven: long enough to acquire a Welsh accent, the words of the Welsh anthem, and a sense of actually being Welsh. Throughout his later career, when people bemoaned his being Welsh and thus confined to playing on the margins of international football, Giggs would reply simply that he was Welsh, and was 'proud to be Welsh'. After leaving Cardiff he would return regularly for weekends and summer holidays. His father, Danny Wilson, signed for Swinton Rugby League Club after making a handful of appearances at fly-half for Cardiff. Ryan moved north reluctantly. He attended Grosvenor Road Primary School in Swinton, shed his Welsh accent because he was teased for it by other kids, and shone as a footballer. From early days he was a natural athlete, with pace, balance and a passion for the game. He played everywhere, was a capable goalkeeper, but gravitated naturally to the left wing. A destiny was emerging.

... In an age where many leading footballers have been unquiet souls – driven by money, agents and uncritical adulation; and unsettled by the pressures of stardom, the cruel scrutiny of the media and the evanescence of their excellence – Giggs has been a more serene figure. True, there have been celebrity girlfriends, fast cars, big houses and stupendous wealth, but he has retained a sense of perspective. Money, he suggested, mattered less when you had more of it. Friendships and family affections are not something to be paraded occasionally for the press, but to be lived and nurtured. In an era when many leading players seemed to regard football as a branch of showbusiness, for Giggs it has remained a sport in the truest sense. He is a professional athlete, and the demands of the game come first. Life is to be lived, but not in ways which compromise his performance on the field. He noticed that Eric Cantona did not drink for four days before a match, and took note. He recognized that natural talent made training more important not less. He knew and said he was 'a flair player', but flair and talent simply gave him a decisive advantage as a professional athlete. Where some, such as Paul Gascoigne, abused natural talent, and others, George Best most notably, were ultimately overwhelmed by it, Giggs was content to hone his skills, preserve his pace and recognize that exquisite skills imposed responsibilities to deliver match-winning moments for the team and entertainment for the fans.

Behind all this lies a more complex and more mature personality than many of his peers. Here, perhaps, Giggs's richer sense of identity was important. Here, perhaps, his Welshness mattered. For many footballers nationality matters relatively little. It is there, inherited, assumed: it does not have to be lived. Giggs's Welshness was different. Different because some people thought it was a negotiable identity; different because he was a Welshman in Manchester; and different because sometimes his commitment to Wales and the Welsh side was questioned. Giggs often referred to himself as 'a local lad', by which, of course, he meant a Manchester lad, a Stretford-ender, a graduate of Greater Manchester schoolboy football. His primary cultural identity was and is Mancunian, and it is this that informs his powerful identification with United as a club and as an institution. United, by now the largest club in world football, casts its spell on most who play for it. For those like Giggs who grew up in its shadow and felt its history, that sense of identification with the club is still more profound.

And yet Giggs has remained persistently and publicly Welsh. His greatest moment of personal pride was in captaining his country. Nothing, he thought, 'would top captaining Wales'. Wales was 'where I was born', Manchester where he grew up, and United which made him a star. As we have already seen, much has been made of Giggs's missing so many friendly matches for Wales. On both sides of the border this has been read as betraying a lukewarm commitment to his country, and as suggesting a sense of regret that his talent was confined on the international stage to representing a minor footballing nation. This is to misread Giggs's motives and to misunderstand his professionalism. The English may have a particular reason for doing this. They, almost to a person, have wished that Giggs had been English. He had captained England Schoolboys, so he could, they thought, have played for England. This sense of loss was misplaced. Giggs is Welsh, wished to represent his country, and was wanted by his country. Nevertheless, this sense of loss was all the more piquant for English supporters and commentators because, throughout Giggs's career, the English have lacked a gifted left-sided forward, and never even glimpsed an English left-winger of Giggs's speed and touch. An English Giggs, the argument went, would have transformed England. Moreover, the English national side would have showcased Giggs's talent in a way nothing else could.

This argument was mistaken on many counts. England throughout the 1990s was a moderate team managed, with the exception of Terry Venables, by men of very moderate abilities. Playing for England Giggs would have won nothing, though he would have played in the final stages of the World and European Championships. Crucially, though, it would not have changed the evaluation of his quality either by contemporaries or by posterity. Giggs, the Welsh international of the 1990s, was in a different position from, say, George Best the Northern Ireland international of the 1960s. Best played in a British First Division in which he dazzled, and in a declining Manchester United team with which he did win once in Europe. Some still suggest that Best was not tested frequently enough at the highest level. For those who saw Best the argument is wilful and his genius beyond question. Still it has been made and parallels have been drawn with Giggs.

Yet Giggs's case is quite different. He has played the bulk of his career in an international Premier League. By the mid-1990s the English Premier League, awash with television money and advertising revenue, was truly an international league. Manchester United despite numerous foreign stars

105

was, in fact, the most British of the leading clubs of the later 1990s and, week in, week out, played against teams expensively assembled through lavish chequebooks from among the world's best players. At the turn of the century, Chelsea often fielded no British players, Arsenal transcended their reputation for remorselessly efficient defensive play by constructing a sparkling team compromising predominantly imported players, and even Liverpool followed suit. Giggs thus played international football every week. He plays for what most critics, at the turn of the century, regard as not only the finest club side in Britain but also probably the best club side in Europe. Certainly United has been a vastly better side than the Welsh teams which Giggs graced, but then they have also been a vastly better side than any England team fielded in the same period. There can be no doubting Giggs's standing on the international stage: he has graced that stage week by week. More than that, his talent has shone against all kinds of opposition. He is a flair player: he has had some moderate games, but even then the threat is always there. In a moment he can, and does, turn a game. The exquisite skills of the natural winger are the most striking aspects of Giggs's game, but to those who have watched closely, and above all to those who have managed and coached him, he has remained throughout a model professional. His work-rate is prodigious, he destroys defences, he delights crowds, and he has repaid his manager's faith one-hundredfold. Performing regularly at this level has been powerful confirmation of his ability and achievement. In the modern game few have displayed a better temperament and more consummate professional-ism, and goals such as that against Arsenal in the 1999 FA Cup semi-final are goals of pure genius. Such moments, shimmering in a career of constant achievement at the highest level, are why Ryan Giggs may come to be remembered as the greatest of all Welsh footballers.

from *For Club and Country* (2000)

Peter Finch

Meeting her lover

I cannot talk to him about football
because I don't know enough. The game
roars on the television like a floundering
ship. I try books but he doesn't respond.
With his fat eyes he looks so dumb.
We try weather it's exciting as
tyre pressures and motorway routes.
Outside the sun is enormous.
His car is shit fast he tells me I
couldn't give a damn. On the
screen the goals mount like fever,
men embracing on the green sward.
You take her then, I say, as
if this woman is still something I
have a hold on. But he's not looking,
the game's being played again,
on and on.

from *Useful* (1997)

FOUR LEGS
AND FEATHERS

Idris Davies

Send out your homing pigeons, Dai

Send out your homing pigeons, Dai,
Your blue-grey pigeons, hard as nails,
Send them with messages tied to their wings,
Words of your anger, words of your love.
Send them to Dover, to Glasgow, to Cork,
Send them to the wharves of Hull and of Belfast,
To the harbours of Liverpool and Dublin and Leith,
Send them to the islands and out of the oceans,
To the wild wet islands of the northern sea
Where little grey women go out in heavy shawls
At the hour of dusk to gaze on the merciless waters,
And send them to the decorated islands of the south
Where the mineowner and his tall stiff lady
Walk round and round the rose-pink hotel, day after day
                                              after day.
Send out your pigeons, Dai, send them out
With words of your anger and your love and your pride,
With stern little sentences wrought in your Heart,
Send out your pigeons, flashing and dazzling towards the sun.

Go out, pigeons bach, and do what Dai tells you.

from The Angry Summer (1943)

George Ewart Evans

Black Diamond

Someone was telling me the other day that Twm Mufti was so mad on whippets that he once overstepped the mark entirely. He was training his famous dog, Black Diamond, for a big race – so the story goes – and he was so nervous about letting the dog out of his sight that he turned his wife out of the bed and took the dog in instead of her. Now I know Twm Llewelyn like the back of my own hand, and I know for sure that he wouldn't do a thing like that. The story just isn't true, and if you can spare a minute or two I'll tell you the real one:

Now Twm bred this dog, Black Diamond, himself; and even when the dog was hardly strong enough to stand on his own legs he knew he'd got a winner, a dog that was worth his weight in gold. He nursed the puppy like a baby. Indeed, if it had been a baby it couldn't have been treated better. It had the best of everything they had in the house, the cream off the milk and the best bit off the meat. He'd never let anyone handle the dog except Eic Caneuon who sometimes took him for exercise, always on the lead and always wearing a muzzle to keep him from picking up stray bits about the lanes and the gutters.

But it was up on to the old Roman Road at the top of Cefn Leyshon that Twm would take his dog. And there you'd see them: Twm, short and a bit bandy in the leg, with a big blue shovel-scar across the bridge of his nose, striding along with the dog loping light as air beside him.

Tim (that was the dog's name: Black Diamond was only a racing name), Tim was a beautiful dog to look at. His coat was ebony and his body was a bit of poetry from the curve of his tail to the tip of his sharp-pointed nose. He was quiet and determined like Twm, not a noisy dog at all, and as compact as a watch.

About this time I am telling you, Twm was training the dog for the big race of his life. Twm had won handicaps with him up and down the valleys on many occasions, but this was to be the race of his whole career. He knew that he had one of the best whippets that had been bred in this valley, and he had entered him for the Thousand Pound Handicap given by one of the big papers, for entrants from all countries. Now Twm Mufti is one of those blokes, once they've made up their minds to do something, the thing's as good as done, even if you'd put it down as impossible. To look at Black Diamond, slight and frail as a bird, you'd think it was a small thing to hang all your hopes on. But Twm knew that he had more than a thousand pounds worth of running in him. He gave all his spare time to the dog, either down at the Welfare Ground exercising and giving him his trials or up on Cefn Leyshon, walking, and occasionally slipping the lead and giving the dog his freedom. The dog came on better than Twm had ever hoped. Eic Caneuon who had slipped all Twm's dogs said he had never handled a quieter dog and a dog who knew his business so well, going straight out of his hands and full into his stride without a turn of his head or a sway of his body – a black bullet straight from the barrel of a rifle.

Twm was very pleased with himself in his quiet sort of

way; but he told no one. Only three people in Llwyncelyn knew he'd entered the dog for the big Manchester race: Twm himself, Eic Caneuon, and Jack James the butcher who was the dog's backer. Whenever they had a trial-run down at the Welfare Ground, it was either early in the morning or late at night, just when it was getting dusk, so that few people knew that there was anything big on. Then about three weeks before the race, the dog had the accident. Twm was taking him along the Roman Road one evening as usual, and just as they came on to the moorland he spotted a couple of rabbits playing a hundred yards or so off the road, not far from the hedge skirting one of Jenkins Tyllwyd's fields. Without stopping to think, Twm slipped the lead off the dog and whispered: '*Ar ei ol e*', Tim [After him, Tim].' (It was his idea to give the dog a bit of sport, but he cursed himself afterwards.) The dog pricked up his ears and went after the rabbits like a streak, but just as he was coming up to them there was a loud report, and he swerved and came whimpering back to Twm. He knelt down, and although he could find no blood on the dog he could feel his heart pounding away like a little machine under his ribs. The shot had just frightened the life out of him.

Then Jenkins the farmer rose from behind the hedge, collected a rabbit and walked towards Twm who was still trying to calm the whimpering dog. Twm was white with temper, and it was touch and go whether there would be trouble there and then. But Jenkins said he never saw the whippet until he'd fired the shot; and Twm knew that he was really to blame for letting the dog off the lead; and he felt thankful that nothing worse had happened to him.

112

So he took the dog home, and next day went on with his training. But the dog seemed to have lost all his zest. He started at the least noise, and when Eic Caneuon caught hold of him to slip him at the trial-run that night, he squirmed and turned in his hands. It was clear that something serious had happened to him; and they called the trial off and Twm took the dog home. That night the dog was worse. He lay down by the fire, refusing all food, and not moving except to raise his head when Twm looked like going out of the room. And when he had gone to bed, the dog whimpered until he came down for him and took him into the bedroom. Next morning when Megan woke up, the dog was sleeping at the foot of the bed. But he was no better, and Twm made up his mind to stay home from work to see what he could do to doctor him. It was no use, although he dosed him and tried every trick he knew. Twm sat in the chair by the fire, watching the dog as he lay there, occasionally looking up at his master with a sad eye. And, naturally, Twm himself was down in the mouth as well. Then his wife Megan said sharply:

'Don't sit by there just looking at the dog! Take him down to Doctor O'Connor. He'll tell you what's the matter with him, if anybody will.'

Now Twm had never heard of taking a dog to the doctor; but there was no vet in Llwyncelyn, and he would have taken Tim to the hospital if there was only that chance of curing him. So he wrapped him in a blanket and carried him down to Doctor O'Connor's surgery. Now old O'Connor was a good doctor but he was as gruff as a bear with chilblains; and when he saw Twm carrying a dog in his arms, he shouted and raved:

'Take that mongrel out of here! What do you think this is, a menagerie?' – and a lot more talk like that.

But Twm knew O'Connor too well, and he knew that it was all only a bit of hard skin, just the rind of the old boy. So he just stayed there till O'Connor asked him what was the matter. Twm told him all about the race, and how the dog had a first-class chance; and Old Irish, being a real sportsman, took the dog on to his table. He opened the blanket and first of all soothed the dog with his hands. Then he started to pass his fingers lightly over the body. The dog lay quite still until he touched a spot on his back. Then he shot his head round as if to bite the doctor's hand. O'Connor said:

'Here it is, my fine fellow!'

And he got a powerful light and some of his instruments, and in no time he had taken a small lead shot out of the dog's back, saying:

'Just in time. Another few days and it would have been a different matter entirely.'

The dog recovered quickly after that, except that he was so nervous he couldn't be left alone. He had to sleep at the foot of the bed each night, in spite of Megan's murmurings. Well, the time drew near for the race, and they had their final trial, with Eic Caneuon slipping the dog, Twm – of course – holding the rag, and James the butcher holding the stop-watch. After the trial everyone was satisfied. The dog had got over the accident fine, was right as rain now, only he was still very nervous of loud noises. Then they were away up to Manchester.

It was a two-day meeting, and on the first day were the

heats. Twm Mufti was a bit doubtful about the dog in spite of his winning his heat quite easily. He was not running as he should have been: he was nervous; every time the gun went for the start of a heat, he showed panic. Now if you've ever been to a whippet meeting, you'll know the hullabaloo that goes on each time the gun is fired. The dogs yap and bark in a fury, and this goes on almost without interruption right throughout the day. Black Diamond had always been quiet, without any nerves at all: he just snuggled down and forgot about things until the time came for him to run. But now he was nervous and as jumpy as a kitten, even worse it seemed than the other dogs. Well, the party went into a conference that night, and Eic Caneuon made the suggestion that Twm should keep the dog out of the grounds until the time came for the semi-finals. They did this on the next day, and the dog skipped into the final. He seemed to have got back most of his old running, going straight into his stride without a falter.

Then came the final. There were two dogs from the north, a dog from London and Twm Mufti's Black Diamond. The London dog had been heavily backed and was an easy favourite. He looked a winner too: he was big, with strong-looking thighs and shoulders. Twm's dog looked puny beside him. They called the dogs out, and there was a hush all round: even the dogs in the stand seemed to have enough sense to keep quiet. It was uncanny, but – mind you – a thousand pounds is a lot of money. Twm brought his dog up from the stand, and he and Eic went to the starting-post. Twm stripped the dog and told Caneuon:

'Keep talking to him, Eic.' Then he whispered confidently to the dog: '*Ar ei ol e', bychan*. We can win it!'

He backed slowly up the course, sweeping his white cloth along the ground for the dog to follow him at the signal. Eic Caneuon knelt, waiting for the gun, firmly grasping the dog by the back of the neck and the tail, and talking softly to him all the time. The starter gave the warning: Eic braced himself; and then there was the report. He threw himself forward and the dog shot from his hands and flew away like a swallow. He was away in front, and the big London dog was after him. Black Diamond! Black Diamond! The London dog made his challenge, but Tim held him off and slowly drew away from him as he regained some of his old running. Eic, racing up the track after the dog, saw him leap up to the cloth in Twm's hand, and swing round until Twm took him up under his arm, still hanging on to the cloth with his teeth. Eic came running up, but neither he nor Twm could speak: Eic for want of breath and Twm for his feelings. Then at last Eic said:

'A thousand pounds, Twm! That's a helluver lot of money.'

But straight after the race, they had to send a telegram home, and that was the hardest part of the business. First of all, Twm wanted Eic to compose the telegram; but Eic said: call again! He'd done his job but he was willing to hold the dog once more while Twm did the writing. Well, at last they decided to do it together. And there they stood in the post office, both scratching their heads, with the girl behind the grill stamping her feet because she was waiting to put the shutter up and go home. They hammered it out at last, and then they were away to get the dog a tit-bit.

Twm's wife Megan received the telegram in Llwyncelyn very late that night. It read: *Buy your self a new clothes-mangle. Home tomorrow with the paper-train. Twm.* So Megan knew they had won, and she would have got the brass-band to meet them, only blowing a trumpet is hard work at any time, and she couldn't really wish it on any man at a quarter past six in the morning.

from *Let Dogs Delight* (1975)

Richard Moore-Colyer

Gentlemen, Horses and the Turf

Like the gatherings of the county agricultural societies, at which gentlemen of good intentions sat down in an atmosphere of warm conviviality to discuss agrarian matters of questionable practical value, the race-meeting provided a means of exercising patronage. Whether it involved charitable donations, educational provision, the granting of land for ecclesiastical building or merely the doling out of gratuities to race-course personnel, patronage in its various forms was viewed as an essential duty of a gentleman. If a vague sense of Christian duty was perceived by the gentry themselves as the prime motivation for the exercise of charity and patronage, in reality other motives were involved, among which the prevention of social discontent and a convenient means of ignoring the root causes of the poverty of their less fortunate fellow men were of importance. An overriding consideration, however, was the

117

compelling need to maintain social status. Under assault from nonconformist radicals who sought to drive a wedge between themselves and their tenants, and beleaguered by mortgage indebtedness and the crippling annuity payments arising from various estate settlements, the notion of status and superiority alone remained of the semi-feudal powers which they had enjoyed in the eighteenth century. It was, in a sense, a matter of clinging on to the wreckage. In rejecting their older cultural and social values in favour of a broader 'English' or 'European' cultural vista, they had severed traditional links with their tenants, abandoned (in many cases, at least) their ancient tongue, and had almost become strangers within their own communities. As a means of counteracting this trend towards alienation, and of attempting to persuade outsiders that they were no longer bucolic squires in a cultural and economic backwater, they struggled to pursue their distinct and privileged lifestyle with ever greater vigour. Hence the remodelling of the old plas on classical or even Gothic lines; hence the harpsi-chords, pianos and family portraits so essential as symbols of status and 'culture', and hence the interest in those equestrian sports traditionally associated with class and privilege.

As Nero fiddled while Rome burned, so did the Welsh gentry pursue their pleasures in the teeth of gathering social, economic and political change. Estates may have teetered on the verge of bankruptcy, yet retrenchment, however compelling the economic arguments in its favour, was repugnant to most men. When W. E. Powell of Nanteos in Cardiganshire reluctantly succumbed to pressure from his trustees and sold his Newmarket-based racing stud in the 1820s, he probably fell to pondering the purpose of being life-tenant of a great estate if a man were denied the wherewithal to enjoy it. Enjoyment, to most Welsh gentlemen, implied outdoor pleasures. Hours spent listening to the ladies of the household wrestling unharmoniously with the piano were regarded as a tedious interval between outdoor activities: walking the fields and woods with agent or bailiff, or engaging in various field sports. As a class they were indefatigable sportsmen, especially dedicated to those field sports tending to emphasize privilege, status and 'rights'. Shooting, confined to those holding certain property and income qualifications, is a case in point, and the protection of game against the predations of poachers and unqualified sportsmen was assiduously pursued. Even the rabbit, traditionally the quarry of the tenant farmers and villagers, was accorded protection under the 1831 Ground Game Act, an iniquitous piece of legislation which effectively widened the gulf between Welsh landlord and tenant. Most real sportsmen regarded the rabbit as a contemptible creature, yet in denying its destruction to all but men of property, legislators once again confirmed the 'rights' of the landed gentry, and thus heightened their own perception of their status.

In theory foxhunting was a more democratic affair in the sense that farmers, tradesmen and others took to the field if their circumstances permitted it. But if there were no strictly defined property qualifications underlying the make-up of the hunting field, the heavy costs involved effectively excluded all but the well-heeled, and for all the much-vaunted talk of unanimity of interest between farmers and foxhunters, hunting was the preserve of the economically privileged. What Mr Jorrocks was to describe as 'the sport of kings, the image of war without its guilt, and only five-and-twenty per cent of its danger', gave the Welsh gentry yet another opportunity to underline their superior condition among men as they galloped through the delectable meadows of Teifi-side or the rock-strewn fields of Anglesey.

Foxhunting, like racing, was intimately linked to the breeding of quality horses, and behind the breeding of the thoroughbred in particular, may have lain a profound, almost anthropomorphic, motivation. The Welsh gentleman, by tradition obsessed with the notion of lineage, would have found much to applaud in Gervase Markham's recommendation to 'get as near as you can true Breed and it will seldom or never bring forth Repentance'. For all the nineteenth-century arguments about the relative contributions of 'nature or nurture' to the constitution of a horse (or, for that matter, a man), the gentry and aristocracy derived considerable comfort from a profound belief in pedigree. In a society characterized by vast disparities in wealth, the idea that a man's social position could be justified not merely on the basis of money and power, but by the hereditary transfer of certain indefinable qualities from some distant ancestor was a highly convenient notion. Breeding thoroughbred horses or pedigree cattle and sheep was a means of celebrating one's belief in the hereditary principle, and in so doing celebrating oneself. Food rioters might ravage the towns, malcontents attack the tollgates and dissenters rail against all manner of iniquities, yet behind the library doors of the 'plas', those rows of stud books nestling alongside *Debrett* and the *Landed Gentry* were both a source of solace and a confirmation of the rectitude of the old order.

from *The Welsh History Review* (June, 1992)

H. M. Vaughan

Tivyside and its Hunts

Oh, the warm greeting we all received at Pantgwyn, and the 'Glad to see you, and you must stay and take pot-luck with us,' that was its immediate sequel. It was an old-world, almost a medieval form of entertainment. The best food and drink for everybody, and the best of hay and corn for your beast. I remember once about Christmas-tide counting twenty cold dishes on the side-board at Pantgwyn. Nor did the Colonel's activities begin and end with sport and good cheer. Nobody was more punctual than he in his public duties, and they were many, whether on the bench, the vestry, or the Cardiganshire County Council, of which he was once chairman. Till within a very few years of his death, the Colonel used to attend the meets of the Tivyside Hounds in pink, though he only rode a quiet cob; and in his button-hole he always sported the little bouquet of violets, which for so long was affected by many members of the Hunt.

Many years before his death Colonel Howell had

resigned the Mastership of the Hunt, and two or three Masters had held this post before it was accepted by Captain Sir Edward Pryse, second son of Sir Pryse Pryse, of Gogerddan. By his marriage with Miss Angharad Webley-Parry, the heiress of Noyadd-Trefawr, Captain Pryse had settled down on his wife's estate in the Tivyside. A more popular master it would have been impossible to find, and Sir Edward Pryse's memory is still cherished apud littora Teivi. A very curious incident, however, took place during the reign of the popular baronet of Gogerddan and Noyadd-Trefawr. Nobody will question the loyalty to the Throne of the squires of West Wales, yet somehow in certain natures the call of sport becomes so imperious as to throw a temporary cloud even over that excellent quality. Thus at the time of Queen Victoria's death towards the close of January in 1901, Sir Edward Pryse and some other keen sportsmen of the Hunt could see no particular harm in hunting on the sly during the tedious interval that elapsed between the great Queen's death and her funeral. So no public advertisement of any forthcoming meet was issued in the papers (as is always done), but a select few met by secret appointment and had a couple of days' quiet sport on their own account during the period of general mourning, when every other pack in the kingdom refrained from hunting. Needless to say, this delinquency came to light in due course, and was followed by a burst of indignation and surprise, Colonel Howell voicing his anger and disapproval in very strong terms.

...It was on the Tivyside Hunt that the social gaiety of the Tivyside gentry during the winter months mostly depended.

There were large fields in those days of riders of every type, of mounts varying from the blood horse to the humble jackass; many carriages attended the meets, and there was a fair sprinkling of followers on foot. The country itself, before the wholesale introduction of barbed wire, was of the most sporting description. Deep wooded valleys, boggy stretches on the uplands and high banks, especially near the coast, to whose rocks Reynard often made for safety. In open weather too the many streams were swollen into torrents, and I remember seeing Mr William Brigstocke of Blaenpant being immersed in trying to cross the Cych when in flood. He disappeared entirely, horse, top-hat and all, in the muddy rushing water, and emerged on the further bank a sad spectacle. The end of the season concluded with the Hunt Week and two public balls in the Guildhall at Cardigan, where about a hundred to a hundred and fifty members of the Hunt and their friends danced cheerily till well into the small hours of the morning. Hulley's string band from Swansea was the popular music of the day. Sometimes after supper the band broke out into song – 'The Jolly Coppersmith' being a special favourite, and of course the final galop of 'John Peel.' Large parties were entertained at the country-houses for these balls, and for the Tivyside Races on the old Cilast course, near Ffynone, which commands one of the finest views in West Wales. Those were merry days, and I am glad to think that I was old enough to enjoy them in the 'nineties; I still consider them preferable to the profiteers' parties of the present years of grace. In those days we were all one huge family, with a few guests thrown in. The Tivyside Hunt Week as a social event

123

collapsed with the South African War, and was never more revived. Already many of the local landowners were feeling the pinch of the hard times that were destined to grow harder. One by one mansions were let or sold to strangers, who disliked or misunderstood the old simple life of their predecessors. What the South African War started, the Great War has speedily finished, and now one may cry 'Ichabod' over the fair valley of the Teifi from Llandysul to Cardigan. This remark only applies to the squirearchy; of course, everybody else is a gainer from its practical disappearance, especially the peasants and cottagers, who now benefit from the proverbial generosity of the profiteer and the got-rich-quick farmer, who are now lords of the Teifi valley.

from *The South Wales Squires* (1926)

Leslie Norris

Hyperion

Hyperion
was hardly a Titan. He stood
a brief inch over six feet, was
sweetly made. Not for his
size am I sent in his just praise
along the measured tracks

of his achievement. Dropped
on the printed turf by Selene,
daughter of Serenissima, he moved

even in his first uncertainty
like one waited for. His birth

was in green April, and he grew
in light, on the fat meadows.
Gently schooled, he delighted
his mentors with his perfect ardour,
honesty, the speed of his response.

Though small, he was quite beautiful,
his chestnut mane burning, his step
luminous. Some doubted his courage,
looking askance at the delicacy
of his white feet, ignoring the star

already brilliant in his forehead.
His heart was a vivid instrument
drumming for victory, loin and muscle
could stretch and flex in eating
leaps. When he ran, when he ran

the rings of his nostrils were scarlet,
the white foam spun away from his lips.
For his was the old, true blood,
untainted in his veins' walls:
two lines to St Simon, two lines

to Bend Or: The Flying Dutchman,
Bayardo, Galopin, all the great ones
back in his pedigree met in him.

He could not fail to honour
his fathers in the proud flood

of his winning. Nine times he left
his crescent grooves in the cheering
grass before the commoners gasped
after him. At Epsom, racing as if
alone on the classic track, he won

a record Derby, at Doncaster the Leger.
He won the Chester Vase, the Prince
of Wales's Stakes. Nor in his fullness,
drowsing in quiet fields in quiet company,
was he forgotten. His children,

sons and daughters of the Sun,
did not allow this. Hypericum,
Sun Chariot, Rising Light, all
were his. And Sun Stream, Midas,
Owen Tudor, Suncastle, many others.

The swift Godiva was his, and in
his image famous Citation, who ran
away with all America. Sportsmen,
all who go to the races, who marvel
at the flying hooves, remember Hyperion.

from *Watervoices* (1980)

126

Tony Curtis

The Mystery of the Homing Pigeon

The mystery of the homing pigeon
is being cracked.
A professor at Cornell tracks
the birds in his twin-engined Commanchie,
asserts the dependence on sun and moon,
what ancient mariners they make;
whilst a computer at the Max Planck Institute
simulates wind, magnetic field and flight.
When I tell you, you say you don't care:
'Good lofts make good birds',
receive the applause of their wings
as they take the air.

from *Album* (1974)

127

BOXING

Leslie Norris

Elegy for Lyn James – killed in the ring
at Shoreditch Town Hall, June 16th 1964

I saw your manager fight. He was
Useful, but his brother had the class.
In shabby halls in Wales, or in tents
On slum ground, I saw your like
Go cuffed and bleeding from a few
Sharp rounds to set the mob aloud
Before the big men came, who had the class.

Even they did not all escape. Tim
Sheehan, whose young heart burst
In a dirty room above a fish shop;
Jerry O'Neill, bobbing his old age
Through a confusion of scattered
Fists all down the High Street; brisk
Billy Rose, blind; all these I saw.

And Jock McAvoy, swinging his right
From a wheelchair. Your murderers hide
Fatly behind the black lines of the
Regulations, your futile hands are closed

In a gloveless death. Down rotting lanes,
Behind the silent billiard hall, I hear
Your shuffling ghost, who never had the class.

from *Finding Gold* (1967)

Richard Llewellyn

Teaching Huw to fight

Up at the house Davy was talking to a couple of men in the back, a couple not generally looked up to, and a surprise to find near our house, for Dai Bando and Cyfartha Lewis were prizefighters, rough but gentle men.

'Come you, Huw,' Davy said, and put his arm about my shoulder. 'You know Huw, Dai.'

'Yes, indeed.' said Dai, and smiled to show one tooth to the side of his mouth. He was not much taller than me, but broad as six, and long in the arm. His face was covered with little punch cuts, all dyed blue with coal dust, and his eyes were almost closed by skin which had been cut and healed time and time again. But his eyes were bright as a blackbird's. They said he had fought more than a thousand fights, and a Marquis had asked him to go to Oxford to teach the students to fight, with the knuckles of course, but he had got drunk in London and put a couple of police in hospital, and landed in jail. So not many had a word for him. Cyfartha Lewis was younger, taller, but tidy in the chest and big in the shoulder, well known to be champion in his weight at the pit head. Instead of going to Chapel he and Dai were off to Town on Saturdays to fight at night, and they used to come back home in time for the morning shift on Monday. But it was certain that whatever they did on Sunday, going to Chapel was not one. 'Dai is going to give you lessons in the art of boxing, Huw,' Davy said. 'I asked him to come up and see if he could do something with you.'

'Strip off, boy,' Dai said, in his high little voice, and making a little move with his hands, that were bumpy and in funny shapes with him, and always half-closed to show the big thumb joints.

So I took off my shirt to the waist, and Dai looked and pinched, as my mother did with a chicken for the pot.

'More in the shoulder, more in the back, more in the forearm,' said Dai, with a look I thought was disgust. 'And his legs want two more pairs like them before they will be going on to be enough, eh, Cyfartha? Hit me by here, boy.'

He put out his chin and poked it with his short finger, but I had a fear to give him a good one. 'Go on, boy,' he said, 'hit to kill.'

'Go on,' Cyfartha said, and smiling. 'A sovereign if you will have him on the floor.'

So I hit, but his head was nowhere near my fist, and I never saw Dai move.

'Nothing to buy a stamp for,' said Dai, 'but he uses his shoulders, and he stands well, eh, Cyfartha?'

'I have seen many a worse one,' Cyfartha said. 'His legs are his trouble. He will never ride a punch with them. And one good clout and they will put him to bed.'

'Look you, now, Dai,' Davy said. 'The boy's legs have

stopped him going to a good school. But you shall teach him enough to fight his way through the school he is in now, legs or not. Yes or no?'

'Yes,' said Dai, and meant it. 'I was up there the night his mother came. God, there is a shocking night it was, too, eh, Cyfartha?' 'Yes, indeed,' Cyfartha said, 'and we built a fire on the rock all night and slid down the mountain to the pit next morning. Say nothing to me of that night, indeed. Twenty pound solid it cost me to have my hands right, with the frost.'

'What time in the morning?' Davy asked, and impatient.

'Half-past four at the top here,' Dai said, 'and five o'clock up the top of the mountain. An hour up there to six, half an hour down, to half-past, and breakfast then, to seven. Eh. Cyfartha?'

'Yes,' said Cyfartha. 'And nothing only water before he comes up.'

'Good,' said Davy, well satisfied. 'You will have lessons from champions, Huw. Now in to your lessons from books.'

So I went from Dai Bando and Cyfartha Lewis, in to Pericles and John Stuart Mill.

That first morning Davy came in to give me a shake and hold down the loose board while I crossed the landing in quiet at quarter-past four in pitch black, and cold to make your teeth chop, no wash because the bucket would rattle in the well to wake the Hill, and only enough in the house for breakfast first thing, then off outside the house into a wind with ice in it, bringing tears to the eyes, and a pain, like the grip of a clothes-peg, to the nose. Dai and Cyfartha came from the lee of the last house, both of them black lumps, and only their boot-falls to tell which was them and which not.

'That you, Huw Morgan?' Dai said, and shouting in the wind, but only a whisper coming.

'Yes,' I shouted back. 'Good morning.'

'To hell,' Dai said, and spat. 'Come, you.'

We went up the mountain together, but I saw in surprise that Cyfartha was following with a dozen or more from the sound, but Dai put his fingers down my neck and swore when I stopped to see. Up we went, quicker than I had ever gone before, but being late for school a couple of times had given me practice in running up, so I was not far behind Dai at the top, and hardly a breath out of place.

'Off with your shirt,' Dai said, and pulling his off, and all the others pulling the clothes from them. So off came mine, and I thought I would freeze, sure, for the wind was high and calling low and strong enough to push you over flat. It was still dark, but above the other valley it was just starting to show grey, black everywhere else, and nothing but black down in the valleys except where Merddyn Jones was getting up, with a little yellow light, and the light in the winding house down at the colliery.

In the coming of the morning Dai Bando was a man to fear.

His skin was pinkish with cold, and with muscle to make you doubt your sight. His arm muscles were bigger than my thigh, and over the top of his trews, six squares, each as big as my two fists together, stood out so that you could have rattled a stick over them. His shoulders had great fat fingers of muscle leading down to the tops of his arms like opening a fan, and behind his shoulders, bunches of muscle lay about the blades, with two great cords going down on each side of his backbone.

I will never forget Dai Bando in that grey light, with night all about him and cold pricking his skin to little pimples as his shirt came from him and he pulled at his trews.

Cyfartha was not much less than Dai, and the boys and men with them were all the same. Only I was skin and bones.

'Come on, boys,' Dai said, and slapping himself hard, 'get the blood going with you.'

For minutes we all danced about there slapping the cold out of us, and hopping and jumping about like mad flies, until the light was coming apple green and orange, with lines of gold, and we could see each other, and the trees taking shape and colours of deep green.

'Down on the back,' Dai ordered, and down flat we went, on the short grass that was smooth as moss, covered with the crystals of frozen dew and sparkling lovely, but so cold it was like red-hot to the back.

'Kick the legs above your heads and back and fore with the arms,' said Dai, and that we did.

'Sit up and lie back, no hands,' Dai shouted, and up and down we went, until nevermind the cold, we were sweating and hot as hot.

'Now pair off, and straight left one, guard the other,' Dai said. 'Huw Morgan, over here.'

Over I went, and while Cyfartha and the other boys paired off Dai put up his fists, and I put up mine, and we did straight lefts and slipping them, and riding them, and ducking, with the punches to counter, and those to score.

Then Dai made me come in close and hit him on those muscles of his in the belly with half-arm blows to strengthen my punching muscles at the back, until I was ready to drop.

'Good,' he said, and smiling he was, 'there is plenty in you, indeed. Run to school and put fat and muscle on your legs. But run, not walk. Strong legs you want, nothing else. I will give you the rest.'

'Thank you, Dai,' I said, and so pleased I could have jumped across the Valley. 'When shall I fight, now?'

'To-day,' Dai said. 'Fight all the time. You will only learn in a fight how much you have got to learn. When you know that, you can come and ask and I will show you. But fight.'

'Good,' I said, 'I will fight to-day.'

'Same time to-morrow,' Dai said. 'Put on your shirt, and run down the mountain home. And fight, is it?'

'Yes,' I said. 'To-day, indeed.'

When I got in my mother had my breakfast ready and when I had washed I sat to it, but she sat beside me and smoothed my hair.

'Did you go out on the mountain this morning, Huw, my little one?' she asked me.

'Yes. Mama,' I said.

'To learn to fight, is it?' she asked me, as though she was hoping I would say no.

'Yes, Mama,' I said.

'There,' she said, and sat back, hopeless. 'I knew it when I heard you go from the house. Right, you. But if you come back with bruises again, not a word shall you have from me. Nothing. Break your old nose and see what I will do. Nothing. Not a word, not a look.'

'But I must learn, Mama,' I said, 'or I shall have them and nothing to stop them coming, and nothing to give back.'

'I am not listening to you,' she said, and over at the fire, now, with her hand over her eyes. 'Breaking your Mama's heart every time you do go from the house. Remember what I say. Not a word, not a look.'

'Yes, Mama,' I said, and finished my tea, and picked up my bag and can, and off.

from *How Green was my Valley* (1939)

Alexander Cordell

Jim Driscoll – and others

The challenger climbed up into the ring with the lazy air of indifference that tells of the professional, and Salem weighed him while he stood in the middle of the ring, grinning at me. He was a smooth one, this; he had big muscles and perky red hair, and he outweighed me by a couple of stones. He might be hard to put away, I thought, and I saw beyond him the white, frightened face of Edie staring up, with Sam still talking vehemently into her ear. The gong went and I came out of my corner.

For the first time in the ring I was afraid; afraid that this man would score at my expense. Unaccountably, it was as if he was standing between Edie and me; that I had everything to lose in this match, and nothing to gain.

I hated him. It was the only time I have known hatred based on fear.

136

'Right, Driscoll, this is you,' said the man, and came in hooking.

I steadied him with a left that knocked him flat-footed. It was a hard punch and his expression wore mute surprise. And, as his guard dropped, I planted my feet and hit him with every ounce of my strength, a right cross that would have floored a donkey. Landing flush upon his chin, it spun him, and he fell sideways into my arms. The vicious crack of the blow was echoing in my ears as I lowered him to the canvas; people rushed into the ring. I heard Salem say:

'Christ, Driscoll, are ye after killin' him?'

The challenger was lying at my feet; he was scarcely breathing.

Badger said urgently: 'Hey, what's up, mun? The man's a novice. What got into yer?' and Sam Boze, standing at my elbow, added:

'That little Edie's gone, Driscoll. The moment that fella dropped she was away home, she said.'

I looked into Sam's face, seeing it, I think, for the very first time. The white cuts above his fading eyes, I saw; the flattened nose and the gummy mouth; his ears, twisted and mutilated, were like bats' wings attached to his nearly hairless skull... a man alive, but a man really dead after twenty years of bad ring punishment. And this, I knew, was why Edie had gone. She saw in Sam the man I might soon be. The black fighter whispered:

'You got to watch that right in the booth, mister, lest you start killin' people,' and a voice from the apron of the ring called up:

'The Yanks would call that baloney, man.' He was a lad

of about fifteen and he jerked his thumb at the slowly recovering challenger. Glassy-eyed, the man moved on stilted legs, supported by Badger and Boy Dando, our latest sensation. The lad said happily: 'He dropped his guard and he came up there for money, Black Sam. He comes up, he asks for it, and he gets it. That's the chance he takes; don't go soft on it, for Christ's sake!'

'Aw, get lost,' I said, and Sam interjected:

'Mind your mouth, boy, this is Jim Driscoll.'

'So what? I'm Frederick Hall Thomas.'

It stilled me, even in the pushing commotion of the ring. This was the amateur lad who was knocking them over from Risca to Pontypridd return journey. His name was on everybody's tongue.

He called himself Freddie Welsh when he fought in the Pontypridd lofts for money, because he didn't want his mother to know. Talk had it that he was emigrating to America and was trying to get hold of the accent. I said:

'Come back in five years' time, lad, and I'll see to you then.'

'I'll do that,' said the boy, and pushed his way through the crowd, and was gone. Sam said:

'Ye know somethin', Driscoll? Ah got a queer feeling in ma bones – you're goin' to see that lad again.'

So had I, but I was looking towards the Leckwith road, trying to see Edie.

... I've seen some packed halls in my time, but nothing like the scene that night in the Athletic Club, New York's equivalent to the National Sporting Club in London. They reckoned that every politician except the President was

138

there, and the ringside seats at fifty dollars a time were filled with major celebrities; the high-society whirl of New York's financial crust, everybody of note in the boxing world, big business and social register: all were there in a haze of cigar smoke and white shirtfronts, packing in from East 24th Street.

Nearly four thousand people were present at the end of the preliminary bouts, and 'Good Eye' White, the referee, called us together after the endless introductions.

'Now a good, clean fight, or not at all, you guys. No butting, nothing with the heel of the gloves, no thumbing, you hear me?' His voice droned on. Abe was staring into my face with the usual tigerish glare he reserved for his opponents; he looked fit and bronzed and bubbling with health, and I remember thinking: Ma will be with me now; aye, she'll be up, though it's three o'clock in the morning back home: all down Ellen Street and Beauchamp the lights will be on, everybody praying for Jim Driscoll, Liz Franklin's boy.

There'd been talk, Edie had written, of a special service in St Paul's, ostensibly to pray for my safety, but somebody had put paid to it; let's pray for Abe Attell like Edie had said, this was Newtown's cry. And Edie? My mind shut out the sudden vision of her face, for Mr White snapped:

'All right, Driscoll, back to your corner!'

'What's wrong, mister,' asked Rastus, before he heaved me up, 'you gone to sleep, or somethin'?'

The bell sounded.

New strength, vital and alive, seemed to flow into me at the sound of that bell; Attell glided out like a cat, suddenly shifted his stance and came in behind a left lead, but I anticipated it and hooked him hard to the body. This drove him back, and as he bounced off the ropes I got him hard with either hand, underneath and over the top, then left-handed him flush on the nose as he retreated around the ring.

It was as if a coffin lid had slammed down over the hall; silence came; a muted, eerie silence interspersed with small gasps of disbelief as I beat Attell constantly to the lead. I was seeing him, in those opening rounds, as a camera shutter sees in slow motion; crisp images on a screen, clarified, distinct; he seemed to stand there waiting until I hit him.

It nonplussed him; I could see it in his eyes, and as if suddenly angered by his inability, he rushed me, got me against the ropes and swung one almighty right that could have taken me out; slipping below it, I saw it whistle over, followed by Abe: his balance gone, the impetus of the blow took him onward, and as I danced clear he floundered about and dropped to his knees at my feet. Humiliation shot to his face. He leaped up, and as he rose I drove him on to the ropes, beat a tattoo of punches on to his ribs and then landed a mind-bender smash to the solar plexus that doubled him up. And as he came forward I laid a right hook upon his chin that staggered him. Eyes glazed, Abe back-pedalled, and I followed, peppering him with straight lefts until he covered up, swaying and ducking.

Meanwhile, he hadn't laid a glove upon me; certainly not to my head. I saw the coal-black face of Battling Siki at the ringside, his white grin, his wink; Johnny Kilbane, a challenger, was there beside the great Ketchel, who stuck up a thumb at me. George Chip, the middleweight champion four years later, was there for experience, I heard; he who later knocked out Greb, the 'Human Windmill', in his first year of boxing. These and a hundred more had their eyes glued to the spectacle – Abe Attell being given the boxing lesson of his life.

It sounds boastful; it is not meant to be; I had some hard bouts in America, fast and skilful flurries against men like Grover Hayes, whom you had to beat out to beat them; Abe Attell wasn't like that. Nor was it because his style suited me, for he was no roundhouse brawler, which are the easiest ones to handle. In retrospect I cannot explain the easy time he gave me; perhaps Rastus did it best every time I came back to my corner.

'You want to give this guy a break, Mr Driscoll – ain't it time he hit you?'

'Just keep doing it,' said Jimmy Johnston between rounds. 'Just keep going out there and do it, again, again and again,' and I obeyed.

Swarthy, gum-chewing, thicker and broader than me, Abe would stalk me like a cat, his strings of muscle bunching up on his shoulders, the eight midriff muscles packing up his body: cold and calculating, he stalked me in the manner of the Old Master, Joe Gans – suddenly to leap in like a panther, only to have his head snapped back as if it was on wires.

Bleeding from the nose, one eye filled up (they had to lance it to stop it closing completely) he stumbled on, his rhythm diminishing within the poetry of hooks and smashes, and had I been really fit, he must have gone out: in the seventh, in desperation, Abe abandoned caution and came in flailing, swinging left and right to the body and switching the attack to the head until I slipped him, side-stepping his bull-like rush; again he fell, sprawling around on the floor, looking as cheap as a nickel. Nobody had seen this world champion fall on his face while trying to land a punch.

Feinting, weaving, ducking, he kept walking on to the jabs, vainly trying to corner the phantom which was one moment there and the next moment vanished. And when, in utter desperation, he got me in a corner for his plastering, all-angle blows, I wheeled him away and he was left fighting himself.

It was not the Abe Attell the American boxing public knew. As the boxing correspondent of the *Daily Telegraph* reported home by cable:

"Driscoll would spring up like a cat, jab Abe on the nose or eye, jump away, and like a flash return with the same punch... and Abe's head was bobbing back and forth, back and forth, when suddenly Jem dropped over a right to the chin, and Attell reeled. He rocked, he shook, but in his anxiety to put another in the same place – this was in the fourth round – Driscoll shot wide and his opponent stalled it out. The crowd was crazy with excitement. The air was full of advice, but Attell managed to weather the storm. His right eye was closing again, and it looked as if he might be put to sleep before the ten rounds was through.

Jem Driscoll left the ring unmarked; Attell's right eye was closed and his nose was all over his face... the face that has for so long worn the championship smile.

Abe Attell, although this was a No Decision match, is no longer the premier featherweight boxer in the world."

When I got back to my corner at the end of the fight the place had gone into bedlam: people were standing up and cheering, hats were flung into the air; the ring was invaded by madly excited fans trying to raise my hands, while poor Abe sat disconsolate, unnoticed in his corner. And Rastus, his big arms about me, protecting me from the invaders, cried:

'Mr Driscoll, you made a right mess o' that now, didn't ye? I told you – remember I told ye? – don't beat him too good, for Gawd's sake. Now ye'll never see the going of him.'

And Jimmy Johnston bawled above the chanting crowd: 'Driscoll, Driscoll, Driscoll.' joining in the unison that was raising the roof. He added: 'You're the featherweight champion of the world, son! Don't just sit there, get up and do something!'

Mr White the referee was calling for silence, and a man came into the middle of the ring. He was big and dressed in a sheriff's uniform. Taking my arm he led me forward, and the crowd went silent, mumbling bassly. The man's name was Bat Masterson, once deputy to Wyatt Earp, and now marshall of Dodge City – come to the fight by special invitation.

His voice rang out: 'Gentlemen, I give you Jem Driscoll. And if I were asked to name this performance of his tonight, I would call it peerless. So I give you 'Peerless' Jem Driscoll!'

The place went mad. Shoulder high they lifted me out of the ring and we went in a run to the dressing room.

'Ah still say you got no real brains,' said Rastus.

'Where's Abe?' I asked. 'I'd like to see Abe.'

'You won't see him no more, Mr Driscoll.'

'Don't you worry, son!' shouted Jimmy Johnston. 'He ain't getting away with that. I'll get him for you, Jem – I promise, I'll get him.'

Meanwhile, they could keep Abe Attell and his world featherweight title; they could keep America.

For all the generosity I had been shown, the only thing in the world I wanted was Edie.

... In the end there was quite a gang of us.

There was Freddy, Tom Thomas and Tom Courtney; Jack O'Brien came, Young Dando, a rising flyweight (until Jimmy Wilde stopped his caper three times) and me, and the old mare clip-clopped her way out of Newtown with the scarlet caravan rumbling along behind, and behind that the two-wheeled cart carrying the booth marquee. And the folks of Newtown turned out to see us off, first stop Pontypridd, Freddy's home town. The Champions' Booth, we called it, and with good reason; the intention was to spoon the takings out of the standard booths – barkers like Cullis and Scarrott, and we did.

Salem Sullivan drove the horse, Badger was cook, and we clopped along out of Cardiff towards Llandaff and the long haul up to the valleys, and the May sun burned down in regal splendour.

There was good money to be earned in the valleys. From Llanerch to Cilfynydd and from Ferndale in the Rhondda to Risca and the Lletty Shenkin in Aberaman, three thousand colliers had been killed since records began, but this didn't quell the fighting spirit of the people. Although the terrible Senghenydd and Gresford disasters totalling another seven hundred dead were yet to come, the will of the coal communities rose like a valedictory flame above the pulverising calamities; as if toughened and refined by pain and baptised in blood, they sought outlet in primaeval competition, man against man; so boxing, like rugby, flourished.

They were a people annealed by adversity. From infancy, small boys fought in the valleys; at times of strike comrades fought on street corners, just to keep warm, or for the fun of it: women fought, too – no scratching hair-tugging females these, but roll-sleeved women who could give their men a run for it.

People fought in the publics, on the patches and in the sporting house yards where Welsh fistiana was born: names like Corky and Pucker-face and Snookey-Boxer abounded in Welsh kitchens: it was six generations of natural fighters spawned in bitterness and nurtured by aggression, and they birthed ten thousand gladiators; the world has seen nothing like it before, or since.

Within the space of ten years the tiny Welsh Principality threw up three world champions and a hundred minor ones, and in Jimmy Wilde they fashioned, pound for pound, the greatest box-fighter who has ever pulled on gloves.

For Celts such as these, their ferocity and gentleness going hand in hand, it was an astonishing performance.

So you'd line up on the apron of the marquee and Salem, our barker, would bawl: 'Who's on? Come on, me lucky lads, try your luck! Here's your chance to fight a world champion!'

145

'Right you, boyo! I'm on!' and some loon in the crowd would snatch down the gloves Salem tossed. 'Will ye give me threes, Salem Sullivan?' for they knew and loved him like a brother.

'Who are ye after, son?'

'Jim Driscoll!' This from an Aberdare fairground brawler. Salem hands on hips now, outraged. 'And you twelve stones if you're a pound? Who d'ye think he is, son – God Almighty?'

'He will be by the time I've bloody done with him!' And up he'd come, big and brawny, a champion of his sporting public, but a roundhouse swinger who was like clay in the hands of the professional.

'How many you done tonight, Jim?' This from Tom Courtney. 'About six.'

'Rest yourself. I'll take him.'

It was the summer nights of the naphtha flares; the smell of frying polonies, of faggots and peas bubbling in the pans, and laverbread, and white-aproned wives of bulging bare arms and large stomachs.

In the valley-town markets they had scrubbed white tables and forms under the canopies of the stalls, and you could sit down there with a saucer-full of mussels; these you'd eat with salt, pepper and vinegar, and no caviare tasted as good. Cockles and winkles went the same way.

They sold cow-heel juice, too, which was the nectar of the gods.

They used to bring the mussels overnight in buckets, fill them up with water, throw in a handful of oatmeal to make them plump and fat and boil them next morning. When boiled, they'd burst open so you could take out the whiskers and the sand drained off.

Along the valley-town high streets they had tripe shops, cow-heel and brawn shops, shops that sold salmon paste with salted farm butter on top; there was faggot and peas shops and rissole stalls; later, the fish and chip merchants arrived, but not then.

In those days the kids used to queue up at these shops with their Coronation jugs clamped against them; screwing up their bare toes to the pavement-stamping boozies in hobnails, waiting for the shops to open. And then the bulging valley wives came, corseted and starched, wielding huge metal spoons with the authority of Robert Peelers, their hair tousled and their chins sweating within the vaporous clouds of steam.

Writing this, I can smell again the sticky-fingered nights of the Rhondda rock, blood-red all down the middle – Porth and Tonypandy written in red fire – I hear again the shrieking children and the music of the Rhondda roundabouts; the red-nostrilled horses I can see again, the chesty colliers looking for ale and trouble, the pale-faced wizened old, the refuse of the collieries.

It was the wearing of the Rhondda like a precious garment – Pontypridd was a hat on sideways; Aberdare, the darling of the Autumn Hiring Fairs; skirts up, showing her drawers. And we, her labouring populations, the cocky tumblers of the rickety, rackety towns, stood on the edge of life's abyss like a collier staring down a pit-shaft.

Above ground the fairground organs blared their martial music; below ground the toilers hawked, sweated, picked, shovelled, grumbled; the discordant shout of Rhondda's song.

And now, with the booth shut and the corpses carried for surgery, we sat together at a table under the brazen Rhondda moon; so big and round on the rim of the mountain that you could raise a finger and touch it: there was Jack O'Brien, Salem and Badger, Freddy Welsh, Tom Courteney and me; there was also Twm Cancelyn, whom others called Tom Thomas.

Tom, though travelling with us, never fought on the apron of the booth: rumour took it that, long back, he had killed a man at a fairground, but I never got the proof of it; now they had to be professionals before Tom would cross gloves with them. He'd fight anything on two legs, this one; on a pub patch, in a sporting house or up on the mountain, for a side stake. He wasn't really one of us, Twm Cancelyn: not lofty or toff-nosed, just different.

A full-time farmer and spare-time fighter, Tom managed his own affairs, taking no talk from anyone save a cousin, a young doctor whom he loved.

In the ring he was a Welsh tiger, and it was said that he invented the rabbit punch, which stopped a man leading with his head (I saw him stop Buller Rees with it in his first professional fight at Aberafon Fair). He was also the possessor of the Twm Cancelyn 'Nose-Wiper', which Freddy Welsh later used on me – a left hook that purposely missed his opponent's chin and which was then whipped back to strike with the elbow, for Twm Cancelyn was never particular how he won in the ring, though Tom Thomas, outside it, was one of Nature's gentlemen.

And now, sitting there in the moonlight with the debris of the fairground around us, Tom was singing, his voice rough but pure. I remember the littered table, the frothed glasses of ale; the roof of the marquee rising and falling in the wind like the breasts of a sleeping woman. And Twm singing 'David of the White Rock'.

Before we left the Badminton Club on one past training session, the press took a photograph of us – Freddy Welsh, Tom Thomas and me; within a year of that day Tom was dead of rheumatic fever, brought on, it was said, by breaking the ice to swim in Cancelyn pond.

He died in London, taken ill on his way to America to fight Billy Papke for the middleweight championship of the world, in the autumn of 1911. Does his soul wander the attic training room of the Gethin in Penygraig? And walk the fields of his Cancelyn Farm?

After my fight with Abe Attell for the world title, an American reporter wrote:

> 'Poor Abe's attempts to hit Peerless Jem
> Driscoll was like a man without a light trying
> to catch a coal black nigger in a coal black
> cellar on a coal black night.'

Which is flattering, but Tom Thomas didn't fight like me: he fought tigerishly, in a shower of blood. I tell you this:

They can talk of Stanley Ketchel and Billy Papke, who beat our Jim Sullivan for the world title – the fight Tom should have had (and Sullivan took Tom's British title and Lonsdale belt off him when he was a dying man...), but had

149

not death snatched Tom away, he'd have given them a run for it on the other side of the Atlantic; my bet would have been on him against any middleweight in the world, except Harry Greb, who blacked his mother's eye at his birth, and beat Gene Tunney.

from *Peerless Jim* (1976)

Jack Jones

The Welsh and the Irish

'This is the place,' said Shenk.

'How do you know?' Glyn asked.

'Well, can't you see one-eyed Ned James scouting along the top there. He can see better and further with that one eye of his than most of us can see with two, and from there he can see anybody coming a mile away. So if the police do happen to get wind of it, Ned'll give us the tip in plenty of time to...'

'Hey, you two,' shouted one-eyed Ned at them, 'don't stand there like a pair of bloody galutes, but get down there with the others out of sight.'

Glyn and Shenk hurried forward to the rim of the bowl-shaped hollow and slithered down to join the huge crowd already seated around its sloping sides. Down there in the hollow the crowd was divided into two sections, the Welsh and Irish sections. Glyn knew most of the Welsh section, bloodthirsty fight-fans all, but he only knew by sight a few of the Irish section. To and fro between the two sections

150

there were a number of men moving along making bets, the sporting landlord of the Anchor being the most active in this. Glyn looked all round without catching sight of Harry, but he could see the redoubtable Tim Flannery standing ready stripped to the waist in the midst of the seemingly light-hearted Irish section of the crowd. Then where was Harry?

'Where the hell is he?' Slasher Evans was asking Will Tavern.

'Damned if I know,' Glyn heard Will Tavern reply.

'The police might have pinched Harry for something or other last night,' said Shenk.

Slasher Evans was wild. 'And Flannery here ready stripped,' he was saying to Will Tavern, 'and these bloody Micks having the laugh on us. Hasn't anyone gone to fetch Harry?'

'Not as I know. He knows where to come to; shouldn't want fetching.'

'No,' muttered the Slasher, making his way up to where one-eyed Ned James was anxiously scanning the road along which Harry should have long before travelled to his corner; and as the Slasher was ascending to the rim of the hollow Flannery attracted everyone's attention by stepping out from the midst of his supporters on to the level piece of sward on which he was to fight, where he stood exhibiting his beautiful body to the crowd. Raising both hands he several times smoothed back his long sandy moustache, and in so doing revealed his muscles in play under the skin of his arms and back.

'Bounce, that's all it is,' muttered Will Tavern. 'But wait until Harry comes; he'll knock all that out of him.'

'Hwat's keepin' tha champeein of yours?' Flannery

151

shouted up to the anxious-looking Slasher who was pacing the rim. 'Has he been overtaken with the shites, or hwat? hadn't ye better be gain' to help the poor feller along, for we can't be stayin' here all day waitin' to lick the likes of him.'

Then with the pace of a stallion he paraded the ring to the accompaniment of his supporters' laughter and encouraging remarks. He and his supporters looked upwards when Slasher shouted down: 'You needn't worry, Tim, he'll be here all right; the longer he is coming, the longer you're allowed to live.'

Flannery replied to this by turning a number of cart-wheels, which delighted his supporters, who roared their encouragement.

'Looks a holy terror, don't he?' said Shenk.

'Yes, Harry looks like having his work cut out this day,' said Glyn.

Will Tavern was standing near and heard what they said. 'Not he, Harry'll eat the bastard and ask for a second helping,' he told them. 'These Irish – the damned lot of 'em – are like the barber's cat, all wind and piss. Big and useless, that's what they are... Haven't I seen a priest whipping hell's bells out of 'em for not turning up to church.'

'I'd like to see the priest as would use a whip on Flannery,' said Shenk.

'Here, are you trying to make me out a liar?' snarled Will Tavern, advancing menacingly on Shenk with fists clenched. Lucky for Shenk was the cry from the rim to the effect that Harry was at last in sight. Those in the Welsh section of the crowd grunted their relief as their champion appeared, and a few cheered and others cried 'Good old Harry' as he bounded down the slope to his corner.

'Where the hell do you reckon you've been?' Slasher wanted to know, pulling off Harry's shirt.

'That Shoni of ours – stole eight shilling out of my pocket, so I had to deal with him before...'

'All right, you can tell us about that after you've dealt with Flannery, who's been bouncing quite a bit; reckoned you wasn't going to turn up, and that you was afraid of him, had the shites and...'

'Afraid of a bloody Irishman.' He spat out the mixture of vinegar and water, 'a rinser', which Slasher, on whose knee he was now seated, had given him to clean his mouth out. 'I could beat a boat-load of the bastards.'

'Don't we know it,' said Slasher, who called out: 'Well, are you Micks ready?'

'Sure, haven't we been ready this hour an' more,' joyfully cried Flannery, springing into the middle of the ring.

'So are we,' grunted Slasher, easing his man up and forward towards his opponent. There was no better second in the district than Slasher. Having himself been a principal in a score of hard-fought battles, none knew better than he the value of caution and restraint in the early stages of a fight; and he also knew the value of a second who knew the ropes as he did. Yes, Slasher knew all there was to know about the handling and nursing of a man through a fight. Flannery was by no means as well served as was Harry.

The number of spectators had grown until the bowl-shaped hollow was filled to overflowing by the time the men were sent up for the first round. What a contrast. Flannery tall, upright, fair, smiling, well proportioned. Harry nearly a head shorter than his opponent, dark, bulky, scowling. They at once got to work, watched by the large and silently excited crowd; but as the two men warmed to their work many in the crowd started grunting, squealing, cursing and fighting empty air. A few there were who yapped like dogs.

Flannery – who played to the gallery quite a lot for the first quarter of an hour – held himself like a guardsman; Harry crouched and moved – and at times looked – like a gorilla. For the best part of half an hour Flannery rushed Harry off his feet, pasted his face with a nasty left, and threw him several times.

'Isn't it time you had a drop of this?' Slasher asked the now rather worse-for-wear Harry, holding his bottle of 'the right stuff' up to his man's lips. Harry took a good swig, blew thick blood out of each nostril of his badly damaged nose. 'That's better,' he said.

'Ay, isn't it,' said Slasher, looking across to where the landlord of the Anchor was pushing his way about shouting odds of two to one against Harry. 'Hear that, Harry?' said Slasher.

'What's stopping me? – but he won't be shouting two to one for long.'

Harry began to steady Flannery with pile-drivers to the body in the next round, and from that round he was relentless – terrible. Flannery couldn't keep him out, he closed in and delivered blows which left their mark on Flannery's fair-skinned body, blows that made the receiver gasp. For about twenty minutes Harry punished his opponent's body before stretching him out with a right under the heart. As Flannery's people were working on him, Slasher gave Harry another swig of the 'stuff' and said: 'The bastard's not as tall as he was, Harry, now that he's trying to protect his body more. So what if you began plastering his mug a bit.'

154

'I think I will,' said Harry, and as soon as he was eased up and forward towards his now swaying opponent he went for his mug. And didn't he plaster it, plastered it until the almost senseless Flannery's nose, moustache and lips were pounded into one piece of blood-soaked hairy flesh.

Glyn bowed his head and closed his eyes long before the 'plastering' of Flannery's mug was completed; he had tried to force his way out of the crowd, but he was wedged in, so he closed his eyes, but he left his ears unstopped, and heard Shenk squeal: 'O, Christ.' Then it was that he raised his head and opened his eyes just as Flannery was being pushed forward by his second to receive the coup de grâce. Smash. He fell, and the blood-drunk crowd yelled before it broke when the Irish admitted defeat. What he had seen caused Glyn's innards to turn a somersault; he was suddenly and violently sick. He crawled up the slope and away as fast as he could...

from *Black Parade* (1935)

Dai Smith

Focal Heroes

It would not perhaps surprise the Englishman who wrote that short masterpiece 'The Fight' that no boxer appears in *The Oxford Companion to English Literature*. It would no doubt have delighted William Hazlitt to learn that the same cannot be said of the *Companion to the Literature of Wales*. This is not because Welsh writers have moved to the same hypnotic rhythms that have entranced American authors from Twain to Hemingway and on to Mailer and Joyce Carol Oates, for there is not much more than one, fine boxing novel by Ron Berry (*So Long, Hector Bebb*, 1970), a colourful, historical fiction by Alexander Cordell (*Peerless Jim*, 1984) and occasional stories and poems by Alun Richards and Leslie Norris. The literary pedigree of Welsh fighters is really attested to by the umbilical cords which once made them emblematic of their society. It would be unthinkable to omit the names of Freddie Welsh, Jim Driscoll and Jimmy Wilde from the standard histories of modern Wales. For if the Edwardian years brought grammar schools, triumphant Welsh XVs and a patina of social cohesion to a booming Welsh world, it was still boxing which continued to seize the imagination of its working class. The progress was neither rational nor harmless but it was certainly triumphant. Tom Thomas from the Rhondda won the first Lonsdale belt for a British middleweight champion in 1909; when he died of pneumonia, aged thirty-one, in 1911 his coffin was carried to the grave by fellow-members of the Labour and Progressive Club; Bill Beynon of Taibach won the British bantamweight title in 1913: he continued work in the pit where he died under a fall in 1932, aged forty-one; Percy Jones of the Rhondda was the flyweight champion by 1914 and dead, after gassing in the war, by 1922. Countless others, more and less famous than these heroes, shared the abrupt origins of their supporters whilst their meteor-like careers were obvious metaphors for a society where sudden death or misfortune, neither rational nor harmless, was all too commonplace. And all of this flashing defiance occurred, and was effectively over, in the first two decades of this century. The young Alun Richards, grammar-school educated and rugby-team trained, was, in the 1940s, already of another world but those sepia-tinted, local champions were, indeed, a focal insight into what his society had been. He knew already that his absent father had once sparred with his fellow townsman, Freddie Welsh, and, later, would learn that the lightweight champion had once sparred with F. Scott Fitzgerald. Boxers were as much the totems of modern life in American Wales as they were in America itself. 'Leaders of thought' may have wilfully missed the point, then and now, but the deep social significance of boxers for societies-in-flux is one that the history of modern Wales amply affirms even if it is imaginative writers rather than historians who hitherto grasped the point...

Freddie Welsh was an athlete whose driven personality caused him, literally, to re-make and re-name himself. He became a totem of that modernity which his fostering society craved, and almost attained. If to be modern is constantly to give up that which you become then Freddie Welsh lived on the knife-edge of that quintessential modern experience. The fact that it was through boxing that his cubist personality was revealed to others only underlines the importance of understanding such appeal to those Welsh who were not, yet, in the early 1900s, socialized by schooling or limited by the boundaries of tradition. Tommy Farr inherited the cumbersome paraphernalia of a made world. Freddie Welsh drew his own maps. Maybe it was the splintering of any assured personal identity that makes him so profoundly reflective of an unsure, cocksure, fragmented Welsh identity.

He was born in Pontypridd in 1886 on the fringe of the coalfield. It was a new town in a new world even if what was to become the Welsh national anthem by the twentieth century had been composed there thirty years before his birth. The town had then been called Newbridge. His real name was Frederick Hall Thomas. His father was fairly well-to-do, an auctioneer and a member of families who farmed in and around the market town before it became a commercial and rail hub for the surrounding, mushrooming colliery townships. Frederick was sent away to school in Bristol. This was no hungry collier boy even if he did become the idol of those who were, like Jimmy Wilde. The boy's father died. His mother remarried and Freddie's home was at The Bridge Inn, Pontypridd. An aunt kept The Bunch of Grapes. Maybe he was now caught up, to an extent, with the sporting world of Pontypridd and even the likes of Georgie Punch. There is no evidence that he did likewise and, certainly, when he ran away aged sixteen he left no reputation behind. He went to Canada. He travelled the rails, like Hemingway's Nick Adams in that early boxing story 'The Battler', until he reached Philadelphia. Maybe he came via Scranton where, in the USA's thirty-seventh largest city, the largest transatlantic contingent of the Welsh had settled to work the mines, damn the Irish and join the Republican Party. He became interested in physical culture and combined it with boxing. It was now that he left his name behind, and, in America, became Freddie Welsh. He

158

practised assiduously. His self-confidence, his self-esteem almost, were fanatical. It was time to go home. It was there that he had to prove himself first.

Freddie Welsh was, at first, treated with some contempt in his home town. He was, in 1907, aged twenty, introduced to a Cardiff manager, Harry Marks, who later recalled how:

> Welsh on our first introduction was a spectacle indeed. Attired in a large black sombrero hat with a long, clerical-looking coat, he seemed a typical foreigner. I took him in hand, however, and I soon found that he was full of British grit.

As virtually an unknown, Welsh made a successful debut at the National Sporting Club. This was the gentleman turned pro with a vengeance and Eugene Corri, a famous referee who handled Welsh's title victory against the American Willie Ritchie in London in 1914, remembered him as a 'dandy-looking Welshman... an ardent student of John Ruskin... all his leisure was spent in reading the best English authors.' Neither this, nor his Americanized accent nor, even less, his American style of fighting endeared him to his home-town patrons. In Pontypridd, they were merely aggravated when on 17 April 1907 he knocked out, all on the same day, Evan Evans in one round, Charlie Webber in two and, with a symmetry he made his hallmark, Gomer Morgan in three. In September the gentlemen of the town put up a purse privately arranged (and this two years after the Evan Roberts religious revival, allegedly the apogee of

Nonconformist Wales) and Welsh fought Joe White, Canadian born but resident in Cardiff and a rated welterweight, for the purse and £100 stakes a side. A loft in a warehouse was provided by a local industrialist for a select, invited audience. An observer remembered:

> There was no secret about the fact that, although in his native town, South Wales sportsmen were longingly hoping that in White they had found one 'to burst the bubble that was Freddie Welsh'.
>
> Freddie had aped everything American as a result of his sojourn 'over the ditch' – in manner and speech; in fact, in every way he had become truly Yankee. His cockiness and his methods, revolutionary in their conception, had rather offended the conservative susceptibilities of the 'sports' of Pontypridd, and they did not conceal their hope that he would get a lacing.
>
> White was a tall, lean lad with a long reach and an expert in ringcraft and generalship – and having most of his fights in America it would appear as if Freddie would be 'hoist with his own petard.'

Welsh knocked him out in the sixteenth. From then on the conservative 'sports' were neither here nor there. He packed crowds in. In 1909 at Mountain Ash Pavilion in front of some 15,000 – the biggest fight crowd assembled to that date in Wales – he beat the Frenchman Henri Piet.

Welsh used 'booster techniques' familiar in the States. He charged for his sparring sessions. He took a percentage of the gate. His defence was immaculate but his speciality was in-fighting and chopping blows on to his opponents' kidneys. When he beat Young Joseph in this way the kidney punch was made illegal by the National Sporting Club. He was British lightweight champion by 1910 and pursued Willie Ritchie across Canada and America until given a chance to challenge him for the world crown. That was in 1914 when Freddie enticed Ritchie into fighting by receiving, himself, no more than his training expenses.

His ring career had run on parallel lines to that of Driscoll. It was inevitable that they meet. The two had become friendly, dandies-about-town, Cardiff town; Welsh lived with and, in 1913, married a waitress he had earlier met in a Cardiff restaurant. A rare surviving photograph shows Driscoll and Welsh together, straw-boatered, bespoke-suited, watch-fobbed and grinning. It seems they had no wish to fight each other. The prospect for others was tantalizing. Over months, in 1910, a whispering campaign and wrangles over money turned the clash into a grudge match. The parallel lines were being forced to converge. Alexander Cordell in his colourful novel *Peerless Jim* rightly makes subtle use of it as a fictional centre piece. It was the real Fight of the Century so far as Wales is concerned. After it the lines diverged.

Welsh and Driscoll met at the American Roller rink in Cardiff for a purse of £2,500 on 20 December 1910. Twelve miles away troops were stationed in Pontypridd to guard the magistrate's court where the leaders of the

Cambrian Coal Strike were being tried for their part in the Tonypandy riots the previous month. Observers commented that the atmosphere was subdued but there was an electric undercurrent amongst the 10,000 assembled:

> The waiting moments were beguiled by a band which played national tunes; but, whereas Rugby crowds amuse themselves, in similar circumstances by bursting into song, there was no vocalism last night, and for once even the familiar Land of My Fathers failed to inspire the musical soul of the Principality.

As for the fight, Welsh was quicker and cleverer than many had suspected. He also enraged Driscoll by holding, boring and kidney punching. Driscoll slowly forced his way back into the contest where the two styles were not proving harmonious when, in the tenth round of the twenty rounds scheduled, to the dislike of contemporaries but the delight of the historian in need of an image, Driscoll, goaded beyond sense, butted Welsh under this chin and across the ring, over and over. The fight was immediately awarded to Welsh on a foul. Time, venue, circumstances and consequences give the event a rich symbolism.

Freddie Welsh was the first to bring a legitimated world championship back to Wales. When he did so – in July 1914 at Olympia before thousands of his fellow country-men, both miners and mineowners – he immediately returned for a triumphal procession in the valleys of South Wales. His message was patriotic achievement, his meaning was global conquest:

When I think of the size of... our little country, and then think again how small that portion of it is that we call South Wales, I am lost in wonderment and filled with pride at the recollection of the things that have been done by the men of our race...

Is there a boxer in the whole wide world who can compare with Jimmy Wilde? There is no class made for him.

South Wales... has bred a flyweight and a featherweight Champion of England... Wales has bred a middleweight champion. Have we no one ready to fill Tom Thomas's place? I believe we can find such a man. And not only a middleweight, but a welterweight and a heavyweight.

Why not? A country where men can play rugby football as Welshmen play it – men who have beaten the best that the world could send against us – can, I am sure, produce boxers with the same qualities of hardihood and skill and courage which have made her rugby footballers famous and feared the world over.

There is no other place in the world, with the exception, perhaps, of France, where boxing has made such rapid advance, in so short a time as South Wales.

Boxing is... the sport which fits in with the Welsh temperament. It calls for quick thinking, for ready hands, and nimble feet... hardy bodies and high courage. I know that

Welshmen have all of these things. I am looking forward to the time when we shall hold a straight-flush from fly to heavy of British boxing championships. Even then the limits of ambition will not have been reached for there will be the world's titles to strive for.

The champion promptly left for America. A short time before Benny Leonard deprived him of that crown in New York City, Welsh had written to the Governor of New York to offer his services in running boxing shows 'at which I will meet contenders for my title and turn the receipts... over to a fund to equip a [sportsmen's] regiment' for overseas service. He added:

If the regiment is organised I am, of course, ready to serve in any capacity. The United States is my adopted country. I have lived here for 15 years; my wife and two children are American, and I feel that the entrance of America into the war is the call to arms for every man who, like myself, has been given an opportunity to earn a living in this great country.

The Americanization of Freddie, and his own 'late' entry into the fray, was reported sardonically by the Welsh press. His popular support remained undiminished.

Nevertheless, Freddie Welsh had become the focal American which the localized Jim Driscoll could not be. Scott Fitzgerald, in 1926, caught the essence of this phenomenon, and its doomed solipsistic heroism, when he created the late Victorian, James Gatz who becomes Jay Gatsby of the American Century by a combination of fanatical self-improvement through physical exercise and study. All given reality by fate:

> James Gatz [of north Dakota] – that was really, or at least legally – his name. He had changed it at the age of 17 and at the specific moment that witnessed the beginning of his career... I suppose he'd had the name ready for a long time even then. His parents were... unsuccessful... – his imagination had never really accepted them as his parents at all. The truth was that Jay Gatsby of... Long Island, sprang from his Platonic conception of himself... So he invented just the sort of Jay Gatsby that a 17-year-old boy would be likely to invent, and to this conception he was faithful to the end.

Fitzgerald's friend, the sports journalist and short-story writer, Ring Lardner, who knew Welsh well and placed references to him in his work, taught the great novelist to see the lineaments of modernity in physical competition and in its mass consumption. The connection is as teasingly tenuous in the 'real' world as it is insistently tenable for all who would truly imagine it. The boxer who once read, and mixed with, the best authors may have read Fitzgerald's masterpiece *The Great Gatsby* before he died, aged forty-one, in a downtown New York hotel room in 1927 and he

may, indeed, have once requested that his ashes be
scattered over Broadway, but there can be no imaginative
doubt that he really meant – Broadway, Pontypridd.

from *Aneurin Bevan and the World of South Wales* (1993)

Anon.

Jimmy Wilde

If the Board of Education's *Famous Welshmen* is gospel, then
Wales produced no eminent fightingmen after the death of
Tomos Prys in 1634. Something less than Higher Criticism
suggests that the writers could not hear the bands go by
because the choir was dealing with the Halleluiah Chorus.
Among the eminent fightingmen they failed to notice
between 1634 and 1934 was Jimmy Wilde, who was born
in 1892 and fated to adorn a profession condemned by
Evan Roberts.

Jimmy Wilde's claim to eminence lies not so much in his
winning the British and World flyweight championships as
in the conditions in which he took them. There have been
many British and World flyweight champions. It is Wilde's
peculiar glory that he won his fights while giving away
more weight than any boxer in British and American
history, and that he lost only four of 864 fights. This is not
a record that can be hidden behind a pile of hymn-books.

Wilde began giving away weight as soon as he could walk
on his sparrow legs. He was born at No. 8 Station Road,
Pontygwaith, Tylorstown, when boys who ran away from

aggressors were chucked into an empty coal-wagon with the challenger while his brothers stood on the grease-boxes to see the family honour redeemed even in defeat. Nobody needed to chuck Jimmy Wilde into a wagon, nor was the family honour even threatened while he carried it – except, of course, in the eyes of those who looked upon a losing fighter as an example of God's justice and a winning fighter as an instrument of the devil.

It is the destiny of small boys, and small men, to get pushed around, but when Jimmy Wilde was pushed he pushed back; the swipe that followed so rarely connected that the bully found it necessary to make a special job of teaching Wilde his place in Rhondda society. Wilde learned early that the smaller boy, if he is to survive, must never be where he is expected, and that if he dodged smartly he would have opportunities of planting his punches where and when he liked. The routine worked when he was seven years old, on tip and street corner, and he never found a better.

He has been called a miracle, but there was nothing miraculous about Wilde; throughout his career, he never did anything which the most sympathetic critic could call original – he did not need to. A boxer is an integrated mass of nerve and muscle, and Wilde was born with powers of co-ordination which few boxers can acquire even after years of training. When his hitting strength was astonishing Britain, a coven of Liverpool doctors prodded, thumped and pinched him for an hour, seeking vainly to discover the secret of that strength; they would have done better, to prod, thump and pinch his opponents, for the strength of Wilde's punches came from his instinctive ability to co-ordinate the efforts of his own tiny body so that the superior weight and strength of his opponent destroyed themselves on a fist which was always swinging in the right place at the right time. The strength of the blow came from the anvil rather than the hammer.

Genes made Jimmy Wilde possible. Environment made him. He was born and bred in a place and age of sullen industrial battle which reached one of many crises in 1911. As a boy he carried his own weight of pilfered coal from sidings to street – never asking who stole the coal from the people – to make a few shillings when a few shillings stopped the hunger-growling of the family guts. The necessary mitching earned him cuffs and kicks from a schoolmaster who, when he was a member of Parliament, took credit for teaching the flyweight champion of Britain to take punishment; the schoolmaster was no more than colliery-owner writ small. The community which gained little but pride from its heroic strikes, pride and a reputation as the most stubborn slaves in the world, found two ways of purging itself of fear and hate: the boxing booth and the chapel. Jimmy Wilde chose the boxing booth and, for his dreams, the mountain fighter. There were no dreams in the everlasting night of Ferndale No. 8 Pit, when Wilde first went underground, weighing four stone, standing four feet six, lost, it would seem for ever, in the cut-down pit clothes of his father; but D. Davis and Sons, Ltd, unaware of the bonus, gave him more than two bob a day with the distant prospect of thirty-five shillings a week to draw him on. They gave him Dai Davies. Wilde realized one day, from the mashed face and torn knuckles of Dai Davies, that he was filling trams for a myth, a mountain fighter. Long before he had heard of Regency prizefighters, he met one in the mangled flesh; an erratic boulder, dropped out of time and place by the hard tide of history. Forty rounds on a mountain top, where the gleam of a policeman's spiked helmet could be seen for five miles, kept up the tone of Dai's muscles for serious fighting, and he would modestly admit, when pushed, that he had fought Ted (Chops) Williams for eighty-four rounds and won on a knock-out where knock-outs were never technical. His home was a microcosm of Rhondda culture, for Mrs. Davies was staunch chapel, and their daughter Elizabeth cried shame on all fighting men. Indifferent to Evan Roberts, Dai pushed the bed against the wall in the back-bedroom, piled the rest of the furniture on the bed, and put young Wilde through his paces on three square yards of worn lino. Circumstances again helped to make Wilde what he became, for the tiny 'ring' forced him to learn to duck and weave with economical precision and contract his stomach and sway till he knew to a fraction of an inch how closely he could ride a punch; given his native endowments, the back-bedroom boy was bound to become front-page news. The girl who sulked over her sewing-machine when she heard the slither and slap of dancing feet over her head, lived to become the first woman to spend a night at the National Sporting Club and, before that, to establish the right of a boxer's wife to take a ringside seat and cheer him on. Elizabeth was a difficult convert, but once converted her blood ran hotter than her husband's. On one occasion when she sat among American toughs, she shouted in Welsh, 'If you don't finish him, Jimmy, I'll come and do it myself. They're giving me a hell of a time here.'

When Wilde was earning three pounds ten a fortnight he married Elizabeth Davies, and the unwritten marriage contract contained a clause forbidding fighting for ever. This was the first and last contract clause broken by Jimmy Wilde. Mrs Wilde was fond of chocolate almonds, and gratified to receive a quarter-pound every Saturday night; gratified at first, then suspicious, for sixpence a week for 'entertainment' does not run to chocolate almonds. Wilde's ringcraft sent him home unmarked from fight after fight from Scarrott's boxing booth, but even an inordinate desire for chocolate almonds cannot blind a Rhondda housewife to the fact that sevenpence into sixpence won't go.

Wilde got his chance at Scarrott's when he was still a lad. Scarrott, asked for a job, contemptuously ordered Jimmy to go round to the back of the tent to stop the other lads from crawling under the canvas. When Wilde had made it clear to the lads that he wasn't one of the lads any more, a dozen came at him like county policemen dealing with a half-pint Tonypandy picket. The battle that followed brought the crowd from inside the tent – they loved a game chicken – and made it unnecessary for the assault party, like the county police on more historic occasions, to send for reinforcements. These, stumbling over the bodies of the slain, would undoubtedly have brought Jimmy Wilde to his knees, but Jack Scarrott's bellow drove them at last from the field, and Wilde was instantly promoted to the tent interior. Marriage itself failed to keep him out of it. Prosperity, however, like love and a cold, cannot be hid, and once Wilde's secret was broken, he found himself in serious domestic trouble. Elizabeth was sixteen, and Wilde seventeen, when they married, and neither could be expected to own a sense of proportion. Elizabeth, at any rate, was not prepared to swop her birthright of respectability for a mess of chocolate almonds. Hardship, however, is notorious for breaking down respectability, especially the front-parlour type, and the domestic difficulties were resolved by a strike. Booth boxing, even at five shillings a fight, brought food into the house for the Wildes and their first child, and Mrs. Wilde realized that her husband was earning more during a strike than he did when working. When, in due course, boxing 'bought' a £500 house, with bathroom (two pounds ten a month to the Building Society), and supported in that house Wilde, his wife, his baby, his mother, and his younger brothers and sisters, the domestic battle was over, the longest and hardest in Wilde's career. Married men will admit that Wilde was giving away weight, as usual.

Booth boxing was business. Wilde and the rest of Scarrott's string ducked under the ropes to take on anything that offered, to make the fight last long enough to entertain the crowd, and short enough to keep Scarrott's challenge money in his pocket. Wilde, however, was forced to give away so much weight that he frequently gave the groundlings short but sweet commons. On more than one occasion he took on a mountain fighter seven stone heavier than himself, and knocked him out in fifteen seconds.

From Scarrott to Ted Lewis, manager of the Millfield Athletic Club, was obviously the miner's next step; and Lewis, not easily impressed by prodigies, was quick to see the making of a champion in Wilde. Wilde himself decided, after taking the seven stone championship of Britain against Billy Padden at Edinburgh, that there was no permanent place for part-time fighters at championship level. In boxing, as in other arts, a lucrative hobby does not make a professional, and only professionalism produces the best. Early in 1913 Wilde drew his last pay from D. Davis and Sons, Ltd, and started on his travels.

The eliminating bouts for the Lonsdale Belt and the flyweight championship of Great Britain, and other fights, first taught the fans that something phenomenal had again come out of Wales. Freddie Welsh already knew it, having been damaged by Wilde in exhibition bouts. The Press hailed him as a miracle, and one journalist wrote of him:

'Wilde's wonderful work lies in his being but six stone ten pounds and giving weight away – a stone upwards to men of boxing repute. We know, of course, that a man of eleven and a half stone can give away a stone or more and not be heavily handicapped. Take Sam Langford and Joe Jeanette, or Sam McVey or, to go further back, Tom Sayers and the Tipton Slasher, and Jem Mace and Sam Hurst. But we must remember that Sayers and Mace were in the neighbourhood of the middleweight limit and were not men of six or seven stone. The lighter a man is, under twelve and a half stone, the less he can afford to give away in weight. A bantamweight ought not to give one fraction more than a couple of pounds, whilst a flyweight must not concede more than a pound, and a seven stone man cannot give anything. But Jimmy Wilde comes along with his six stone ten pounds and puts paid to the account of good men scaling a full stone more. Never has such a thing been done or heard of in the annals of the old prize-ring, or in those of the modern boxing ring, and I am justified in saying that Jimmy Wilde is the greatest fistic marvel the world has ever seen.'

This was good reading for Wilde, and Elizabeth cut it out and pasted it into a scrap-book. Wilde knew that the secret lay in his timing and his footwork. Scorning to dazzle by dancing, he never tired himself by covering more ground than was necessary. Working at exactly the right range, he placed his long left-hand punches with astral precision to wear down his man, and finished the job with a meteoric right. Nothing illustrates more clearly the delicate nervous balance of Wilde's fighting than his form when he fought with a cold in his head. He became second-rate instantly, and courage never yet saved the second-rate from destruction. A common cold broke Wilde at his first attempt at the British flyweight championship against Tancy Lee in January, 1915. A year later, in perfect health, he took the championship against Joe Symonds, and at Christmas, 1916, the World championship against the Zulu Kid. Those who saw him fight then or afterwards can look down their noses at those who saw Irving in 'The Bells.'

After entering first-class boxing, and before joining the Army, Wilde fought thirty bouts a year, which requires almost as much stamina as playing in a repertory company, but when he tried to enlist, early in the war, he was rejected as physically unfit. In 1917, he was at last accepted, but only as a P.T. instructor. The Army, of course, made things difficult for him as a fightingman, but his business flourished, and five shillings from Ted Lewis became £5,000 from C. B. Cochrane. In 1919 Wilde sailed for the

United States, the profitable purgatory of British champions. Purses were not so fat then as now, but even then they were too fat to jingle. His American prize-money amounted to £23,000, but his expenses were sky-scraping. Miners are, of course, excessively familiar with 'deductions,' and there were no expenses in America which hurt so much as 'boy, cash advances, checkweigher, rent; house-coal, tools, and helves, powder and safety, doctor, institute.' Wilde's last fights, against Herman and Villa, at the mature age of 31, though both were lost and Villa nearly killed him, earned Wilde £21,000, and he retired with a nest egg of £70,000, a sum which even a colliery owner might envy.

Unfortunately, Wilde lacked the colliery owner's flair for keeping his cash, even in defeat. A Starting Price business at Cardiff got off well, but was pipped at the post and Wilde was no luckier at making bets than at taking them. His cinemas in the Rhondda lost their plush and paint when the slump deprived miners of their last comfort – fourpennorth of dreams – and Wilde lost heavily when Jimmy White took his friends' investments to the grave. Journalism, like the insurance book, is often the last hope of the physically or financially crippled, but Jimmy Wilde has flourished in Fleet Street, and it is a testimony to the magic of his name that he is a commercial asset to a newspaper twenty-five years after his last and losing fight. The Archangel Gabriel himself is a sucker at judging men, compared with a newspaper editor, and in all material affairs the last edition is more important than the last trump.

To hold a by-line over boxing articles for twenty years is enough to put a man in a class of his own, but this is no good reason why Welsh biographers should crown him lord among lords, if not lord of all. It is, however, a reflection of the fact that Jimmy Wilde's fighting life has become a golden myth in his own lifetime, part of the folk-culture of Wales and the world, for eminence in the eyes of an editor is evidence that the people have spoken and the sêt fawr had better shut up. When the *Welsh Dictionary of National Biography* is published, paying tribute at last to General Picton and to the immortals of Rorke's Drift, Mametz Wood and Arras, there may well be space, not too far from Colonel Dai Watts-Morgan, for Wilde, James (Jimmy).*

from *The Welsh Review*, Winter, 1948
*(There was, – see *Welsh DNB,* 1959. GW)

Ron Berry

Hector Bebb, British Champion

Hector:
Round 2: 'How's it going?' says Sammy.

I'm failing to think who Jesse reminds me of, the past won't click forward. Fact is Jesse's five kinds rolled into one. Jesse's a real handful.

Round 3: Again from Sammy. 'How's it going son?'

I says, 'Time will tell in this fight.'

'He's nutting you a bit,' says Sammy.

'Jesse works rugged inside,' I says.

Sammy agrees. 'He'll try anything, the bastard. We're doing all right, Hector, we're doing fine.'

Comes 4, 5 and 6. Round 6 I meet a short bolo in the mouth. Blood. Gumshield away. Behind the bolo his other glove heeling upwards. I thought, aye, Jesse'll fling all the rough stuff if I let him. By and by he'll take some medicine.

Round 6: 'I'm not worried' says Sammy. 'Here, it's salted.'

'Thanks,' I say, the salt stinging, stinging, washing the blood taste away.

'Listen, son, lay on him next round. Try some elbow in the old throat. Teach him, right?'

'Why not,' I says.

Jesse and me, we're about equal in height. Close-to I lower off on his right side, blocking that arm because he's faster with it. Only southpaws hit faster right-handed but like I said, Jesse's this much more awkward. I can't make it work though. He follows my crouch, prepared to sacrifice that right arm, instead grinding his nut at my eyes and mouth. As Sammy mentioned, it's nothing to worry about, the cut inside the mouth.

Round 7: 'Hector, now listen, he's slow on the break. He's waiting for you, get it? Son, let him break.'

I thought, definitely, it's Jesse's method, he's all come-on. The referee says, 'Break,' tapping my left arm same as in every previous round. I'm expected to break first. I've made the pattern for this slow-minded referee. Now I kept Jesse tangled inside. 'Break,' he says again. 'You, Markham, break,' and pushing him off. By the end of round 7 they're shouting insults for more action. Faces outside the lights, faces with holes in them.

Round 8: 'He's fretting,' says Sammy. 'Let him break first.'

The referee walks over. 'Tell your man to box.'

Abe takes the warning comfortable as a bus inspector. 'Pass the word to Markham's corner,' he says.

Jesse comes his boring and barging in the 10th, but he's wilder, swinging more, hoping to land a softener. 'Jesse,' I tormented into his ear-hole, 'there'll be 5 more to go after this one.' He's so surprised I send in a nice right hook low down, safe on the mark, shoot the repeat at his head but he's too near, grunting under my chin. 'Break!' comes the order. He's expecting interference from the ref. I'm easy. It's Jesse's move. 'Another 5 Jesse,' I says.

The referee does his job, all Belle Vue bellacking for blood. Mine mostly. This is Jesse's home patch, his crowd.

Round 10: Sammy smears a real grease pack above and below my eyes. The referee wipes it off, Sammy reaches under his wrist where he's got the jelly balled like wads of chewing gum, and it goes on again. He says, 'This time don't wait for the referee, try catching him on the break. Understood, son? You break first, then whap, then double-handed. Try it.'

I says, 'What's the score?'

Abe takes his hand off my shoulder. 'Near enough even by my count. Feeling strong, Hector?'

I says, 'Fair, pretty fair.'

Just before the bell Sammy rips open the telegram, a copper standing by the delivery boy. 'From Pont Fawr,' he says, grinning all over his chops. 'Listen, son. 'Warmest congratulations. Hector Bebb. British champion. Jane and Prince.'

I think to myself, great, that's bloody great, then the bell rings. Near the end of the round Jesse connects twice. We're in his corner where they've sloshed water over him. He's half-way through the ropes on his own. I'm skating till I land on both knees. Safe. We clinch. At the break I step back, shunt forward and Jesse's watching it coming without being able to dodge it. Whap, as Sammy said, bang on the angle. Jesse grabs out but this is my chance. I'm unloading as he tries to smother, over and under his arms, unloading my lot, everything right to the bell.

Round 11: Sammy rubs my stomach. 'You know what to do, son,' he says. 'Get stuck fast into him. He's yours.'

I piled in till the third man stopped us in the 12th, which goes to show how twp-witted some officials are. He allowed the crowd to influence him. It isn't for me to comment on Jesse, whether or not he could defend himself. He took three counts: six and twice down for eight. After the opening rounds I foresaw this fight would wear through to the last stages. Jesse knew all the tricks. You couldn't connect full wallop on a fighter like Jesse Markham. We made him lose confidence on the breaks. Until the 11th I'll admit he hurt me more than I hurt him. This Jesse knew his business. He had everything, everything bar a man like Sammy John in his corner. Sammy analysed the move. Abe and Len Jules were there, true, swabbing and rubbing down, but me and Sammy worked the British title off Jesse Markham.

Tommy Wills:
It looked to be even-stevens up to the 8th. After the 8th I suspected something. They go into tight wrestling, deliberate the way it came from Hector, almost asking to be

disqualified. Not only that, you'd believe Markham was in charge. Great dog of a scrapper, Jesse Markham. Genuine all-in dog, like he was reared hungry same as my father and his father before him. By the 10th I'm thinking Hector's losing the verdict. He's done nothing but hold for 3 rounds, yet I'm still waiting to be convinced, still half expecting him to pull something out of the bag. One of those short-arm digs that deadens the nerves. I'm drawing beer when he falls down in the 11th, every customer in the bar willing to spill the commentary better than Barry Dalby. Less polite than Dalby, all effing and blinding since it's been MEN ONLY in our public bar since before my time. A ruling my wife resents, by the way.

Markham turns from the ropes. He comes forward. They're head to head again as usual, Markham swinging blind from all angles. I see the ref moving in, we all see it, Markham trying to back off, Hector driving in from close range. Bomb of a punch. Real beaut, yet simple as ABC. Because Jesse can't box there's some more wrestling, maul, maul, Jesse hanging on, hanging on, only until the bell he's soaking it.

Hector's left hook banger kept in reserve, as I suspected.

Last round it was a question of strength, with Markham not having enough to box him off. Jesse's down, he's down, he's down. It's all over.

As I say, we've produced some good Welsh boys through-out past years, boys who've supplied safe thrills for those rich-fed bastards with gold tiepins and Larranaga cigars filling the ringside seats. Hector Bebb from Cymmer, he's the king. Definitely king. Now I see in today's *Express* how he's committed a murder. Some dirty prick knocking off his missis while he's winning the title for us up in Belle Vue. If a man can't trust his own wife, where's the point? Mark her for life he should have, put her nose out like mine is. Where's the satisfaction in duffing the bloke? You take the average youngster, he'll grab anything offered. Only natural. Granted, here I'm speaking for myself, but if it's vice versa what you've got is a wanker.

Anyhow, Hector Bebb, we'll be arguing about him for years. He's more important than any bloody peke yapping in some newspaper office. Nobody remembers fight reporters, scores of the bastards who've scribbled their blind ignorance about Dempsey, about our little Jimmy Wilde, or Maxie Baer or Joe Louis. Parasitic bastards they are without exception. Never tell me any fight reporter, any so-called boxing expert can explain what happens when a fighter's put to sleep. For a start it isn't sleep, and that's a mystery. Watch anybody sleeping, father, mother, brother, missis – they're not there. Neither can you be where they are. It's the same when a man takes solid pummelling. Same as regards dipping your wick, intercourse as they call it.

Two morning papers and one evening paper every day here in The Lion. Three main Sunday papers. Fridays we take the *Racing Handicap*. We take *Reveille*. We take *Y Cymro* for our old-timers, seven regulars who stink out our snug with their Condor and Franklyn's. Nineteen inch telly in the bar. All channels. My daily crust costs me roughly seventy hours a week on my feet. Everybody's lackey. Remember, this comes after eighteen years in the game. Now, when these papers splash Hector's face all over their front pages, calling him a brutal murderer, I suggest it's time we members of the general public came to realise that life isn't a monastery garden with nightingales hopping about in the bushes. Fall back on politics or religion in any kind of argument, and straightway you fall back on murder. It's us as we are. It's you and me, it's one and all. We can do for men, women and kids with punches, with bullets, bombs, or by signing our autographs. Like these big blabs in the press. When they catch Hector, when that happens I hope the officials who sit in judgment on him, I hope they trot back home to wives who've taken to buggery with their family pets, preferably Alsatians. That's my recommendation. It's been done here in Tosteg. I say it takes a lot of real experience to ram this murder talk where it belongs, slap-bang inside all of us. I've sampled my share legally, wearing 6 to 8 ounce gloves. As I see things, this old world's just about fucked. There's no right nor wrong in the press or on telly. It's all yap, signifying nothing, with nowhere coming at the end of it. First though, a man's got to go through the mill, find out what it's all about.

from *So Long, Hector Bebb* (1970)

Geoffrey Nicholson

Billy Eynon

Even today, with its houses strung across the head of the Taff Valley at odd angles and levels, as though its terraces had been rearranged by an earthquake, Merthyr seems like some frontier town of the welfare state. It is literally on the industrial borders. Southward there are works and collieries all the way to Cardiff; to the north lies the green prettiness of Brecon.

Once when I was there the *Merthyr Express* had this headline on the obituary page: 'A Pipe-smoking Nonagenarian.' It was remarkable only for the fact that it referred to a mother of twelve children, 'An interesting feature of Mrs. T.'s life,' the text explained, 'was that sixty years ago, being in delicate health, she was advised by her doctor to take up pipe-smoking. She did so, and never suffered from a chest complaint afterwards.' It's hardly surprising that several sons of so indomitable a woman should have taken up boxing, or that one of them had some success in the professional ring.

Merthyr, because it was a kind of industrial Klondike in the last century, attracted to itself boatloads of Irishmen and probably more Jews than is common for a town of its size in South Wales. In a later wave came the Italians. They intermarried and today form a radical, lively community which speaks – with hardly a pause – in a broad valley accent yet is distinctive from Welshier areas. It is a soccer town, for instance, whereas Ebbw Vale, Mountain Ash and Pontypridd, all within a dozen miles, are fanatically devoted to Rugby Union (in fact Merthyr was one of the towns that at the turn of the century gave further offence by running a Rugby League side). You're soon reminded that in 1938, when England were beaten 4-2 at Cardiff, there were six Merthyr men, led by the marvellous Bryn Jones, in the Welsh team. The town side still does fairly well in the Southern League, but hates playing at home because the pitch and the tongues of its supporters are so rough.

It is boxing, though, that carries the greatest prestige. People in a town that produced the press barons Camrose and Kemsley, the composer Joseph Parry, the novelist Jack Jones and innumerable bards and choirmasters, think far more highly and frequently of Billy Eynon who can be seen almost any morning exercising his dog at a steady clip through the park. Billy Eynon? Unremembered outside, he is honoured in Merthyr as the man who fought Jim Higgins in 1921 for the British and Empire bantamweight titles – and in the opinion of almost everyone except the referee, beat him.

Eynon is seventy-one now: small, slight, wiry and as bright as a bird. The only visible mark of his 250 fights is that one eye behind the round National Health spectacles is artificial – and that was the result of an accident in the gym.

When I visited him he was living in a back street of the town, alone. You stepped off the pavement into a room which had been empty of furniture since his son, a school teacher, moved with his family to a more modern house. He had been pressed to go with them, but said 'You're better off by yourself.' The back room he took us into had a modern paraffin stove and a television set; it was warm and quiet.

When he was a small boy they were still hammering away with bare, brine-pickled fists on the tips around the town, very often Irish against Welsh, sometimes Irish against Irish, you couldn't be too choosy. The fights would be picked in the pubs at night and settled on the following morning. They might go on for hours until only one man was left standing. Or the police might arrive. Then the fighters would run for it and escape into the Taff. The police drew the line at getting their uniforms wet.

Eynon never got mixed up in anything like this, coming from a respectable non-conformist family. Local legend lays down that his career began when his parents began to send him to violin lessons. He sold the violin, bought a pair of boxing gloves and used to smuggle them out of the house in the case. He smiled indulgently about this, not confirming or denying it. His version was that he came into boxing when he was working in the pits at fifteen. He quarrelled with his butty, they had a scrap, and this boy told a local fight promoter that Eynon was pretty useful.

'Well, this promoter approached me,' said Eynon, speaking slowly and carefully at first, but soon quickening into an almost unpunctuated monologue. 'And he asked me if I'd like to box for him. So I said yes and the next Saturday he put me in against Bert Harding who was the best kid in Merthyr. Well, I knocked him out in the first round – five bob I got for that. I'd told the boys I'd buy them raspberries and ice-cream if I won, so I was just leaving the hall to buy them their raspberries and ice-cream when the seconds said what about us? I had to give them two shillings each. Left me with a bob. After winning my first fight I couldn't even treat the kids to raspberries and ice-cream. But anyway who should have been in the hall but a manager from Pontypridd, and he asked me if I'd go and fight for him. So of course I said yes. And in a month a letter came to the house saying I was fighting on Saturday at Tonypandy.

Thirty shillings for six rounds. Well, I got a bloody hiding. But it was a good fight. They were standing on their chairs at the end. Draw it was. So the manager comes round afterwards and says he wants me to fight the next Saturday. I've had a bloody miff, I say. Well, I'm bruised all over and aching. Look, he says, you fought the best kid in the Rhondda tonight. I wanted to see what you could do. Next time I'll pick you a little lemon. No, I'm giving up boxing, I say. But the next day the bruises begin to go and I feel different about it. So I go back and win easy. What did I tell you he says afterwards. And I've got another little mug for you next Saturday. And that's how it went on, ten Saturdays in a row. And that's how I started boxing.'

Eynon's gym was in the old Taff Brewery, or in the Globe or the Tiger. Most pubs had a ring of sorts in the back room, and Merthyr had more pubs per head than any other town in Wales. 'There were so many boxers in those days, and everyone doing it for the love of the game not for money.' What with this, and with the regular weekly promotions, Eynon need hardly have gone outside the town to get a regular fight with men of his class. Certainly he needn't have gone outside the valleys. But he was ambitious, so at seventeen he spent a year with the boxing booths.

Until the thirties, the booths were the meal-ticket of the hungry fighters; and old-timers say that their decline is the greatest blow the game has ever suffered. They taught boxers to cope with anything on two legs. Eynon described his life with them: 'You'd pitch in a certain place, at a fair or the seaside. Might be a week or just a day. Then you'd stand out the front of the booth with your hands crossed,

185

and a feller'd be telling the tale, you know. And maybe one of you'd be punching the ball. And you'd wait for someone in the crowd to challenge you. They came from all over, the boxers – Yorkshire, Birmingham, even had a black feller. Be fifteen, twenty houses a day, and you got two shillings each time you fought. I was all right. I was small, see, smaller than the others, so they'd always pick on me. And you had to take them on, didn't matter what weight. I had a black eye or cut lip most of the time. Yes, I always did pretty well in the booths.'

He darted out of the room to fetch some press cuttings and a wallet which held nothing but a photograph. It was of his fight in Salonika in the Great War when he won an Army featherweight championship. Two tiny figures were caught in mid-punch in an open-air ring. The faded, indistinct background was a mass of spectators. 'Two hundred thousand soldiers and sailors – biggest crowd ever to watch a boxing match. They were on banks, well, hills if you like, all around. They got the idea for Wembley from there.'

He folded out the sheets of newspaper, which were already becoming dry and brittle: 'There, these will tell you better than I can.' Then he was beginning to talk again, this time about his first fight in London. 'I was walking down the street in Merthyr when this chap came up and said are you Billy Eynon. I said yes and he said I've come all the way down from London to see you. I want you to fight in The Ring at Blackfriars. So I went up. And who should I meet in London but Jim Kendrick. He was the bantamweight champion of England. He used to live around here. I used to see him boxing down the Garth. He knew me. Well he said, what are you doing up here? I said I was fighting Gaines at the Blackfriars Ring. You're fighting a good kid, he said. Can you fight? I hope you can fight because he's the best bloody kid in London. I tell you what, I'd better come in your corner.

'Well they were a funny crowd at The Ring. They started booing because I was a Taff, see. But Kendrick said don't worry. And he said don't go into Gaines at the start. Just keep up close and try and beat him to the punch. You win the first round and they'll all be shouting for you. So I did what he said and I won the first round. And I did the same in the second round and I won that one. What did I say, he said. And now they were all shouting for me. That's the bloody way. Come on, Taff. Kill the bugger. It went to twenty-three rounds and I won on points. They were always on my side after that fight. I was a big idol of The Ring for years.'

In that period he fought everyone except Jimmy Wilde, and he sparred with him in the gym, but so ferociously that Wilde always avoided him after that. It was a rough life. If there's one thing he envies modern boxers, it's that they have 'to box only ten rounds'. He had to box twenty-three, and not much account was taken of injuries. 'I've seen them fighting with one ear hanging off. And if someone's eye was swollen, well often the seconds would lance the swelling with a knife. Then there were the gloves. They get new gloves now to fight with, and they're eight ounces. They were four when I started – sometimes three ounces, so much of the hair had come out of them. They'd throw two pairs of

187

gloves into the ring. Might have been used a dozen times. Blood on them, and stiff. You'd toss for first choice, and your second would choose the ones that didn't have so much hair in them. Cut eyes, though, we didn't get so many of those. I blame these helmets they train in. They come out of them a bath of sweat. I've seen little Winstone steaming when he took his off. Stands to reason it must soften their heads.'

He was out of the pits by this time. 'I injured my finger one day, and when I came home I said, 'Mam, I'm not going down there any more.' He became a fishmonger and fruiterer.

His fights were less frequent and better paid now. He was getting forty and fifty pounds, which was big money. 'Top of the bills were coming down from London and Liverpool for only fifteen shillings or a pound. And they'd take that back off them at cards before they left.'

Then in 1921 came his title fight against Higgins. Unpleasant rumours still surround it. On the day of the contest he was over-weight – a fact that wouldn't normally have escaped his manager's attention. Merthyr drew its own scurrilous conclusions about whose side the manager was on, but that didn't help Eynon. He had to take a Turkish bath to reduce, and while Higgins was comfortably at rest, he was skipping in heavy clothes before an open fire. He went back to be weighed, but still he hadn't quite made it. 'Higgins's manager put a penny on the scales. That was all there was in it. Take it off, he said. I was as dry as a chip after that. I'd fought a twenty-round fight before I'd even got into the ring.'

For all that, Eynon appeared to beat Higgins on points,

and it wasn't only Merthyr that thought so. A record of £300 in 'nobbins', made up of sovereigns and five-pound notes, was thrown into the ring by the crowd to help console him. Several times a return fight was arranged, but on each occasion Higgins broke down in training. Then, a year later, Eynon had the sparring accident that cost him the use of his eye. It was the end of his career.

'I had about two thousand saved. I'd had three fights at £500 in a year. And I spent the lot. I was a bloody fool, really, but I thought I might lose the sight of the other eye and go blind altogether. I went up to London, stayed in the Strand Palace, went round the races. It soon went. I should have opened up a business with the money. But there we are.'

Not that it would occur to you to feel sorry for Eynon. Forty years on, people in Merthyr would still turn and look after him when he passed.

from *The Professionals* (1964)

John Morgan

Dying Demonology

'Punch, Jesus, punch!' shouted the Mexican in the aisle seat at Earls Court. In a pool of light in the centre of the stadium the Mexican Jesus Saucedo was doing badly against a thin Scot, few in the crowd paying much attention, except the Mexican spectator, who really cared. Suddenly there was a roar of joy, a sound more savage than the roar for a goal, the pleasure angrier, almost bitter. Jesus was down. His leg would twitch occasionally, otherwise he was still. A man looking like a doctor came into the ring and then St John's Ambulance men with a stretcher. They carried him through the crowd who cheered in what's known as a sportsmanlike way. He was in a coma and, for all we knew, near death. My neighbours, discussing the situation in Welsh, observed that the Mexican had been behaving peculiarly during the fight: he had twice walked to the wrong corner at the end of the round. The pageantry of the world title-fight that followed immediately afterwards seemed tawdry and distasteful.

Recorded trumpets blew a fanfare. Two searchlights in the roof broke the darkness, searching for the challenger, Howard Winstone, and finding him in a scarlet robe surrounded by men in white carrying flags, one the Welsh Ddraig Goch, the other the Union Jack. The banners drifted in the smoke while national anthems were sung, the Welsh, naturally, with most the 18,000 crowd had come up from Wales in the hope that Winstone, the Merthyr featherweight, would be the first Welshman ever to win a world title.

I wouldn't care to defend boxing against the usual charges; that it is crooked, that betting men and gangsters move in the shadows of the game, fixing and threatening; that men die in the ring, damage their brains, stumble through the rest of their lives. A few weeks ago I talked to an old boxer, once adulated, who now confused the decades in which he fought, burst into tears from time to time, and needed to hold his drink with both hands. Neither would I care to peddle the line that it's a useful substitute for brawling in life, that a polite society needs its public punchers to sublimate and expiate its violence. (See Mailer on Clay versus Liston for a brilliant analysis of this.) I don't much go either for the thesis that pro-boxing is an extension of the Theatre of Cruelty, offering Artaud-like insights into those truths of hatred and passion which respectability conceals. If I shared that view, I suppose I would have been delighted to discover one evening two years ago, when Howard Winstone and Brian Curvis, two Welsh British champions, were on the same bill at Wembley, that my ringside seat was covered with the blood of two heavyweights who had just finished a preliminary bout. Here was 'reality', involvement; hypocritically, no doubt, since boxing is bound to be bloody, it made the occasion revolting. Yet here I was again, and there was a Mexican being carried away on a stretcher. The defence I would offer is that it is hard to escape from the demonology of a particular kind of industrial society, and hard for anyone brought up in a British coalfield to see boxing quite in the fashion it appears to more genteel regions. Boxing offered miners riches beyond the avarice of shop-keepers; nothing else did, not even professional football. Good boxers became famous. When I was a small boy, we would see champions walking around the streets. An uncle of mine used to run a 'boxing academy' – he wasn't, we gathered, well enough to work down the mine. We would gather on Saturday mornings on the first floor of disused colliery workings, probably illegally, and wave our feeble fists at one another while he recalled the skills of Driscoll and Wilde. Beneath the ring were the cold waters which had flooded the pit years before and drowned a few miners.

Old champions then, and later, endlessly recounted or invented anecdotes. One day a few leading pugilists – or so the story went – organised a small crowd that threw a mob of policemen into the River Towy at Llandeilo during the General Strike. They all pleaded guilty at the Assizes but the jury found them not guilty, at which the judge fell down foaming in an epileptic fit. There was more admiration for the elegant boxer than the big puncher, and a romanticism about bygone stylists. Was it not passing brave to be the champ and ride in triumph through Tonypandy?

Nationalist pride in Wales has always been inextricably involved with poverty; it's easier to see now that poverty promotes fighters, and that the United States has the best because it still has the hungriest. The crowd at Earl's Court last week seemed, in a way that's hard to specify, seedier than one remembered. Society is being cured of boxing as it is being cured of poverty and its supporters come to have the air of men enslaved to some lewd anti-social taste: apologetic, conscious of being near the fringe of society rather than, as in the first 40 years of the century in British industrial communities, near the heart of it. This is why Howard Winstone had been a bonus for the dying sport. He has a sensible manager, Eddie Thomas, once a British champion himself. He trains and lives simply in Merthyr. He has saved his money, having made £60,000 in the past six years, and plans to open a motel in the Brecon Beacons. More than that, he boxes in an old 'classical' style, and makes the sport look like an exercise in high skill. Against the world champion Saldivar at Earls Court he needed to fight defensively since he was less strong – this wasn't clear until about the ninth round at which point Winstone still seemed to be holding his own – but he fought that kind of fight at extraordinary speed with the footwork of a dancing master. He lent to a rough and dubious profession an athletic grace. So long as there was grace, it has been possible to enjoy boxing's hilarious rascality.

No British fighter or manager quite matches up of course, to a pair like the American middleweight of the century's first decade, Stanley Ketchel and his handler Wilson Mizner. Said Mizner of Ketchel's famous fight with Langford in 1910: 'Why, it was written like a play. We had it surge to and fro like a melodrama. First, Ketchel in dire distress, then Langford, then Ketchel, and so on. It's the old, old plot.' Ketchel disliked punching people he regarded as nice and had to be persuaded they were unpleasant. At a New York brothel he was discovered weeping in front of a picture called Lost in the Storm, 'showing a sheep lost in a blizzard'. Runyon wrote: 'Ketchel prejudiced the judgement of everyone who ever associated with him. They can see no other fighter'. He was murdered at the age of twenty-four.

I wouldn't like to suggest the British boxers of one's acquaintance live lives so baroque. They have become earnest, introspective about tactics and motives; but I remember the trainer of one British champion for a week before a bout, sleeping like a dog outside the champ's bedroom door to keep this boy's wife from 'draining his juices' as he put it; and another one keeping dogs at a door to stop a pugilist sneaking out, not for gin, but for ice-cream. Feckless, gambling wildly, gaily disrespectful of themselves and the future, pugs and their handlers were keen for company and great men for funerals, when they would weep unashamedly. The trick doesn't work any more. Nothing is so distasteful as a dead romance. Jesus Saucedo lies in a semi-coma at the Atkinson-Morley hospital: 'his condition is unchanged.' He may live. Boxing may not.

from the *New Statesman* 17 September 1965

Leslie Norris

The Ballad of Billy Rose

Outside Bristol Rovers Football Ground –
The date has gone from me, but not the day,
Nor how the dissenting flags in stiff array
Struck bravely out against the sky's grey round –

Near the Car Park then, past Austin and Ford,
Lagonda, Bentley, and a colourful patch
Of country coaches come in for the match
Was where I walked, having travelled the road

From Fishponds to watch Portsmouth in the Cup.
The Third Round, I believe. And I was filled
With the old excitement which had thrilled
Me so completely when, while growing up,

I went on Saturdays to match or fight.
Not only me; for thousands of us there

Strode forward eagerly, each man aware
Of tingling memory, anticipating delight.

We all marched forward, all except one man.
I saw him because he was paradoxically still,
A stone against the flood, face upright against us all,
Head bare, hoarse voice aloft, blind as a stone.

I knew him at once, despite his pathetic clothes;
Something in his stance, or his sturdy frame
Perhaps, I could even remember his name
Before I saw it on his blind-man's tray. Billy Rose,

And twenty forgetful years fell away at the sight.
Bare-kneed, dismayed, memory fled to the hub
Of Saturday violence, with friends to the Labour Club,
Watching the boxing on a sawdust summer night.

The boys' enclosure close to the shabby ring
Was where we stood, clenched in a resin world,
Spoke in cool voices, lounged, were artificially bored
During minor bouts. We paid threepence to go in.

Billy Rose fought there. He was top of the bill.
So brisk a fighter, so gallant, so precise!
Trim as a tree he stood for the ceremonies,
Then turned to meet George Morgan of Tirphil.

He had no chance. Courage was not enough,
Nor tight defence. Donald Davies was sick

And we threatened his cowardice with an embarrassed kick.
Ripped across both his eyes was Rose, but we were tough

And clapped him as they wrapped his blindness up
In busy towels, applauded the wave
He gave his executioners, cheered the brave
Blind man as he cleared with a jaunty hop

The top rope. I had forgotten that day
As if it were dead for ever, yet now I saw
The flowers of punched blood on the ring floor,
As bright as his name, I do not know

How long I stood with ghosts of the wild fists
And the cries of shaken boys long dead around me,
For struck to act at last, in terror and pity
I threw some frantic money, three treacherous pence –

And I cry at the memory – into his tray, and ran,
Entering the waves of the stadium like a drowning man.
Poor Billy Rose. God, he could fight
Before my three sharp coins knocked out his sight.

from *The Loud Winter* (1967)

Hugh McIlvanney

Merthyr v. Mexico 1965

If Howard Winstone beats Vicente Saldivar of Mexico and takes the featherweight championship of the world at Earl's Court on 7 September, the people of Merthyr Tydfil will see it as merely the fulfilment of the natural law. They are already infectiously convinced that Merthyr is in possession of some kind of cosmic championship, that the town and its sons have established firsts or bests in all the significant fields of human endeavour. When Eddie Thomas, Winstone's manager, reminds you that Britain's first coal was dug out from Merthyr hillsides and that the town was once 'the industrial capital of the world' he is simply introducing you to a mounting scale of claimed distinctions which ends in bizarre magnificence: 'First man Albert Pierrepoint hung threw a woman down those coke ovens over there.'

Charles Jones, the Merthyr poet, a man of sharp intelligence and uproarious humour who has elected himself bard and jester to Thomas's court, starts by telling you solemnly in the main street at lunchtime that 'for its size Merthyr has more beautiful girls than any other place in the country, without a doubt'. He finishes at 11 p.m. over a lager and lime in a working men's club by reassuring you with the information that the town 'has the most expert abortionists in the world'. When the club closes there is still a long way to go. Land-locked in a natural bowl 20-odd miles north-west of Cardiff, Merthyr maintains a defiant insularity against most outside influences,

197

including the licensing laws. And Eddie Thomas is one of the few men who can go through a session on two glasses of Advocaat and lemonade and half a dozen pineapple juices and still be offering to sing 'Speak to me, Thora' at 4 a.m. The Advocaat is the response to the discovery that he has an ulcer. 'I only hope some of the boys don't start to fancy me when they see me on this stuff.'

The major reason why Howard Winstone is fighting for the world title is that he is the most skilful boxer in Britain, but to understand the real nature of his challenge – his own quiet, unnervous dedication and the support that would have taken three planeloads of his neighbours to Mexico City if the match had been made there – it is necessary to know Merthyr. The simplest way to know Merthyr is to know Eddie Thomas.

Thomas, who held the welterweight championships of Britain, the Empire and Europe, was secure in the town's folklore before he took on Winstone. Now in his 40th year, nearly three stone heavier than he was when he won the titles, he goes around with an open, slightly amused expression, accepting his fame with the affectionate pleasure of a boy who is being praised by the family for passing an exam. In the street he is greeted every few paces and when he drives he is constantly giving toots of recognition on the horn of his red Corsair. It is almost new but already has a dusty veteran look from being driven with rough skill around the tips where ballast is being excavated by the firm he runs with his brother and a friend. Thomas's life is geared to his own impulsive rhythm and he is fantastically unpunctual. His friends can predict where he will turn up but never when. 'He is incredible,' says Charles Jones. 'He is a wild man and yet there is a broad streak of the puritan in him. He is impossible, but he is pure gold.' He is also pure Merthyr, a conscious guardian of the old values that grew mainly out of the mines, where his father lost an arm and where Thomas himself worked even while he was a champion. When we gathered for a training walk on the hills above the town it was beside the row where his father lives and Thomas went in to change into enormous boots, denim trousers and a heavy V-necked sweater worn next to his skin. Winstone wore shoes, slim-fitting trousers and a suede waistcoat over a white shirt. It was sensible enough clothing – he was out to stretch himself, not to sweat – but it emphasised a striking difference between two men who have much in common.

Winstone is absolutely loyal to his environment and says he would never leave it but there is a sense of the modern young man about him that contrasts with the traditionalism of his manager. Winstone likes fashionably cut suits; Thomas wears heavy navy-blue serge. Thomas sings seriously and usually picks songs that have been favourites for 50 years; Winstone is always half-joking when he gives out random lines from contemporary musicals. He leans forward into your face suddenly, affects a deep brown voice and sings: 'We'll find a new way of living. We'll find a way of forgiving.'

Thomas's lurcher followed us on the walk and almost immediately it began to chase sheep. 'Come back, you bugger,' he shouted. 'I'll warm you. I'll warm you,'

'One word from Ed and it does as it likes,' said Colin

Lake, one of two Londoners who have been sparring with Winstone. Lake and the other sparring partner, Don Weller, team up with Winstone when he plays his game of baiting Thomas. They call him Jethro, after a television hillbilly, and like to tell about the time they went to a bowling alley in Blackpool and he started to hurl the bowls down two-handed with a fury that threatened to wreck the building. Thomas enjoys it all.

I asked Lake what it was like to spar with Winstone. He jerked his head sideways as if he had developed a twitch and said out of the side of his mouth, 'It's great, just great.' That evening in Thomas's gym it was easy to see what Lake meant. Winstone was sharp even by his own standards. If one left hand missed, he followed with five or six more that didn't, and he threw over his right with an eagerness that forced Thomas to restrain him. 'Box, don't fight,' he was told from the corner. He did eight rounds with Lake and Mick Laud, who must have weighed nearly ten stone. In one of them Lake said something and Winstone suddenly drove him into a corner and punished him with a stream of savagely accurate punches.

'Got him wicked then, didn't you, Col?' said Thomas as the round ended.

'That's what I wanted,' said Lake. 'Best way, innit?' Most of the crowd who had paid half-a-crown to see the workout stayed to watch the long session of callisthenics. Even those who had seen it all before drew in their breath as Winstone moved across the floor by bouncing his stomach up and down on the medicine ball. It was a brutal demonstration of fitness. His new headguard had produced a reddening above the left eye during the sparring and it encouraged Thomas to give him two or three days out of the ring. 'How are the legs, hard?' he asked the masseur in the dressing-room afterwards. 'Lovely, coming along nice.' 'Yes, he's there.' Thomas said quietly, 'He's getting nasty now in the ring. He's ready. So I'll give him a whiff. All we want now is to keep his edge.' Howard Winstone, Eddie Thomas and Merthyr Tydfil would all rather be nice than nasty. But for Vicente Saldivar they are determined to make an exception.

Decided Long Ago

The world championship contest between Vicente Saldivar and Howard Winstone was one of those fights that are settled in the womb. Saldivar was born with much more natural strength and all Winstone's years of physical discipline, all the dazzling skills and utter fearlessness, could not compensate for that one fundamental discrepancy between the challenger and the champion.

The essence was as simple as that but the event was more complex, which is why it seems worthwhile to recollect Tuesday night's emotion in tranquillity. Even Saldivar's superior power would not have kept his featherweight title if he had not been a southpaw. Because he leads with his right he reduced the effectiveness of Winstone's superb left hand by at least 30 or 40 per cent. The target area was reduced and many of the best jabs were smothered or shut out by the Mexican's right arm and shoulder. As Winstone's manager, Eddie Thomas, pointed out afterwards, the Welshman had to throw a much higher proportion of left hooks and right crosses than he normally would. That was why it was fatuous for people to complain that Winstone was rashly deserting his usual jab-and-move routine. Since the opportunities for jabbing were curtailed he had to stay around and attempt other punches.

The important fact, of course, was not that Winstone met a southpaw but that he met an exceptional southpaw, the only one who holds a world championship at the present time. Saldivar is a good champion: strong, determined, brave, intelligent. Even under pressure he sets himself carefully for the punch, getting in close before he starts work. His basic policy is to do more than his opponent, and if he cannot throw good punches he is prepared to throw indifferent ones. That is why he hits rather often with the inside of the glove, which in turn is why some people thought Winstone might have won. My own view is that Saldivar delivered enough legitimate blows and mounted enough legitimate aggression to win clearly. I thought he took seven rounds to Winstone's five, with three level.

Winstone's wife scored it differently. In the dressing-room, as she kissed her husband's bruised right cheek, she said, 'You won it, lad.'

'No, he just got there,' said Winstone. 'But never mind.' Aside to the rest of us in the crowded, sweaty room, he added, 'You know what women are.' He was lying back on a rubbing-table wearing nothing but a jockstrap. He had just signalled one of his helpers to wave a towel over him but Eddie Thomas said no. As Thomas turned away, Winstone nodded mischievously to urge that the cooling should continue, but Thomas's brother, who is one of the corner-men, said, 'No you don't, you sod.' Winstone gave him an old-fashioned look and a quick kick on the arm with a bare foot. Another friend came forward to the table and Winstone said, 'Here he is, only man in Wales who can eat one spud more'n a pig.'

'Look at 'im,' said somebody beside me, slightly awed. 'He's still wicked.' In Merthyr Tydfil the highest tribute you can pay anybody is to say he is 'wicked'.

Next day, at a lunch given by Winstone for the press, the promoters and some other friends, the tributes were less ironic. He was described as one of the most talented, most sportsmanlike and most popular boxers who ever stepped into a ring. The astonishing thing was not that it was all sincere, but that it was all justified. Winstone and Thomas are such appealing people that it is scarcely possible to do them justice without embarrassing everybody, them most of all.

Johnny Owen's Last Fight 1980

It can be no consolation to those in South Wales and in Los Angeles who are red-eyed with anxiety about Johnny Owen to know that the extreme depth of his own courage did as much as anything else to take him to the edge of death. This calamitous experience could only have happened to an exceptionally brave fighter because Lupe Pintor, the powerful Mexican who was defending his World Boxing Council bantamweight championship against Owen, had landed enough brutal punches before the 12th and devastatingly conclusive round to break the nerve and resistance of an ordinary challenger. The young Welshman was, sadly, too extraordinary for his own good in the Olympic Auditorium.

In the street, in a hotel lounge or even in his family's home on a Merthyr Tydfil housing estate, he is so reticent as to be almost unreachable, so desperately shy that he has turned 24 without ever having had a genuine date with a girl. But in the ring he has always been transformed, possessed by a furious aggression that has driven his alarmingly thin and unmuscular body through the heaviest fire and into the swarming, crowding attacks that gave him a record before Friday night of 24 victories, one defeat (avenged) and one draw in 26 professional matches. That record was built up in Europe and its reward was the European bantamweight championship and acceptance as a contender for the world title. Given the basic harshness of boxing as a way of earning a living, no one could blame Owen or his father or his manager, Dai Gardiner, for going after the biggest prize available to them, but some of us always felt that the right to challenge Pintor in Los Angeles was a questionable privilege. Making some notes about the background to the fight on Friday morning, I found myself writing: 'Feel physical sickness at the thought of what might happen, the fear that this story might take us to a hospital room.' This scribble was not meant to imply any severe criticism of a match which, on the basis of the relevant statistics, could not be condemned as outrageous. Indeed, the apprehension might have been illogically excessive to anyone who set Pintor's career figures of 41 wins, seven losses and a draw against the fact that Owen's one defeat had been a blatant case of larceny in Spain and the further,

204

impressive fact that he had never been knocked off his feet as a professional boxer.

Yet it is the simple truth that for weeks a quiet terror had been gathering in me about this fight. Perhaps its principal basis was no more than a dread that the frailty that the boy's performances had hitherto dismissed as illusory would, some bad time in some bad place, prove to be terribly real. There is something about his pale face, with its large nose, jutting ears and uneven teeth, all set above that long, skeletal frame, that takes hold of the heart and makes unbearable the thought of him being badly hurt. And, to my mind, there was an ominous possibility that he would be badly hurt against Pintor, a Mexican who had already stopped 33 opponents and would be going to work in front of a screaming mob of his countrymen, whose lust for blood gives the grubby Olympic Auditorium the atmosphere of a Guadalajara cockfight, multiplied a hundred times.

No fighters in the world are more dedicated to the raw violence of the business than Mexicans. Pintor comes out of a gym in Mexico City where more than a hundred boxers work out regularly and others queue for a chance to show that what they can do in the alleys they can do in the ring. A man who rises to the top of such a seething concentration of hostility is likely to have little interest in points-scoring as a means of winning verdicts. So it was hard to share the noisy optimism of the hundred-odd Welsh supporters who made themselves conspicuous in the sweaty clamour of the hall and brought a few beer cups filled with urine down on their heads. But they seemed to be entitled to their high spirits in the early rounds as Owen carried the fight to

Pintor, boring in on the shorter, dark-skinned champion and using his spidery arms to flail home light but aggravatingly persistent flurries of punches.

The first round was probably about even. Owen might have edged the second on a British scorecard and he certainly took the third, but already Pintor's right hooks and uppercuts were making occasional dramatic interventions, sending a nervous chill through the challenger's friends around the ring.

It was in the fourth round that Pintor's right hand first struck with a hint of the force that was to be so over-whelming subsequently, but this time it was thrown overarm and long and Owen weathered it readily enough. He was seen to be bleeding from the inside of his lower lip in the fifth (the injury may have been inflicted earlier) but, since both Pintor's eyebrows were receiving attention from his seconds by then, the bloodshed seemed to be reasonably shared. In fact the laceration in the mouth was serious and soon the challenger was swallowing blood. He was being caught with more shots to the head, too, but refused to be discouraged and an American voice behind the press seats said incredulously: 'I don't believe this guy.'

Pintor was heaving for breath at the end of the fifth but in the sixth he mounted a surge, punished Owen and began to take control of the contest. The official doctor, Bernhard Schwartz, checked the lip for the second time before the start of the eighth, which made the abrupt disaster of the ninth all the more painful.

Pintor smashed in damaging hooks early in the ninth but their threat appeared to have passed as the round moved to its close. Then, without a trace of warning, Pintor dropped a shattering right hook over Owen's bony left shoulder. The blow hurled him to the floor and it was here that his courage began to be a double-edged virtue. He rose after a couple of seconds, although clearly in a bad condition. There was a mandatory eight count but even at the end of it he was hopelessly vulnerable to more hooks to the head and it took the bell to save him.

By the tenth there was unmistakable evidence that the strength had drained out of every part of Owen's body except his heart. He was too tired and weak now to stay really close to Pintor, skin against skin, denying the puncher leverage. As that weariness gradually created a space between them, Pintor filled it with cruel, stiff-armed hooks. Every time Owen was hit solidly in the 11th the thin body shuddered. We knew the end had to be near but could not foresee how awful it would be.

There were just 40 seconds of the 12th round left when the horror story started to take shape. Owen was trying to press in on Pintor near the ropes, failed to prevent that deadly space from developing again and was dropped on his knees by a short right. After rising at three and taking another mandatory count, he was moved by the action to the other side of the ring and it was there that a ferocious right hook threw him on to his back. He was unconscious before he hit the canvas and his relaxed neck muscles allowed his head to thud against the boards. Dai Gardiner and the boxer's father were in the ring long before the count could be completed and they were quickly joined by Dr Schwartz, who called for oxygen. Perhaps the oxygen might have come rather more swiftly than it did but only if it had been on hand at the ringside. Obviously that would be a sensible precaution, just as it might be sensible to have a stretcher immediately available. It is no easy job to bring such equipment through the jostling mass of spectators at an arena like the Auditorium, where Pintor's supporters were mainly concerned about cheering its arrival as a symbol of how comprehensive their man's victory had been. The outward journey to the dressing-room, with poor Johnny Owen deep in a sinister unconsciousness, was no simpler and the indifference of many among the crowd was emphasised when one of the stretcher-bearers had his pocket picked.

There have been complaints in some quarters about the delay in providing an ambulance but, in the circumstances, these may be difficult to justify. Dr Ferdie Pacheco, who was for years Muhammad Ali's doctor and is now a boxing consultant with NBC in the United States, insists that the company lay on an ambulance wherever they cover fights but no such arrangements exist at the Auditorium and the experienced paramedics of the Los Angeles Fire Department made good time once they received the emergency call. Certainly it was grief and not blame that was occupying the sick boy's father as he stood weeping in the corridor of the California Hospital, a mile from the scene of the knockout. A few hours before, I had sat by the swimming-pool at their motel in downtown Los Angeles and listened to them joke about the calls Johnny's mother had been making from Merthyr Tydfil on the telephone they had recently installed. The call that was made to Mrs Owen from the waiting-room of the California Hospital shortly before 7am Saturday, Merthyr time (11pm Friday in Los Angeles), had a painfully different tone. It was made by Byron Board, a publican and close friend of the family, and he found her already in tears

208

because she had heard that Johnny had been knocked out. The nightmare that had been threatening her for years had become reality. She can scarcely avoid being bitter against boxing now and many who have not suffered such personal agony because of the hardest of sports will be asking once again if the game is worth the candle. Quite a few of us who have been involved with it most of our lives share the doubts. But our reactions are bound to be complicated by the knowledge that it was boxing that gave Johnny Owen his one positive means of self-expression. Outside the ring he was an inaudible and almost invisible personality. Inside, he became astonishingly positive and self-assured. He seemed to be more at home there than anywhere else. It is his tragedy that he found himself articulate in such a dangerous language.

The doctors' struggle to rescue Johnny Owen from deep coma proved to be hopeless and he died in the first week of November 1980. His body was brought home to be buried in Merthyr Tydfil.

from *McIlvanney on Boxing* (2000)

Leslie Norris

A Big Night

I used to train at the Ex-Servicemen's Club three nights a week, Tuesdays, Wednesdays, and Fridays. Training began at six, but I was always late on Tuesdays and Wednesdays because of homework. I used to like getting there a bit late. As I hurried through the long passage that ran beside the room where the old, dry miners – hardly any of them ex-servicemen – were drinking away their age and disappointment, I would hear above me the slithering feet of the other boys as they moved around the ring or the punch-bags and the pungent smell of the liniment would come greenly down the stairs to meet me. I would watch them working out a bit first, looking particularly for my friends Bobby Ecclestone and Charlie Nolan, before going into the dressing room to change into my shoes and shorts. I used to wear black shorts with a yellow band round the waist and a yellow stripe at the side of each leg. In Warrilow's Sports Emporium they had satin boxing shorts, immaculate and colourful. Mine were home-made. Most of the time I used to skip. I loved that rope and I could do some very fancy skipping, very fast and for a very long time. Tiredness was something I'd only heard about. Then I'd box a few rounds with Charlie and Bobby, and sometimes with one of the older and more skilful boys. They were always very kind, showing me how to slip a left lead, or how to move on the ropes. I hardly ever used the heavy, shapeless punching bags; when you're thirteen years old and weigh eighty pounds it doesn't seem very necessary. Then I'd do some exercises on the mat and finish off with another burst of skipping.

Boxing with Charlie Nolan was best of all. Charlie had been in school with me, in the next desk, until he'd moved to another district. He was almost the same age and size as I was and his footwork was a miracle of economy and precision. His feet brushed the floor like a whisper as he moved perfectly about me, in a kind of smooth ritual. I, on the other hand, would jig up and down in a flashy and wasteful way, careering around the ring at top speed and not caring very much where I got to. But Charlie's hands were slow. They would sit calmly in front of him, now and again mildly exploring the space between us, and I would hit him with a variety of harmless punches that left him blinking and smiling. As he passed us, Ephraim Hamer, our trainer, would say, 'Well done, Charlie!'. He rarely said anything to me. After we'd showered we'd sit about listening to the bigger boys, or boasting quietly between us. Bobby Ecclestone would tell us about his work in a grocer's shop; he was errand boy in the shop where we bought our groceries and I often saw him sweeping the sawdust boards, or staggering out with huge loads to the delivery van. It was Bobby who had first brought me to the Ex-Servicemen's Club. He was fifteen and the best boxer among the boys.

One Friday evening after we had finished working out and we were sitting warm and slumped on the benches, Bobby asked me if I was going to the weigh-in the next day. I didn't even know what it was. I was always finding that there were whole areas of experience, important areas too, about which I knew nothing and other boys everything.

'Where is it?' I said carefully.

'Down at the Stadium. One o'clock,' said Charlie. 'I'm going.'

Everything fell into place. Next day at the Stadium our local hero, Cuthbert Fletcher, who everyone said would have been featherweight champion of Wales except that he was coloured, was to fight Ginger Thomas, the official champion.

'Are you going?' I asked Bobby.

'Of course,' he said. 'It's my dinner-time. See you outside at ten to.'

All Saturday morning I hung about in a fever of anxiety in case my lunch wouldn't be ready for me in time to meet Bobby and Charlie at one o'clock outside the Stadium. But it was, and I was the first there, although Charlie was not long behind me. He hadn't had his lunch and was eating a huge round of bread and jam which he'd cut for himself from a new loaf. Bobby wouldn't let us go inside the Stadium until Charlie had finished eating. A few men hung about in a corner of the empty hall, their hands deep in their overcoat pockets. They whispered softly and tunelessly and they all carried an air of vast unconcern, but when Cuthbert and Ginger Thomas appeared, they hurried forward to greet the boxers, talking excitedly to them. It was exciting too. I don't know why it should have been so, but we all felt a curious tightening of the air as the boxers smiled formally at each other. Cuthbert stepped on the scales first, and a great fat man adjusted the weights, flicking them up and down the bar with finicky little movements of his enormous fingers before he called out, in a high voice, 'Eight stone and twelve pounds, gentlemen'.

Cuthbert smiled, ducked his round, crinkly head at his friends, and moved away. Ginger Thomas was a lean, pale man, elegant and graceful, his mahogany hair brushed smooth and close to his head. He, too, stood on the scales and his weight was called in the tat man's brittle tenor. Everybody shook hands and at once the place was deserted.

'That's all right then,' said Bobby.

'Nothing in it for weight,' said Charlie.

We stood together silently, for a long time.

'Are you going to the fight?' asked Bobby.

'No,' said Charlie, 'my father won't let me.'

Bobby looked at his shoes as they scuffed the ground in front of him, first the right shoe, then the left one.

'I can't go,' he said. 'Don't finish in time on Saturdays.'

'I expect I'll go,' I said, 'if I want to.'

'Will you?' said Charlie, his eyes big.

'I expect so,' I said, although I knew I couldn't.

At eight that evening I was in Court Street, one of the crowd milling around the Stadium, knowing I could not get in. Slow, comfortable groups of men with money and tickets moved confidently through towards the entrance, talking with assurance about the fights they had seen in the past. On the steps near the door Trevor Bunce danced up and down, his wide, cheeky face smiling as he asked the men to take him in with them. An arrogant boy and leader of his gang, Trevor Bunce was bigger than I was. You could see him everywhere. Incredibly active, his string-coloured hair hanging over his eyes, he bounced with energy through a series of escapades wherever you went. The street lights came on suddenly, and we all cheered. I knew with certainty that Trevor Bunce would get in somehow.

Now the whole road was thick with people and the few cars prodding through to outlying districts honked and revved with impatience and frustration. I moved cautiously to the pavement. I saw that, prudently, they had built a temporary barrier of corrugated sheets of metal above the low wall which separated a little yard, belonging to the Stadium, from the road. On lesser occasions many daring boys had climbed this wall – an easy feat – and run through a nest of little rooms into the hall itself. There was even a large door, always locked, which led directly into the raucous noise where even now the first of the bouts was being decided.

As I looked at the new metal sheets, Trevor Bunce threw himself past me, leapt on the wall, and, with unbelievable strength, forced back the long edge of the barrier. For a moment only, it was wide enough for a boy to wriggle though and Trevor Bunce did just that. But before he was half clear, the inexorable metal wall snapped back, pinning him at the waist, his legs kicking wildly; and even as we looked, we heard clearly and without mistake, a sound as of a dry stick breaking. Then Trevor Bunce began to scream.

In seconds, it seems to me now, we had ripped away the corrugated wall and its wooden framework, and men's gentle arms carried Trevor away. I saw him as he went, his face white and wet, but his eyes were open. He cradled his right forearm carefully, because it was broken.

By this time many of us were in the yard itself, aimlessly stacking the six-foot sheets of tin in an untidy heap near the wall. There must have been forty or fifty of us; boys, young workless men, and a few older men who were there by chance, it seemed. Yet, haphazard and leaderless as we were, we suddenly lifted our restive heads and, like some swollen river, streamed for the door that led to the Stadium's lesser rooms.

I didn't want to go with them. Some shred of caution tried hard to hold me back, but my treacherous legs hurried me on, gasping. We met nobody, except in a corridor an old man wiping saucers with a wet cloth. He pressed himself against the wall, his mouth wide open, and we were past him before he got a word out. And then we were in the great hall itself, our force broken against the huge weight of the legal customers. We lost ourselves among them at once.

The noise, the heat, the immense, expectant good humour made the whole place intoxicating, but I could see nothing except, high overhead, a blue, unshifting cloud of cigarette smoke. Agile though I was, I could not push or wriggle another inch nearer the ring. It was Freddie Benders who came to my help. Freddie didn't fight much, because he was nearly thirty years old. His ears were rubbery and he had few teeth, but he often came down to the club and sometimes he'd let us spar with him. You could hit him with everything you had, right on the chin, even, and he'd only laugh.

When he saw me he shouted out, 'Make room for the boy there, let the boy get down to the front'.

Grumbling and laughing, the men inched more closely together and I squeezed my way almost to the ringside.

'That's right,' shouted Freddie. 'That boy is going to make a good 'un. Keep your eyes on Cuthbert tonight, boy!'

I saw the fight. I saw every moment of the fifteen rounds, and it was a great fight, I know it was. Yet all the time it was on, all the time incisive Ginger Thomas moved forward with a speed and viciousness I had not imagined, what I really saw was Trevor Bunce's white face, what I heard was the stark snapping of his bones. When the fighters moved around the ring, the crowd was silent and absorbed and at the end of each round there was a great sigh before they clapped and

215

shouted. I think Ginger Thomas won, but at the end the referee held Cuthbert's arm up and we all cheered, with relief and pride rather than with certainty. Ginger Thomas stood in the centre of the ring, aloof and unmoved; his pale eyes glittered in the arc-lights, and then he turned and swaggered easily away. His lack of emotion disturbed me more than the terrible, precise fury and venom of his attacks.

When I got home my parents had nothing to say to me. I was so late, my crime was so enormous, that all they could do was to point to the stairs; I hurried up to my room to shiver gratefully under the icy sheets. I knew I should never sleep again and, even as I realised this, fell at once to sleep. When I awoke all was dark and confusing, and my right forearm was throbbing with pain. Struggling with darkness, I found the fingers of my left hand tight in a cramping grip around my right arm. The pain made me think of poor Trevor Bunce, in hospital surely, and I felt with quick relief the whole, frail bones in my own arms.

The following Tuesday I was late getting to the Club, but only because I had found my French homework particularly difficult. I waved to the boys, changed eagerly, and soon had the old skipping-rope humming away. Everything began to feel fine. It wasn't until I put the gloves on to spar with Charlie Nolan that I realised that something was wrong. I kept on seeing Ginger Thomas, destructive and graceful, his hands cocked, moving into Cuthbert, as he had on the Saturday night. I could see his face, relaxed and faintly curious, the sudden blur as he released three or four short punches before sliding away. I knew too that I was doing this to Charlie, but I couldn't stop. Charlie was bleeding from the mouth and nose and he was pawing away with his gloves open. I could tell he was frightened. Yet I kept on ripping punches at him, my hands suddenly hard and urgent and the huge, muffling gloves we used no longer clumsy. I could hear Mr Hamer shouting as Charlie hid in a corner and then somebody had me around the waist, throwing me almost across the ring. Charlie was crying, but in a little while Bobby Ecclestone put an arm round Charlie's shoulders, talking to him softly. Nobody said anything to me and I sat on the bench. I thought I was quivering all over, but when I looked at my legs they were all right. I felt as if I were going to be sick. Nothing seemed to matter very much. I walked to the dressing room and began to change. I was so tired that it was an effort to take off my ring clothes, and when I pulled my vest over my head I could feel my face wet with my own tears. I took a good look at the room before I went out, then I shut the door behind me, very quietly. It sounded just as it always had, the slithering of the shoes around the ball or the heavy bag, the rhythmical slapping of the rope on the boards as somebody did some lively skipping.

Nobody saw me go. As I went down the stairs I could see through the window little groups of quiet drinkers in the room below, but they could not see me in the dark passage.

I never went back there. Sometimes when I went for groceries, some cheese maybe, or some canned stuff, I would see Bobby Ecclestone in the shop. He didn't say anything to me and I didn't say anything to him. It was as if we had never been friends.

from *Sliding* (1976)

Carolyn Hitt

A Palpable Hit

'Boxers are the most docile men in sport,' Henry Cooper once said in the era before Mike Tyson liked to supplement his diet with a little fresh ear-lobe. It's one of the many paradoxes that make boxing such an intriguing sport. Others strange ironies include:

1. Women who love boxing. Nice girls don't surely. Wrong. You may think two men rearranging the alignment of their respective jaws is anathema to the feminine instinct but a surprising number of females love it. It's proper pugilism, not like that nancy-boy wrestling your nan used to love Dickie Davies introducing on a Saturday afternoon. Yet there was a time when boxing rated alongside kitten-drowning and Jim Davidson on my disgust-ometer – that was before I actually watched a live fight. Within five minutes, the banshee-like scream of 'Knock his brains out Chris!' mysteriously emitted from my person, as the lisping one went in for the kill. Like it or not, watching boxing can arouse something rather primeval in one's nature.

2. Promoters who promote themselves. How can you keep your eyes on the boxer at the pre-fight press conference when he is totally upstaged by the flamboyance of his management entourage? Don King set the standard with a look that could only be emulated by attaching yourself to a couple of jump leads. The suave Frank Warren, meanwhile, prefers the

immobile barnet and country gent chic of a character from a 1960s cult British television series. One of these days, he'll turn up with Diana Rigg on his arm in a leather catsuit. As for the assorted minions and hangers-on, you'll hear them before you see them as they arrive sporting more chunky chains than Jacob Marley. Bling Bling Round One.

3. Boxing and Posh Writers. It may be the sport of the ghetto but boxing has inspired the most high-brow heavyweights. From poetry to fiction, essays to drama, no other sport can boast a similarly prestigious literary line-up. In the blue corner we have Norman Mailer, Joyce Carol Oates and William Hazlitt. In the red corner we have... er Nick Hornby?

But it's still the paradox summed up by Henry Cooper's comment that 'boxers are the most docile men in sport' that is the most difficult to comprehend. Our Enery certainly practised what he preached. Outside the ring, he revelled in his mildness, imploring us to 'splash it all over' with a kind of sleepy charm. Inside the ring, the great smell of Brut gave way to the scent of brutality. It's a weird one. How can the nicest men pack the hardest punches?

Tyson apart, Cooper's verdict is still true of many modern fighters. Particularly Welsh ones. I interviewed Steve Robinson several years ago on the topic of women boxers. 'I've nothing against ladies who box. I just hate the thought of them getting hurt,' said the soft-voiced Robinson with genuine concern. Nicky Piper looked like someone who would approve your bank loan rather than knock your front teeth out. Going further back into Welsh boxing history, Howard Winstone's humility was as legendary as his right hook, while Johnny Owen's fragile frame was matched by his shy and gentle nature.

The current crop are continuing the trend. I met Joe Calzaghe and Jamie Arthur, the young Commonwealth Gold medallist, this week at the press conference for tonight's big fight at the CIA. Again, two perfect gentlemen who if you didn't know better, you could never imagine inflicting serious pain. They both cited bullying as the motivation for becoming boxers – as did Calzaghe's opponent Byron Mitchell. 'It's quite common in boxing,' an American sports photographer told me as we filed out of the Marriott. 'I know a fighter who took it up because he was bullied so badly in school, his sister had to fight his battles for him. Then she'd hit him too because she was so frustrated that he wasn't sticking up for himself.' Perhaps the bullied skinny kid who turns into the champion fighter is the sweetest boxing irony of all. And whatever Henry Cooper reckoned about mild-mannered fighters, from the second Joe Calzaghe steps into the ring tonight it's no more Mr Nice Guy.

from the *Western Mail,* 30 June 2003

CRICKET

John Arlott

Cricket at Swansea

From the top of the hill-top pavilion,
The sea is a cheat to the eye,
Where it secretly seeps into coastline
Or fades in the yellow-grey sky;
But the crease-marks are sharp on the green
As the axe's first taste of the tree,
And keen is the Welshmen's assault
As the freshening fret from the sea.
The ball is a withering weapon,
Fraught with a strong-fingered spin
And the fieldsmen, with fingers prehensile,
Are the arms of attack moving in.
In the field of a new Cymric mission,
With outcricket cruel as a cat
They pounce on the perilous snick
As it breaks from the spin-harried bat.
On this turf, the remembered of rugby –
'The Invincibles' – came by their name,
And now, in the calm of the clubhouse,
Frown down from their old-fashioned frame.
Their might has outlived their moustaches,
For photos fade faster than fame;

And this cricket rekindles the temper
Of their high-trampling, scrummaging game:
As intense as an Eisteddfod anthem
It burns down the day like a flame.

from *The Cricketer's Companion* (1960)

John Arlott

Valete Wilfred Wooller

It was in 1937 that Jack Mercer said, in his softly confidential manner, 'Do you know the best swing bowler in England is playing club cricket in North Wales?' Pressed, he named him as 'That young Wooller, the rugby player; a big lad, he gets a lot of pace off the pitch and moves it about'. Born at Rhos-on-Sea, Wilfred Wooller went to Rydal School, played for Denbighshire, and in winning Cambridge sides in the University matches of 1935 and 1936. In 1937, however, he was too busy making a living in the coal trade to find much time for cricket. Maurice Turnbull, an old rugby team-mate, persuaded him to turn out for the county, but he could contrive only seven matches in 1938 and nine in 1939; nevertheless, he matured and developed steadily as an all rounder.

Rugby, though, was his main pre-war sport and he... won eighteen caps as a determined, high-kneed, extremely fast runner, at centre-three-quarter, and a spectacularly long and accurate kicker.

In 1942 he was captured, with his Royal Artillery unit,

222

at Singapore. During three years as a prisoner of war of the Japanese, his immense determination, not only to live himself, but to carry his fellows through with him, won him the lifelong devotion of many of them.

By the same inflexible purpose and his immense natural physical resilience, he pushed himself back into action for the 1946 cricket season when, under John Clay, Glamorgan finished sixth, the highest Championship position they had ever achieved. In the next year he took over the captaincy; and, ninth then, they went on, in 1948, to win the title for the first time. If many knowledgeable judges were surprised by their success – for there were certainly several stronger batting and bowling counties in the country – they needed to look to the new captain. For more than a decade Wilfred Wooller lifted his side, again and again, to heights greater than the sum of the players' individual ability.

Memory will always recall him in those years, his wide, heavy shoulders slightly stooped, shambling down the pitch to his place, little more than a stride from the batsman, at forward short leg. There, eyes intent under his high forehead, jaw jutting, fists jammed truculently down on hips between deliveries, he dominated the outcricket. More than one batsman cracked under this psychological pressure; some were undoubtedly talked out by the exchanges between the captain and his wicket-keeper, Haydn Davies. Others, attempting to drive him away with aggressive strokes, were surprised by the speed of reaction of the large, fearless man who caught them. He was not alone in the practice of gamesmanship; but, unlike some, he accepted it in the same unyielding spirit as he indulged it. He was possessed of divine impatience; perhaps, indeed, he was temperamentally better suited to rugby than to cricket. Sometimes when he was frustrated by a cricket match that was going nowhere, it seemed likely that, in a sudden fury, he would buckle down with his fieldsmen and sweep the umpires, opposing batsmen and stumps over the boundary line to resolve the issue once and for all. He cursed opponents roundly and fiercely, but without malice. Many were amazed that one so belligerent on the field was so convivially generous off it. Again it was the rugby player showing through. He followed Maurice Turnbull in seeing catching as the means which lifted a team to competitive heights; he drilled his sides in fielding as a rugby captain might exhort a scrum: and he held 409 catches himself.

It is fair to say that, although the specialists of the pre-war Gloucestershire under Beverley Lyon had approached it, no other county side had ever before caught so well as his of 1948; they set a fresh standard. The evidence of one who watched every ball bowled, with the confirmation of several who took part in it, argues that Wilfred Wooller virtually lifted Glamorgan to win the decisive game against Hampshire – in that Championship season. They had only one more match to play against Leicestershire – which they expected to lose – and did – because Jack Walsh was so deadly against their numerous left-hand batsmen. After losing most of the Saturday at Bournemouth to rain, Glamorgan reached 315 on the mild Monday pitch. In terms of cricketing probability, they simply had not time to win. Then, with no alteration in the conditions, after a few overs of the new ball, Wooller ostentatiously rubbed it in the dust, waved six fieldsmen closely about the bat. With no apparent technical justification, he called up his spinners – and in an hour, six Hampshire wickets went down for 24 runs. The rest was psychologically inevitable.

After the war his bowling was never more than medium in pace, but he consistently took good wickets (958 altogether) by his accuracy, variation of pace, movement either way and sheer hostile persistence. His batting looked heavy-handed, but he five times scored over a thousand runs in a season; 13,593 altogether. He could play either way as he judged the game demanded; defend doggedly and safely – as he did to save the match against the Australians in 1953 – or hit powerfully, especially to leg (108 in two hours against Lancashire in 1947). He played twice in strong Gentlemen's teams against the Players, but most of his cricket was for Glamorgan. He was invited to tour South Africa in 1948-9 but had to refuse because of the demands of his business; and, immeasurably the finest captain in the country at the time, he should have taken the 1950-1 England team to Australia. An extremely durable cricketer, he performed the double in 1954 when he was forty-one, was forty-seven when he gave up the captaincy after fourteen seasons; rising fifty when he returned to the side for a single match in 1962.

In 1946 he became County Secretary; and for the next thirty-one years he exerted more influence over Glamorgan cricket than some committees would permit. He stood in a strong tactical position. He came from North Wales; and, in consequence, while he could not be rejected as a non-Welshman, West Wales could not question him as being

225

Cardiff; nor Cardiff for being West Wales. He rode out some turbulent times; made some wrong decisions, but more that were correct, and rarely one which did not stem from conviction and enthusiasm.

One story often told about him dates from 1948. Glamorgan had never beaten Middlesex when they met them at Cardiff in that triumphant year; thanks to the bowling of Hever and Wooller, they took a first innings lead of 138, and eventually set Middlesex 275 to win. Wilfred, opening the bowling, had a series of 'shouts' against Syd Brown the Middlesex opening batsman, each of which was refused by that idiosyncratic but wise umpire, Alec Skelding. At length, after his fourth or fifth appeal, Wooller turned on him with 'What was wrong with that, you blind old bastard?' 'He was not out, Mr Wooller,' said Skelding, 'and it is true that my eyesight is not good; that is why I wear these strong glasses; but I can assure you that my mother and father were married; and, I'll tell you something else, Mr Wooller, I don't think you're going to win this cricket match.' He never gave a decision against Syd Brown, who made 150 not out in a score of 275 for eight (no one else got as many as 30) and Middlesex won by two wickets. Some years later, when the county secretaries discussed the position of Alec Skelding – who was already over age – on the umpires list, Wilfred Wooller was the most vehement supporter of his reappointment, which was duly approved...

from *Another Word from John Arlott* (1985)

Leslie Thomas

Daffodil Summer

In the fading August of 1948, on a day by the southern seaside, J.C. Clay, the gentleman of Glamorgan, bowled a measured off-break which struck Charlie Knott, of Hampshire, on the pad. The story has it that Dai Davies, the umpire, a brown, beaming man, raised a dramatic finger and, unable to contain himself, bellowed at Knott: 'You're OUT – and WE'VE won!'

Glamorgan had indeed won. Not only a remarkable match, but the County Championship, and for the first time. On that dun afternoon in Bournemouth the pavilion trembled with Welsh singing, voices that floated over the English regular roses, causing raised eyebrows among the gardens and where the band was playing by the sea.

For Johnnie Clay, the lean, grey man, wise as a heron, the triumph had come in his fiftieth year and after seasons of failure, disappointment, even ridicule, for his beloved county. I remember that day, trotting on my trivial rounds as a junior reporter on a local newspaper in Essex, hearing the wonderful news on the radio while I was cross-examining a lady about the thrills and spills of the Women's Institute flower arranging contest. 'Why,' she asked briskly, 'are you grinning like that? Flower arranging is no laughing matter.' 'I'm sorry,' I remember saying, knowing she would never understand. 'I'm doing it because I'm happy.'

Happy indeed I was, along with a throng of others. Of the four hundred telegrams sent to Arms Park, Cardiff, the next day was one from an exile in Paris. The news, he said, had made him decide to return home to Wales. What, after all, had Paris to offer?

For me the love affair was new. It is a confession I hesitate to make, even after these years, but, brought up in wartime Newport, I hardly knew of the existence of cricket, until I was gone twelve years. Then, after the war – after I had heard about it and was growing in love for it – one day in 1947, I went for the first time to Lord's and had scarcely had time to place my spam sandwiches and myself on one of the free seats (as they were loftily called) below the heads of the trees at the Nursery End, when I witnessed the most exquisite sight of my youthful life. Willie Jones, small as a button, batting against Middlesex, leaned back, folded his body like a spring, and square cut to the boundary. The ball hit the boards with an echo I can hear now. It was as though he had waited for my arrival, after all those unknowing years. From that moment – and although I had left the Land of my Fathers and my birth – I had Glamorgan written on my heart.

… Meanwhile Glamorgan appeared to have lost their way. They fell to Middlesex and to Leicestershire and there came a faltering series of drawn games, partly through the summer weather turning sour. The game with the Australians never came to any flourish, although with lumpy rain clouds hanging on the Bristol Channel and not an inch of room in the ground, Keith Miller made 84 in the only innings, which came to a stop in a downpour with the tourists at 215 for three. In another July game Gunner G.A.R. Lock, playing for Combined Services, the only squaddie in the parade of

228

Lieutenant Colonels, Squadron Leaders and Commanders, took six wickets for 43, a taste of the great days that were to come for him with Surrey and with England.

A victory against Warwickshire, at Neath, kept Glamorgan's nose near the top of the table and then came, in mid-August, with the Welsh weather mending, a wonderful and crucial victory against Surrey at Cardiff. Wilfred Wooller's brave batting, driving and hammering square cuts, ensured a Glamorgan total of 239 – Wooller scored 89, his best of the season. Then Johnnie Clay, coming into the team in the absence of Watkins, and having reached the age of fifty, bowled out one of the strongest counties in England for fifty runs. Clay took five wickets and when Surrey followed on took another five. The long, tall, silver man was almost bowled over himself as the Arms Park Welshmen charged across the pitch at the end to acclaim him and the Glamorgan team. The smell of success was in the Cardiff air and very sweet it was.

And so to the final match against Hampshire, at Bournemouth – not the last match of the season but the one that had to be won. 'It needed to be then,' remembered Wilfred Wooller laconically. 'Because the last game was at Leicester.' Jack Walsh, the Australian-born spin bowler, played for Leicester and Wooller's team knew they would be pressed to scrape even a draw on the home side's wicket. (So it proved for, having secured the Championship, Glamorgan went to Leicester and were soundly beaten by an innings – the second time that the Midlands county had defeated them that season.)

The habitual champions, Yorkshire, who might have

finally overtaken Glamorgan, were engaged against Somerset at Taunton, on the other side of Dorset, and Glamorgan began their innings at Bournemouth with conspiratorial clouds on the sea. Arnold Dyson, on holiday from his school coaching, was asked to play because Phil Clift was injured. Johnnie Clay came into the side instead of the Test-match-bruised Allan Watkins. Both replacements played crucial roles in the events of the next two days.

Emrys Davies and Dyson went forth to bat. Emrys's wife went off to walk around the town. As she shopped she listened for sounds from the ground.

Only ten minutes after the innings had begun dull summer raindrops sent the players to the pavilion and there they remained for the rest of the day, staring out at that most glum of views, the English seaside in the wet.

Sunday was spent wondering. On Monday the skies appeared kinder and once more Emrys and Arnold went to the middle. There now remained eleven and a half hours to win the match. The pair batted steadily as the clock turned, but knowing that the time would come for acceleration. Dyson was out for 51, trying to force the tempo, and at lunch Glamorgan were 99 for one wicket. Willie Jones emerged (tentatively) and, locking up his dashing shots, stared long and anxiously down the wicket at the fiercely advancing Shackleton, one of England's finest pace bowlers.

In mid-afternoon Emrys stroked (yes, stroked) a six, an extravagance greeted with almost chapel-like pursed lips from the Welshmen present. Emrys smiled apologetically. Willie sidled his way past his fifty, and when Emrys was eventually out for the most important 74 he had ever accumulated, the unassuming little man from the Valleys assumed the mantle, stitched his way patiently through the whole innings while Wooller and Len Muncer and Norman Hever, at the tail, threw their bats. The side were all out for 315, Jones returning, smiling unsurely, with 78 not out.

It was still only early evening and the Hampshire openers, Arnold and Rogers, went out with over an hour left for play. Wooller and Hever bowled. In the captain's second over Rogers played a true leg glance and Gilbert Parkhouse, who had failed with the bat, swooped like a local gull to catch the ball an inch from the ground and no more than three yards from the bat. It was the catch that made Glamorgan really believe they could do it. Before the end of play on that brief evening six Hampshire batsmen were back in the pavilion. Glamorgan went to bed looking forward to the morning.

There seemed hardly room or time to breathe on that ground the next day. Not long ago I played in a match there and I sat after the game, in the lemon sun of the evening, years later, trying to imagine how it had been. Wooller, seriously, sent a telegram to Somerset playing Yorkshire at Taunton. The two counties, having for so long been treated lightly, disdainfully, had a mutual bond, and the message 'Hold on to Yorkshire. We're beating Hants.' was received and understood. 'Don't worry,' came the reply. 'We're beating Yorkshire.'

With that assurance Glamorgan set about the Hampshire second innings. Every so often a whisper would go from the pavilion around the crowd that Somerset were keeping their word.

John Clay had been out early to sniff the salty air. He

pressed his finger tips into the wicket and knew everything would be all right. The information he kept private. He and the oval-faced Len Muncer finished Hampshire for 84. There were now four hours during which to get them out a second time.

Arnold and Rogers batted without any crisis for twenty minutes and four hours began to look a short time indeed. Then young Hever got one under Rogers' bat, pitched right up and moving a shade. Clean bowled. Hope rekindled.

Desmond Eagar, a fine player, charged the Glamorgan bowlers, hitting Willie Jones for a six that came near to disturbing people on the beach. But Muncer and Clay came back and that was enough. Muncer curled one around Eagar's feet to bowl him. The next man Bailey was promptly run out and the two spinners, so disparate in physique and style, whittled their way through the tail. Muncer had claimed five wickets in the first Hampshire innings and Clay three. Now it was the tall Johnnie's turn. The man who had played in Glamorgan's first county match in 1921, bowled as he had never bowled before. By the time he had Knott lbw, and had received the historical affirmative from Dai Davies (Knott swears to this day that the umpire appealed as well!), he had taken six for 48. It was still only mid-afternoon.

So there it was. The miracle at last... It was wonderful that time long ago. That Daffodil Summer.

from *County Champions* (1982)

Dannie Abse

Cricket Ball

I watched Glamorgan play
especially Slogger Smart,
free from the disgrace of fame, unrenowned,
but the biggest hit with me.

A three-spring flash of willow
and suddenly, the sound of summer
as the thumped ball, alive, would leave
the applauding ground.

Once, hell for leather, it curled
over the workman's crane
in Westgate Street
to crash, they said, through a discreet
Angel Hotel windowpane.

But I, a pre-war boy,
(or someone with my name)
wanted it, that Eden day,
to scoot around the turning world,
to mock physics and gravity,
to rainbow-arch the posh hotel
higher, deranged, on and on, allegro,
(the Taff a gleam of mercury below)
going, going, gone
towards the Caerphilly mountain range.

Vanishings! The years, too, gone like change.
But the travelling Taff seems the same.
It's late. I peer at the failing sky
over Westgate Street
and wait. I smell cut grass.
I shine an apple on my thigh.

from *On the Evening Road* (1994)

Tony Lewis

Sober Reflections

There are always key teachers. Sam Evans was one. A Welsh-speaking Rhondda man, he could always be seen and heard on the rugby fields, blasting on the whistle and shouting, 'Free kick, boy. Dull play.' He was in charge of the under-fourteens when I first encountered him. I sold a dummy in the centre, ignoring the winger outside, and sprinted for a try under the posts. The whistle was shrill, his voice taut and high. 'Come here, show-pony. A man outside you and you sold a dummy. You're a show-pony, boy. Take a spell on the touchline for five minutes and remember rugby football is a team game.' I could not believe it and, as I wandered off, looked back to frown. The whistle blasted again and he trotted over.

'Right, boy, stay off for ten minutes and learn a bigger lesson. D'y know what it is?'

'No, sir.'

'It's this, Lewis. Life is frequently unfair.' He blew again and was gone.

Our paths crossed again when I decided to study history in the sixth form. Sam Evans was the senior history master. Within weeks he built in me a love of history that I have always retained. He was the first to explain that the study of history centred on asking the right questions, not squeezing facts into my head.

He was positive about my rugby, deciding that I was a scrum-half. After a couple of seasons being kicked about at the base of the lineout, I moved to centre and first made the school team in that position. Speed, or rather the lack of it, was my problem and so I took the advice of the new rugger master Roy Bish, the Aberavon centre, and retreated to full-back where I felt completely at ease for the remainder of my playing days. We were lucky to have such an analyst of the game as Roy. After he had finished playing, he became one of the foremost coaches in Europe, ahead of his time in the analysis of the game.

To give you an idea of the precedence rugby took at Neath Grammar School, I must relate the story of Walter Thomas, the senior French master. 'Waller' was a big man with a love of literature and a strong way with words. His brother Gwyn Thomas, author, playwright and broadcaster, was a deal more famous, but Waller lacked nothing of Gwyn's sharp eye and shattering phrase.

One day he prepared to conduct a lesson with the upper sixth in Room Five, which overlooked the rugby pitch. 'Les Fleurs du Mal,' he announced, noisily clearing his nostrils; he suffered from sinusitis. 'Baudelaire.' He flipped open

235

the textbook. 'Turn to "La Charogne", the dying carcass. Filthy stuff but compulsory.' Then, glancing sideways, he saw one of our tiniest school sides taking the field against local opposition – a proper match.

'Who are they and who are they playing?' Waller inquired.

'The under-thirteens, sir, playing the technical college from next door.'

He raised his index finger. 'Come.' He walked out of the room indicating that we should follow. A dozen of us trailed along the corridor not knowing where we were going. Just at the end of the building Waller turned into the senior lavatories, marched smartly across to the window and lit a cigarette.

'Right,' he proclaimed. 'We will remain here in the senior bogs for the next two periods where you and that dirty sod Baudelaire will be far more at home, and I can witness the delights of the under-thirteens.'

... At the end of August 1968, Garfield Sobers, then captain of Nottinghamshire, hit six sixes in an over, the first ever to achieve that feat in first-class cricket. I was the fielding captain; it had nothing to do with field placing.

In fact, Glamorgan were waiting for a declaration as Notts moved on untroubled to 308-5 – when Gary came down the steps at the St Helen's ground in Swansea. This was the moment for me to give Malcolm Nash, our excellent left-arm swing bowler, the chance to prove that he could bowl cutters. By the late 1960s, Derek Underwood was confirmed as the outstanding slow bowler in England, although not in the style of Tony Lock. He was quicker through the air, but that is not to say that his flight lacked deception. He could wrap his fingers round the ball and turn it on the more helpful surfaces, but day by day his superb accuracy came from rolling the ball or cutting it; some turned, some did not. Batsmen often got in a terrible tangle as close fielders preyed and Alan Knott, the finest wicket-keeper I have ever seen, demonstrated his wonderful skills. Underwood and Knott were a magical duet to watch but not so much fun to play against. I have watched a ball pitch on middle and off and turn past the outside edge of my bat, followed by a ball looking the same but going straight on to shave the inside edge of my bat and landing in Knotty's gloves down the leg side. Malcolm Nash believed that if he tried the Underwood style, he too could top the national averages. This was the day of his promised opportunity.

At first, he was treated with caution by the Notts batsmen, who we could see had their eyes on being not out when the innings was closed. Gary Sobers was different of course. He lost patience with his men and after playing sweetly but safely he decided to get on with it. There was a cracking shot to square-leg that sent the ball screaming into the concrete terrace at the Civic Centre end and bouncing back on the first bounce to the square-leg umpire. A second six followed, swung to leg towards the Cricketers' Hotel. Then Malcolm shifted his line to outside off stump. This third ball was lofted on to the straight terraces, just wide of mid-on. It was then that I went to talk to him. The match situation did not matter all that much but I wanted to give him the chance to end the experiment and get back to the seam and swing bowling that would get him 991 first-class wickets in his career. He was a good performer, capable of ruining a whole innings if there was a hint of swing in the air.

'If you want to go back to your usual stuff, Malcolm, and whack it in the block hole, that's fine by me,' I told him. 'Look after yourself now.' But Malcolm had entered the dangerous area where pride moves in, but on rubber legs.

'I can handle it, Captain. Leave him to me.' It was as if he was fighting Muhammad Ali and refusing a stool after being knocked down three times in the last round.

Alas for Malcolm, the next ball, still delivered à la Underwood from round the wicket, disappeared over his head on to the pavilion terraces. The fifth ball was wide and Gary failed to middle it. St Helens, however, had a short straight boundary and although Roger Davis held a brilliant catch at long off, he carried the ball over the line for a fifth six. The towel should have gone in then, but like the rest of the team, I was stationed far away on a boundary. The ball was pulled down short and the rest is history, the only dispute still open being how far the ball was hit over straight midwicket down King Edward Road. Malcolm was only twenty-three and had a longer career ahead than he could have imagined – in the record books.

There was huge excitement in the pavilion and in the dressing room, and leg-pulling for Malcolm Nash.

'Don't worry,' he responded. 'I'll make a fortune out of it. They'll make a movie.'

'What will they call it, Mal, Gone with the Wind?'

Wilf Wooller's television commentary for BBC Wales was so emotional he had lost his way during the over, and it took days of editing and re-editing to fix it for posterity.

Gary Sobers was a great sportsman on the day, embracing Malcolm, buying him a drink, saying how it nearly happened to him one day, well, for a few balls anyway.

from *Taking Fresh Guard* (2003)

Gareth Elwyn Jones

Don Shepherd

Don Shepherd played for Glamorgan between 1950 and 1972, retiring at the age of 45. He bowled over 21,000 overs for the county alone, taking 2,174 wickets at an average of 20.95, figures for which most modern bowlers would do a Faust. He passed that magic mark of 100 wickets in a season twelve times. Near medium-pace or not, an action which looked as if it had a regular application of machine oil allowed him to bowl long spells – nearly 58 overs in one innings against Derbyshire in Swansea at less than two an over, still the record for the county. In a magic season, only a year after his conversion to spin bowling, he took 168 wickets for Glamorgan at an average of just over 14, reaching 100 wickets by 2 July, the earliest ever in the county's history – and representative matches took him to an incredible 177, another record. He took a first-class hat-trick, and some of his figures are more fitted to *The Wizard* than Wisden – five wickets for two runs in ten overs against Leicestershire at Ebbw Vale, 1964, seven for seven in one innings against Hampshire in 1966.

...Shepherd took his wickets on all the English grounds

as well as in Wales but somehow what we saw, what we read and what we remember gel into an image of him playing 'at home'. In days when Glamorgan players were as peripatetic as instrumental music teachers he bowled out strong batting sides in Ebbw Vale, Llanelli and Neath. He bowled superbly at the Arms Park in Cardiff. But his ancestral home ground was St Helen's in Swansea where he invariably bowled from the Pavilion end, up the slight slope so that he could 'feel' his left foot landing. He knew the St Helen's square like no other. This was his patch, and even if all the spectators did not actually know him personally they acted as if they did. The expectation when he began a spell was almost tangible. It was here, so fittingly, that he most often made history.

Our memory prompt for Don Shepherd, then, is endless overs on the Swansea ground. If the Romans had built an amphitheatre at St Helen's they would have done a tidier job (an amphitheatre's stone seating would not have been noticeably less comfortable than the precarious wooden benches which, for years, ringed the east side of the ground, and the more permanent wooden pews in the rugby stand, with squabs at ninety degrees, which still test the resilience of the most ample spectator). But the amphitheatre image, however strained, remains. Around three quarters of a small ground tiers of seats rise steeply. Members can perch high behind the bowler's arm at the pavilion end. From the 'rugby' stand, separated from Swansea's beach by little more than a road's width, there is another almost perfect vantage point, made so by the very short boundaries at both wicket-ends. Spectators at

St. Helen's get a superb view of the cricket. Even with just a few hundred in the ground the atmosphere can build into something special. Tens of thousands have occasionally turned it into the Colosseum.

A combination of small ground and the occasional turning wicket, together with the tradition of hosting touring teams over August bank holidays, has provided a mix for some memorable days. Best known across the world, of course, is Sir Garfield (Gary) Sobers' achievement, in Nottinghamshire colours, of hitting six sixes in one over but it was here, too, that Clive Lloyd equalled the record for the fastest double hundred in a first-class match, in the process managing to rocket one ball out of the ground, across the road and right through the open first-floor French window of 'The Cricketers' hostelry. So there was symmetry in Swansea providing the perfect platform for Don Shepherd, a cricketer who has played for Glamorgan in more matches than anyone else. Whenever he came on to bowl, there was expectation; now something positive was going to happen even if it was a long haul. When he came in to bat there was also a sense of expectation, though the time-frame was briefer. His Glamorgan batting average was under 10. But now and again the council could have run a film of a Shepherd innings rather than bother with the traditional municipal fireworks display on the next door Recreation ground. The most memorable was in 1961, when he scored an eleven-stroke half century in a quarter-of-an-hour against the Australians, a record which gave way years later only to a travesty of a contrived innings.

From then on, the Australians (shortened to Australia

241

when Glamorgan win) would have done well to take out an insurance policy against Shepherd as he lived out two of his three finest hours against them. The 1964 August Bank Holiday (it came at the proper time in those days) made nationalists of the whole of Wales. Just down the Mumbles Road the National Eisteddfod was dispensing its brand of poetry while the cricketers produced another. It was as if Don Shepherd and his team mates were personifying those of us of a certain age who regarded Australia as the ultimate cricketing enemy. There cannot ever have been a humiliation quite like that wrought by the Australian tourists in 1948. It was compounded by an exhausted Bradman opting out of the game against Glamorgan in Swansea, so depriving me and 30,000 (and that was just on one day) others of the chance to see the greatest batsman of all time. We had to be content with Lindwall and Miller before a regulation Swansea thunderstorm ensured that the game was drawn, and there were more draws in 1953 and 1961, as well as a defeat in 1956.

The 1964 Glamorgan team did not look any more like Australia-beaters. Tourist games are traditionally used to blood a few young players and this game was no different. Still, a fine August Bank Holiday was bound to mean a great weekend for St Helen's aficionados. We just didn't know how great. Glamorgan batted on a wicket which was always going to be helpful to spin bowlers and, at first, there seemed to be the awful inevitability almost inherent in a county side playing a strong touring team. Alan Jones, as always, was a class act for his 33 runs but surely, with Tony Lewis out for a duck, the side would disintegrate. Then came two sterling performances, one from Peter Walker who got 41 and a top score from Alan Rees, with 48. It was obvious what was happening because two spinners, Veivers and Martin, took seven wickets between them. The delight of the St. Helen's ground is that if you position yourself just to the side of the sea-end sightscreen the boundary is so short that you might just as well be on the pitch. From this vantage point I vividly remember watching Martin bowling to Peter Walker and realising just how sophisticated is the technique of top county cricketers against spin bowling on a helpful wicket, and just how quick their reactions. That ball was turning square, and quite quickly. After almost every ball a slightly wry grin of satisfaction registered Walker's sense of achievement in having kept the ball out. Still, a total of 197 was not exactly promising.

Glamorgan did have a couple of rather handy spinners in the Swansea/Gower pair of Shepherd and Pressdee, but our reasoning was more focused on Australia having rather handy batsmen, names to conjure with even at this distance in time – Lawry and Redpath to open, Norman O'Neill at number three and captain Bobby Simpson at number five. Glamorgan's bowlers were rather less impressed than the spectators. Ritual alone decreed that fast medium Wheatley and Cordle opened the bowling, although their analyses were remarkable enough – 9 overs for 8 runs between them.

This was only the rather accomplished playing of the overture. Now the performance proper, Shepherd at the pavilion end (he had already hammered 24 runs in Glamorgan's innings) and Pressdee at the sea end. What happened next was almost beyond belief. Ian Redpath, elegance personified, steered Jim Pressdee elegantly to Peter Walker. Still at my vantage point behind the bowler's arm at the sea end, I watched cavalier O'Neill clattering down those interminable pavilion steps, change angle abruptly at the bottom and march out as if he owned the place. I cannot recall now whether he survived for one or two balls but I do remember the ball from Pressdee that got him – inviting, slow, a flurry of footsteps as he came out of his crease to get to the pitch of the ball, again slow-motion as he was beaten in the flight, the ball turned sharply away from him, then a second lightning movement as Eifion Jones took the bails off and he, in unison with a few thousand others, appealed for the stumping.

Six times, as day faded, this noise erupted. At the pavilion end Shepherd's brand of off-spin, delivered at pace, made him impossible to play. At the close of this opening day Australia were an incredible 39 runs for six wickets – a great day for Glamorgan, but the pessimists among us decided it could not last. It did. The Australians managed 101, Pressdee took six wickets and Don Shepherd four, from 17 overs, 12 of which were maidens, and conceded only 22 runs. That economy proved crucial.

Glamorgan's second innings on this spinner's paradise produced five wickets for leg-spinner Simpson and a total of 172. With plenty of time left, a team containing some of the best batsmen in the world needed 268. It was an incredible last day. Swansea was in an early version of gridlock, thousands at St Helen's complemented by thousands down the road at the Eisteddfod. It is a pity that there is no record of how many of the traditionally cricket-loving Gorsedd 'bunked off', but spiritually the whole of Wales was at St Helen's. Alun Williams, the BBC man at the Eisteddfod, was fed the score from the BBC man at the cricket, and no competition was ever more tense. The crowds on the maes gravitated less to the pavilion than to the BBC stand, with its black-and-white television pictures from the arena up the road. Lawry lingered, Veivers was skilfully violent. Australia came within 37 runs of winning but Shepherd and Pressdee again took charge. Don Shepherd's contribution came not only from the five wickets he took but also his amazing, crucial economy – 52 overs for 71 runs. *'A oes heddwch?'* No fear. This was victory in the arena, David had beaten Goliath, Wales had beaten Australia which taught those English a thing or two, thousands cheered, the singing turned the cricket ground into the eisteddfod pavilion and the adjudicators joined in.

from *Morgannwg, 2004*

SPEED AND SRENGTH

Harri Webb

Guto Nyth Brân

He was born on the mountain, he breathed its pure air
And nourished his frame on the good mountain fare
And in all our proud country there was no one who ran
Who could ever catch up with bold Guto Nyth Brân.

Make way on the mountain, make way down below
For one who ran swifter than strong winds that blow,
Give a cheer as he passes and catch him who can
For the fastest of runners is Guto Nyth Brân.

High over the Rhondda the farmstead is seen
Where Guto kept sheep on the hillside so green,
He needed no sheepdog, now beat this who can,
He out-ran all his flock, did fleet Guto Nyth Brân.

From Wales and wide England the challengers came
To the valleys all drawn by his peerless fame,
But however they laboured, all-comers he'd tan –
They hadn't a hope against Guto Nyth Brân.

Twelve miles in an hour, seven minutes to spare,
From Bedwas to Newport, not turning a hair

And back as a winner according to plan
Was just one of the races of Guto Nyth Brân.

At the end of the race, his fair sweetheart, 'tis said,
Kissed Guto all breathless, and our hero fell dead,
So heed what I tell you, each young sporting man
And be warned by the fate of poor Guto Nyth Brân.

He died long ago and two centuries have gone
Since he ran his last race but his legend lives on,
And still at Llanwynno his gravestone we scan
And at Brynffynnon Inn drink to Guto Nyth Brân.

from *Rampage and Revel* (1977)

ATHLETICS

George Ewart Evans

The Powder Monkey

'DAVEY! Davey John! Where are you, boy? You'll be late for school.'

The small boy looked up as he heard the shrill voice from the house below. He had been shooting marbles and he licked his knuckles and wiped them quickly on his trousers before he shouted down over the wall of the back garden,

248

'I'm up here, Mam.'

'Hurry now.'

The house was one of the top row in the village and the bracken of the hill-side grew up to its back gate. As the boy gathered his marbles from the ground he looked up towards the hill; his eye lighted up and he pocketed the marbles quickly and shouted down towards the house,

'It's early, our Mam; there's Johnny Edwards Powder-house coming down the green path. He's never late; I'm going down with him.'

'Hurry then. Be off with you,' the harassed voice called back as the boy scuttled through the bracken to reach the path down the hill. When he stood on the path he made a trumpet out of his hands and shouted up to his friend in a yodelling sing-song,

'C'mon to school, Johnny; I'll shoot you marbles. I've got a *blem taw*.'

The small figure waved his hand. He came down the hill-side steadily, as he did every morning. He wore a thick, blue jersey and corduroy trousers. His face was round and his black hair stood out in bristles on his scalp. He carried his lunch in a neat, paper parcel tucked under his arm.

'How be, Johnny,' his friend greeted him.

'How be. Show me that *taw*, Dai. I bet he's not so good as mine.'

The two boys walked together down the hill. They saw the school below them in the valley, laid out as in a plan. The schoolbell began to ring, the urgent tongue filling the valley with its clangings.

'Will we be late?' asked Davey John hopefully.

'No that's the first bell. There's another ten minutes, yet.'

The bell stopped immediately, spent out by its quick frenzy, Davey John said,

'Tommy Price said your house was full of powder; 'nough to blow up the whole of Pentre, the whole of the valley and Splott Docks, Cardiff as well.'

'Tommy Price is a liar.'

'Isn't it right then, Johnny: haven't you got blowing-up-powder in your house then, all in sacks and big barrels?'

'No, we only got Indian corn for the chickens in sacks, and we haven't got a barrel at all 'cept a treacle-barrel sawed in half, with handles, for a washing-tub. My father has his bath in it in front of the fire every night after work.'

'Can I come up and see?'

'Doesn't your father have a wash after work?'

'Ay, but not in half a treacle-barrel; we got a proper bath.'

'There's no difference, really.'

'Can I come up, Johnny?'

'No, my father's bad.'

'My Dad says your father's bad a lot.'

'Ay, it's his chest,' said Johnny, 'he's been working in a rough place and the tubes in his chest have got clogged up. C'mon, race you to the schoolgate.'

They had reached the road leading down to the school and they raced along the pavement making the flagstones ring with their nailed boots.

At the end of afternoon school Johnny Edwards called at the shop for the swedes and the potatoes and climbed slowly up the hill. A fine mist had descended onto the hill-crest and his home was up there somewhere, lost in it. The mist trailed down the path of green turf that led through the bracken, pouring down into the valley in a gossamer stream. As Johnny walked into the mist he felt the chill of the moisture-drops upon his face. He remembered the game of 'making tears come' – blinking quickly so that the tiny drops of mist collecting on the eyelashes ran onto the cheek; and he was still playing this game when he came in sight of his home. The old Powder-house was a low one-storey building of rough grey stone and slate. A shelf had been dug into the steep slope to contain it and the hill rose sheer from its back wall and fell away precipitously from its front gate. It had been built during the sinking of the coalpits below in the valley, to store the explosives that are needed in the mining of coal. But as the village grew and the long narrow streets crept steadily up the hill, the Powder-house became less remote; and it was decided that the powder had better go further away, although Davey John Hughes' house, the nearest house in the village, was nearly half a mile from it. A new Powder-house was built, right on the top of the mountain, surrounded by high railings with curved metal spikes sprouting from the top. The people down in Pentre were glad to see the powder go higher up the mountain, because, as they said, there was always a chance that one morning, with the powder just where it was, they'd be up much earlier than they expected. But now it was in its new place right on top of Twyn-Dolan mountain it was all right; although if some-thing went wrong up there the powder would surely blow

251

the roof off God's heaven. But God could take care of himself, no doubt; and, in any case, it was no use worrying about God's business. After the powder was shifted the old house was empty for a while, and then the colliery company had the idea of changing it into a dwelling-house. Two small windows and a fireplace were built in and at the back they dug a bit more out of the mountain and added a small lean-to shed. Luther Edwards brought his wife and small baby to live there as the first tenants. Johnny very soon had a brother and a sister and the Powder-house was as full as it had ever been. But Luther Edwards was the only bit of powder left in it, and he was getting a bit damp. Fifteen years before he'd been one of the liveliest colliers in Pentre Pit: he was a good workman and a good sportsman. In the boxing ring he could hold his own with anyone of his own weight; and his speed on the track was known in four or five valleys. He was small and wiry and beneath his broad forehead was a thin face, ending in a pointed chin; his eyes were very dark and never still. But the dust had got into his lungs and had dulled his eye and taken the spring out of his step. He was still working although he was often away from work for long spells through his sickness.

After the evening meal Luther Edwards seemed to wake up out of his drowsiness and he said to Johnny: 'Come on, Jack; we'll take a turn on the road to Berth-Capel.'

They climbed the steep slope behind the house. Johnny had to wait for his father who panted so much that he had to stop every twenty yards of the climb. They reached a point where the hill sloped more gently and, going through

252

a gate in the long dry wall, they left the bracken behind them and walked through a field of short, springy turf. Beyond this they passed through another gate and came out on a metalled road which ran along the spine of the hill, up past Berth-Capel, a farm with a long straggling group of out-buildings. As they got onto the road, Luther Edwards pulled his cap down over his forehead and buttoned up his coat; then, first of all moving his arms rhythmically across his chest, he broke into a slow trot. Johnny looked at his father and thought: this is a fine game; and trotted alongside him. But they had scarcely run fifty yards when Luther Edwards halted, his face white and his hands to his chest, gasping for breath. Johnny watched as his father staggered about coughing: he wasn't frightened because he'd seen him like this before: it would stop suddenly, he knew. His father straightened up and wiped the sweat from his forehead, 'It's no use, Jack bach, my running days are finished, but I thought I'd like to try out the old legs again. They're fine, he said, tapping the hard muscles of his thighs; 'It's my wind that's gone. I've not got enough to blow out a birthday candle.'

As they walked on Johnny said, as though to console his father, 'I can run, Dad.'

'I can see that,' the man answered looking at the lad and nodding to reassure him.

'I'm the best runner in our class. Shall I run just now to show you?'

'Ay, run you; let's see your paces.'

The boy bent his arms, imitating his father, threw back his head and scampered up the road. Luther Edwards whistled when he'd run about fifty yards; Johnny stopped.

'Now come back; but keep your head down.'

The boy ran back towards his father, picking up his knees like a young horse, his face set with the effort to show he was a runner.

'That's the way, mun; keep your head down, lower still. Don't slack up.'

He waved the boy to run past the spot where he was standing and then he whistled him to a halt.

'Well done, Jack.'

The boy came back happy as a sheepdog to hear the words of praise.

'We'll make a runner of you yet, Jack. Never slack up by the post, though; always run well beyond it. You've got the idea, fine.'

They turned back towards Berth-Capel and Johnny chattered about the spiked shoes the runners wear, and the big gun that went off behind them; he'd seen them practising in the Welfare Ground. There was one runner who made a noise like a snake as he was running; he carried two pieces of cork in his hands and he clung on to them tight in case he would lose them. As Johnny babbled on, Luther Edwards thought: why shouldn't the kid make a sprinter? He's strong and he's keen. I'll take him down to Rhondda Parry. When they got home he said to his wife,

'We're going to make our Jack into a runner, Mam. He's got the idea already. We'll have him winning handicaps in no time.'

His wife noticed the change in him: his eyes had lost some of their dullness. She was glad to see him look more like a live man than he had done for weeks.

Every afternoon after tea Luther Edwards took Johnny up onto the hill, along the road to Berth-Capel and taught him how to run. All his own enthusiasm for the game returned and became focussed on his son; and when they came down from the hill just before dusk, he would send the boy to bed and take down a box from the top shelf of the dresser. This held a sheaf of dusty, much thumbed sports programmes. They were the records of the meetings he had taken part in between ten and fifteen years before. His name was there printed in the programmes with his heat and handicap and, written in pencil, the times the various heats were won at, and where he himself finished. It was all recorded there and the blood came into his head as he ran his races over again! But it was the boy's handicaps which he now studied; and he pictured his son in each one of them. Johnny was as keen on the running as his father. He told Davey John Hughes,

'I'm going to be a runner, Dai John; every night I practise up on the mountain with my father. Soon I will be winning cups and medals too, and real money like my father.'

When Luther saw that the boy had some running in him he got Rhondda Parry to have a look at him. Rhondda was the expert trainer of runners; he had men and boys in his 'school', and if a boy could put one foot before the other and Rhondda took an interest in him, that boy would go a long way. The next time Rhondda Parry was going over the mountain to a sports meeting in the next valley, he stopped to see Johnny run. He told his father, 'He's not very big with you, Luther, but he looks as if he's got some running in him. Bring him down to the Welfare next Friday night

255

and we'll put the gun on him. I got a boy down there he can run against.'

On Friday night after school Johnny put on his best jersey and went down into the valley with his father. When they got to the Welfare Ground, Johnny saw a boy called Billy Biggs. He was two classes higher than Johnny at school; he was dressed in running knickers and vest and had real spiked shoes on. He was prancing about the field like a young colt who's just found out how green the grass is. Rhondda Parry came up to them and he asked,

'How old's the boy, Luther?'

'Let me see now...' Luther scratched his head,

'Eight years three months,' Johnny answered quickly.

Rhondda Parry had a fresh, rosy face like a farmer's and he grinned and said,

'That's the way, bach. We'll give you some start on Billy here. But come over and have a look at the gun first. We'll put the gun on him, Luther.'

Rhondda took Johnny and showed him the gun: it was an old pistol with ramrod attached to the barrel. 'It makes a big bang but that's all, no harm. It's like my old 'oman: all shout but no bite in her at all. Just go down by there like your father showed you. On your mark! – Get set!'

Johnny felt the crash of the gun in every nerve of his body: it was as if a thousand shouts were going round in his head, and the bang was still there when he stopped running. But Rhondda started him with the gun twice more, with Billy Biggs alongside picking his knees up enough to touch his chin, and each time the bang sounded less. Then he called to Johnny's father and Walter Drew the whippet man, 'I'm going to run 'em forty yards. Put the wool up will you Walter?'

Rhondda then put Billy on his mark and took Johnny up, 'A couple of yards extra till we get you some spikes.' Run right past the tape, full pelt. Go after him, Billy.'

Johnny never heard the gun this time but he was away like the wind, afraid that he should see Billy Biggs out of the corner of his eye. He could hear the crinch, crinch, crinch, of his spiked shoes digging into the turf behind him. But he didn't see Billy for some time. He felt the wool across his chest and as he slacked up, Billy came alongside-him. He said, 'Rhondda gave you a lot of start 'cos you're new. You wait till we're both off level, though.'

After this Johnny went to sports meetings with his father, Rhondda Parry, Walter Drew and anybody else who was going along. They all piled up in a car, all mixed up with whippets and running clothes and bottles of embrocation. He became a favourite with Rhondda who used to call him the Powder Monkey because he was small and quick. They got him a pair of running shoes and a pair of black shorts and a red vest. The men at the meetings came to know him; he was one of the smallest boys on the track, and where you'd think from his size that his father would have to take him by the hand and show him his mark, Johnny used to prance up and down the track to limber up, picking his knees up like a stallion; and when he was ready he'd take up his mark as though he'd been doing just that since his first birthday. He had plenty of start, standing well up the track from the other boys. Some of the back-markers were as big as men, with black hair sprouting on their lips and chins. He'd never won a handicap though; he'd reached the semi-final of one but he was beaten by a big, lanky boy called Raker who came from another valley and who used to chase after small boys as if he'd eat them. Luther Edwards was getting impatient and kept asking Rhondda whether there was any chance at all of Johnny winning a handicap. Rhondda told him, 'There's no hurry is there, Luther? He can win all right when the time comes. We'll let him go one day and then you'll see the colour of the money he'll be winning.'

Luther's chest was so bad now that he had to give up work altogether: he could get down into the valley without much strain but it was a struggle for him to get back up the hill. He'd reach the Powder-house with a white face and the sweat thick on his forehead. His wife shook her head at him and said, railing at him with sharp kindness,

'Killing yourself you are, man. What do you think we shall do if you get tied there to the bed? There's a fine look-out that will be.'

Luther wiped the sweat off his forehead with the back of his hand: 'Don't you worry about that, old gel. It's only a bit of asthma; the chest will come all right again.'

Fair play to Luther; he wasn't the sort that would do their dying in bed. If there was any dying to be done at all he'd be standing up on his feet: he'd go to bed to sleep not to spend his time looking at the tops of his toes making a mound in the blankets. Yet, if Luther didn't go to bed, he was tied to the armchair by the fireplace and his steps became as slow as an old man's. The more he was anchored to the house the more interest he took in Johnny's running;

and every time the lad came back from a practice or a handicap, he would have him by his chair and question him as closely as the head deacon would a new minister.

Johnny's running was improving, and in the middle of August, Rhondda brought him up after one of the practices. He sat down opposite Luther on the other side of the fire, first of all taking off his tie and loosening the collar from his neck.

'How's the chest with you, Luther?' he asked; but he didn't wait for a reply; nor did Luther think of giving one since it was one of those questions that are asked not for the sake of knowing but for the sake of proper feeling.

'I came about Johnny: I've entered him for a big handicap down the Vale.'

'Penybont?' asked Luther, his eyes lighting up for the moment.

'Ay, Penybont. You remember it I can see. Well, I've seen the programme and Johnny can win it. A fair prize, Luther, a Twenty-Pound Handicap. Besides we may be getting him to carry a bit of money as well. Shall we let him go?'

Luther shifted in his chair, raising his arms in a resigned way. 'You see how I am, Rhondda: on my backside. If you think he can win, let him go. I only wish I could borrow a good pair of lungs, just for the day like, to be down there with you to see him win.'

It was a fair day for the meeting at Penybont. The meeting was one of the best of the year: it was held on Bank Holiday. The course was on a moorland surrounded by the green, undulating garden of the Vale. There was a Galloway as well as the usual Whippet and Foot Racing;

and besides the calls of the bookmakers, and the yapping and howling of the dogs at every shot of the gun, there was the dull thud of the hoofs as the horses exercised on the side of the enclosures. There were the colourful jockeys too; and a sprinkling of Vale farmers and their folk who were never seen in the meetings in the valleys. The heats for the Boys' Handicap was the first event of the afternoon and as Johnny came prancing out in his red vest the holiday crowd took a fancy to him; they roared at the small boy pacing up confidently between the cords with all the motions of a veteran. One of the regular crowd recognised him and shouted, 'It's the Powder Monkey! He's going to show us how to run today.'

The crowd took up the cry and shouted, 'C'mon the Powder Monkey!' But Johnny took no notice; he was doing a job and he'd had his instructions from Rhondda. The cry went up again and one of the bookmakers, a fat, red faced man at the end of the row, shouted the odds on Johnny, 'Evens the field! Evens the field! Evens the Powder Monkey!'

He chalked up Powder Monkey on his board. Then Raker, Johnny's old rival came loping out, a big greyhound after a puppy. Johnny didn't turn a hair; he knew Raker was in his heat and Rhondda had told him just before he sent him out, 'Raker's his name, Johnny, but you'll be doing the raking today and it's him will be getting the cinders in both his eyes. He won't catch you, not if he's got wings.'

And Johnny didn't think he would either. But the bookmakers took one look at Raker and then at Johnny and they changed their shout to, 'Evens bar Raker ! Evens bar Raker!'

260

The crowd hesitated to put their money on Johnny, seeing the giant on the track beside him; and that was the moment Rhondda and Walter Drew were waiting for; they went in and got good odds about Johnny and they laid their money to bring home some profit. There were two other boys in the heat but the real contest was between Raker and Johnny. The gun went off sending a white puff of smoke over the heads of the back-markers, and Johnny rose off the ground like a bird. He got into his stride straightaway and his legs worked away like pistons. The crowd roared and, although Raker was eating up the distance between them, it was plain that this time he wouldn't catch Johnny who breasted the tape a good two yards in front. The crowd cheered,

'Well done, the Powder Monkey!'

And the big bookmaker looked up as he was paying out the money to one of Rhondda's crowd and shouted with a scolding voice as Johnny trotted back from the winning post, 'There he goes, the little Powder Monkey; as quick and as cunning as you make 'em.'

The money was as good as in Johnny's pocket after the heat, because there was no one else in the handicap who had a chance of catching him; and he won the semi-final, and the final with a couple of yards to spare. Going home that night, Rhondda put the prize-money in an envelope and with a safety-pin he pinned it in Johnny's pocket. When they reached Pentre, they stopped the car at the foot of the hill and Rhondda walked with Johnny up to the Powder-house. On the way Johnny looked down, and saw Davey John Hughes making a tent with bracken just behind his wall. He whistled with two fingers, then with four; but Davey John didn't hear him.

Luther Edwards was waiting for them; his wife had seen them climbing the hill, and had tidied her hair and put a clean white cloth on the table. Just before they got to the house Johnny could hold himself in no longer and he ran in front shouting, 'I won, our Dad, won! Mam, there's enough money in my pocket to start a bank!'

Rhondda Parry came in after him saying to Luther as he shook hands, 'Well, he pulled it off, Luther. He ran like a champion and if he grows a few inches we'll make a runner of him.'

While Johnny was struggling to get the pin out of his pocket to give his mother the money, Rhondda had taken a small roll of notes and placed them under the tea-caddy on the mantel-piece saying casually, 'Walt Drew got 'threes' about Johnny in the heat.' And when Luther attempted to refuse, Rhondda waved his hand, 'You rest there; the lad has earned more than the prize-money.'

After Johnny had got the money out of his pocket and handed it to his mother, he asked eagerly, 'Can I go out and play with Davey John?'

While his mother was raising her hands and complaining;

'Won't the boy ever get tired,' Johnny had taken a piece of bread and butter from the table and was off, bowling down the green path, chanting as he ran,

'Dai John, Dai John. I got a knife to cut the fern with. I got a knife to cut the fern with.'

from *Wales*, February–March 1948

Gerald Davies

Lynn the Leap

I shall never forget, I don't think, that bleak Sunday evening in Japan. Not that I was there, but such is the indelible image that has seared itself into my memory, that I have begun to think over time that I was there. The black and white pictures which migrated across the continents to reach our homes made the Meiji stadium look bleaker than it in fact was. Lynn Davies from Nantymoel cut a lonely figure in the windswept and rain-soaked Tokyo night; the local boy so far from home, as we all thought of him, and playing to win the long jump against overwhelming odds. It was the stuff of dreams and adventure. This was the Olympics, sport's greatest theatre, when a Welshman stood on the edge of immortality.

We are accustomed in Wales to seek our heroes on the playing fields, more particularly in both the football codes of soccer and rugby union. Perhaps this is partly because we can translate the strong sense of belonging and togetherness which we have traditionally found in our communities into the team spirit which inspires these games. Much like silver bands and choirs, we find that they are shared experiences. No doubt we also enjoy the thrills and spills that rugby and soccer excitingly provide.

In 1964 Wales found for itself a different kind of hero, one who ran on a track, not grass, and who wore a delicate pair of spikes on his feet, not a ponderous pair of football boots. Lynn Davies stood as a solitary figure who chose a

263

different route to the status of a legend in Wales and beyond. He pursued his talent on the athletics track, isolated and single-minded.

Others had chosen this path and had themselves made their genuine and unforgettable mark. No one, however, had won an Olympic gold medal on the athletics track. The only other famous gold medal, so the wits would have it, could be said to have been won on four not two legs. (The great Harry Llewellyn had won his on a horse, Foxhunter).

Against the outstanding favourites to win – Ralph Boston of the USA and Igor Terovanesyan of the USSR – Lynn was meant to dent their reputations, not overcome them. The newspapers show the famous leap with a head-on picture, arms swirling in the air, while the moving image on our flickering television screens showed how, after accomplishing his successful jump, he turns and takes a little skip of knowing delight. The gold medal was his.

It was a remarkable achievement. As a new millennium commences, he remains Wales' single athletics gold. In Tokyo's gloom Lynn Davies left the vivid air signed with his honour.

from *Welsh Sporting Greats* (2001)

Peter Finch

The Runner

To make myself younger I run.
The gun metal sky soaks me so my chest

heaves through my t-shirt and my glasses
mist over so I see nothing
except their rims.

I lope along the brook near the quiet street
where I once lived, where the slick
of dumped sump slips through the reeds and
the locked park toilets cower quietly
their entrance lamps smashed to
smithereens.

For a moment the grass turns me sixteen
and I feel the sap engulfing my body
like a wet dream. I'm outrunning dogs,
yes, but they reach me,
snapping my heels, in the end.

The road back is a numb bone with heat
at both ends. The rain in sheets like a
power shower. I'm half blind
and I'm breathing half-century rasps
yet the world is leaping.

I don't age while I'm moving. No flake
amid the sweat. The blood is bright
it remembers. The years only roar
again when I cease.

from *The Yellow Crane* (2005)

SWIMMING

Phil Steele

Martin Woodroffe

'Fancy going to the 'baars' on Saturday?'

For the uninitiated, the 'baars' was Cardiffian dialect for 'The Swimming Baths'. As an eight-year-old growing up in Cardiff in the late 60s, such a jaunt entailed rolling a pair of hand-knitted woollen bathing trunks cylindrically inside a minute towel, extorting half a crown (12p) from my father, and catching a number 17 from Ely to the Central Bus Station. From there it was but a short, gleeful jog to that famous landmark hugging the banks of the River Taff and the scene of a thousand childhood pilgrimages – The Wales Empire Pool.

So why visit a swimming pool where the legendary coolness of the water could induce hypothermia in a polar bear, whilst simultaneously inflicting several varieties of verruca on unsuspecting patrons, when for the same financial outlay a sport-mad youngster could watch Gareth Edwards strut his stuff at the Arms Park, or admire John Toshack's aerial dominance at Ninian Park – not to mention Tony Lewis's captivating elegance at Sophia Gardens? The answer lay in the exploits of an eighteen-year-old swimmer from Fairwater, Cardiff at the 1968 Mexico City Olympics,

On the morning of Friday, October 25th I sat transfixed as our grainy old 'Rediffusion' black and white television showed 'Uncle' Frank Bough on Olympic Grandstand informing the nation of Martin Woodroffe's achievement the previous evening. A silver medal in the 200 metres butterfly in a time of 2 minutes 9 seconds - merely 0.3 seconds behind gold medal winner Carl Robie of the USA. And he (Woodroffe) actually trained at my Empire Pool – unbelievable!

It was the first ever Olympic swimming medal to be won by a Welshman and how we celebrated! That evening, it seemed that every child in Cardiff descended on The Empire'. Not that butterfly is the easiest stroke known to mankind! As I remember, the pool became a boiling cauldron of thrashing limbs and piercing shrieks as we all tried to emulate our hero; four hundred children heaving through the water like arthritic frogs.

I never did master 'butterfly', and regretfully if I swim these days it is in the characterless setting of an excessively warm health club pool, the Empire Pool having been sadly demolished to make way for the Millennium Stadium. But nothing can erase the memory of those blissful childhood days, crouching with toes curled over the edge of the waterside anticipating the cool, chlorinated shock and challenging a friend, 'Come on, I'll race you. One length, I'll be Martin Woodroffe!'

from *Welsh Sporting Greats* (2001)

MOTOR RACING

Griffith Williams

Swan-song of Babs

Within a month I was back again in Pendine. This time it was to cover Parry Thomas's latest attempt on the record, an attempt that was doomed to result in such an unhappy ending.

Thomas was already in Pendine when Flash and I arrived there. Although it was only the beginning of March, the weather was fine, even warm. The beach was in grand shape in the early sunshine and the prospect of an immediate start seemed likely.

It was almost a year since I had covered the first Parry Thomas record at Pendine, and I looked forward with great eagerness to this, his latest attack on the world land speed maximum. The figure of 174-plus seemed a difficult one to beat, but Thomas had already done 171 mph in Babs, and we all felt that he had more than a sporting chance.

Would he be the first man to realise Malcolm Campbell's own forecast that 200 miles an hour was the next objective in the world record race? We all wondered.

It was just as well that we had little time to wait before the attempt took place, because Flash was inclined to get impatient at any delay. The last time the plough had provided him with something unusual to work upon. Now there seemed to be nothing new for him.

'Roll on tomorrow,' he said. 'Let's get this job over and go back to town. I'm bored stiff.'

'Wouldn't you like to live down here?'

He shook his head. 'Not on your life. I'd go nuts. Nothing to see but miles of sea and gulls everywhere.'

'You could get some wonderful pictures of bird life,' I suggested.

'Not me, m'lad. I'm a student of human life, not the bird variety. Action pictures I want. Speed with a capital S.'

'You'll get that tomorrow.'

He nodded. 'For once, Davies,' he said with great solemnity, 'I believe you're right. That's why we're here, anyway.'

'There's one thing I don't like very much,' I said seriously.

Flash looked at me sharply. 'What's that? Nothing wrong with the car, is there?'

'No, but there is with Parry Thomas.'

'What d'you mean?'

'He's had flu, and he hasn't recovered from its effects yet.'

Flash grinned. 'I don't suppose that will make any difference to him,' he remarked shrewdly.

He was right. It didn't.

By the next morning the Welshman was all ready for his attack on the record. The weather was bright and, indeed, apart from the after-effects of flu, the prospects seemed almost to favour Thomas.

Those close to him, however, thought otherwise and considered he was in no fit state to undertake such an ordeal and risk an attempt on the world speed record. But Parry Thomas was a strong man and his mind was made up.

He was going for the record.

I remember watching him climb into the car for the first run along the beach, a tall man, quiet, efficient, and dedicated to the one mission dominating his life – speed.

And now once again he was putting that ambition to the test. His hand moved over the gears, the car roared into vigorous life and moved swiftly off the mark.

Soon it was no bigger than a distant speck on the sky-line.

Flash and I followed with the rest of the cars, making for the measured mile.

At first everything seemed to be going well. Babs charged along the sands at terrific speed on several test runs. Seagulls rose in screaming protest before its spinning wheels, their wings white against the deep blue of the sky. The sunshine danced on the sea, and the sound of the car's engines was like a song of speed on a fair spring morning.

Parry Thomas did not seem satisfied, however. Babs stopped and there were hurried consultations between the driver and his mechanics. We were too far away to know what was happening.

Suddenly, the sun went behind a cloud and a chill breeze ruffled the surface of the distant sea. Over the bay to the west the pattern of the sky was changing to a sombre grey.

Flash yawned. 'I don't like the look of things,' he said. 'It's going to rain soon. Wonder what's keeping him this time?'

It was strange. Already there had been a much longer

delay than was usual when Parry Thomas was behind the wheel.

Flash sat down on an upturned box, which had been washed ashore, and fiddled with his camera.

'What's his last speed? Can't we find out yet?'

'Not for a while. Have a bit of patience. There's plenty of time.'

There was a sudden roar. We jumped to our feet. The car was on its way again.

All at once we could see it, heading towards the measured mile at very high speed. Flash grabbed his camera and started to focus in readiness. I leaned over the bonnet of our car and waited while Babs scorched up the beach.

It was the beginning of the ill-fated run.

What happened next took place in a fraction of a second and almost defied accurate description.

Babs appeared to run into a tremendous skid, the offside wheel went careering towards the sea and in the next instant the car burst into flames.

For a moment there was a stunned, terrifying silence. Then we scrambled into our car and dashed towards the burning wreckage.

But we all knew we were too late. Parry Thomas had died instantly at the wheel.

from *Sands of Speed* (1973)

271

Tony Curtis

The Death of Richard Beattie-Seaman
in the Belgian Grand Prix, 1939

Trapped in the wreckage by his broken arm
he watched the flames flower from the front end.
So much pain – Holy Jesus, let them get to me -
so much pain he heard his screams like music
when he closed his eyes – the school organ at Rugby
Matins with light slanting down
hot and heady from the summer's high windows.
Pain – his trousers welded by flame to his legs.
His left hand tore off the clouded goggles -
rain falling like light into the heavy trees,
the track polished like a blade.
They would get-to him, they were all coming
all running across the grass, he knew.

The fumes of a tuned Mercedes smelt like
boot polish and tear gas – coughing, his screams rising
high out of the cockpit – high
away back to '38 Die Nurburgring.
He flew in with Clara
banking and turning the Wessex through a slow circle
over the scene – sunlight flashing off the line of cars,
people waving, hoardings and loudspeakers, swastikas
and the flags of nations lifted in the wind he stirred.
She held his arm tightly, her eyes were closed.
He felt strong like the stretched wing of a bird,
the course mapped out below him.

That day Lang and Von Brauchitsch and Caracciola
all dropped out and he did it – won
in the fourth Mercedes before a crowd of half a million
– the champagne cup, the wreath around his neck,
An Englishman the toast of Germany.
The camera caught him giving a Hitlergruss.
Waving arms, shouts and faces, a mosaic
laid up to this moment – La Source – tight – the hairpin
the trees – tight – La Source – keeping up the pace
Belgium – La Source hairpin too tight.

With the fire dying, the pain dying
the voices blurred beneath the cool licks of rain.
To be laid under the cool sheets of rain.
A quiet with, just perceptible, engines roaring
as at the start of a great race.

from War Voices (1995)

CYCLING

Wil Jon Edwards

The Funeral of Arthur Linton, 1896

I remember one evening when Twm and Dai came home
from the pit... they had a legitimate reason for coming out
early. They wanted to attend the funeral of Arthur Linton,
the champion cyclist of the world in his day. There had

been a good deal of talk about this funeral which, in its way, had international significance; and my curiosity had been excited to such an extent that I became far from sure whether I, so young and small, was worthy to attend the funeral of so distinguished a man. I thought it wisest not to leave the question for my mother to decide.

I recall the event most vividly. It was the largest funeral I have ever seen, stretching for two miles with thousands of people lining the route from the town to the cemetery. Apart from local people, the mourners seemed to have come from every country in Europe. Many of the wreaths were designed in the form of cycles; but perhaps the most impressive sight, apart from the actual wreath-decked coffin, was a Frenchman (I knew he was a Frenchman because he wore a beard) riding a bicycle immediately behind the coffin, the form of the bicycle being cleverly outlined in flowers. Being too young and small, I was jostled here and there until I found myself more or less settled in a prominent position immediately behind a brass band playing a solemn tune which I have since identified as the 'Dead March in Saul'. I was blissfully unaware that a fairly large hole in the seat of my pants permitted a good deal of shirt to emerge, but in the sombre glory of the occasion perhaps this was not noticed as much as my mother evidently feared it had been with consequent disgrace to the family...

People talked of this funeral and the famous people who attended it for weeks after. I heard Twm tell Dai that he had seen no less a person than Jimmy Michael; and Dai told Twm that he had seen Tom Linton, the late champion's brother. Both became world champions later.

And I remember hearing our lodger, Harry John, telling a highly interested group of people how Arthur (the late champion) had trained on Haulier's Tip before going forth into the world to beat all rivals and to become its champion.

from *From the Valley I Came* (1956)

CLIMBING

R. Merfyn Jones

The Mountaineering of Wales

It was a London Welshman who was to make the greatest impact on British climbing – Owen Glynne Jones. Jones's importance in the history of the sport has been widely acknowledged for it was he who produced the first genuine rock-climbing guidebook, *Rock Climbing in the English Lake District* in 1897. In 1910, when another Welshman was Chancellor of the Exchequer, he was described by one of his climbing companions as a sturdy, muscular Welshman, heart aglow with fierce enthusiasm, and features bespeaking unmistakably that keen Celtic courage and determination which conquers crags and builds Budgets. Such was Owen Glynne Jones. This formidable and immensely strong climber had left his mark on climbing in Wales, as well as Cumbria. He was especially active in Wales in the final months of his life and, had he not fallen to his death on the Dent Blanche in the Swiss Alps in 1899 when he was thirty-two years of age, this London school-teacher would have published his own rock-climbing guidebook to north Wales. Jones had started his audacious climbing career on the Cyfrwy on Cader Idris (which he climbed by himself in 1888) while on one of his many visits to his cousin's house in Barmouth which Jones came to treat as a second home. Shortly before his death he established classic climbing routes on the Milestone Buttress and elsewhere on Tryfan and was clearly set, with the enterprising Abraham brothers of Keswick, to revolutionize Welsh climbing.

So prominent are Welsh climbers, and those living in Wales, in the early history of rock-climbing in Snowdonia that it is difficult to understand why the sport continued to be viewed as the preserve of the English. Perhaps the explanation lies in the fact that many of these Welsh mountaineers were, either because of geographical or social mobility, marginal to the mainstream of Welsh culture. It was certainly the case that members of the exiled Welsh communities were unusually prominent and they often seemed to find this mountain exploration the most compulsive. In addition, it has to be recognized that mountaineering bore the indelible stamp of the public-school and university-educated English intelligentsia, for whom mountaineering and climbing carried a special significance. These pressures and the impact of social and geographical mobility can be clearly discerned in the academic and climbing careers of the most intriguing and significant of the early twentieth-century Welsh climbers, Humphrey Owen Jones.

Born in Goginan, in rural north Cardiganshire in 1878, H. O. Jones moved as a child to Ebbw Vale and attended the Lewis School in Pengam from where he went up to Aberystwyth in 1894. He became one of the early graduates of the newly founded University of Wales and then proceeded to Cambridge where he graduated in 1900, becoming a demonstrator in the University's laboratories and then, in 1902, a Lecturer and Fellow of Clare College. He rapidly established a reputation as one of the leading chemical researchers of his day and, in 1912, he became a Fellow of the Royal Society.

Jones was one of the brilliant successes of the Welsh educational system; he was also an accomplished and courageous mountaineer. He started climbing in his late twenties following a chance meeting with Thomson in Pen-y-Pass and rapidly established himself as a climber of great skill and dedication. He accompanied Thomson on two of his first ascents on Lliwedd in 1907 and, in 1909, succeeded in putting up two new ascents of his own – Paradise Climb and Slanting Gully Rib. He visited the Alps on a number of occasions and, in 1911, attracted the admiration of the climbing world with his audacious first ascent, with Geoffrey Winthrop Young, of the exposed west ridge of the formidable Grandes Jorasses, one of the most challenging mountains in the Alps.

H. O. Jones, a Welsh-speaking Welshman, was now recognized as one of the outstanding climbers of his generation; apart from his Alpine expeditions, he climbed almost exclusively in north Wales. He never climbed in the Lake District and his passion was indisputably for Snowdonia. 'It was', commented the *Journal of the Climbers' Club*, 'primarily in his own mountains of Wales that he discovered his peculiar powers... [where his] highly trained mind and the enthusiasm of the Celtic nature found their most challenging expression. Geoffrey Winthrop Young was later to refer to him as 'an accomplished Welshman, the youngest F.R.S. of his time, and a brilliant climber and mountaineer, he was the most sympathetic and sensitive of Alpine colleagues.'

In August 1912, H. O. Jones married Muriel Gwendoline Edwards of Bangor, a scholar and his rival in love of the mountains. Her academic achievements matched his own: receiving first-class honours in science at the University College of North Wales, Bangor, in 1910 she went up to Newnham College, Cambridge, and became a demonstrator in the laboratories. The first woman Fellow of the University of Wales, she was also a fine athlete and a climber who had, amongst other achievements, led all-women teams of rock-climbers on the Cwm Idwal slabs. She was also a member of the most combative and high-profile Anglican family in Wales. Her father was vicar of Bangor; H. T. Edwards, scourge of nonconformity, had been her uncle; Alfred George Edwards, the first archbishop of Wales, was another uncle. The wedding of these two brilliant Welsh scientists and climbers at Bangor Cathedral was one of the most notable events of the year in north Wales.

Their married life was to be tragically short for, a fortnight later, setting out from the Refugio Gamba, on the Chatelet plateau above Courmayeur, on the Italian side of the Mont Blanc massif, in an attempt to climb the rocky Mont Rouge de Peuteret their guide slipped from a rock chimney and, roped to the newly-married Welsh couple, he dragged them over the cliff to fall a thousand feet onto the glacier below. The three were buried together in the cemetery at Courmayeur in a service attended by many of the leading British climbers including Eckenstein, Young, Pope, Mallory and Todhunter. The coffins were carried to the grave by mountain guides bearing ice axes.

Had the two Joneses, Humphrey Owen and Owen Glynne, not died so young – O. G. Jones died in 1899 at the age of thirty-two, H. O. Jones in 1912 at the age of thirty-three – it is quite possible that the Welsh contribution to the development of mountaineering would have been recognized as widely within Wales as it was within the climbing fraternity, but that was not to be. Along with Muriel Gwendoline Edwards, they were both highly educated products of the university system and pre-war mountaineering clearly appealed most to the university educated, both for social and intellectual reasons. The universities, particularly Oxford and Cambridge but also London and, in this context, Bangor, offered the social networks which allowed for mountain 'meets' and intellectually they fostered that quest for higher meaning and purpose which mountaineers so espoused. As Wales developed its own stratum of university-trained intellectuals by the end of the century, it is not surprising to find a number of them turning to the mountains for solace and inspiration, although no other came close to matching H. O. Jones's achievements.

However, the youthful and, in some eyes, romantic, deaths of these young Welsh mountaineers did not succeed, in Wales, in creating the kind of martyrology which climbing offered to the English. Death was an accepted risk for the mountaineers and their acceptance of the risk was part of what could be defined as both the private code and the popular ideology of mountaineering: that climbers were willing to risk their lives in pursuit of self-fulfilment and, in part at least, for the honour of their nation. Throughout Europe conquering mountains was considered to be a highly visible symbol of a nation's courage and virility. The fact that H. O. Jones and G. M. Edwards failed to be celebrated as Welsh hero and heroine, in the same way as Mallory came to be in England, is intriguing and raises a number of questions.

In part the explanation might lie in the simple fact that the intellectual stratum to which they belonged was too thin and emasculated in Wales to be able to sustain their heroic status. The federal University of Wales had not, after all, been established until 1893. It might also be the case that the triumphalist ideology associated with mountaineering, with all its references to sacrifice and national superiority, had less purchase in Wales than in England. But caution needs to be exercised here; it was the *Carnarvon and Denbigh Herald* which, in response to the fatalities in Snowdonia in 1910, offered a spirited defence which eloquently expressed the reverence in which mountaineering was held in the ideology of race and Empire:

> Nothing compassable daunts him, no peril shakes his iron nerve; he climbs for the sheer joy of the exercise. Not that he neglects any necessary precaution, because he knows... that

a slip of the foot on a piece of unstable rock, a loosening of his grip on a jagged edge, or a too slippery bit of holding, means inevitable injury and probably death ... The cragsmen need no moralising upon the danger or the folly of their pastime. They seek it of deliberate choice because the pursuit of the pleasure keeps their bodies fit, their minds alert, their nerves wrought to glorious tension. When the race becomes decadent we shall not have to lament these dreadful tragedies; but a vastly greater tragedy will have overtaken them.

For those who pursued the sport, mountaineering was often an introverted search for individual challenge and spiritual uplift, but climbing also had its public and political face and the 'glorious tension' of the mountaineer was clearly identified as expressing a nation's finest qualities. The death of George Mallory and his youthful colleague, A. C. Irvine, within sight of Everest's summit in 1924 was a private tragedy but it became transformed into a public celebration marked by a service at St Paul's Cathedral, commemorated in a memorial window at Chester Cathedral and etched into every English public-schoolboy's mind. The preface to one of the biographies of Mallory claims 'that the mere mention of the name is enough to strike a haunting chord in the minds of most adventurous Englishmen for Mallory is part of our national heritage.'

Humphrey Owen Jones did not abjure that public ideology of martyrdom and patriotism. As one of his friends was to testify:

> He believed that life, to be worth living by the race or by the individual, must be lived, both as an example and as personal realisation, at the fullest exercise of vitality and manhood. He accepted, for himself as for others, the necessity involved in so stringent a code of the occasional sacrifice of the individual.

Jones might even have accepted his own, and his wife's, death as necessary sacrifices to this code, but it was a code that apparently found little resonance within popular Welsh culture. Memorial services were conducted for the young couple – at St Mary's Church in Bangor and at the Welsh Presbyterian Church in Abergavenny, attended by the Mayor of Ebbw Vale – and a plaque to mark his scholastic achievements was erected in Jones's old school in Pengam – but Humphrey Owen Jones and Gwendoline Muriel Edwards did not become popular Welsh martyrs to the mountaineer's code of national honour and personal sacrifice.

This mountaineering ethic apparently had less purchase in Wales than in England and Welsh climbers could appear foreign even on their own mountains. In part, this was undoubtedly a matter of class and education, as suggested by Ioan Bowen Rees in his pioneering study. Climbing before the First World War was, in Britain, a largely upper or middle-class pastime which neither industrial workers nor local slate quarrymen and tenant farmers had either the leisure or the resources to enjoy. But there were wider cultural considerations too, for climbing at this time appealed to a kind of middle-class athleticism which often possessed an intellectual, aesthetic or even Bohemian bent. The Edwardian climbing parties were accustomed to sleeping rough in dormitories and mountain refuges, to late mornings and late nights, to swimming naked in mountain lakes. The climbers, when they came to Snowdonia, and despite their wealth, would sport untidy, often ragged, old clothes, ancient but 'favourite' blazers and boots. Mixed parties of young men, women and even children were common and these group expeditions were marked by exuberant socializing as well as by clever talk and informed comment. Such relaxed social and intellectual behaviour must have seemed foreign indeed in nonconformist Snowdonia. Access to this exclusive group required sophisticated intellectual and social skills. J. A. Thomson, the quiet schoolteacher, found it a hostile and difficult environment, but Humphrey Owen Jones was perfectly confident in this elite company to which his intellectual and physical prowess granted him access. Winthrop Young confirmed this impression of Jones's integration into this socially exclusive group. At Pen-y-Pass, he recalled,

> The long evenings of impromptu songs and varied entertainment were alternated, as whim dictated, with gymnastic feats in the hall; when the casual visitor might enter to find Eckenstein hanging upside down by his hands on a rope; H. O. Jones, or Miss Bronwen Jones [his sister] kicking over the matchbox with incomparable finesse; Leslie Shadbolt, Harold Porter or Miss Sanders (later Lady O'Malley) swinging easily up onto the window-sill.

These people shared a common geographical space, the mountains of Snowdonia, with the slate quarrymen of Llanberis and Bethesda, the tenant farmers of the Welsh uplands, the chapels and their congregations and ministers. But they occupied a different cultural space, whether they themselves were Welsh or not, and that formidable ideological construct, Welsh nonconformist culture, could neither contain them nor fully identify with them in their triumphs and their tragedies.

The Welsh contribution to the development of climbing in Wales should not be overstated. The input of English climbers was immense and many of the Welsh mountaineers were themselves exiles of one sort or another. But, equally, it is important to stress that there was a significant Welsh contribution to mountaineering in Wales from the 1880s onwards. The reluctance of contemporary Welsh popular culture more generally to identify with the mountaineers, let alone to celebrate their sport, for which Wales itself was so ideally suited, should not be allowed to obscure that fact.

from *The Welsh History Review*, June 1998

Arnold Lunn

Accident on the Cyfrwy ridge

The day was perfect. The burnished silver of the sea melted into a golden haze. Light shadows cast by scudding clouds drifted across the blue and distant hills. The sun flooded down on the rocks. I slid down the crack and reached the top of the steep face of rock above 'The Table', The usual route dodges the top fifteen feet of this face, and by an easy traverse reaches a lower ledge. But on that glorious afternoon I longed to spin out the joys of Cyfrwy, and I found a direct route from the top to the bottom of this wall, a steep but not very severe variation.

It was one of those days when to be alive is 'very heaven'. The feel of the warm, dry rocks and the easy rhythm of the descending motion gave me an almost sensuous pleasure. One toyed with the thought of danger, so complete was the confidence inspired by the firm touch of the wrinkled rocks.

I was glad to be alone. I revelled in the freedom from the restraints of the rope, and from the need to synchronize my movements with the movements of companions.

I have never enjoyed rock-climbing more. I have never enjoyed rock-climbing since. ...

I had just lowered myself off the edge of 'The Table'... There was no suggestion of danger. Suddenly the mountain seemed to sway, and a quiver ran through the rocks. I clung for one brief moment of agony to the face of the cliff. And then suddenly a vast block, which must have been about ten feet high and several feet thick, separated itself from the face, heeled over on top of me and carried me with it into space. I turned a somersault, struck the cliff some distance below, bounded off once again and, after crashing against the ridge two or three times, landed on a sloping ledge about seven feet broad. The thunder of the rocks falling through the hundred and fifty feet below my resting-point showed how narrow had been my escape.

from *The Mountains of Youth* (1925)

Alan Hankinson

Archer Thompson: mountaineer

It was after seven when they completed the climb, already growing dark and bitterly cold. They decided to follow the longer but less dangerous path to Llanberis and reached the Dolbadarn Inn at 10.30, their clothes in tatters and one of Archer Thomson's hands so badly frost-bitten that he was unable to use it for several weeks.

Archer Thomson was to dominate the progress of Welsh climbing for the next decade and longer. He came to know many of its cliffs, and the intricacies of Lliwedd in particular, better than anyone else. When he climbed it was almost always as leader on the rope, and it was primarily his example that carried the sport out of the gullies and on to the ridges and buttresses where the holds were as small as the sense of exposure was great. 'He evolved,' Geoffrey Young was to write in 1915, 'the somewhat specialised type of climbing which has been principally responsible for the extraordinary advance made in the standard of difficulty during recent years; the slow controlled movement, depending on a fine balance rather than grip, and identical in pace and security upon easy crags or on the hardest passages.'

Thomson was a skilful and daring climber but also a very cautious one. He chose his companions carefully and would not climb with novices. He was punctilious about the nailing of his boots. He had no time for the technique, much practised by the Lake District men, of closely investigating a proposed new line by climbing down it with the protection of a top rope before venturing to climb up it without protection from above. Such a method, he said, was unfair; it imposed on the second party to attempt the route a harder task than had faced the first. He was prepared to spend a long time contemplating the next moves on a difficult pitch. 'Poised on nailholds high upon a steep slab,' wrote Geoffrey Young, 'he would lean right back from his waist, mutely meditating upon the difficulties above for minutes together.' And Haskett Smith said, 'He was like one of those great chess or billiard-players who are never happy unless they can decide their play ten or twelve moves in advance.' Although he did much climbing, in Wales and on Skye and in the Alps, he never had a serious fall.

He was, in this respect and in almost every other, the antithesis of O. G. Jones. Jones relied on the strength of his arms rather than the delicate placing of his feet, on muscle rather than balance. Thomson's keen eyesight and careful observation made him an accomplished route-finder, while Jones, dangerously combining myopia with impatience, would hurl himself at the problem, trusting in his arms and his boldness to overcome the unconsidered difficulties, with the result that all too frequently he fell off. Jones' climbing was full of clatter and chatter, while Thomson was possibly the most taciturn man who ever climbed.

Stories about Thomson's capacity for silence have become legends. One man claimed to have spent a whole day on Snowdon with him without getting a word out of him. When they arrived back at Pen-y-Pass in the evening, the man held out his hand and said 'Goodbye'. Thomson shook his hand, and smiled. On another occasion, it is said, he spent a day in the hills with a professor from Bangor University who had heard of Thomson's reputation and was determined to match it. They walked all day and neither said a word. But when they came to part that night, it was the professor who broke. 'I have a brother,' he said, 'who is even more silent than myself.' Thomson acknowledged the remark with a glance, but said nothing.

In a talk to the Alpine Club in 1918, Haskett Smith said, never was there a man who felt more intense delight in the rocks than Archer Thomson; never was there one who displayed it less. Sometimes he would pass a whole day without uttering a word and even without changing the expression on his face. A Swiss who climbed with us once for half a day conceived an immense admiration for him and declared that he was more wonderful than the blind man who some years ago went up Mont Blanc. We were rather puzzled by the comparison till we realised that the speaker had never suspected Thomson of being anything but deaf and dumb.

Archer Thomson gave away nothing about his climbing or his feelings about it in conversation, and only a little more in his writings. He wrote many articles for The Climbers' Club Journal and the Club's first two guide-books, but it is only rarely that he gives a glimpse of his inner feelings. His writing style was factual and incisive and cool, sometimes witty and always idiosyncratic, showing a schoolmasterly taste for precision and erudite allusion. He meticulously avoided any hint of heroics. He was an intensely reserved and self-concealing man.

He might have lived longer had it been otherwise. Accelerated perhaps by greater professional responsibilities – he was promoted to be headmaster of Llandudno County School in 1896 – his introversion was to grow into a fatal neurosis. But... in the mid-1890s and the years immed-iately following, Archer Thomson was the most consistently active and creative and venturesome climber in Snowdonia.

from *The Mountain Men* (1977)

Jim Perrin

A Sense of Place

On a rainy April morning over twenty years ago, a young boy was walking along the road between Pont y Pant and Dolwyddelan in North Wales. Mist wraiths skirled amongst dwarf oak woodland on the hillsides above, and the rain marched in gleaming columns down the valley, beating an incessant counterpoint of downpour and drip. A steady trickle ran from the boy's hat-brim on to his oilskin cape, to which his rucksack gave a curiously tilted and purposeful parasol shape as he plodded up the road, veering to the crown here and there to avoid stippled puddles or encroaching pools. Down to his left winterblack trees formed cutwater vees on the spreading plain of flood, and little island pastures were newly green where they rose from the grey watersheen. The boy's boots had taken on the texture of wet cardboard, and the baggy flannel trousers he wore were dark and sodden from thigh downwards. For all that, there was an obduracy and resolution in his step as he paced forwards. Hearing the sound of an engine, and tyres splashing along the road behind him, he eased up from his hunched stride, leant left-handed against a wall, half-turned and stuck out his thumb. The grey Morris van drew up beside him, he thrust himself in, and they set off, worn gearbox clicking and whining through the ratios, along the streaming road. A mile or so farther on the van turned down a steep, rough track and pulled up in front of a large house. Driver and boy emerged, and the latter was ushered through a white door into the kitchen beyond.

Before I take you into that kitchen, I will tell you something about this boy. He has just turned thirteen, and for all the usual reasons of adolescence and some which are uniquely his own, he is painfully self-conscious. He lives in Manchester, in the very middle of that grimy, smog-ridden city, in a flat above a city-centre office-block of which his father is the caretaker. The streets in which he grew up were bulldozed away three or four years beforehand, their groundplan quite gone, their place taken by harsh crescents of concrete flats, where once there were damp rosettes and the smell of soot, dirt and the closeness of crumbling brick. He attends a grammar school in a middle-class area of his home-town and, caught between snobbery and allegiance, hates something about this weekday, workaday scenario which he cannot quite define, though he hates it with excruciating, bitter hostility. On the day of which I write, he probably has a week or so of his Easter holiday left, perhaps a pound in his pocket, and in his rucksack a couple of packets of porridge, a paraffin bottle, blanket, pan, and primus stove. He will sleep where he can – barn or shed, bus shelter or forestry plantation – and intends making for Ffestiniog or Bala on this night, to climb Arenig Fawr on the following day.

In the kitchen, the driver sat the boy down while his wife threaded and fussed through the room's clutter of furniture with the practised dexterity and hipswerve of a Welsh fly-half taking on the Irish pack. The kettle boiled, tea was made and handed round, the boy's flannels steamed and turned pale by the fire, and the talk began. You should understand that there was a need in this boy for a landscape carved from rock and spirit and the natural responses of men – more than a need, a passion for such. There was a craving in his soul for beauty and poetry and permanence to set against the transience and squalor of his own beginnings, the harshly mechanistic uncomprehendingness of school and home society. This was a willing listener, and the talk had begun.

291

Preliminaries differ the world over. An Indian will ask you if you are married and how many children you have. Englishmen ask for the Test Match score. This Welsh couple, old, childless and kindly, asked where I was from, what my religion was and then told me – their proudest boast – of the preachers who had lived in the house. And the conversation went on from there: the castle above; the pulpit rock of Rhys Goch in Cwm Cynfal; the slate-ranked generations in the chapel yard from this single house; the fable of a society in whose composition doctor and vicar, quarryman, cowman, shepherd, drunkard and fool were distinguished by richness of language, imagination, and humanity alone.

There is a vivid picture in my mind of the wife standing at her door and waving; small, bulking a little at bosom and hip, her wrinkled face shrewd and gladdening as the man and boy set off back to the delivery round. And I have vivid flashes of the places, the talk, the people of that day from time to time, for it was one of continual magic. I will describe one incident, to serve for the rest.

Some time about lunch, they stopped in the straggling grey downhill, upland village of Trawsfynydd. The boy's new friend stood bareheaded in the still-falling rain by the statue of Hedd Wyn to tell him the story – poet and farmer's boy from Cwm Prysor, killed in France in the Great War, news of his death arriving on the morning he was awarded the bardic chair at the 1917 National Eisteddfod, which thereafter was known, from its black-draped chair, as 'Eisteddfod y Gadair Dhu'. The thrill of feeling which shot through the boy in response to this

292

story, its charge of raw sentiment, remains with him still, its pulses still travelling along the arteries of belief, its presence more archetypal than actual now in his mind.

But to return to that day in the rain – the man and boy standing by the statue, and the boy asking for some lines of Hedd Wyn's – to which request the man obliged by repeating the following quatrain:

> Dim ond lleuad borffor
> Ar ffin y mynydd llwm,
> A sŵn hen Afon Prysor
> Yn canu yn y cwm.

(Nothing but the purple moon on the end of the leaden mountain, and the sound of the old River Prysor singing in the valley.)

It was a 'nothing but' which carried with it a desired magical everything. It set the grey universe humming as, drawn up to his full five-and-a-half feet of height, hair plastered thinly to his scalp under the glistening copper statue, he breathed and whispered it out to the clean wind of a wet Welsh street. Little more need be said. If you have listened attentively, you will know what the day brought. But I will add a coda, lest you think impressionable youth incapable of discernment. Very recently, I met the old man again, sat by his fire through the space of an afternoon as the light faded and night fell. He was retired, his wife was ten years dead, and daily he sat by his fire reliving the days. He had aged and shrunk, but still seemed sweet at the core though his skin was shrivelled and seamed. The voice I remembered was a little tremulous now across the deep

293

basses, but its images were fresh and clear. He talked of frost-crystals hanging from wires in the winter I was born, 'like notes of music written on a page', and voiced his thankfulness for having lived his life in such a place, 'I look up at Moel Siabod; it is different every day, a different light every time I look, and they try to tell me there is not a God!'

The mechanics of our speech might bring us contradiction now, but his knowledge and his vision were an education to me once, when the need was there to be fulfilled. They imparted to me a sense of place, a richly-informed love of a particular landscape, they were a catalyst, a creative agent. What blooms in the imagination lives on in the perceiving eye, glows out through words and memories that others may share its colours and fragrance, is passed on, translated, and perhaps eventually dies.

from *On and Off the Rocks* (1986)

TEE BREAKS

Sheenagh Pugh

'147'

It's the magic number: seven more
than black despair, and that last black
has to be the hardest. He poises
his cue, and we all feel sick

with certainty: he won't make it.
That black is every job interview
we failed; every final step
we tripped on. It's every no

we heard when we needed to hear yes,
and it's going to happen again,
it's bound to... There's the contact: too late now,
it's paused on the lip; we all breathe in,

and it's down, and everyone's going mad,
because destiny's taken a day off
and we've won. His laughter radiates
out at the audience; they mirror love

back to him, and everyone wants
to hold him, touch him, touch the Jack,

in case it's catching. He did it
for all of us; he put down the black.

from *Beware Falling Tortoises (1990)*

GOLF

John Morgan

Sad news about the Welsh

That Golf is not a game had always been my opinion. Having played it for the first time that remains my view. But, chancing my incorrect arm, how was I to guess that it has become a Welsh game - one quietly like so much else in Welsh life, shattering the past and so transforming long-accepted social and perhaps political attitudes. Fellow-citizens, I tell you, strange things are happening. Where shall I start? There was irritation in the roads around the St. Pierre course at Chepstow last week when hot shots like Ballasteros, Woosnam and Langer were at play and I was held-up in traffic-jams. That was not important. More to the point was the discovery raising the subject with friends, at serious news about rugby clubs in South Wales, about which more later. A revelation also was playing a round myself.

Humankind is clearly divided into those who like hitting a moving ball and those who like hitting a static ball. Similarly, the division makes clear, there are those who like playing a game or match against other human beings, and those who like playing a match against themselves. Most of us belong in the first category I think: golfers among the rest. I had always assumed that Welsh people, given their political history, would choose the amiably combative exercise against themselves. Obviously there would be exceptions: we can think of a few Welsh narcissists, always playing by themselves. Historically, though, Welsh sport has involved a team against a team. Our heroes and heroines have been thought of as playing for Wales, or involved in a match. Therefore when I came to my first round of golf I was firm in my view. Always, although abandoning some forms, due to the infirmities of time and mode of life, I had been a rugby, cricket, tennis, table tennis and snooker player. Only the last three are now possible, and only then through the cunning devices of experience to dismay the dashing young.

That in my golf round I should be matched with a glamorous woman is a different chance, properly equalised by her being some sort of champion. Had I been a male chauvinist kind of fellow I would have been dismayed at her hitting the ball from the tee out of sight straight down the course. Since I am not and, indeed in other ways, stupid – no wonder some males pretend to be feminists in political fields – I spent the afternoon under instruction. It was no good. When we reached territory that demanded a seven iron and reached the green and putting was required I wasn't bad at all. She had to hit the ball for me to be near enough for a seven-iron. It was no good my trying to hit the ball as if this was cricket. The arm, you dope, has to be differently held. There is, I was told, the exercise. The fresh air is good for you. At which, I'm afraid, being accustomed to walking the country, and suffering too much fresh air at home I hired a buggy. Golf is not a game. This, for any student of politics and literature, is a stunning piece of news. Lloyd George was determined golfer. I was even present myself at a Harold Wilson putting practice in Downing Street. P. G. Wodehouse's work has hilarious golfing tales. Among my friends, a most applauded Welsh bard finds the game a sole means of escape – although I'm told he swears a lot while playing. A composer I'm working with wears fake Scots tartan to dismay opponents and believes golf the only route to a simple battle with nature and the elements. (His wife has just discovered a device to rescue abandoned golf balls from the lake at the Rolls course in Monmouth). Golf teaches man his imperfections, men golfers say. The women who play golf tell me it makes them feel serene. Work that out. Could be I just know some strange people, except that all people are strange.

Many aesthetic points may be raised by this confirmation of the nature of golf. More relevant than an understanding of its tortured and tormenting role as a personal struggle is the class and political revelation offered by its growing popularity in Wales. Once upon a time, I used to think, golf was what freemasons, brewers, aspiring school teachers, barristers, bank managers, university professors and that sort of people did. Builders, of course, and town clerks; solicitors, no doubt. But not the rest of us. Now, I'm told, there are rugby clubs in Wales where more of the members play golf than play rugby.

What does this mean? I find it difficult to believe that they find the game satisfactory as a game: golf is for those who do not understand games. Can it therefore be the case that those who once enjoyed the comradeship of the team, now search for satisfaction in being solitary? There is no harm in that, except that it is different from the past. Can it be that golf is an activity that defines the bourgeois? That it carries a class memory, one not to be abjured but embraced? If so, then this really is a mark of social and political change. For myself, I'm sticking to tennis, table-tennis and snooker as long as the puff lasts, and yet find it sad that Wales should be a golf-playing nation.

from the *Western Mail* 20 May 1987

Tony Curtis

The Spill

After days of rain on the course
each bunker has black and blue
shapes drawn in its sand.
Something has been washed and rises

to glint polished black in the sun.
This stuff dredged from the Channel,
brought for cheapness, carries grains
from a century of coal.

Mardy, Britannia, Ferndale,
Maritime, Parc and Dare,
Nantgarw, Bargoed Steam,
Senghenydd, Lady Windsor.

All that power firing the Empire,
two world wars, spilled from the ships
and their loading – ghosts under
the big rise and fall of the western sea.

As we line up our shots on the fifth hole
the distant dazzling sea is a silver divide:
black coal built the Welsh side,
black chained muscle built the English.

I punch my ball out of the sand
and before putting the iron back in my bag
spit on the club face and wipe away
the grooves' black dust with my hand.

from *Last Candles* (1989)

Dai Rees

Golf in Wartime

...Later in the year, I qualified again for the matchplay
championship, sponsored by the *News of the World*, at
Oxhey. In the early rounds I played inspired golf and, in the
semi-final, I gave Percy Alliss, then one of the most

prominent of British golfers, a lesson in how to get the ball into the hole.

Percy, like his son Peter, was a magnificent striker. But, on that particular day, he must have thought my putter was bewitched.

The final was against Ernest Whitcombe, another of my idols, who had won the matchplay in 1924 and that same year had been runner-up in the Open to Walter Hagen at Hoylake.

My parents, and many members of my former clubs, made the long journey to London from Wales to support me. My work on the greens lacked its usual efficiency on the morning round and I went into lunch four down.

Just before I put on my shoes to go out again, I overheard one member tell another, 'I think you should phone your wife and tell her we'll be back for tea. Young Rees won't last to the turn with Whitcombe in this form.'

My Welsh blood boiled and I was in fighting mood as we teed off for the second round. But Ernest showed no sign at all of cracking and four halves left me still four down. At the fifth, I chipped neatly into the hole for a winning birdie and this sparked off an extraordinary run of seven threes in nine holes. My putter was like a live thing in my hands, hitting the ball unerringly into hole after hole. It was enough to make an angel blush.

The putt that finished off Ernest came at a hole where the green lay in a quarry, which I was told by local people had once been used for cock-fights. Ernest outdrove me from the tee and, after I had hit what I thought was a good approach, he followed with a shot that produced a burst of applause from the spectators sitting on the slopes of the quarry. When I got to the green I found that my ball had stopped at the very foot of the steeply rising green. It was at least twenty-five yards from the flag and there was a borrow of about nine or ten feet. Whitcombe's ball lay eight feet from the hole.

I strode straight up to my ball and, after a quick look at the line, rapped the ball on a curving line straight at the flagstick. It went up and on and finally down and into the hole as if I had it under some kind of uncanny control.

Poor Ernest was flabbergasted, and my friends in the crowd set up a most tremendous roar of applause which could not have been helpful to his by now extremely difficult task of getting down his eight footer for the half. He missed, of course, and we were level, and I won the match and the title by hitting my approach at the last hole to within five feet of the flag for a birdie three, and returned home, elated with a cheque for two hundred pounds and an invitation to play in the Dunlop Masters tournament.

Looking back, I am awed by the fact that I possessed that kind of confidence on the putting green. There is probably more nonsense talked about putting than about any other department of golf. I feel certain that more important than any style or method, is CONFIDENCE. If you have confidence, you can hole out better with a broom-handle than a pessimistic golfer can with the newest gimmicky putter from the United States.

... My service was spent mainly in France and, later, in Holland. On one occasion I had the privilege of driving Sir Winston Churchill from Eindhoven Airport to meet Air

Marshal Broadhurst and Eisenhower. While stationed at Eindhoven I was also lucky enough to be able to play golf fairly regularly.

One foggy November morning in 1944, I was told to report urgently to the commanding officer.

'Corporal Rees,' said the boss briefly. 'You will play golf this morning.'

'Sir?'

'With His Majesty the King.'

'Yes – sir!'

King George the Sixth had been visiting his troops in the field and his return to England by air had been delayed because bad weather had grounded all aircraft. He had requested to play some golf and so I partnered him against our C.O. and Field Marshal Montgomery's aide-de-camp. The King treated me with the utmost graciousness. His Majesty played a pretty good game.

I had seen the King, as Duke of York, playing at Sunningdale with his brother, Prince 'Teddy', before the war when they were both very keen. Many years had passed and the King's game had grown a trifle rusty, but he played still to a useful ten or twelve handicap. We covered nine holes in thirty-seven shots and won the match. One hole, I know, gave His Majesty particular pleasure. After I had hit a good drive, the King really got into a number three wood shot and hit the ball into the middle of the green. I holed the four-yard putt for an eagle three.

'Good show, Rees,' said His Majesty. 'We played that hole rather well, don't you think?'

We chatted about golf matters generally and he asked me about the professionals who had been at clubs around

Windsor during his youth; Sunningdale, Wentworth, and the Berkshire at Ascot.

Also at Eindhoven I had the good fortune to play with 'Monty' shortly before the Germans launched their last big counter-attack of the war, 'the Battle of the Bulge'. We had reached the sixth hole, with 'Monty' more than having held his own, when an aide-de-camp rushed out on to the course.

'Monty', facing an eight-foot putt, looked up inquiringly at the perspiring and excited officer, and nodded permission for him to speak.

'The Germans have attacked, sir, at five points along the front in the Ardennes.'

'Monty' stayed cool.

'Very well,' he said briefly. 'I'll be along directly.' He lined up his eight-footer carefully. He holed out.

from *Thirty Years of Championship Golf* (1968)

Gwyneth Lewis

A Golf-Course Resurrection

Mid morning, above the main road's roar
the fairway's splendid – eighteen holes
high on a mountain, which should be all slope,
too steep for a stretch of evenness or poise.
By logic this layout shouldn't work at all
but all the best places are untenable...
and the greens are kind as mercy, the course
an airy, open paradox.

304

The golfers move like penitents,
shouldering bags and counting strokes
towards the justices of handicap and par.
The wind, as sharp as blessing, brings its own tears.
Just out of sight is the mess below:
deconsecrated chapels, the gutted phurnacite,
tips reshaped by crustacean JCBs,
tracts of black bracken that spent the night on fire.

There is a light of last things here.
These men have been translated from the grime
of working the furnace with its sulphur and fire
into primary colours and leisurewear.

They talk of angles, swings and spins.
Their eyes sprout crows' feet as they squint to see
parabolas and arcs, an abstract vision, difficult to learn,
harder to master, but the chosen ones
know what it is to play without the ball
when – white on white – against the Beacons' snow
the point goes missing, yet they carry on
with a sharper focus on their toughest hole,
steer clear of the bunkers, of their own despair,
sinking impossible shots with the softest of putts
still accurate, scoring an albatross
as around them the lark and the kestrel ride
on extravagant fountains of visible air.

from *Parables and Faxes* (1995)

SNOOKER

Sheenagh Pugh

Man getting hammered between frames

Black hair soaked in sweat,
face flaming, he lights up
one after another: stares
with set eyes at the defeat
inside him. They call this pressure,
he calls it humiliation,
and it isn't over. He must go
out soon, and take some more of it:
smile when it's finished; tell
his tormentor how well he played.
And you could try saying
it's only a game, but he
wouldn't hear you for the hammering
in his head.

Exhibition

He's playing trick shots to entertain
the crowd, because the match finished early.
And why was that? He was comprehensively
hammered, that's why; he didn't win

a frame. Now it's all going well:
now it doesn't matter, he can knock
them in from anywhere. There's a wisecrack
from the audience; he looks a bit pale,

small wonder, but he's right in there
fighting back, turning the laugh, as if
no-one just hurt most of the life
out of him for some hours. He's a master

now, showing them how to do it,
the skills of which most of us just dream,
courage, class, humour. That's the game
in the end, and he's a player all right.

from *Selected Poems* (1990)

Philip Davies

Cue Dracula

Happiness in 1969 Harlech consisted of two empty Corona bottles, worth 6d at Siop Gwyndy. Tough call – Elvis on Snowdon Cafe's jukebox, Batman from Maidments or the dark cool haven in the basement under the library and institute? Working men and spotty teenagers didn't mingle in coastal Merionethshire. Only briefly at Ysgol Sul, the bandroom, whist drive or the touchline of Harlech FC home games. During daytime we were allowed into the musty slate-clad snooker room, the bastion of maleness.

Then chalking two straightish cues (with tips), unfolding the cloth, setting the table in the gloom, sliding scoreboard to zero, heads, a nod, dropping the coin into the slot, twisting the dial with a satisfying click. Twenty whole minutes of snooker, the arena lit up like White Hart Lane on cup night. 'I'll be Reardon, you be Spencer, Pullman or Davis.' Later, men arrived in overalls, cardigans and baggy pants. Beatle-fringed teens were relegated to scorers or the corner brag school. Maybe an invitation to make up a doubles team. Between shots PC 142, Twm or Dai South whispering reverentially about Pontins – exhibition – beat all comers – trick shots – ex-constable, ex-miner, and world champion. Ray Reardon from Tredegar down south'. Hang on, world champions came from USA, Russia or Brazil, surely?

Then BBC2 and *Pot Black* arrived, whispering Ted and Mr Reardon. Always immaculately attired, waistcoat pocket for his own chalk, dramatic Dracula-like widow's peak, Brylcreem glistening under the lights and that lupine grin, the same in defeat (rarely) and victory (always). A gentleman in total command, controlling the table like a chess grand master. Relaxed, joking and avuncular until the cue slid between finger and thumb of the spread hand, staring cobra-eyed at the target ball.

A true colossus of the game – Raymond Reardon: World Champion 1970, 1973, 1974, 1975, 1976, 1978.

from *Welsh Sporting Greats* (2001)

Sheenagh Pugh

Forgiven

Bad boy, going on fifty, trace the bones
through your skin; you're like some consumptive

from old times. Your starry eyes,
your paper face. And it s still a child's,

was always a child's face. Lit
with brilliance. Jesus, I'm good at this,

I'm fucking great. Cursing and spitting,
then crumpling afterwards. You didn't mean it,

nor the drunken threats, the head-butts;
you were baffled as any child

by adult anger. But I said sorry.
And it didn't make things all right.

Wives walked away; you cried their names
in the night. TV sets crashed

through first-floor windows: you too, once.
A sarky plod sneered, 'No real damage,

luckily he landed on his head'.
But I remember you winning a match

on crutches, hopping round the table,
looking sick with pain. And I remember

days you couldn't hit a ball wrong,
you with your hopeless stance, your head

jerking on the shot, your shining
bloody genius. Hey there,

you with the stars in your eyes,
the cancer burrowing and nesting

in your throat. Your ghost-voice,
still bruised, still plaintive: why me?

All your life, people have softened
to that child's wail, fed you

more vodka, more nicotine, more tabs,
because the joy of talent demands

forgiveness. Wrecked you, it did,
and now, what can anyone say

to a hurt that can't be made better
but it's all right, you're forgiven?

from *The Movement of Bodies* (2005)

RUGBY

Harri Webb

Vive le Sport

Sing a song of rugby,
Buttocks, booze and blood,
Thirty dirty ruffians
Brawling in the mud.

When the match is over,
They're at the bar in throngs,
If you think the game is filthy,
Then you should hear the songs.

from *The Green Desert* (1969)

Richard Llewellyn

The Rugby Match

A healthy sound is the tamp of the leather ball on short green grass and pleasant, indeed, to watch it rise, turning itself lazily, as though it were enjoying every moment of the trip up there, against blue sky, and coming down against the green in a low curve right into the ready hands of a back.

A whistle from Ivor, and the captain on the other side takes his run and kicks, and as you watch the ball climb you see the teams running into position to meet one another underneath it.

A forward has it, but before he can so much as feel it properly, he is flat on his back, and the two sides are packing over him. A whistle from Ivor, and the first scrum, and shouts for Davy as he lifts his arms to bind his front men. In goes the ball, and the tight, straining muscles are working, eight against eight, to hold one another and then to push each other the length of the field, but the ball comes free behind the pack, and their fly-half has it so fast that nobody knows till he is on his way toward our goal line with his three-quarters strung behind him and nothing but our full-back in his way. Shout, crowd, shout, with one voice that is long-drawn, deep, loud, and full of colour, rising now as the fly runs pell-mell and Cyfartha Lewis dances to meet him, and up on a rising note, for inches are between them, louder with the voice in an unwritten hymn to energy and bravery and strength among men.

But Cyfartha is like a fisherman's net. The fly has been too clever. He should have passed to his wing long ago, but he is greedy and wants the try himself, and on he goes, tries to sell a dummy, and how the crowd is laughing, now, for to sell a dummy to Cyfartha is to sell poison to a Borgia. The fly is down and Cyfartha kicks the ball halfway down the field to our forwards, and has time to offer his hand to poor Mr Fly, who is bringing himself to think what happened after the mountain fell on him.

And my father is laughing so much that his glasses are having trouble to settle on his nose. Owen and Gwilym are shouting for all they are worth, for Davy has the ball and his forwards are all round him to push through the enemy. Shoulders and knees are hard at work, men are going down, men stumble on top of them, fall headlong and are pinned by treading, plunging boots. Red and green jerseys are mixed with yellow and white, and mud is plenty on both. On, on, an inch, two inches, bodies heave against bodies, hands grab, legs are twisted, fall and crawl, push and squirm, on, on, there are the white posts above you, but red and green jerseys hide the line and form a wall that never shows a gap. On, yellow and white, pack up behind and keep close, pull the ball into the belly and shield it with your arms, down with your head, more shoulder from the pack, keep closer at the sides, push now, push, push, push. A red and green down in front, another, who carries away a third. Another push now, and the ball is slipping from him. A hand has come from the press below and grasps with the strength of the drowning, but a wriggle to the side and a butt with the hip loosens it and on, on, half an inch more, with an ankle tight in the fist of red and green who lies beneath two yellow and white and only enough of sense and breath to hang on.

Down with the ball now, full flat, with eight or nine on top of you, and there is the whistle.

The ball rests an inch over the line.

Then see the hats and caps go into the air, and hear a shouting that brings all the women to the doors up and down the Hill, and some to lean from the back windows.

Again the whistle, and Maldwyn Pugh looks up at the posts, makes his lucky sign, and takes his run at the ball that rests in its heeled mark, and kept there by the hand of Willie Rees, who lies full length in the mud with his face turned away, not to be blinded by the slop that will come when the boot leaves his hand empty.

Empty it is, and the ball on its way, and the crowd quiet, with the quiet that is louder than noise, when all eyes are on the same spot and all voices are tuned for the same shout.

The ball travels high, drops in a curve, turns twice. The crowd is on its way to a groan, but now the wind takes it in his arms and gives it a gentle push over the bar, no need for it, but sometimes the wind is a friend, and there it is. We are a try and a goal, five points, to the good.

from *How Green Was My Valley* (1939)

W. J. T. Collins

The Greatest Player of All Time

All my life through I have had a capacity for hero-worship. Whenever I have found greatness of character, intellect, skill, or kindliness it has been a joy to pay tribute

314

to it. Yet, side by side with willingness to admire and praise (in connection with Rugby football and all else), has been an inability to ignore faults and shortcomings. In the early 'Nineties I thought Arthur Gould the greatest Rugby player I had ever seen. Today after sixty years of football criticism I think of him still as the greatest player of all time. There were days when he fell short of his own standards, and I criticised his play accordingly (much to the annoyance of some of his idolatrous admirers); yet, in spite of occasional defects, he seemed then, and to me remains, the master of supreme achievement. How wonderful were the days when Arthur Gould was the bright particular star of Invincible Newport and Invincible Wales! Under the heading of 'The Prince of Players', I wrote in 1893 or 1894 two articles which gave a full account of his career till that time. Its completeness was due to the fact that I had access to a newspaper cutting book in which Arthur Gould's admiring sister had kept records of most of the matches in which he had played. His career was remarkable in its variety. Though Newport was his home, and early and late he played for the Newport team, he spent long periods in other districts, part of the time associated with a brother who was a public works contractor. He played for the Southampton Trojans, the London Welsh, and Richmond; for Hampshire, South Wales, and Middlesex; from 1885 till 1897 he was assured of his place in the Welsh team, of which he was the accepted captain for years. Those who never saw him in his heyday can have little conception of his physical powers and the keen brain which directed and controlled them. He was a track sprinter only two yards outside evens; and a great hurdler who several times was second in the English championship. As a footballer he had all the gifts, and they had been developed by thought and constant practice. Some boys when they begin to play Rugby football find that they dodge, swerve, and side-step naturally – it is not a question of thought, it is an animal instinct. Arthur Gould was one of them. He dodged or swerved away from a tackler instinctively; but before he had gone far he had learned to study the capacity of his fellow players and the defensive powers of his opponents, knew what he was doing, why he did it, and how it was done. Other players, on their inspired days, have gone through their opponents – swerving, side-stepping, dodging with easy mastery which made the defence look silly; other centres have made perfect openings and unselfishly given their wings chances to score; other men have nipped their opponents' attacks in the bud by the quickness with which they smothered man and ball, or by intercepting passes; others have tackled man after man or compelled them to pass to avoid being taken with the ball; but no threequarter I have known has maintained the high level of attainment in attack and defence so long and so consistently as Arthur Gould – no man has shown such uniform brilliance and resourcefulness over so long a period of years. He was in first-class football from 1882 till 1898; he first played for Wales against England in 1885, and his last game was against England – at Newport in 1897 – twenty-seven matches, at that time a record. And when comparison is made with the records of other players it must be remembered that in his day there were no matches with

316

France, New Zealand, South Africa, or Australia to swell the record, and that he was in the West Indies in 1889. As a boy he played at three-quarter, but it was as a stop-gap full-back that he entered the Newport XV. His first game was prophetic. 'Kick, you young devil!' shouted the Newport Captain, for he was playing a three-quarter game; but twice he ran through the Weston-super-Mare team and scored tries. As a full-back he played for Newport for three seasons; he got his cap for Wales first as a full-back; but when he had a chance to play at three-quarter he soon made his mark. In those early days he was famous as a kicker, and one season dropped twenty goals; but he was known also for his speed and elusiveness, and for the wonderful quickness of his punting. Thereby hangs a tale. Arthur Gould was left-handed and left-footed; he kicked instinctively with his left foot. But when his opponents found that he could kick only with one foot, they played on him from their right and smothered his kicks. When he found what was happening, he practised kicking with his right foot so assiduously that he became as good with one foot as the other, and the late W. H. Gwynn, of Swansea, Secretary to the Welsh Rugby Union, who told the tale, concluded, 'And you simply couldn't prevent him from getting in his kick.' Never did a rugby player work harder to improve his natural gifts and perfect his technical equipment. As time went on, he became sparing of his efforts to drop goals, and concentrated upon running through the defence or making openings for his wings. In his closing years his defence was criticised, and it is true that often in those late days he would not go down to the ball, and obviously avoided clashes with big forwards who were bearing down on him; while too often he tried to intercept a pass instead of going for the man with the ball. This of course was a defect – it counts against him. But he had taken a lot of battering, and had suffered many injuries in the earlier years, when his defence was the admiration of friend and foe. Indeed, after the Welsh victory over Scotland at Newport in 1887-8, Charles Reid, the greatest of Scottish forwards, said publicly that he had never known a man who did more for his team than Gould did that day. When Gould ran, he carried the ball in both hands; often as he side-stepped an opponent he raised the ball at arm's length above his head; sometimes from that height he gave a downward untakable pass. I mention faults developed late in his career, because if they are ignored I may be charged with praising this great player blindly or dishonestly. But, when all is said, Arthur Gould is to me the greatest rugby footballer who ever played.

from *Rugby Recollections* (1948)

Terry McLean

The Greatest Match of All

... And so the game began. Straightway was remarked a strange lethargy about the All Black movements. Because they had travelled so much and understood each other so well, the New Zealanders glossed over their mistakes with a kind of professional competence. But there were mistakes, all the same, and alone among the teams of the Kingdom the Welsh had the wit to perceive and the knowledge to employ the means of capitalising them. So often in the past the ball had flashed from the scrum into the hands of Roberts and gone from him in smooth movement to Stead, to Hunter at the start of a weaving run and thence into the three-quarters and sometimes back to where Seeling and O'Sullivan and McDonald and Glasgow hunted and hungered like black panthers. Now, there were awkward movements, fumblings, slow passes and aimless runs which drifted across the field into touch. Time and again Gillett hefted the ball and more often than not it swerved into midfield so that All Black heads rolled and began to hang as they chased hither and thither.

Where Gillett aimed and misfired, Winfield, steady as a rock, planted the ball unerringly ahead of his forwards into touch. Where Mynott stumbled outward, Percy Bush nipped and jigged. And while the All Black forwards for the main part had the advantage, this was slight. Wales had deduced that the New Zealand formation of seven forwards, seven backs and Gallaher as half one and half the other was more elastic and hence more dangerous than the standard formation of eight forwards and seven backs, and with that imitation which is the sincerest form of flattery they had made their Cliff Pritchard a rover, too. His roving here and there was the ruin of a number of attacks at their inception; and when he was beaten on the tackle, the Welsh backs, all enduring, thudded into their markers and put them down as comprehensively as if the Leaning Tower itself had bitten the dust of Pisa.

So the play went for half an hour. As someone afterwards remarked, keen, strenuous and intensely exciting,

319

yes. Brilliant, no. Then Wales breached the New Zealand 25 and heeled from a scrum somewhat to the right of the posts. It was the moment to execute the planned attack. Owen feinted to the right, to the blindside, and in the confusion seemed to run a yard or two wide of the scrum. The All Black defence bore across, rapidly massing. In a moment, Owen flung back a pass to Pritchard to the left of the scrum. Away went Wales. Now Gabe in the centre had the ball and was thrusting ahead. As a tackler loomed he passed onward to Morgan on the left wing. Years later, Morgan's mind seemed to grow clouded on issues of the game and a famous statement of his on events was taken as gospel truth – as it might have been – and made thousands of New Zealanders embittered. At this moment, all that mattered was the present and in it Morgan was at the height of manhood and dangerously quick in his running. Clasping the ball, he sped around the lumbering stretch of Gillett and flew a few yards onwards for a try. Forty thousand Welshmen screamed their delight. Teddy! Teddy! Did you see it, man, did you see him get the ball and go! Lord, what a run! And did you see Gabe, man, and Cliff Pritchard? And Owen, Dicky Owen. He fooled 'em. Dicky fooled those bloody All Blacks, man.

Winfield could not manage to goal, but it was Wales 3 and New Zealand 0 and so it remained at half-time which, proclaimed two minutes too soon, caught the New Zealanders storming at the Welsh goal-line and battering down the defence, too. Now was seen the almost professional competence of the All Blacks. Though Bush once caused swelling screams of joy and hope as his dropkick soared

320

toward, and only just dropped short of, the posts, the attack was principally delivered by New Zealand. The old, smooth, rippling movement of men and ball toward the goal-line wanted in rhythm and fluency, but its substitute, an honest, almost tormented endeavour, seemed too strong for Wales. McGregor once placed the ball back in mid-field from the centre and with a surer grasp anyone of half a dozen forwards could have had the ball and a try. Another time Roberts snapped the ball to Mynott with the goal-line only feet away; but Welsh hands turned Mynott for the time being into the Leaning Tower of Taranaki and struggle as he might he could not score.

And then came the moment which was to stand not only this match but all of Rugby on its ear, not for a spell but for generations, which was to engender a feeling that New Zealand had been unfairly used and which, when all the pros and cons had been argued into eternity, was to be the greatest event in the history of New Zealand Rugby because it provided a basis, a starting-point, a seed of nationalism upon which all aspects of the game were to depend in succeeding years. Wallace the Nonpareil dashed in and, gathering the ball, set off from near halfway, bearing to his left and weaving and swerving away from the tiring mass of Welsh players. Nothing that this genius ever did on the field was marred by gross miscalculation or foolish blunder and now, with the light in his eye and the honour of New Zealand to save, his flying run shouted of death and destruction, no matter how much Wales might or could endure.

Striding up to join him ran young Deans, the powerful centre, and as they rushed onward in concert the youth sensed that Wallace might be covered. He called and the pass came swiftly to him as he thundered for the goal. He dived – And then, of course, all hell let loose.

Gabe tackled Deans. It was certain that they lay a moment. It was also certain that soon Welsh reinforcements were pulling the two back into the field and not wasting any time about it, either.

The question was whether Deans had grounded the ball across the tryline, or not.

Gabe felt that he had not, because he could feel Deans straining forward as they lay on the ground. Wallace and other New Zealanders swore that he had. The Welshmen, of course, were far too busy. Never were traces of a crime – and, in Wales, it is a crime to score against Wales – so swiftly expunged.

And the only man in all the world whose yea or nay meant anything at all was, poor fellow, in a state of utter confusion. Poor Mr Dallas, a Scotsman, had taken the field as referee heavily clad and without bars to his boots. He was not in fine training. The pace of the game was great. At this vital moment when all he needed to do was to be there and to see for himself, giving a judgment which all would have to respect, he was not present. Like a blunt-nosed trawler shipping steep seas, he was trudging along a good 30 yards behind the play. When he did get up, Deans and Gabe lay in the field. The Welsh expungers had been diligent at their task. Mr Dallas blew his whistle; but it was not for a try.

You may, if you wish, even now embroil yourself in the aftermath. Gabe has stated that he said to Deans, after the game, 'Why did you try to wriggle onward?' There was no reply. There is evidence that Gallaher had no complaint. But the next day, at 10.26 a.m., Deans handed in to the Cardiff Post Office a telegram to the London *Daily Mail*. 'Grounded ball 6 inches over line,' he wrote in it. 'Some of Welsh players admit try. Hunter and Glasgow can confirm was pulled back by Welshmen before referee arrived.'

Deans was a man of complete probity. It was unthinkable that he would deliberately falsify the issue. And, years later, the issue was bedevilled still further when Morgan, now Dr Morgan, wrote on a programme that it was a try. Fifty years later, those few, those gallant few, who remained of this incomparable team were treated to a reunion by the New Zealand Rugby Union and, as is the custom, gathered in a hotel bar to drink and talk. It was a moving experience to hear Hunter say to Stead, while the years peeled off their shoulders back to the days when they were stalwart and strong and without compare, 'Without you, I should have been nothing. You were the finest player of all.' But it was also wryly moving that the gathering had scarcely got going before Wallace was producing a diagram which purported to show where he had run, when he had passed, and how Deans had scored. The old men grouped about it. 'Yes,' they said. 'That is right. That was how it happened. It was a try.'

In all this seriousness, there is a touch of the comic, if not irreverent, in the evidence of George Nicholson, an Auckland forward who had not won a place in the match. 'Billy Stead,' Nicholson said, 'was touch judge. Bill felt the call of Nature. He asked me to take over. When Wallace began to run, I went with him. I was only yards away when

Deans got the ball. I was whooping along. And then I saw the dive and the tackle.'

'And what was it?'

'Ah,' said George. 'It was a try, true enough.'

So it can go and has gone on. And yet, what did it matter? What does it matter? Only one man in all the world could decide and he said no. That was the end. The place of the 1905 All Blacks in history is secure. No other team ever approached their back play. By modern standards, Seeling and McDonald and Casey and O'Sullivan and the rest were small forwards; but so powerful were they, so husky, so well trained, so tough, that for all time they fulfilled Falstaff's dictum that it is the spirit and not the size of the man that counts.

It is fascinating, if fruitless, to speculate on the might-have-beens if the try had been awarded and Wallace, as he would almost certainly have done, had kicked the goal. Would Rugby in New Zealand have remained the national game? Would the rivalry with Wales still be of a special quality which none but New Zealanders and Welshmen can ever properly understand? One speculates and gets no further. Was it a try? Of course not. The referee said so.

Fifty years later – and in fifty years you can cover most of the arguments – Stead said, almost as if he were ruminating, 'We did not deserve to win. Wales had the better team on the day.' When wisdom speaks, let all other tongues be silent.

New Zealand: G. A. Gillett (Canterbury), D. McGregor (Wellington), R. G. Deans (Canterbury), W. J. Wallace (Wellington), J. Hunter (Taranaki), S. J. Mynott (Taranaki), F. Roberts (Wellington), D. Gallaher (Auckland), captain; A.

McDonald (Otago), C. Seeling (Auckland), J. J. O'Sullivan (Taranaki), F. Newton (Canterbury), F. T. Glasgow (Taranaki), G. Tyler (Auckland), S. Casey (Otago).

Wales: H. B. Winfield, W. Llewellyn, Gwyn Nicholls (captain), R. T. Gabe, E. T. Morgan; Cliff Pritchard (extra back); P. F. Bush, R. M. Owen; W. Joseph, C. Pritchard, A. F. Harding, J. F. Williams, G. Travers, J. Hodges, D. Jones.

Referee: Mr J. D. Dallas (Scotland).

The day was fine, but the pitch was heavy. The attendance was 40,000. Wales scored 23 minutes after the start. This was the 28th match played by the All Blacks in three months.

Footnote: The discussion over the 'Deans' try became an international affair to which every Welshman desired to be a party. It has been calculated, from the vehemence of their arguments and the apparent sincerity of their statements, that some 2,000,000 Welshmen were present at Cardiff Arms Park at the time. One writer even claimed to be sitting within six yards' of the spot where Deans was grounded.

Many years later, Seeling and G. W. Smith, who after the tour both played Rugby League in Lancashire, were taken on the turf of Cardiff Arms Park. Seeling dug his umbrella into the turf and with tears streaming down his face said, 'This was the spot.' (But it was Seeling who, not long after the tour, exclaimed that the All Blacks had lost because 'they done their nuts.')

The 1953 All Black team streamed on the field at its first visit to Cardiff and a local guide headed purposefully for a corner. 'Here it is,' he exclaimed. He dug his heel into the turf. 'Away out here?' said an All Black wonderingly. 'Golly, not even Billy Wallace could have kicked the goal from here.'

'No, no,' said the Welshman. 'This was where Morgan scored.'

from *Great Days in New Zealand Rugby* (1956)

David Parry-Jones

Prince Gwyn

If one criterion of sporting 'greatness' is the ability to exert innovative influence, the other vital one concerns the capacity to achieve victories consistently. This was what Gwyn Nicholls was now able to do with Cardiff, whose captain he had become for the 1898-99 season. Besides leading the Blue and Blacks to twenty-two victories and three draws out of twenty-eight games, he drew praise from the generally restrained Charles Arthur: 'Nicholls' form this season was probably the best he has ever shown in all his long and brilliant football career'. People evidently thought of him now as an old-established, 'ever-present'; yet that career was not much more than five years old. His team's unbeaten record lasted only until the third game and defeat at Neath; but thereafter only Gloucester and Newport, with home advantage, lowered its colours. The captain's form was tremendous. He scored twice against Bristol. He opened the scoring against Newport with a brilliant single-handed try: 'showing infinite cleverness, dash and determination', wrote the Press. After his try in Cardiff's 3-3 draw at St Helen's a Swansea journalist observed, 'One opportunity seems to come his way in every match, and I cannot remember when he failed to use it. As a defender he is like a centre half in Association Football – always able to look after an attack that comes down the middle, in addition falling back and relieving threats on either right or left wing.'

The club's three quarter line performed superbly under Nicholls' guidance. Co-centre 'Pussy' Jones scored nine tries, while wing Huzzey was sent in eighteen times by the captain, who would total sixteen tries himself. Gloucestershire, the county of his birth, mindful of his Westbury roots chose him twice during the season in what seem to have been fairly pedestrian games – including a 0-0 draw with Devon.

In Wales, the nation was girding itself for the annual tussle with England, which would return to its traditional month, January, in 1899 and take place at Swansea. Although the Saeson led the series 11-3, and had been cruelly superior in 1898, Wales were steadily cultivating a 'David' mentality which told them that Goliaths were there to be overthrown.

The ever-strengthening hold exercised by the Game on the Welsh imagination was acknowledged in enhanced Press coverage and build-up. Distinguished scholars, usually content to pontificate in the columns of the popular Press on the origins of Celtic words and phrases, found them-selves spellbound by the new sporting magic gripping the south, and impelled to write about it. Such a figure was 'Morien', an Archdruid who contributed to the *Western Mail*. Here is his description of the media of the day in action at an International match: 'Behind me sat, ranged

327

along a long, narrow table, fifty or sixty journalists. Further back was a Grand Stand flanked on both sides by seething multitudes. On opposite sides of the field were solid rows of people forty lines deep and extending at least a distance of 200 yards... It was interesting to watch the army of nimble-fingered shorthand writers jotting down the incidents of the game. With raised face and pencils at the ready they all gazed with earnestness at the contending athletes as if a Waterloo were being fought before them.'

Back at the subs' tables the efforts of the location reporters were being ever more steadfastly supported by page designers and graphic artists. A *South Wales Daily News* chart portrayed a Rugby pitch with the thirty players' names printed in their positions.

Today's media may have made it more vivid, but the excitement and expectation that accompanies the start of Rugby's European championship season can scarcely be more intense in our own day than was the case a century ago. The air is full of threat and counter-threat, boast and counter-blast, and an all-pervading tension. Hope is dominant in the minds of players and spectators alike.

from *Prince Gwyn* (1999)

Rowe Harding

Reminiscences and Opinions

There is a typically Swansea man, a typically Cardiff man and a typically Newport man, but none of these is typically Welsh. On the other hand, the inhabitants of Neath and Llanelly are typically Welsh, and these are the only two Rugby towns of any size where the typical Welsh Rugby supporters may be found, and it is in a match between Neath and Llanelly that one gets an atmosphere more nearly approaching the atmosphere of an international match: beer and argument and betting and singing, and perhaps a free fight or two.

To English ears all this probably sounds rather disgusting, and I suppose it is impossible for an Englishman to see the Welshman's point of view as the Irishman is able to see it. The typical Welshman who goes to a football match is usually a small, sallow man, emotional, talkative and, if need be, abusive. He probably has a scarf of outrageously clashing colours, a cloth cap which accentuates the dead whiteness of a face which perhaps does not see daylight for forty-eight hours in the week, and if it is an international match he wears a leek of gigantic proportions, and smells of leeks and beer in about equal strength. He used to know Rugby better than any other spectator in the world, because he had been in the habit of seeing the best Rugby in the world, and his subtle, quick-witted brain saw the movements engineered and executed with a cunning which the less agile English mind could not appreciate. Nowadays, I am afraid, [1920s] the less agile English brain has at last devised a system of defence against which our three-quarters have squirmed and twisted in vain. Guile for the time being has been subdued by speed, and the Welsh supporter goes up to Twickenham complete with mascot and leeks, and cannot understand why England continues to beat us. I am confident that the reason will not elude him much longer. Some of the characteristics I have mentioned are not likeable ones: a taste for bizarre colours, beer and argument, allied to a national emblem of such strong-smelling properties, do not form a pleasant combination; but these are the results of an emotional, imaginative and ardent temperament which, if properly directed and controlled, would produce an artistic genius. These same Irish characteristics which, misdirected, make a drunken sot of an Irish navvy, make a genius of Sean O'Casey, and the outwardly unpleasant characteristics of the rude Welsh miner are merely the results of an uncontrolled emotionalism. In the rustic Englishman the characteristic phlegm of the best type of the Englishman becomes stupidity; in the Welshman characteristic buoyancy and fervour become noisy self-expression.

If anybody wants the full flavour of a Welsh international match, let him stand in the crowd on the cheap side of the field, forget all his prejudices about bad language, and listen to the drollery of the Welsh wits in the crowd. He will learn to tolerate the Welshman's faults and appreciate a type of humour which has no counterpart anywhere – it has a spontaneity and dry subtlety, a capacity for looking at things exactly as they are, which are, I think, unequalled by Cockney or Lancashireman. I shall always remember a conversation I heard in a London hotel between the Boots, who was a Cockney, and a somewhat squiffy Welshman. The Boots asked the Welshman if he came from Wales. He replied that he did. 'Then,' said the Boots, 'I suppose you know Morgan Hopkins, the butcher, from Wales.' The Welshman looked at him with sublime pity and said, 'Good God, do you think Wales is a bloody street, or what?' I must tell one story against the Welshman, lest it be thought that I am blind to all but his virtues. Two miners from a Monmouthshire village went up to London to see the English-Welsh match, and one of them who was slightly lame got lost in the crowd. His friend looked for him in vain for some time and then sought the aid of a policeman. 'Have you seen my butty, Will Evans?' he asked. The policeman replied that it was possible, but that he did not know him. 'Don't you know Will Evans?' was the astonished question. 'He's got a cap on, and he walks like this.'

... No ground except Newport presents such terror for a visiting team as Stradey when there is an important game, and more than one colonial team has had to bow before the fury of the Llanelly onslaught, urged on and encouraged by the fierce enthusiasm of the spectators. The Stradey atmosphere is worth ten points to the home team, and I know of no ground where the spectators exercise such an influence upon the players. No side ever won at Stradey without a terrific struggle, and, except Newport, no side has suffered defeat at home less often than the redoubtable Scarlets at Stradey Park since the war.

The history of Llanelly's post-war Rugby is bound up with the name of Albert Jenkins. Since the war Llanelly has produced many fine players, forwards and backs. Many of them have played for Wales, but the greatest of them is a puny figure compared with the gigantic rugby stature of Albert Jenkins. To my mind, he is the finest centre three-quarter I have ever seen, judged on his all-round excellence. Outside Wales, unfortunately, he is a myth, because for some reason, probably lack of support, he has never quite touched his best form in international matches. That is not to say that he never played a good international match. Some people say his best match was against Ireland at Cardiff in 1920, when he and Bryn Williams, his club partner, played so magnificently; but personally I consider his performance against Scotland at Swansea, in that famous match [1921] when the crowd broke on to the field, the best individual display I have ever seen. I am not forgetting Jerry Shea's wonderful achievement on the same ground against England in 1920, but he was great and a lucky player playing in a great side. Jenkins was playing a lone hand in a bad Welsh back division. In defence and attack alike he was magnificent. The length of his punting was phenomenal, his tackling was heroic, and more than once he cut across to hurl Sloan into the crowd, when that extremely fast Scottish wing seemed certain to score. At half-time Scotland led by eleven points to nil. In the second half the Welsh pack was beginning to exercise a dominance over the Scotch pack, and Wales were getting the ball. Jenkins made opening after opening only to see his efforts nullified by the ineptitude of his colleagues. Finding that victory by orthodox methods was hopeless, he took the game into his own hands, and in ten minutes he had dropped two goals, and narrowly missed dropping two more. Wales were now pressing on the Scotch line. It looked as though victory would be merely a matter of time, when the crowd broke on to the field again and the Scottish pack got a much needed breather. Almost immediately after the resumption Jenkins was hurt, and while he was off the field a Scottish movement, started in their own twenty-five, resulted in Sloan scoring a final try which decided the match; but Jenkins' game that day stands out in my memory as the finest piece of single-handed courage and skill I have ever seen.

No man was ever more completely equipped to be a great rugby centre three-quarter than Jenkins. He was of ideal build, five feet eight inches in height, with the chest and shoulders of a bullock, powerful thighs, and the trim, well-turned calf and ankles of a sprinter. His pace for thirty yards was terrific. I saw him overtake Lowe at Swansea when that fast runner seemed clear away. His punting, drop kicking and place-kicking were alike extraordinary, and he won game after game for Llanelly by the accuracy of his place-kicking or by an opportune dropped goal. His timing of swift, accurate passes was uncanny, and I never saw a man with such an instinct for doing exactly the right thing. His tackling was all-enveloping, but scrupulously fair, and he was a master of the art of running an entire three-quarter line into touch and smothering the helpless wing as he received the ball. The greatness of Llanelly from 1920 to 1929 was the greatness of Albert Jenkins, and the moral effect of his presence upon his own side was amazing. He was the keystone of the team, the whole structure seemed to be built around his powerful frame, and even when he was himself subdued the team seemed to draw inspiration from his presence. Llanelly players have told me that they felt a supreme confidence when Jenkins was playing, and a corresponding sense of insecurity when he was absent. Like all men of genius, he sometimes confounded his colleagues by his unorthodoxy, and he never got a partner who fully understood him after Bryn Williams went north. Personally, he is a quiet and taciturn man, and shows little evidence of that extreme quickness of thought and action which characterises him on the football field. The list of the truly great is a short one, but however exclusive that list, it will not be complete without the name of Albert Jenkins of Llanelly, tinplater and rugby footballer, a genius in his own sphere.

from *Rugby Reminiscences and Opinions* (1929)

Rhys Davies

Canute

As the great Saturday drew nearer most men asked each other: 'Going up for the International?' You had the impression that the place would be denuded of its entire male population, as in some archaic tribal war. Of course a few women too intended taking advantage, for other purposes, of the cheap excursion trains, though these hardy souls were not treated seriously, but rather as intruders in an entirely masculine rite. It was to be the eternal England versus Wales battle, the object now under dispute being a stitched leather egg containing an air-inflated bladder.

The special trains began to leave round about Friday

midnight, and thereafter, all through the night and until Saturday noon, these quaking, immensely long vehicles feverishly rushed back and forth between Wales and London. In black mining valleys, on rustic heights, in market towns and calm villages myriads of house doors opened during the course of the night and a man issued from an oblong of yellow light, a railway ticket replacing the old spear.

The contingent from Pleasant Row, a respectable road of houses leading up to a three-shafted coal-mine, came out from their dwellings into the gas-lit winter midnight more or less simultaneously. Wives stood in worried farewells in the doorways. Their men were setting out in the dead of night to an alien land, far away from this safe valley where little Twlldu nestled about its colliery and usually minded its own business.

'Now be careful you don't lose your head, Rowland!' fretted his wife on their doorstep. 'You take things quiet and behave yourself. Remember your trouble.' The 'trouble' was a hernia, the result of Rowland rescuing his neighbour, Dicky Corner House, from a fall of roof in the pit.

Rowland, grunting a repudiation of this anxiety, scuttled after a group of men in caps. 'Jawl,' shouted one, 'is that the whistle of the 'scursion train? Come on!' Out of the corner house ran Dicky, tying a white muffler round his neck. Weighted though they all were with bottles for the long journey, they shot forward dramatically, though the train was still well up the long valley.

The night was clear and crisp. Thousands of stars briskly gazed down, sleepless as the excited eyes of the excursion hordes thronging all the valley's little stations. Stopping every few minutes, the train slid past mines deserted by their workers and rows of houses where, mostly, only women and children remained. It was already full when it stopped at Twlldu, and, before it left, the smallest men were lying in the luggage-racks and sitting on the floor, placing their bottles safe. Some notorious passengers, clubbing together, had brought crates of flagons.

Dicky Corner House, who was squat and sturdy, kept close to Rowland, offering him cigarettes, or a swig out of his bottle and a beef sandwich. Ever since Rowland had rescued him he had felt bound to him in some way, especially as Rowland, who was not a hefty chap, had that hernia as a result. But Rowland felt no particular interest in Dicky; he had only done his duty by him in the pit. 'Got my own bottle and sandwiches,' he grunted. And, 'No, I am not feeling a draught.' The train rocked and groaned through the historic night. Some parts of it howled with song; in other parts bets were laid, cards played, and tales told of former Internationals.

Somewhere, perhaps guarded by armed warriors, the sacred egg lay waiting for the morrow. In its worship these myriads had left home and loved ones to brave the dangers of a foreign city. Situated in a grimy parish of that city, and going by the name of Paddington, the railway terminus began to receive the first drafts at about 4 a.m. Their arrival was welcomed by their own shouts, whistles and cries. From one compartment next to the Pleasant Row contingent a man had to be dragged out with his legs trailing limply behind him.

'Darro,' Rowland mumbled with some severity, 'he's

started early. Disgrace! Gives the 'scursionists a bad name.'

'Hi!' Dicky Corner House tried to hail a vanishing porter, 'where's the nearest public-house in London?'

'Pubs in London opened already, then?' asked Shoni Matt in wonder and respect, gazing at 4.30 on the station clock.

'Don't be daft, mun,' Ivor snarled, surly from lack of sleep. 'We got about seven hours to wait on our behinds.'

A pitchy black shrouded the great station. Many braved the strange dark and wandered out into it. But in warily peering groups. A watery dawn found their numbers increased in the main thoroughfares; early workers saw them reconnoitring like invaders sniffing out a strange land.

'Well, well,' said Rowland at ten o'clock, following his nose up the length of Nelson's Column, 'how did they get that man up there? And what for?'

'A fancy kind of chimney-stack it is,' Dicky declared, 'A big bakehouse is under us.' He asked yet another policeman – the fourth – what time the public-houses opened, but the answer was the same.

'Now, Dicky,' said Rowland, in a severe canting voice like a preacher, 'you go on behaving like that and very sorry I'll be that I rescued you that time. We have come here,' he added austerely, 'to see the International, not to drink. Plenty of beer in Wales.'

'I'm cold,' bleated Shoni Matt; 'I'm hungry; I'm sleepy.'

'Let's go in there!' said Gwyn Short Leg, and they all entered the National Gallery, seeing that Admission was Free.

It was the Velasquez 'Venus' that arrested their full attention. 'The artist,' observed Emlyn Chrysanthemums – he was called that because he was a prize grower of them

337

in a home-made glasshouse – 'was clever to make her turn her back on us. A bloke that knew what was tidy.'

'Still,' said Rowland, 'he ought to have thrown a towel or something across her, just by here... '

'Looking so alive it is,' Ivor breathed in admiration, 'you could smack it, just there...'

An attendant said, 'Do not touch the paintings,'

'What's the time?' Dicky Corner House asked the attendant.

'Are the pubs open yet?'

'A disgrace he is,' said Rowland sharply as the contingent went out. 'He ought to have stayed home.'

By then the streets were still more crowded with gazing strangers. Scotland had sent tam-o'-shantered men, the North and Midlands their crowds of tall and short men in caps, bowlers, with umbrellas and striped scarves, concertinas and whistles. There were ghostly-looking men who looked as if they had just risen from hospital beds; others were unshaven and still bore the aspect of running late for the train. Many women accompanied the English contingents, for the Englishman never escapes this. By noon the invaders seemed to have taken possession of the metropolis and, scenting their powerful majority, they became noisy and obstreperous, unlike the first furtive groups which had arrived before dawn. And for a short while a million beer taps flowed ceaselessly. But few of the visitors loitered to drink overmuch before the match. The evening was to come, when one could sit back released from the tremendous event.

At two-thirty, into a grey misty field surrounded by huge

walls of buzzing insects stickily massed together, fifteen red beetles and fifteen white beetles ambled forward on springy legs. To a great cry the sacred egg appeared. A whistle blew. The beetles wove a sharp pattern of movement, pursuing the egg with swift bounds and trim dance evolutions. Sometimes they became knotted over it as though in prayer. They worshipped the egg and yet they did not want it: as if it contained the secret of happiness, they pursued it, got it, and then threw it away. The sticky imprisoning walls heaved and roared; myriads of pin-point faces passed through agonies of horror and ecstasies of bliss. And from a great quantity of these faces came frenzied cries and urgings in a strange primitive language that no doubt gave added strength to the fifteen beetles who understood that language. It was not only the thirty below the walls who fought the battle.

The big clock's pallid face, which said it was a quarter to midnight, stared over the station like an amazed moon. Directly under it was a group of women who had arranged to meet their men there for the journey back. They looked worried and frightened.

And well they might. For surely they were standing in a gigantic hospital base adjacent to a bloody battlefield where a crushing defeat had been sustained. On the platforms casualties lay groaning or silently dazed; benches were packed with huddled men, limbs twitching, heads laid on neighbours' shoulders or clasped in hands between knees. Trolleys were heaped with what looked like the dead. Now and again an ambulance train crawled out packed to the doors. But still more men kept staggering into the station from the maw of an underground cavern and from the black foggy streets. Most of them looked exhausted, if not positively wounded, as from tremendous strife.

But not all of them. Despite groans of the incapacitated, grunting heaves of the sick, long solemn stares of the bemused helplessly waiting for some ministering angel to conduct them to a train, there was a singing. Valiant groups of men put their heads doggedly together and burst into heroic song. They belonged to a race that, whatever the cause, never ceases to sing, and those competent to judge declare this singing something to be greatly admired. Tonight, in this melancholy place at the low hour of midnight, these melodious cries made the spirit of man seem undefeated. Stricken figures on floors, benches and trolleys stirred a little, and far-gone faces flickered into momentary awareness. Others who still retained their faculties sufficiently to recognise home acquaintances shouted, embraced, hit each other, made excited turkey-cock enquiries as to the activities of the evening.

A youngish woman with parcels picked a zigzag way to under the clock and greeted another there. 'Seen my Glynne, have you?' she asked anxiously; 'I've been out to Cricklewood to visit my auntie. Who won the match?' she asked, glancing about her in fear.

'You can tell by the state of them, can't you!' frowned the other.

Another woman, with a heave of hostility, said, 'Though even if Wales had lost they'd drink just the same, to drown the disappointment, the old beasts. Look out!' The women scattered hastily from a figure who became detached from a knot of swaying men, made a blind plunge in their direction, and was sick.

'Where's the porters?' wailed one woman. 'There's no porters to be seen anywhere; they've all run home... Serve us right, we shouldn't have come with the men's 'scursion... I'm feeling ill, nowhere to sit, only men everywhere.'

Cap pushed back from his blue-marked miner's face, Matt Griffiths of Gelli bellowed a way up No. 1 platform. He was gallantly pulling a trolley heaped with bodies like immense dead cods. 'Where's the backwards 'scursion train for Gelli?' he shouted. 'Out of the way there! We got to go on the night-shift tomorrow.'

'The wonder is,' said a woman, fretful, 'that they can find their way to the station at all. But there, they're like dogs pointing their snouts towards home.'

Two theological students, solemn-clothed as crows, passed under the clock. They were in fierce converse and gesticulated dangerously with their flappy umbrellas. Yet they seemed oblivious of the carnal scenes around them; no doubt they were occupied with some knotty biblical matter. The huddled women looked at them with relief; here was safety. 'We'd better get in the same compartment as them,' one of them said to her friend; 'come on, Gwen, let's follow them. I expect they've been up for a conference or an exam.' Soon the two young preachers-to-be were being followed by quite a band of women though they remained unconscious of this flattering retinue.

'That reverse pass of Williams!' one of the students suddenly burst out, unable to contain himself, and

341

prancing forward in intoxicated delight. 'All the matches I've been to I've never seen anything like it! Makes you want to grab someone and dance ring-a-ring-o' roses.'

Elsewhere, an entwined group of young men sang *Mochyn Du* with an orderly sweetness in striking contrast to their mien; a flavour of pure green hills and neat little farmhouses was in their song about a black pig. On adjacent platforms other groups in that victorious concourse sang *Sospan Fach* and even a hymn. As someone said, if you shut your eyes you could fancy yourself in an eisteddfod.

But in the Gentlemen's Convenience under No. 1 platform no one would have fancied this. There an unusual thing had occurred – the drains had clogged. Men kept on descending the flight of steps only to find a sheet of water flooding the floor to a depth of several inches. They had to make-do with standing on the bottom steps, behind them an impatient block of others dangerously swaying.

And this was not all. Far within the deserted convenience one man was marooned over that sheet of water. He sat on the shoe shine throne which, resting on its dais, was raised safely – up to the present – above the water. With head lolling on his shoulder he sat fast asleep, at peace, comfortable in the full-sized armchair. Astonished remarks from the steps failed to reach him.

'Darro me,' exclaimed one man with a stare of respect across the waters, 'how did he get there? No sign of a boat.'

'Hoy,' another bawled over, 'what train you want to catch? You can't stay there all night.'

'Who does he think he is,' someone else exclaimed in an English voice – 'King Canute?'

342

The figure did not hear, though the head dreamily lolled forward an inch. Impatient men waiting on the crowded steps bawled to those in front to hurry up and make room. Soon the rumour that King Canute was sitting below passed among a lot of people on No. 1 platform. It was not long before someone – Sam Recitations it was, the Smoking Concert Elocutionist – arrived at the bottom step and recognised that the figure enthroned above the water was not King Canute at all.

'I'm hanged if it isn't Rowland from Pleasant Row!' he blew in astonishment. 'That's where he's got!... Rowland,' his chest rose as in a recitation, 'wake up, mun, wake up! Train is due out in ten minutes. Number 2 platform...'

Rowland did not hear even this well-known Twlldu voice. Sam, himself not in full possession of his faculties, gazed stupidly at the sheet of water. It looked deep; up to your calves. A chap would have soaking wet socks and shoes all the way back to Wales. And he was appearing at a club concert on Tuesday, reciting four ballads; couldn't afford to catch a cold. Suddenly he pushed his way through the exclaiming mob behind him, hastened recklessly through the platform mobs, reached No. 2 platform and began searching for the Pleasant Row contingent. They were sitting against a kiosk plunged in torpid thought. Sam had to shake two or three of them. 'I've seen him!' he rolled. 'Your Rowland! He isn't lost – he's down in the men's place under Number 1, and can't budge him. People calling him King Canute... '

They had lost him round about nine o'clock in crowded Trafalgar Square. There the visiting mob had got so

343

obstreperous that, as someone related later at a club in Twlldu, four roaring lions had been let loose and stood lashing their tails in fury against these invaders whose nation had won the match; and someone else said that for the first time in his life he had seen a policeman who wore spectacles. While singing was going on, and two or three cases of assault brewing, Rowland had vanished. From time to time the others had missed him, and Dicky Corner House asked many policemen if they had seen Rowland of Twlldu. Sam Recitations kept on urging them now. 'King Canute?' repeated Shoni Matt in a stupor. 'You shut up, Sam,' he added crossly; 'no time for recitations now.'

'He's down in the Gents under Number 1,' Sam howled despairingly. 'English strangers poking fun at him and water rising up! He'll be drowned same as when the Cambrian pit was flooded!' He beat his chest as if he was giving a ballad in a concert. 'Ten minutes and the train will be in! And poor Rowland sitting helpless and the water rising round him like on the sands of Dee!'

Far off a whistle blew. Someone near-by was singing Cwm Rhondda in a bass that must have won medals in its time. They shook themselves up from the platform, staring penetratingly at Sam, who was repeating information with wild emphasis. Six of them, all from Pleasant Row. Awareness seemed to flood them simultaneously, for suddenly they all surged away.

By dint of pushing and threatening cries they got down all together to the lower steps of the Convenience. Rowland had not moved in the shoe-shine throne. Still his head lolled in slumber as if he was sitting cosy by his fireside at home after a heavy shift in the pit, while the waters lapped the dais and a yellow light beat down on the isolated figure indifferent to its danger. They stared fearfully at the sheet of water.

'Shocking it is,' said Gwyn Short Leg, scandalised. 'All the Railway Company gone home, have they, and left the place like this?'

'In London too!' criticised Ivor, gazing below him in owlish distaste.

Then in one accord they bellowed, 'Hoy, Rowland, hoy!'

He did not stir. Not an eyelid. It was then that Shoni Matt turned to Dicky Corner House and just looked at him, like a judge. His gaze asked, 'Whose life had been saved by Rowland when that bit of roof had fallen in the pit?' Dicky, though he shivered, understood the long solemn look. 'Time to pay back now, Dicky,' the look added soberly.

Whimpering, Dicky tried to reach his shoe-laces, on the crowded steps. But the others urged excitedly: 'No time to take your shoes off. Hark, the train's coming in! Go on, boy. No swimming to do.'

Dicky, with a sudden dramatic cry, leapt into the water, foolishly splashing it up all round his legs. A pit-butty needed to be rescued! And with oblivious steps, encouraged by the applause of the others, he plunged across to the throne. He stepped on the dais and, being hefty, lifted Rowland across his shoulders without much bother. He staggered a bit as he stepped off the dais into the cruelly wet water.

'Careful now,' shouted Emlyn Chrysanthemums; 'don't drop him into the champagne.'

It was an heroic act that afterwards, in the club evenings, took precedence over tales of far more difficult rescues in the pits. Dicky reached the willing arms of the others without mishap. They took Rowland and bore him by his four limbs up the steps, down the platform and up the other, just as the incoming train was coming to a frightened standstill. After a battle they got into a compartment. Dicky took off his shoes, hung up his socks over the edge of the rack and wiped his feet and calves in the white muffler that had crossed his throat.

'Wet feet bad for the chest,' he said fussily.

All the returning trains reached the arms of Wales safely, and she folded the passengers into her fragrant breast with a pleased sigh of 'Well done, my sons'. The victory over her ancient enemy – it was six points to four – was a matter of great Sunday celebration when the men's clubs opened in the evening, these having a seven-day licence, whereas the ordinary public-houses, owing to the need to appease old dim gods, were not allowed to open on Sundays.

The members of the Pleasant Row contingent, like most others, stayed in bed all the morning. When they got up they related to their wives and children many of the sights and marvels of London. But some weeks had passed before Rowland's wife, a tidy woman who starched her aprons and was a great chapel-goer, said to him in perplexity, 'Why is it people are calling you Rowland Canute now?'

Only that evening, Gwyn Short Leg, stumping to the door on his way to the club, had bawled innocently into the passage, 'Coming down, Rowland Canute?' Up to lately Rowland had been one of those who, because he seemed to

346

have no peculiarity, had never earned a nickname.

'Oh,' Rowland told his wife, vaguely offhand, 'some fancy name or other it is they've begun calling me.'

'But a reason there must be for it,' she said inquisitively. 'Canute! Wasn't that some old king who sat on his throne beside the sea and dared the tide to come over him? A funny name to call you.'

'What you got in the oven for my supper?' he asked, scowling at the news in the evening paper...

from *Boy with a Trumpet* (1935)

Dannie Abse

Shouting and Swearing

These big rugby matches were great fun. The kind Welsh crowd would pass us down over their heads, hand by hand, laugh by laugh, right to the front. And then there would be a band playing and the fat man banging the fat drum. Tiddle-um, tiddle-um, tiddly um tum tum. Hoo-ray, Hoo-ray. And they sang the Welsh songs that floated sadly, but joyfully, into the air over Cardiff Arms Park, as little dark-headed men invaded the field in an attempt to climb the goalposts and hang there the all-important leek. There would be the ritual of the crowd shouting 'Boo' and 'Shame' when the policemen ejected the intense spectators from the holy pitch. The policemen knew they were unpopular. They tried to shoo the invading spectators away-with dignity, but the spectators ran round them towards the goal-post, jigging and dancing, putting their thumbs to their noses. What a laugh it was. Yet nobody succeeded in attaching the leek to the crossbar. As one of the men next to us said, 'The buggers have greased the poles.' England came out in their white shirts and the crowd clapped politely, but the real applause was reserved for the men in red shirts as they strutted out from the players' tunnel, cocky and clever. The roar subsided as the band played *Land of My Fathers*. Fifty thousand people… stood with their hats off at attention. When the National Anthems were over there was another roar. Somebody said, 'Jawch, England 'ave an 'efty team, much bigger than ours, mun.' The whistle blew, and soon after England scored. 'There seem to be two of theirs to one of ours,' the man with the wart said. Another remarked, 'In the old days Wales really had a team, not a bunch of students.' 'It's the referee,' added his companion. 'Look at that, offside if there ever was one.' At last Wales equalized. 'What a movement, what a movement,' said the man who had been talking of the old days. 'Just like in 1923 when …' Three spectators near us wore red shirts and banged silver, saucepans, urging the players to victory with screams of Llanelly encouragement and scathing criticisms. And we shouted too, oh how we shouted … When the noise was loudest we swore and nobody could hear us.

from *Ash on a Young Man's Sleeve* (1954)

Dylan Thomas

Enoch Davies and a stranger

... The Blue Bull, the Dragon, the Star of Wales, the Twll in the Wall, the Sour Grapes, the Shepherd's Arms, the Bells of Aberdovey: I had nothing to do in the whole, wild August world but remember the names where the outing stopped and keep an eye on the charabanc. And whenever it passed a public-house, Mr Weazley would cough like a billygoat and cry, 'Stop the bus, I'm dying of breath!' And back we would all have to go.

Closing time meant nothing to the members of that outing. Behind locked doors, they hymned and rumpused all the beautiful afternoon. And, when a policeman entered the Druid's Tap by the back door, and found them all choral with beer, 'Sssh!' said Noah Bowen, 'the pub is shut.'

'Where do you come from?' he said in his buttoned, blue voice.

They told him.

'I got a auntie there,' the policeman said. And very soon he was singing 'Asleep in the Deep'.

Off we drove again at last, the charabanc bouncing with tenors and flagons, and came to a river that rushed along among willows.

'Water!' they shouted.

'Porthcawl!' sang my uncle.

'Where's the donkeys?' said Mr Weazley.

And out they lurched, to paddle and whoop in the cool, white, winding water. Mr Franklyn, trying to polka on the slippery stones, fell in twice. 'Nothing is simple,' he said with dignity as he oozed up the bank.

'It's cold,' they cried.

'It's lovely!'

'It's smooth as a moth's nose!'

'It's better than Porthcawl!'

And dusk came down warm and gentle on thirty wild, wet, pickled, splashing men without a care in the world at the end of the world in the west of Wales. And, 'Who goes there?' called Will Sentry to a wild duck flying.

They stopped at the Hermit's Nest for a rum to keep out the cold, 'I played for Aberavon in 1898,' said a stranger to Enoch Davies.

'Liar,' said Enoch Davies.

'I can show you photos,' said the stranger.

'Forged,' said Enoch Davies.

'And I'll show you my cap at home.'

'Stolen.'

'I got friends to prove it,' the stranger said in a fury.

'Bribed,' said Enoch Davies.

On the way home, through the simmering moon-splashed dark, old O. Jones began to cook his supper on a primus stove in the middle of the charabanc. Mr Weazley coughed himself blue in the smoke. 'Stop the bus,' he cried, 'I'm dying of breath!' We all climbed down into the moonlight. There was not a public-house in sight. So they carried out the remaining cases, and the primus stove, and old O. Jones himself, and took them into a field, and sat down in a circle in the field and drank and sang while old O. Jones cooked sausage and

mash and the moon flew above us. And there I drifted to sleep
against my uncle's mountainous waistcoat, and, as I slept,
'Who goes there?' called out Will Sentry to the flying moon.

from 'A Story' in *A Prospect of the Sea* (1955)

Gwyn Thomas

Padded up for action

I've just emerged with a torn pelt from a furious faction
fight between supporters of rugby on the one hand and
soccer on the other. Until that meeting I had no idea of
what it would feel like to emerge at speed from a burning
kraal. Now I think I know.

Rugby, as played by the Welsh, is not a game. It is a tribal
mystery. This fancy for violent movement, for suddenly
scragging a fellow human who is trying to pass you,
probably goes back far into time. It might have been a
device to fool the Normans into thinking that we were
constantly mobilising for another round of playing it up
around Chepstow.

If the place had been flat, it would not have been so bad,
but time and again, in the deeper valleys, teams have
played on pitches with a slope of one in three, where they
take their half-time slice of lemon in an oxygen tent, and
have rubber barricades at the bottom of the ramp against
which players and referee can be bounced back into play
when they go hurtling down with their brakes burned out.

351

Strategic use was often made of these conditions. A visiting team would turn up at the changing room on a Saturday afternoon. The changing room was almost invariably a pub. Hospitality would be lavish.

A tidal wave of ale would hit the new arrivals, laced on high occasions with meat pies like cannon-balls. Then beer-logged and replete, the visitors would be led to the field. The road could well be a thousand feet of up-winding goat track, and committee men would course like corgis on the flanks of the convoy, keeping the glassy-eyed gladiators on course.

Up on the plateau, the referee would go around making sure that the players were facing in the right direction. When the massive bodies met in direct assault you could hear the glug two valleys away. When the fire of battle had been stoked to a maximum, and the referee had been crushed out of sight in a marshier section of the pitch, the committee would then nip in and remove the ball to save wear and tear.

Back in the pub there would be a specially darkened room for the handing back of limbs.

My own experience as a young rugby player was brief and rugged. My impulses as a sportsman were not dynamic. I did a little with a game called 'catty and dog', played by beating a short stick sharply with a long stick. I also made occasional appearances as a very casual cricketer, emerging as a bowler with a special line in balls that went in and off the gas-works container that overshadowed our minute pitch.

I also went in for a simple version of quoits played with stones and later taken over by a rockery tycoon.

But at grammar school I was singled out by a Rugby

Union dervish who had soccer and cricket tabbed in the same category as yaws. He had seen me once in spectacular flight from a wild dog. It was about my only burst of speed. Normally I move very slowly except when frightened at the prospect of rabies. The master told me that with my type of springy, bandy leg I could develop a body swerve that would fox even Interpol.

He foxed me. The school pitch was a kind of gravel and coke dump. If you took a series of falls (and the sensible ones took just one fall and then stayed down, groaning and quietly burrowing out of sight into the coke) you got up looking like a fuel briquette, and spent the following lesson winkling bits of coke out of the skin.

The field ended, on the school side, in a sharply sloping bank. Whenever I broke into a run I seemed to be within inches of this slope. As soon as I got the ball, the master would urge me loudly to use my natural body swerve. I would disappear over the bank, and genuinely glad of the trip.

There was only one player on the field more inept than myself. He was a monster of about 15 stone, who spent most of his time standing stock still in a corner, turning his head slowly and trying to figure the whole thing out.

One day when I was coming down the field at some speed, galvanised this time not by a rabid hound but by the coach – who was barking in a way that would have had Pasteur worried – I rammed the monster. He didn't budge. I went flat. And then, quite solemnly and without malice, he boarded me as if I were a bus. Honourably injured, I was allowed to go back to quoits and corrupting indolence.

The incident left me with nothing worse than a curious psychosomatic limp, which I am still able to summon when wishing to deepen perplexity or to explain my distrust of strenuous sport.

from *A Hatful of Humours* (1965)

Alan Watkins

Ups and downs of a climber

This week I propose to write the brief life of a rugby player, R. H. Lloyd-Davies. He came from my native village, Tycroes, Carmarthenshire, and was seven years older than I was. His full name was Rheinallt Lloyd Hughes Davies, but he was known locally as Hugh Lloyd Davies. The initials and the hyphen came later, for Hugh, despite his many outstanding qualities, was a bit of a climber. His family owned one of the two bus companies operating from the village, Tycroes being particularly well-endowed with this form of enterprise. Though the family were prosperous, they were not ostentatious or grand. His father worked as a conductor on the family buses to give himself an occupation.

Hugh, along with his brother and sister, attended the Amman Valley County (subsequently Grammar) School, Ammanford. When he went up to Cambridge later, and was asked where he had been at school, he would reply: 'Ammanford, actually', placing the accent on the second syllable. A peculiarity of his childhood was that he was brought up by his grandparents, who lived just down the road,

354

while his siblings remained with his parents. Anyway, it was said that Hugh was spoiled. He was, however, denied a bicycle. He was told that, as he could travel free on the buses at any time he liked, he did not need a bicycle.

As a sixth-former he had an affair with the French mistress. This was prosecuted vigorously during bouts of fire-watching, a duty which teachers and senior pupils were required to undertake. They married when he was in his early twenties. Hugh had always enjoyed (or suffered from) a sexual drive well above the average. Like most successful practitioners in this field, he was both bold and undiscriminating. He was also handsome, with pale, smooth skin, black curly hair that grew in a peak, very bright eyes and very white teeth. He possessed loads of charm. In drink, however, he could turn verbally vicious.

He was a fast, adventurous full-back, and a schoolboy international. From school he was conscripted into the RAF, where he soon became a pilot officer. He played in the great inter-service and representative matches at St Helen's, Swansea, and for Wales, first against New Zealand, the 1945 Kiwis, and then against England in the 1946 Victory International. In neither match were his experiences particularly happy. Against New Zealand he kicked the ball straight at J. R. Sherratt, who promptly scored. Against England another wing, R. H. Guest, evaded him to score two tries. Hugh resented the non-award of caps for this match, and kept claiming – what was morally true but factually incorrect – that he was a Welsh international. However, he confidently expected to be in the post-war side. But the selectors preferred Frank Trott of Cardiff, less spectacular but much safer.

From the RAF, Hugh went up to Trinity Hall, Cambridge, to read law. He won the university match of 1947 by kicking two penalties, six points to Oxford's nil. On the morning of the game he had been roused from a deep slumber by two friends, given a shower, dressed and poured on to the team coach. Shortly afterwards he was sent down from the university. He was in a pub, a proctor arrived, and ordered him to leave. The proctor, Trevor Thomas, was not only a law don at Hugh's college but came from Swansea. Hugh addressed him familiarly in Welsh, telling him not to be so silly. Thomas was not amused.

Nevertheless he joined Gray's Inn and played for London Welsh and Harlequins, where, he said, you met a better class of girl. Finding himself short of money, he joined Barrow – the first Cambridge Blue to go north. He was paid £1,000, played a couple of matches and then promptly decamped to Paris.

Returning to London, he had several encounters with the law, culminating in a nine months' prison sentence for attempting to pawn stolen jewellery. During the early 1950s, he was in Tycroes, doing odd labouring jobs. He then went back to London. There were reports of sightings. He was passing himself off as a colonel; had gone bald; was sleeping rough; was a gardener with the Islington council. A few months ago, I was told that he had died last year.

from *The Independent* 23 October 1987

J. P. W. Mallalieu

After the Singing, January 1953

There is a supreme moment in international rugby football; but it comes only once every two years. Sometimes it is one of hope, sometimes of fear; but always it is one of dedication. It flowed through me at 2.44 p.m. last Saturday. That moment comes at Cardiff Arms Park when, before the kick off, the Welsh and English teams stand stiffly facing each other and the Welsh crowd sings 'Land of My Fathers'.

That Welsh crowd will sing 'Land of My Fathers' against Ireland, Scotland and against France. But it sings best against England, for, against England, there are old scores to be paid off, scores which were notched against My Fathers long before rugby was first played. When England comes to Cardiff, the fathers of 'My Fathers' thunder from their graves that this beloved land is and always shall be, to Englishmen, foreign; and the thunder from the dead becomes mingled with the exuberance of the quick, the quick who earn their living in a foreign land but return to the land of their fathers on this one day, and find how wonderful it is. Maybe they are ashamed that they come home so seldom and wish to assert their nativity; maybe they are stirred by the warmth with which their families greet them at the station, a warmth so seemingly unbroken that they feel they have never been away. Whatever the cause, these Anglo-Welsh, home again for the match against England, sing with a fervour which their home-staying brothers can only try to emulate.

But of course neither subconscious politics nor conscious delight at being home alone accounts for the ecstatic solemnity with which 'Land of My Fathers' is sung at this biennial moment. rugby comes into it too. We think of the Welsh as people who can hew a bit of coal, pour a bit of steel or decant a bit of song. But in fact, before all these things, we ought to think of them as inspired players of rugby. Welshmen were made for Rugby. They have in them a blunt but insidious cunning which shuns the light of day, which is designed to work deviously underground and which is ideal for operations on the blind side of a tight scrum. They have that hot-blooded sense of kinship which sends them, unthinking, as a mass, against the enemy, and is just right for loose forward rushes; and they have that genius which, here and there, carries a singer or a poet beyond the stars and here and there evokes a Bleddyn Williams.

So when they sing, just before the kick-off, the Welsh crowd sing not only of past wrongs now to be righted, not only of home long lost but now found again, but also of the game which they know expresses their instincts, of the game which they know to be, peculiarly, theirs. Before the great moment arrives, there are many things to do and see and hear. There is the singing on the football special from Paddington. There is the moment outside Cardiff Station when brother meets brother and each is made awkward by overwhelming affection. There are jumping crackers to be thrown at the staid-looking policemen who, every fifteen yards, face the crowd from the greyhound racing-track which surrounds the field. There are leeks to be worn as emblems or used as missiles against the same staid-looking policemen;

and there are flags – red flags – to be planted in mid-field when for a moment these staid-looking policemen, with wide grins on their faces, turn aside on the pretence of attending to some duty or other. There are the loud-speaker announcements begging Mr Thomas of Pontypridd to return to work immediately or, even more hopelessly, imploring Mr Jones to meet Mr Williams out-side the ground at once; and there is the band, playing 'Cwm Rhondda' and 'Ebenezer tôn-y-botel' and 'Crimond' and 'Sospan Fach' and 'Onward Christian Soldiers' and 'I Can't Give You Anything But Love, Baby'. The Welsh crowd joins in all this, showing its independence by keeping one beat behind the band-master, but these are only working-up exercises in preparation for the supreme moment that is to come. Then at last the teams emerge, England in white jerseys, Wales in red, and there they stand while the crowd gives out its resentment of the past, its joy in the present and its hope for the future.

I wish that, at the end of that moment on Saturday, I could have left the ground. But unhappily I stayed on and saw Welsh Rugby below its best. England won this match by eight points to three, and Englishmen like myself had several things to cheer. There was, for example, that glorious first try by Cannell after a burst of passing and a run by Bazley. There was that glorious screwing kick from the touchline with which England's captain, Hall, converted this try. In the second half there was that forty-five-yard penalty goal kicked by Woodward. But Wales had only one thing to cheer, and that was the performance of their young National Service full-back, T. E. Davies, playing his first international.

Some 3,000 men, women and children live in Davies'

village. From that village there were 1,800 applications for tickets for this match as soon as Davies' selection was known. Only 200 applications were granted, but those who had to stay outside at least knew that young Davies would be in good hands. That Welsh crowd, all 56,000 of it, looked after Davies as a mother looks after her child. His first job was to take a penalty kick for touch. As he received the ball, he was given a great cheer and when he kicked it safely to touch he was given an ovation. Then, with his first international cap only ten minutes old, he was given a chance to kick a penalty goal from forty yards out. As he ran to take the kick someone near me sneezed. Fifty-six thousand other people at once said, 'Hush!' The kick failed; but four minutes later, from the same position, Davies tried again and the ball sailed effortlessly, gracefully between the posts and the world exploded. But that was the end of Welsh cheers. What followed was not tragic – for nothing forseeable and inevitable is ever really tragic. What followed was just sad.

Of all the golden lads in rugby football the one who has shone brightest in my eye has been Bleddyn Williams. He could see openings when no openings seemed there. He could sidle, or jink or glide through a forest of opponents without touching one tree. He could flash to the left, taking all his opponents with him; then flash to the right leaving all his opponents behind. For ninety minutes he was unruffled grace, and all I could wish to see. But on Saturday he was no more. Except just once. With ten minutes to go for time, and England leading by eight points to three, the ball came to Bleddyn on the half-way line, and suddenly Bleddyn became what he used to be. A shake of one hip, a twist of one shoulder, and his immediate opponent was grasping the January air while Bleddyn was wisping himself towards the England line.

On the twenty-five line he passed to Thomas who drew the fullback and passed to Ken Jones. Ken Jones can run as fast on a rugby field as he can when on the track he is sprinting in the Olympic Games. He has an experienced head – for this was his twenty-seventh consecutive appearance for Wales. But as Thomas's perfect pass came to him, Ken Jones lifted that experienced head, dropped the pass, and gave away a certain try and all hope of victory. I could have cried. Thousands of Welshmen did, not from bitterness, but just from sadness that this one last flash from their golden lad could not have brought one last glorious triumph before the post-war glory of Welsh rugger crumbled to dust.

I look back now to that moment at 2.44pm when silence and stillness pervaded the field, when the bandmaster raised his baton and the crowd began to sing. I wish then that when the last notes had died away we could have converted the cricket notice 'No further play. Rain' into 'No further singing. Rugby' and left it at that.

from *Rugby Football: an anthology* (1958)

John Morgan

Wales v New Zealand 1953

This was what we had come for, the myth-in-action, the men in scarlet and the men in black, prancing from under the stands on to the field of Welsh praise, now standing at attention for our National Anthem, our noise too great to be heard except when the wind swirls suddenly back from the wide, high stands, the sound of a passionate affirmation that at the back of every Welsh mind lives a blind patriotism, uncaged only for rugby internationals, for the only battles Wales has fought alone for centuries.

The 'excursion' from Swansea had been full; flagons were bandied about. We all knew what we were talking about. We named the team which had beaten the Newsy-landers in 1905, and were told by the asthmatical old man in the corner, who said he had seen the game, as every old man says he saw the game, how Dr. Morgan had scored the only try. We couldn't name the team which was beaten in 1924, but we could name the winning 1935 team. Hadn't we all heard the B.B.C. broadcast last night? The excerpt from the recordings of the game? The pontiffs pontificating; the centre three-quarters earnest and nearly word-perfect at their scripts? We recited the great names – Bancroft of the very old days, Nicholls, Gabe, Owen of the golden days, Wooller, Davey, Tanner, Willie Davies, Cliff Jones. They are names of the light and air of rugby; not, oddly, of the vicious in-fighting, the massive heave and crack of bone in the scrummage. A fan, about fourteen years old, produced a print of an old photograph. It was

362

the 1905 Welsh team, solemn men, all looking much older than they must have been at the time. We passed it round the compartment, we discussed prospects. We all thought it a pity in a way that the Newsy-landers had lost to Cardiff, and a shame in a way that they couldn't beat Swansea. We wanted it as it had been in 1905 when only Wales beat New Zealand. We wanted to curl up in the historic precedent. We all thought the Welsh backs would be better than the enemy's. We shook our heads over the forwards. 'Oh,' said the fourteen-year-old, 'Oh, I hope it'll be a memorable game.'

Before the game began, the crowd swayed behind me and I fought against the swell. I missed the kick-off. My first clear and honest memory of the 1953 game is of a line-out in the shadow of a grandstand, the only shadow on the sunlit ground. Two years ago I stood in almost the same place and was crushed against a crush-barrier. It was the day Wales lost to South Africa, and an old man standing a yard in front of me had been taken ill, overwhelmed by the heat and the stench, and had been lifted up by the crowd and passed, overhead, to the touch-line, hand to hand, being sick all the way.

The hallucination, no matter how hard you fight it, is total; if we didn't want it to be, we wouldn't be here. These men are heroes. That tall, athletic young man is a student; that short, black-haired, wild-eyed, vital man is a salesman, his partner a company director; the burly, incredibly energetic man is a boiler-maker; the well-built, surprised-looking man now placing the ball on the ground near a white line is a school-teacher; that slim, young man who is going to kick the ball in a moment is a doctor; that tall, older-

363

looking man over there, with a streak of grey in his hair, is a Justice of the Peace. A middle-class bunch? One of the ways of becoming middle-class in Wales is to play for a big rugby club. There are certainly few manual workers in the team but there are many sons of manual workers, the Grammar school boys. There are also sons of the bourgeoisie. (Look on the programme for the men with three initials.) The crowd look, as an Englishman once told me, like a soccer crowd. Not here the tweedy, bescarved, sun-burned hearties, the pretty, healthy girls – they are Stand-people, not Field-people. Here are the blue-suited or brown-suited men, off the peg, who know what it's all about, this game, and didn't learn it at a Public school. A characteristic Welsh ground has steelworks at one end and a ribbed, overhanging mountain the other; the banks are coal-tips and the stands are made of zinc; the spectators are as ready to boo as to cheer. Playing the game doesn't mean exactly the same thing.

Something has gone wrong. The Welsh lead disappears. The Newsy-landers are ahead and we have nothing to shout, a lot to be quiet about, a quiet that can be heard all over Cardiff. New Zealand camp, as they say, on the Welsh line, a brawling, hectic camp, under tents of massive men, with one sentry more than any other, the Welsh fly-half, Cliff Morgan, running and kicking and tackling, the smallest man, one of the most intense and talented rugby players ever seen. Griffiths, the young centre-three-quarter, leaves the field, injured. The quiet is profound. The players' shouts echo back from the stands and the massed heads that have turned to stone. But New Zealand seem unable to score and gradually we all realise that this refusal by our side to allow a score is, in its way, heroic and memorable. Griffiths comes back on to the field and immediately runs, confidently, elegantly, through the New Zealand defence and rouses us all. Wales score. Ten minutes to play and the scores level. Where I am becomes a jostling, mauling, howling place. I am kicked behind the knee. People are throwing other people's hats in the air. The crowd sways and fights bitterly against the sway. The Welsh team have gone wild, perhaps because we have gone wild. The noise must impel them like a great gale. Cliff Morgan avoids Clarke again. The Newsy-landers are tired. He kicks towards the corner-flag. Elsom of New Zealand catches it but Rowlands tackles him. Oh, Rowlands! Thomas picks up the ball. He's in touch. No. Yes. He's not. Oh, what's he up to, kicking across the field like that. There's no one there. But there is – Ken Jones, Olympic sprinter. He's caught the ball. He's run around the full-back. He's going to score. He scores and we've won. Five minutes to play, and we've won, and Jones has become immortal with a try.

from *The New Statesman* 2 January, 1954

Richard Burton

The Last Time I Played Rugby

It's difficult for me to know where to start with rugby. I come from a fanatically rugby-conscious Welsh miner's family, I know so much about it, have read so much about it, have heard with delight so many massive lies and stupendous exaggerations about it, and have contributed my own fair share, and five of my six brothers played it, one with some distinction, and I mean I even knew a Welsh woman from

365

Taibach who before a home match at Aberavon would drop goals from around forty yards with either foot to entertain the crowd, and her name, I remember, was Annie Mort and she wore sturdy shoes, the kind one reads about in books as 'sensible', though the recipient of a kick from one of Annie's shoes would have been not so much sensible as insensible, and I even knew a chap called Five-Cush Cannon who won the sixth replay of a cup final (the previous five encounters, having ended with the scores 0-0, 0-0, 0-0, 0-0, 0-0 including extra time) by throwing the ball over the bar from a scrum ten yards out in a deep fog and claiming a dropped goal. And getting it. What's more I knew people like a one-armed inside half – he'd lost an arm in the First World War – who played with murderous brilliance for Cwmavon for years when I was a boy. He was particularly adept, this one, at stopping a forward bursting through from the line-out with a shattering iron-hard thrust from his stump as he pulled him on to it with the other. He also used the mis-placed sympathy of innocent visiting players who didn't go at him with the same delivery as they would against a two-armed man, as a ploy to lure them on to concussion and other organic damage. They learned quickly, or were told after the match when they had recovered sufficiently from Jimmy's ministrations to be able to understand the spoken word, that going easy on Jimmy-One-Arm was first cousin to stepping into a grave and waiting for the shovels to start. A great many people who played unwarily against Jimmy died unexpectedly in their early forties. They were lowered solemnly into the grave slow version of 'Sospan Fach'. They say that the conductor at these affairs was noticeably one-armed but that could be exaggeration again.

As I said, it's difficult for me to know the end. The last shall be first, as it is said, so I'll tell you about the last match I ever played in.

I had played the game representatively from the age of ten until those who employed me in my profession, which is that of an actor, insisted that I was a bad insurance risk against certain dread teams in dead-end valleys who would have little respect, no respect, or outright disrespect for what I was pleased to call my face. What if I were unfortunate enough to be on the deck in the middle of a loose maul... they murmured in dollar accents? Since my face was already internationally known and since I was paid, perhaps overpaid, vast sums of money for its ravaged presentation they, the money men, expressed a desire to keep it that way. Apart from wanting to preserve my natural beauty, it would affect continuity they said, if my nose was straight on Friday in the medium shot and was bent towards my left ear on Monday for the close-up. Millions of panting fans from Tokyo to Tonmawr would be puzzled, they said. So to this day there is a clause in my contracts that forbids me from flying my own plane, skiing and playing the game of rugby football, the inference being that it would be all right to wrestle with a Bengal tiger five thousand miles away, but not to play against, shall we say, Pontypool at home. I decided that they had some valid arguments after my last game.

It was played against a village whose name is known only to its inhabitants and crippled masochists drooling quietly in kitchen corners, a mining village with all the natural beauty of the valleys of the moon, and just as welcoming, with a team composed almost entirely of colliers. I hadn't played for four or five years but was fairly fit, I thought, and the opposition was bottom of the third class and reasonably beatable. Except, of course on their home ground. I should have thought of that. I should have called to mind that this was the kind of team where, towards the end of the match, you kept your bus ticking over near the touchline in case you won and had to run for your life.

I wasn't particularly nervous before the match until, though I was disguised with a skull-cap and everyone had been sworn to secrecy, I heard a voice from the other team asking *'Le ma'r blydi film star 'ma?'* (Where's the bloody film star here?) as we were running on to the field. My cover, as they say in spy stories, was already blown and trouble was to be my shadow (there was none from the sun since there was no sun – it was said in fact that the sun hadn't shone there since 1929) and the end of my career the shadow of my shadow for the next eighty minutes or so. It was a mistaken game for me to play. I survived it with nothing broken except my spirit, the attitude of the opposition being unquestionably summed up in simple words like 'Never mind the bloody ball, where's the bloody actor?' Words easily understood by all.

Among other things I was playing Hamlet at that time at the Old Vic but for the next few performances after that match I was compelled to play him as if he were Richard the Third. The punishment I took had been innocently compounded by a paragraph in a book of reminiscence by Bleddyn Williams with whom I had played on and off (mostly off) in the RAF. On page thirty-seven of that volume Mr Williams is kind enough to suggest that I had distinct possibilities as a player were it not for the lure of tinsel and paint and money and fame and so on. Incidentally, one of the curious phenomena of my library is that when you take out Bleddyn's autobiography from the shelves it automatically opens at the very page mentioned above. Friends have often remarked on this and wondered afresh at the wizardry of the Welsh. It is in fact the only notice I have ever kept.

Anyway, this little snippet from the great Bleddyn's book was widely publicized and some years later by the time I played that last game had entered into the uncertain realms of folk legend and was deeply embedded in the subconscious of the sub-Welshmen I submitted myself to that cruel after-noon. They weren't playing with chips on their shoulders, they were simply sceptical about page thirty-seven.

I didn't realize that I was there to prove anything until too late. And I couldn't. And didn't. I mean prove anything. And I'm still a bit testy about it. Though I was working like a dog at the Vic playing Hamlet, Coriolanus, Caliban, The Bastard in 'King John', and Toby Belch, it wasn't the right kind of training for these great knotted gnarled things from the burning bowels of the earth. In my teens I had lived precariously on the lip of first-class rugby by virtue of knowing every trick in the canon, evil and otherwise, by being a bad bad loser, but chiefly, and perhaps only, because I was very nippy off the mark. I was 5ft $10^{1}/_{2}$ ins in height in bare feet and weighed, soaking wet, no more than $12^{1}/_{2}$ stone, and since I played in the pack, usually at open side wing-forward and since I played against genuinely big men it therefore followed that I had to be galvanically quick to move from inertia. When faced with bigger and faster forwards, I was doomed. R. T. Evans of Newport, Wales and the Universe for instance – a racy $14^{1}/_{2}$ stone and 6ft $1^{1}/_{2}$ ins in height – was a nightmare to play against and shaming to play with, both of which agonies I suffered a lot, mostly thank God, the latter lesser cauchemar. Genuine class of course doesn't need size though sometimes I forgot this. Once I played rather condescendingly against a Cambridge college and noted that my opposite number seemed to be shorter than I was and in rugby togs looked like a schoolboy compared with Ike Owen, Bob Evans or W. I. D. Elliot. However this blond stripling gave me a terrible time. He was faster and harder and wordlessly ruthless, and it was no consolation to find out his name afterwards because it meant nothing at the time. He has forgotten me but I haven't forgotten him. This anonymity was called Steele-Bodger and a more onomatopoeic name for its owner would be hard to find. He was, I promise you, steel and he did, I give you my word, bodger. Say his name through clenched teeth and you'll see what I mean. I am very glad to say that I have never seen him since except from the safety of the stands.

In this match, this last match played against troglodytes, burned to the bone by the fury of their work, bow-legged and embittered because they weren't playing for or hadn't played for and would never play for Cardiff or Swansea or Neath or Aberavon, men who smiled seldom and when they did it was like scalpels, trained to the last ounce by slashing and hacking away neurotically at the frightened coal face for $7^{1}/_{2}$ hours a day, stalactitic, tree-rooted, carved out of granite by a rough and ready sledge hammer and clinker, against these hard volumes of which I was the

370

soft-cover paper-back edition. I discovered some truths very soon. I discovered just after the first scrum for instance that it was time I ran for the bus and not for their outside-half. He had red hair, a blue-white face and no chin. Standing up straight his hands were loosely on a level with his calves and when the ball and I arrived exultantly together at his stock-still body, a perfect set-up you would say, and when I realized that I was supine and he was lazily kicking the ball into touch I realized that I had forgotten that trying to intimidate a feller like that was like trying to cow a mandrill, and that he had all the graceful willowy-give and sapling-bend of stressed concrete.

That was only the outside-half.

From then on I was elbowed, gouged, dug, planted, raked, hoed, kicked a great deal, sandwiched and once humiliatingly taken from behind with nobody in front of me when I had nothing to do but run fifteen yards to score. Once, coming down from going up for the ball in a line-out, the other wing-forward – a veteran of at least fifty with grey hair – chose to go up as I was coming down if you'll forgive this tautological syntax. Then I was down and he was up and to insult the injury he generously helped me up from being down and pushed me in a shambling run towards my own try-line with a blood-curdling endearment in the Welsh tongue since during all these preceding ups and downs his unthinkable team had scored and my presence was necessary behind the posts as they were about to attempt the conversion.

I knew almost at once and appallingly that the speed, such as it had been, had ended and only the memory lingered on, and that tackling Olivia De Havilland and Lana Turner and Claire Bloom was not quite the same thing as tackling those Wills and Dais, those Twms and Dicks.

The thing to do I told myself with desperate cunning was to keep alive, and the way to do that was to keep out of the way. This is generally possible to do when you know you're out-classed, without everybody knowing, but in this case it wasn't possible to do because everybody was very knowing indeed. Sometimes in a lament for my lost youth (I was about 28) I roughed it up as well as I could but it is discouraging to put the violent elbow into the tempting rib when your prescience tells you that what is about to be broken is not the titillating rib but your pusillanimous pathetic elbow. After being gardened, mown and rolled a little more, I gave that up, asked the Captain of our team if he didn't think it would be a better idea to hide me deeper in the pack. I had often, I reminded him, played right prop, my neck was strong and my right arm had held its own with most. He gave me a long look, a trifle pitying perhaps but orders were given and in I went to the maelstrom and now the real suffering began. Their prop with whom I was to share cheek and jowl for the next eternity, didn't believe in razor blades since he grew them on his chin and shaved me thoroughly for the rest of the game taking most of my skin in the process, delicacy not being his strong point. He used his prodigious left arm to paralyse mine and pull my head within an inch or two of the earth, then rolled my head around his, first taking my ear between his fore-finger and thumb, humming 'Rock of Ages' under his breath. By the end of the game my face was as red as the setting sun and the same shape. Sometimes, to vary the thing a bit, he rolled his head on what little neck he had around, under and around again my helpless head. I stuck it out because there was nothing else to do which is why on Monday night in the Waterloo Road I played the Dane looking like a Swede with my head permanently on one side and my right arm in an imaginary sling intermittently crooked and cramped with occasional severe shakes and involuntary shivers as of one with palsy. I suppose to the connoisseurs of Hamlets it was a departure from your traditional Prince but it wasn't strictly what the actor playing the part had in mind. A melancholy Dane he was though. Melancholy he most certainly was.

from *Touchdown* (1970)

Emyr Humphreys

Post-match analysis

Packed tight between the south stand and the car-park the crowd oozed good-humouredly towards the Westgate Street gates. Collectively it was digesting the game like a good meal. Wales had played with resolution and the necessary flashes of brilliance and they had won by two converted tries to a penalty goal. Eruptions of laughter and shouting from groups whose enthusiasm was still unspent caused some to turn their heads in the hope of extracting the last drops of pleasure from the expiring occasion. The wave of movement halted. There was a solid block of humanity at

373

the gate, all facing east, several thousand necks protected by collars and scarves against the stiff breeze that had kept the rain off for the duration of the match. It was possible to squint upwards and wonder how much lower the clouds could sink before the rain fell; but impossible to pull a hand out of a coat pocket and bend an elbow to insert the stem of a pipe between the teeth. Friends who had not stuck close together from the moment they moved from their position in the stands or the enclosures would not see each other again, unless they had made prior arrangements to meet at precise rendezvous and at precise times. More than a couple of yards apart and the faint illusion of controlling your own destinies dissolved completely.

Individuals were no more than corpuscles, obedient in the stream that controlled and conditioned their immediate existence. The skin and clothing in which each was wrapped served to emphasise their unity: as if they had been made up in a factory into shapes that gave the maximum cohesion.

Professor Amos, Doctor Hudson and Gwilym Tist were wedged together contentedly enough but beyond talking. (In such a crowd, at such a juncture, it is often easier to talk to a stranger than a friend.) Amos was the tallest. He looked ahead shrewdly but in fact saw little more than a further expanse of heads sprouting densely in the width of road beyond the gates. The professor's curly grey hair fluttered freely in the breeze and seemed a badge of his hardy open-air outlook and pursuits. Tist was a young lawyer who appeared regularly on television. He was so well wrapped and pale he could have been in disguise for this public occasion. He was also a parliamentary candidate who hoped to speak for the claims of Wales in the ranks of the Labour Party and he made it his business to look calmly patient. Doctor Hudson was a frail middle-aged scholar, a reader in Comparative Religion. Professor Amos looked down on him with brotherly concern. He called Dr Hudson 'Huddy' and addressed him in the familiar but friendly manner he always felt compelled to adopt when on a visit to Cardiff.

All three were members of an advisory council which tended to meet in Cardiff on dates that coincided with important rugby football occasions. Usually it was Professor Amos who would call out under 'any other business' – Mr Chairman, before you come to the date of our next meeting, may I point out that the French match takes place on Saturday the twenty-sixth! In the capital city! and then there would be laughter and winking among the council members around the long table as they fingered the thin pages of their pocket diaries. At first Dr Hudson had been unaware of the significance of these jokes. He had gazed absently at his colleagues over the top of his reading glasses and then hurried away to catch his train....

The crowd began to move again, inching its way nearer to the gate. Helmets of policemen appeared, bobbing up and down like upturned boats moored on a narrowly limited horizon. Suddenly, out on the street, the crowd broke. The Professor placed himself in front of Dr Hudson and they were swept along towards the Angel Hotel. When it was at last possible to stop, the professor stopped and turned around. 'Where's Tist? Where's Gwilym Tist?'

He sounded fussed and anxious. Dr Hudson looked down at the toes of his boots and smiled. Most of the things the professor said and did seemed to give him a mild form of amusement. 'Don't tell me we've lost him?'

Inexplicably Gwilym Tist was ahead of them. Out in the Cowbridge Road, in the centre of an oasis of unpopulated road surface, the well-wrapped figure beckoned them to join him.

'Academics!' he said. 'Out of training both of you. Come on now while the going's good.'

'Not the back bar of the Park for God's sake,' Professor Amos said. 'It's full of boys and girls in college scarves who look too young to be there.'

'Couldn't we have a cup of tea somewhere?'

Dr Hudson's slow North Wales accent sounded even more tentative than usual.

'Come on Huddy! In the interest of science. You've got to carry out your researches into the Ritual unto the bitter end. 'Bitter' end. That's good GT. Did you hear that? The 'bitter' end.'

They hurried down the street, hopping on and off the pavement to avoid people, and keeping Gwilym Tist in sight. He turned to wave them on and then dived into a side street. When they caught up with him he was already in conversation with the manager of the steak-bar who had kept a corner for Mr Tist and party as promised.

'What it is to have influential friends,' Professor Amos said.

He was rubbing his hands and sniffing the smell of meat cooking on a grill in the far corner of the long room.

'Soft lights and sweet music!'

Professor Amos nudged Dr Hudson.

'Make a note of this Huddy. Just the place to bring one of those birds of yours.'

Dr Hudson winked at Gwilym Tist who smiled indulgently. Pints of bitter appeared on the table as if by magic. 'I can't drink one of these,' Dr Hudson said. 'Good for your kidneys,' Amos said.

He drank down more than half his tankard in deep grateful gulps. 'Now then. Now then Huddy boy, what about your impressions?'

'Impressions of what?'

'Oh for God's sake man. Here you are. Just been taken to your first rugby international. First ever. Now then. What have you got to say about it?'

'It was very interesting.'

'Interesting! Interesting! I'll tell you something Huddy. You are a complete mystery to me. What about all that stuff you were regurgitating after lunch about the nature of crowds?'

'I've forgotten what it was I said...'

Again Hudson winked slyly at Gwilym Tist. The professor waved his hand as if he were feeding a reluctant student in a seminar.

'What kind of a crowd was it to begin with? Tribal? Religious? Power-directed? Destructive? Constructive?'

'I know one thing,' Gwilym Tist said. 'I wished I'd stayed at home and watched it on television.'

'Gwilym!'

Professor Amos sounded horrified.

'You're getting soft man. A boy of your age. It's disgusting.'

'Seriously. I hardly saw anything of the first half. And my knees were cold. And I'm fed up with being washed in a sea of nostalgic song. You're quite right. I am soft. Sad, isn't it?'

'It was a good crowd.'

Dr Hudson made the statement solemnly.

'Shush! The oracle is speaking. That's the trouble with these North Wales wizards. You have to wait so long before they pronounce. Look at this.'

His knife was already in his hand as he pointed at the garnished steak which had been placed before him.

'They're laying this on for you, Gwil. All out to impress you, eh? The TV star!'

He nudged Dr Hudson.

'I hope you realise, Huddy, we're living in GT's reflected glory.'

'I'm afraid we got them their licence. It was quite a battle.'

Gwilym Tist looked around the interior and shook his head sadly.

'The owners don't have too good a reputation.'

Professor Amos chewed hard at his steak.

'The bubble reputation...'

'I'm afraid you have very few illusions if you work in a law firm.'

Dr Hudson was staring apprehensively at the size of the steak on his plate.

'There's far too much here for me you know. I eat very little meat.'

'Scruples?'

The professor was chewing hard at his mouthful.

'Most over-rated dish in the world, I'd say,' Gwilym Tist said. 'It's just a great big tasteless cult for retarded adolescents. Really now, I mean it.'

'Well, on behalf of the retarded adolescents may I say this is very good? Get some beer down you, boy,' the professor said. 'The world will look better then. Don't you know Wales has just scored a famous victory?'

Gwilym Tist lifted his glass in a silent toast. They ate and drank, enjoying their meal after two hours in the open air. Amos unbuttoned his waistcoat and spoke appreciatively of the comfort and the good food. It was the middle of the meal before he remembered to press Dr Hudson once again for his view of the match.

'It's an impressive sight,' Dr Hudson said. 'The green arena. The stands and terraces packed with eighty thousand people. The entire population of my county. And thirty young gladiators in peak of fitness, ready to do battle.'

'Ready to set right Wales's ancient wrongs, eh? Ready to pulverise the oppressor. Ready for the sweet scent of victory.'

Dr Hudson shook his head.

'No. It wasn't that. What impressed me was the longing in the stands for a vanished youth. That was one thing. Rows and rows of grey-haired men with red faces from drinking, smoking and overeating, reliving an idealised youth, identifying with the young heroes in the arena. To see that collectively, that was interesting. I would have thought that was the core of the cult really.'

'Beating England, man. Or anybody. All comers...'

'No.'

Dr Hudson pushed shreds of meat out of his top teeth with the tip of his tongue.

'No. Not winning. Avoiding losing. Avoiding failure.'

'What's the difference?'

'There is a difference. Not losing means avoiding failure. Avoiding the common fate. Analogous to postponing death. This is why the ritual is not really religious. And not so much sublimated warfare either. It's probably more sexual.'

'Oh-oh, here we go.'

Dr Hudson frowned as he chewed. He was thinking aloud.

'I suppose the sources of aggression are the same. I shall have to give it rather more thought. But you asked me for my impressions. It was interesting. Of course I didn't understand the finer points of the game. It's quite complicated really. But of course that would be part of the pattern. Make it difficult. The testing of the hero. A mythological category.'

'Comedown to our level, now,' the professor said. 'What did you like about it?'

'That thing you called the 'Garryowen',' Dr Hudson said.

He smiled and with an unstraightened finger prescribed an uncertain parabola in the air.

'The old 'Up and Under',' Professor Amos said.

He became consciously daring.

'Well that's sexual if you like.'

He laughed noisily and Dr Hudson, with his eyebrows raised to acknowledge the unexpected validity of the point, nodded sagely.

'The hero is subjected to certain tests and trials. Like the labours of Hercules and so on.'

380

'Now there was a hooker for you!'

The professor's face flushed convivially. Three helpings of fresh fruit salad and cream appeared before them. The professor smacked his lips and Dr Hudson looked pleased.

'I eat a lot of fruit,' he said.

from 'The Hero' in *Natives* (1968)

Phil Melling

Billy Boston

Wiganers have had a long affair with overseas wingers. They have loved their style: Springbok, Aboriginal, African, Welsh. A scan of the team lists of the 1950s and 1960s is most revealing with almost every continent, bar Asia, represented in rugby league. This seemed to suit Boston's personality and made him feel at home. It reminded him, perhaps, of the world he had left behind, the ethnic communities he had mixed with in Tiger Bay, the interracial atmosphere that drew him as a youth to the Cardiff International Athletic Club.

In the 1950s the CIACS were a cosmopolitan side formed in the heart of Cardiff's dockland with a huge range of players from many backgrounds: Greeks, Italians, Maltese, Arabs. According to Billy, they were a motley crew in coloured shirts but they helped break down ethnic barriers and gave him some of his happiest moments on a rugby field. Many of the CIACS players, like Johnny Freeman and Colin Dixon, also went North and had glittering careers at

Halifax and Salford. While these players were not entirely free of prejudice in rugby league, the prejudice they did encounter tended to come from overseas; occasionally from New Zealand, and more especially in South Africa, where, on the 1957 tour, Boston was the victim of a colour bar.

If the streets of Wigan were uniformly white in the 1950s its rugby fields were not. Yet in its own way Wigan replicated the close-knit community of Tiger Bay and the raucous warmth of its streets, where Bill had been friendly with Joe Erskine and Shirley Bassey. In Ince, Wallgate, Whelley and Scholes, Billy could enter once again a tight, labyrinthine world of back-to-backs, Irish communities and rugby lovers in their pubs and in clubs like Wigan St Patricks. Martin Ryan, second only to Sullivan as Wigan's greatest full-back, is convinced that the protective, communal environment of a place like Wigan, with its extended family structure, was an ideal breeding ground for the hard school of rugby. 'It bred loyalty,' says Ryan, 'and whatever the drawbacks and the deprivation, it gave you the character to play a physical contact sport.' 'The team I played in after the war was just like a family,' he adds. 'We relied on each other; shared our grief as well as our grub.' Ted Ward who played with Ryan, also made the same point when I met him in Garnant in the late 1970s. 'Our trainer was a farmer, Frank Barton. After the war rationing was still on and Frank used to give us a side of pig to share out after training.' Billy and Ted Ward felt at home in Wigan. The CIACS motto: UNIS ET IDEM, one and the same, went North with them.

The real problem for those who stress [Ellery] Hanley's

382

limitations has nothing to do with his nonconformity on the field, and the people who are critical of him know this as well as anyone. The real problem with Hanley, is that, unlike Boston, he did not play like a Wiganer nor did he act like one. Hanley was considered by some to be anti-social and ill-mannered, his behaviour a kind of implied critique of the relationship that Billy accepted between player and fan. To them, he was too self-regarding, which is why he had to leave Wigan, or wanted to leave Wigan, before his time was up. Billy became part of the family, while Hanley was a loner with an iron will. You could see it, say his critics, in the way Hanley followed play around... in the way he took the last pass.

Whether or not it was a weakness, Billy Boston managed to resist the last pass; he could leave it alone. He did what was needed, and he was more than willing to share his tries with his centre partner, Eric Ashton. Hanley appeared to snub Wigan; he seemed unwilling to let the town love him, when all it wanted was to box him up and stroke him like a pet. Hanley was too cool for all that. He was an 80s man. He had Thatcherite values whereas Billy was old Labour – game for an outing on the St Pat's 'away' coach – Ellery Hanley played for Wigan. Billy Boston became Wigan. Boston brings to mind Garrison Keillor's Lake Wobegon's code from his novel *Wobegon Boy*: 'Do your job, don't tell lies, don't imagine you're exceptional even if you are, be glad for what you have done, don't feel sorry for yourself.' Once in Australia, in 1954, Billy let rip: 'I wish Australians wouldn't make such a damned fuss of me', he said. 'I've been lucky. I've got a long way to go. I've got the tries. But they were laid on for me by better players than I am. I hope the Australians will drop this attitude of wanting a spectacular show from me every time I play.' Jack Winstanley, Billy's biographer, makes the point clearly: 'Billy had a nice smile. He liked kids. He had a great degree of humility about him. That's why he was asked to open church bazaars and crown rose queens. Wiganers took to Billy Boston.'

In 1996 a joy-rider hit Billy Boston outside his home in Poolstock. Billy suffered serious leg injuries. Sentencing the young offender the magistrate placed him under a curfew order. 'I'm doing this for your own good,' he said. 'There are people out there who are very unhappy with what you've done. If there's one person you don't knock down in Wigan, it's Mr Boston.' Billy, who was inundated with flowers and get-well cards, was in hospital for a few weeks. The car was a write-off.

from *Heart and Soul* (1998)

John Morgan

Excursion Train, 1955

The rain eased last night five minutes before the excursion train to Scotland for the Welsh Rugby match was due out of Swansea. The men who had been pretending they were waiting for the rain to ease ran from the ex-international's pub across the station yard swinging their flagons or carrying their crates like soldiers rushing ammunition to the guns. In the hallway an undergraduate stood holding a bunch of delicately wrapped leeks, looking very much like a man waiting for his mistress in a sensitive British film, but not talking like one. He had lost his ticket.

After a man had rushed through our crowded Pullman car shouting 'Moses, Moses, where are you Moses?' we settled down quietly for the twelve-hour journey through the night. Young men played cards for fun. In another car a frail middle-aged man with his false teeth on the table in front of him joined in singing 'I Believe', obviously not knowing the words. When 'Calon Lân' began he put his teeth back in his mouth. In the mixed car – the girls being of most ages – there was some shouting and a bonhomie so humid that, transmuted, it trickled down the window panes.

Two men, both over seventy years of age, at my table, after establishing that they had a mutual acquaintance of preachers and minor bards, began a recondite philological discussion in Welsh. The man in the grey suit and brilliant white collar, his face scrubbed until it shone had postulated this argument: some Englishmen and some renegades say that Welsh is a dead language because it borrows from the English. Well then, what about telephone? 'What about telephone indeed,' said his new friend, the man in the navy blue suit and striped flannel shirt.

'Telephone is from the Greek.'

'Those Greeks were a brilliant lot.'

'What is the English for telephone?'

'Ask you may.'

'Telephone!'

While they considered this point the man in the white collar offered me a Minto and his friend offered a Cymro

385

Mint. I accepted both and offered a swig from my flagon. 'Strict T.T.,' they said.

'There is no 'th' in the Welsh alphabet,' said the white-collared man.

'You are quite right,' said the other.

'In Ireland they spell the word telephone with an 'f'. Now then.'

I left them to their discussion and their bags of sweets and moved down the train where men were arranged to sleep in remarkable postures. I settled myself down as some town passed by in the darkness and the rain. A stranger offered me a Scotch to drink and talked about opera until he suddenly fell asleep when explaining to me the plot of Don Giovanni. Sometime around five o'clock the familiar cry of a Welsh woman calling her friend sounded through the compartment. Marie was the friend's name. The sound was more like a cockerel crowing in a quiet valley at dawn than anything else.

A young man was pounding the table and shouting, 'I'll never leave Wales again.' He had been ill all through the night. At another table a freshly shaved man was drinking beer out of a pint pot, eating last night's sandwiches, and reading about Formosa. The lady found her friend; the boy gave up pounding; the car became very quiet.

What does a man do when he arrives on a bitterly cold winter's morning in Edinburgh before dawn? He trails, hot sand in his eyes, in the train of tradition. He hands his bag through the luggage hatch and helps two solemn-faced jokers to lift their crate of Guinness into the same place. He then walks up Princes Street to Scott's Memorial, warms at a brazier, turns about and walks back in the dawn to a restaurant that opens at seven.

'Would you find this in Swansea? Would you find this in Cardiff?' demands a Welshman gone native. He has been here before and knows about this restaurant and is proud of that.

A man eats two breakfasts and reads what the native experts have to say about the match. He notes that the Scots have taken to trusting in miracles.

It is then time to gawk at the Firth of Forth bridge, be restored by the first breezes and to ride back through the countryside into a city awake and alive with Welshmen. We join up with compatriots who have been in Edinburgh two or three days, and walk the streets and the shops staring at everything and listening to the people who actually speak with a Scotch accent as they do in the films.

Most of us have either scarlet berets or scarlet and white scarves, or leeks or daffodils. Some have all these things and also carry saucepans. Everyone is tremendously polite and cheerful. Even the rain stops and the sun shines. People in the know tell us that we must be at Murrayfield by two o'clock if we want a good view of Scotland being trodden into her own turf. And while, of course, we all feel sorry for poor Scotland, we don't feel all that sorry. 'Have a good journey up?' asks a man selling views of the Castle. 'Quiet,' says a customer.

'A very quiet journey, but God help us to-night if we win,' he pauses. 'Or especially if we lose.'

from *The Observer* 5 February 1955

Gwyn Thomas

The Great Shrine

Cardiff is a city of the most inexplicable draughts. Around the General Station in particular, a family of winds has got itself stuck and there has been no one to show them the way out. They reproduce in their tempo and sound the tumultuous anxieties of the travellers inside the station.

It is quite a place, that main terminal in Cardiff. South Wales has been one of the classic lands of emigration. If a South Walian wants to look at his motherland he has to keep turning, for his brothers are everywhere. And it is on the platforms of Cardiff General that the shattered heart reassembles. One could not count the number of times one has seen two or more Welshmen come out of their train, and as they hurry on to the next stage of their journey, one hears them shout, 'See you in Cardiff the day of the match. In the Park, the Queen's, the Grand, the Royal.' Or whatever bar or cinema front takes their fancy.

Cardiff is the settled Zion of the Welsh Israelites. A face you may have glimpsed in Maerdy, Ammanford, Treharris, Blaencwm, and thought never on this earth to see again, be sure that one winter's afternoon it will come again into view in the swift river of people that flows down Quay Street towards the gates of the Arms Park.

The Arms Park is the great shrine. The memories of the great games that have been played there have been worn as smooth as pebbles by every talking group in the taverns and clubs of the region. They have become, for many, a sort of ritual incantation which has come close to ousting the theological and political jousts of yesteryear. Men who were not born at the time will come to blows over who scored the try that beat the All Blacks in 1905. The only person in the nook who was really there says nothing. After thirty years of recounting the epic he shut up for good in 1935.

If you have that over-forty feeling and are quietly dusting your policies, come and stand in a capacity crowd at the Arms Park when they sing one of the great hymns. The sadder the hymns the better, because that allows the boys to dig deep for their harmonies. It is typical of us that if the hospitality is lavish, we are often married and buried to the rhythm of the same superb graveside chants. At the Arms Park it is like being caught up in some mighty natural force; it gives you a taste of what it must have been like to be caught up in the fierce, hypnotic frenzies of tribalism.

Even notoriously discourteous spectators, whose banter has peeled the paint off the old stand, have been so over-whelmed by this experience they have gone through the entire match glassy-eyed and opening their mouths only to advise the referee to wear longer knicks when the colder weather comes. But our choral tradition is crumbling some-what. The vast anthems of yearning melancholy are often displaced by flimsier tunes, and the folk on the two-bob bank, being chilled, sing to a brisker measure than the cosier choristers in the stands, and the first group can often be well into the third verse when the rearguard is still edging its way out of the overture. This, in so vocally conscious an area, is going to cause some heavy neuroses. But even now, on form, the lads can blow a hole in heaven and reduce a complete military band to the status of a solitary fifer on an upland.

from *A Welsh Eye* (1964)

Alun Richards

Fly-Half

'You're drinking!' she said, 'My God...'

'Oh, for goodness sake, I just met some people.'

'Have you seen what you look like this morning? Your eyes? Well, you should have seen yourself when you came in last night? A man your age. You weren't just squiffy, you were paralytic. Simply dreadful. It took the Under-Manager and a porter to carry you up the stairs.'

'It didn't?' He was small and chubby, run to fat now, pear-shaped and pink, and his sharp, pale little eyes narrowed with concern as he looked at her, immaculate in white shorts and tennis shirt, her rather severe face and pointed features browned by the sun, her hair still thick and lustrous, her shape good, still youthful, that detached, untouchable air of the well groomed woman remaining with her even in the casual clothes which she wore on holiday. She remained a Miss Muffet in appearance even though they had been married for seven years. There was still something pristine about her, and trying to alter her had exhausted him. If it could have been done at all, it should have been a younger man, he thought. The seven years between them was too much. And now she was getting waspish. It wouldn't be long until she did it before other people like the other one. Neither of his marriages had quite worked out as he'd hoped, but perhaps that was because he hadn't enough to give them. He wasn't blaming anyone and he wasn't complaining. The fact was, he'd had his moment and his time, and he'd doubted if she'd understand either. He never spoke about it anymore. He'd have to say something though, if she went on in that vein. Her voice... God save him from ageing head prefects.

But in the event, he controlled himself.

'Steady... Play it close to the chest now, boys. Keep it tight first half.' What a hell of a night it had been though! 'Sospan Fach' in Portuguese... What about that?

'They had to carry you up the stairs,' she continued. 'The lift wasn't working and they had to manhandle you. Where were you? You weren't in that place again? Not with that disgusting lecher, the dirty joke person? Not him? Not in that bar?'

'It came on to rain,' he said. He didn't seem to have the energy to make up good excuses any more.

'Can't you understand that they're just hangers-on in that bar? I'll bet you paid for every drink.'

'I didn't, I...' but he'd really filled his boots, he remembered, and now a pain like a marble seemed to roll down his intestine.

'Every drink! Only you haven't got the sense to see it. I'm sure they laugh at you behind your back anyway. They take one look at what's coming, and just know they're on a good thing. Well, be your age. There are fifty-two weeks in the year and we're just over here for two.'

'They're rugby men.'

'Rugby men?' That again, she thought. 'They're any kind

of men you want them to be, provided you're paying.'

'Where's the Alka-Seltzer?'

'By your bed.'

'Have you got a spoon?'

'Can't you do anything for yourself?'

'There's no need to be like that,' he said.

But there was every need, she thought. It was more than just another night out with the boys this time, it was their annual holiday, and she hadn't come abroad just to have a repetition of what went on at home, his finding exactly the same kind of places and people as those with whom he normally cavorted on his night out. It was absurd to think of having a night out on your own when you were on holiday with your wife anyway. What was wrong with wives as part of the human species? But to be fair, it hadn't begun like that this time. She'd wanted to see some pottery in a display they were putting on in the hotel, and then she'd taken coffee with some women who were staying there and he'd said he was going to take a stroll down to the village. But the stroll meant another visit to a Tavern and a session, and he was on the tiles again, her husband.

That was how it started, a little thing like that, but the trouble was, as she well knew, she was the second wife, and being the second wife, she had to cope with the impossible as far as she was concerned, his memory of the first wife who as the years had slipped by had become a hallowed figure in his mind, she was sure. He had that capacity for romanticising the past and although he checked himself from actually mentioning her name now, in his private thoughts it was still Lil this, Lil that, Esme was sure. Even the difference between their two names was chalk and cheese. Lil was valleys and Esme was Cardiff, a Tory Lord Mayor's daughter and that again was part of the problem, one of the many things which stood between them. The other was that she had not known him in his heyday, for he was something very special then, she was given to understand, and indeed, people who had known him, men now in their late forties, spoke of him as a special being whose darting heels and will-of-the-wisp figure had made him the idol of the crowds. For he was that rarest of beings, a much capped Welsh fly-half, one of the greatest according to journalists who kept bringing up his name in their columns, a man to be put amongst the immortals, Trew, Willie Davies, the two Cliffs, and head and shoulders above the recent crop, even 'King' John who did other things better, but could not beat a man off either foot and shirked a physical game. He sneaked through anyway like a thief in the night, but her husband could beat a man openly and make him look a fool. It was this beating a man off either foot which was apparently important. In thirty years only two men could do that, one was Bleddyn, and the other was her husband and that was something according to the connoisseur. He had an eye for an opening, and more important than anything else, absolute confidence, a wicked acceleration over twenty yards, and a wonderful pair of hands. He had once sold a dummy which deceived even the referee who blew up for a forward pass and could not then reverse the decision, or so the legend ran.

People who knew went on for hours and hours in this vein, and at first, she was not averse to listening. She had played games at school herself, and she thought physical elegance an excellent thing in itself. But that was in school. She did not think it reasonable that a prowess at games should haunt you all your life, but rugby was not a game where they lived, it was a religion, and a Calvinist religion at that. She went with him occasionally to internationals, and listening to the roar at the Arms Park and watching the seething faces beside her, she had felt rather sorry for the All Blacks until they started a little bit of this and that, to use his phrase, but that only made them more like the others, in her book. But for their jerseys they were indistinguishable from the Welsh side as human beings, and if people looked at her as if she had committed treason when she said things like that, she did not care. It was no longer a joke and it had got past the point of irritation. The game, the past, his continual wallowing in it, aided and abetted by everybody he seemed to meet even here in Portugal, added up to a kind of cancer which she wished she could exorcise.

But she couldn't.

from *Dai Country* (1973)

Dai Smith and Gareth Williams

Cliff Morgan

The succession [in 1951] of William Benjamin Cleaver by Clifford Isaac Morgan as Triple Crown fly-half confirmed a long-held suspicion that, years ago, one of the lost tribes of Israel had somehow wandered into South Wales. Cliff always played with the passionate urgency of a man trying to get out again. With the ball held at arm's length in front of him, his tongue out almost as far, his bow legs pumping like pistons, eyes rolling, nostrils flaring, and a range of facial expressions seldom seen north of Milan – either at the opera house or the soccer stadium – the dark-haired, Celtically-constructed, perky Morgan was, at 5 foot 7 inches and 12 stone, the identikit Welsh outside-half. But no-one could have assembled Cliff; he was an amalgam of the social and cultural forces that had shaped modern Wales and of the currents that were defining Welshness anew in the second half of the twentieth century. Cliff came from Trebanog, a precipitous offshoot of the Rhondda, on whose windy ridge people clung together for warmth and safety lest the storms of the world blew them away; he would never lose a sense of this induced Welsh, almost cosy, togetherness. His was the Welshness of a nonconformist home where Mam ruled and Sunday was for chapel, which meant that Cliff was humming snatches of oratorio before he was out of the shawl. The rugby crowds of the 1950s – strong, now, on 'Blaenwern', 'I bob un', 'We'll keep a Welcome', and 'The Holy City' ('… lift up your gates, and sing') – were the last of the harmonious generations brought up on choir practice and the Band of Hope. If there had been room on the terraces to dance then the incessant rain of the fifties would have completed a mass Welsh imitation of the era's favourite Hollywood musical; and if that international crowd could have managed something from the *Messiah* – as, in the fifties, sections of it still could – the chorus best calculated to inspire Cliff Morgan would have been 'Let us break their bonds asunder'. It might have been written with him specifically in mind – South Wales is liberally endowed with Handels – for Cliff's india-rubber face typified the unbelievable springiness of his whole body: a favourite ruse of his for evading the clutches of opponents who had managed actually to lay hands on him was to go limp in their embrace; then, as the tackler momentarily relaxed his grip, Cliff jumped out of the tackle with an agility that made Harry Houdini look arthritic, and scurried away.

Born in 1930, Cliff had gone to Tonyrefail G. S. and came under the sensitive care of sportsmaster E. R. Gribble. It was 'Ned' Gribble who in 1956 would lead a W.S.S.R.U. party – with Alan Rees (Glanafan G. S.) and Clive Rowlands (Ystradgynlais G. S.) at half-back – to South Africa, where it won seven of its eight matches. His reputation as a rugby mentor was established by his nurturing of the effervescent genius of the boy Morgan, whom he guided to international schoolboy honours just after the war. It was not only the joys of rugby that Cliff discovered in school, but his own Welsh identity. Writing on the occasion of the Urdd Jubilee Match (Gêm y Dathlu), played, to celebrate the fiftieth anniversary of its founding, at the National Ground in April 1972, where both teams were selected by two other former Urdd members and international fly-halves, Carwyn James and Barry John – it was 'The King's' last appearance and he left as a lingering memory a ghostly fifty-yard solo try – Cliff Morgan recalled what Urdd Gobaith Cymru (the Welsh League of Youth) had done for him. 'It was around the age of 11 or 12 that I became a member of the Urdd at Tonyrefail Grammar School. D. J. Williams ran a flourishing branch with a variety of activities. Visits by Dr Iorwerth

Peate, the doyen of Folk Life Studies, Cliff Jones, the Welsh rugby international, a trio from University College, Cardiff, and a Folk Group from Pontlottyn. We had dances and discussions, Noson Lawen and Mabolgampau [sports]. But it wasn't until I went to the Urdd camp at Llangrannog about 1945 or 6 that I really felt a sense of Welshness and of belonging. It's easy to fall in love with Llangrannog with its beaches and the green-blue sea...' Cliff had fallen in love with a Welshness that was, culturally and geographically, distinct from the one he knew in his native Rhondda. His reinforced sense of identity reflected a muted national awareness of broken links that rumbled off-stage during the 1950s. Lacking the sharp edges, the readiness to defy authority and challenge power structures that became features of Welsh political and language movements in the sixties and seventies, the mini-nationalism of the fifties – the Parliament for Wales movement led by Lady Megan Lloyd George, ex-Liberal and Labour M.P. for Carmarthen from 1957 to 1966, and S. O. Davies, Labour and then Independent Labour M.P. for Merthyr from 1934 to 1972; the Welsh Schools movement that made inroads into anglicized Glamorgan (though, as late as 1951, most Welsh speakers still lived there); the campaign for the formal recognition of Cardiff as Wales's capital city – was most agreeably personified on the rugby field by Cliff Morgan.

His international career – he played his first home game for Cardiff at nineteen against Oxford University in October 1949 – extended from the drawn match with Ireland in 1951 to the historic 16-6 defeat by France at Cardiff in 1958. During the course of his twenty-nine-cap career he

397

adjusted his play to the changing requirements of those years. By instinct an attacking player of unquenchable spirit, he played his finest running game for Wales in 1952 against Ireland. His most memorable Welsh try was also against Ireland in 1955 when a generally lifeless game was transformed in its last quarter when Wales suddenly ran up 18 points in as many minutes to turn a 3-3 stalemate into a 21-3 demolition job. The points avalanche included one furiously individualistic try by the Trebanog terrier as he tore into a thicket of defenders, got lost, and shot out the other side and over the line. But there was more to his game than just pyrotechnics. Though sometimes as unpredictable as a jackie-jumper, he generally jumped with a purpose. He spent his whole rugby career working endlessly for an extra half yard of space; when he failed to pierce the defence himself, his pass often did, and he gave a masterly exposition of his skill as distributor, as well as dodger, in partnership with England's Jeff Butterfield in South Africa in 1955, when his pass in itself often put that gifted centre into the gap. From that year on, he revealed extra qualities as tactical kicker and tireless coverer. In 1958, his creativity increasingly at the mercy of tighter back-row defences and ruthless midfield marking, he harnessed the notorious Twickenham swirl and dominated the match tactically to earn an injury-hit Wales a 3-all draw by kicking cleverly and insistently to the right-hand corner in the lee of the west stand. Beneath the lilting voice and warm personality there was a decisive streak that later took him to the Head of BBC Outside Broadcasting. In the scarlet jersey he learned decisiveness the hard way. Against

Ireland, on his debut, he faced Jack Kyle. He was rightly apprehensive of the Irishman's reputation, but as the game progressed and Kyle seemed reluctant to do anything much, Morgan allowed his attention to flicker. Kyle sensed it and was suddenly past him for a crucial, equalising score...

from *Fields of Praise* (1980)

J. B. G. Thomas

South Africa v. British Isles 1955

Conditions were perfect when Ernie Michie and his pipes led the Lions out on to the beautifully green springy turf, closely followed by Stephen Fry and his green-and-gold-jersied Springboks. The sun shone brilliantly and again I wondered what the five most important South African officials, the selectors, were doing sitting on the touchline!... There seemed to be hundreds of cameramen, two ballboys and ambulance men ready for the off when Ralph Burmeister put his whistle to his lips. Pheep... and the great match was on!

Cameron kicked to the left touchline and the Springboks' forward allowed the ball to roll into touch. Soon Basie Van Wyk was away and then Phil Davies brought down Vollenhoven, but the Springboks attacked strongly. Sinclair short-punted and Retief was nearly over before Gentles went away in menacing style from a scrum. It was a case of the Lions back on their heels, defending bravely, and when Van der Schyff essayed a drop at goal the Springboks were rampant. Luckily the ball sailed wide and the Lions countered with a good attacking movement – which saw Tony O'Reilly move with speed and power up the touchline. He was stopped by a bunch of players and hurled into touch thirty yards out on the right. From the throw-in Rhys Williams jumped to gather cleanly, half turn and drop a quick pass into the safe hands of waiting Dickie Jeeps. Out went the ball to Cliff Morgan, who drew his man and handed on to Phil Davies running hard and straight. Phil got through between Des Sinclair and Vollenhoven and handed on a pass to Jeff Butterfield, a little behind the Northampton man.

Jeff put his right arm behind and scooped the ball into his side and while running at full speed brought it to his front. When challenged by Van der Schyff, Jeff timed an accurate pass to Cecil Pedlow, who ran hard to dive over in the left corner. A good try and a good start to the Test. Angus Cameron failed to convert but his kick was not too far off the target. Unfortunately three minutes later, after a quarter of an hour's play, the Lions went down into a loose maul and Jimmy Greenwood in his eagerness to get the ball back played it with his hands and Van der Schyff had no difficulty in landing a lovely 40-yard goal. This levelled the scores but the Springboks took the lead when three minutes later, at another loose maul, nearer to their line, the Lions were penalized and Van der Schyff raised tumultuous cheers as he kicked his second goal.

Chances came the way of the Lions but Angus Cameron and Cecil Pedlow both fell short with long-range penalty attempts, and Angus just failed with a long high drop at a penalty goal. Then came a real thrill as Cecil Pedlow intercepted just inside the Springboks' half and raced towards the left touchline in a bid to get through the closing gap between the touchline and Van der Schyff. We thought in the Press Box that he would get clear before Van der Schyff launched his tackle and Pedlow crashed to the ground. Back came the Springboks and after 30 minutes' play went further into the lead. Heeling from a scrum 20 yards from the Lions' line and half-way out on the right, Fry broke wide as Gentles gathered the ball and set off round the blind-side. The move was so well timed as to flavour of a prearranged plan, and when Gentles was challenged Fry was ready to accept the pass outside while running between Gentles and right-wing Briers.

Fry took his pass and drew his man before sending Briers away, for the wing to swerve inside Cliff Morgan and dive over for a fine try. Van der Schyff landed a lovely goal and the Springboks were well in the lead. Vivian Jenkins murmured to me, 'We're in trouble now, boy!' and I almost agreed when suddenly I saw Cliff Morgan streaking away for the outside gap and immediately the pulse quickened, for it was the first time the little Welsh wizard had really gone on his own. He made a half-break before handing on to Phil Davies, who straightened the line immediately and cleverly put an over-head pass to Tony O'Reilly. As usual it took several players to stop Tony outside the line and all three rolled into touch temporarily winded or dazed!

No try, but a sign of the shape of things to come. Cliff Morgan had tested the Springbok midfield defence and found it wanting, and so from the next scrum near the centre of the field Cliff set off again to his right and making the half-break handed on the ball. Butterfield, with hands holding the ball out in front of him, swerved outside his man and then straightening up to catch the defence moving across him on the wrong foot, he veered inside Van der Schyff beautifully and was away beneath the posts for a great try. Angus Cameron had no difficulty in converting and the Lions were well in the match again and raring to go for more points, but the referee's whistle went and the interval brought relief for many folk, not forgetting two anxious Welshmen in the Press Box! Trying to remain neutral with the Lions in trouble was not easy, but the closing minutes of the first half had proved a timely reviver, and there was hope for better things to come. We were not disappointed!

The Lions attacked from the restart and Tony O'Reilly was bundled into the corner flag after being sent away by Phil Davies. Tony thought he had scored, as did the referee who stood on the goal-line and pointed to the line of conversion, but the South African touch judge was waving his flag and the referee changed his mind to call for a line-out. While jumping in this line-out Reg Higgins further injured his right knee and had to leave the field, this time for good. A scrum followed and the ball was whipped out to Cliff Morgan, who shot away like a rocket, half-hesitated as if to check and deceive the defence, and then away outside his man and through a bunch of coverers to leave his old enemy Basie Van Wyk standing as he crossed the line to touch-down near the posts. It was a brilliant try and just what the Lions needed at the time; after Angus Cameron had kicked an easy goal the Lions were in the lead.

Having captured the initiative the Lions reacted quickly, particularly the seven forwards, who enjoyed an inspired spell to gain valuable possession of the ball for their try-hungry backs. The whole side rose magnificently to the occasion as Robin Thompson called for an all-out effort. It was now or never, as the Springboks appeared to suffer reaction. First Morgan kicked a high punt down the blind-side of a scrum to catch Van der Schyff well away from the right touchline. He raced across but the ball bounced awkwardly back across him and Tony O'Reilly was up to gather and race for the corner. Near the line he was overwhelmed by weight of superior numbers and fell just short of his objective, but the ever-ready Jim Greenwood was up, and deftly playing the loose ball with his foot gathered to dive over for a try. This was intelligent thinking and Angus Cameron landed a beautiful goal to put the Lions well in the lead.

Van der Schyff was short with a 6-yard attempt at a penalty goal before the Lions attacked again. Jim Greenwood gathered in the loose and kicked on down the right touchline to worry Van der Schyff once more. The full-back mistimed the ball and Tony O'Reilly was up to kick on smartly, before scooping up the ball majestically and crashing over the line for a good try. Angus Cameron made a nice cradle for the ball and banged it over with admirable style and accuracy to leave the Lions 12 points in the lead.

The seven Lions' forwards, with the Welsh front-row packing and hooking magnificently, the second-row shoving and binding like six men, and the flankers putting their shoulders into the scrum, like voor-trekkers pushing their ox wagons out of the mud, held their own. The question uppermost in our minds in the Press Box was – How long would the Lions seven last against the Springbok eight? Van der Schyff went short with a penalty and there followed a long maul on the far side of the field between the half-way line and the Lions' 25. Finally the referee blew up for proper scrum and the Springboks heeled smartly for Gentles to break wide to open side and then shape as to find touch near the blind-side corner on the Lions' line. Cameron was moving the other way at the time to cover the attack and turned to find the ball not going into touch but rolling towards the goal line with Swart in hot pursuit. Just as the ball got to the goal line Swart gathered it up and dived over to score. Van der Schyff missed the goal kick but there was still 19 minutes to go and the Springboks only nine points behind. The Lions held on bravely as the Springbok forward effort gathered momentum, and all fourteen players tackled and fell like heroes before Gentles and his forwards, as they interpassed cleverly. The end of the match was in sight but there was injury time to be played and bang on time, with the Springboks swarming in the Lions' 25 area, Chris Koch proved himself to be one of the great forwards.

He gathered up the ball 20 yards out and dived, swerved and barged through at least five tackles before he fell over the Lions' goal-line amidst deafening applause. It was a magnificent effort and when Van der Schyff landed a good goal, to leave the Springboks only four points behind, they made another tremendous effort. Less than half a minute remained and away came the Springboks again as forwards and backs combined to shake off the weary Lions. Ulyate and Fry were in the movement which worked the ball out to Briers on the right-wing. He took the pass well and swerved his way past Pedlow and Cameron to dive over as he was tackled by Butterfield. All seemed lost for the Lions as Van der Schyff prepared his mark for the kick.

The giant crowd was strangely silent and all fourteen Lions behind the goal-line moved nervously – some indeed were almost on the point of crying, they told me afterwards – as the ball was put in the placer's hands and Van der Schyff walked backwards four yards and halted to line-up his angle. Then he moved off and his long foot carried through, but in his anxiety his head moved up a little and the ball veered to the left outside the far post. The kick had failed and immediately the whistle went for time – the Lions had won! We stood in the Press Box, and as Vivian and myself shook hands the crowd swarmed across the turf and carried the players shoulder high to the dressing-room. Many needed such generous aid, as they had played themselves out in a magnificent match. Typewriters hanged away in the Press Box as we began our messages, and racked our brains for suitable adjectives to fit the great occasion – seven forwards – one point – last minute – magnificent – match of a generation and so on.

...People stood in the stands long after the end and one man dropped dead as he left the ground.

from *The Lions on Trek* (1956)

Cliff Morgan with Geoffrey Nicholson

The Irrepressible Cliff

I'm also thankful that my international career overlapped with Cliff Davies's... to play in an international with Clifton Davies was something else. If you imagine his typical Saturday – coming off night shift in the pit, walking home for a bath and breakfast, walking another half-mile or so to the main road to catch the express bus into Cardiff and playing in the front row for Wales that afternoon – then Cliff, too, would cut an improbable figure in today's professional game. And I must say that rugby is all the duller for the loss of the kind of player that Cliff represents.

Cliff was a great prop forward, one of the tireless 'mules of Kenfig Hill'. But beyond that he was a marvellous story-teller, singer, entertainer and a very droll man with a gift for inventing phrases that still stick in your mind forty years on. Often he didn't realise just how funny he was being. He wasn't educated in the formal sense, but his education came from an ability to listen and converse with people, from reading books and working in the pit every day. He was a part-time undertaker as well, and used to tell us unbelievable tales about funerals he'd arranged.

When we were on away trips Cliff wasn't one of those people who liked sitting around in the bar, playing cards or endlessly discussing rugby. He preferred to sing or have a proper conversation about something. Cliff used to remind me of one of those minstrels in the Middle Ages who went around the big country houses entertaining the company.

Known among us as the Bard of Kenfig Hill, he was always coming out with these little lines of verse he'd written to amuse us:

Me and Tamp do love our wives,
And we will love 'em all our lives.

Tamp was Bill Tamplin, who had played at lock for Wales just after the war, and one evening he said to Cliff, just to get him going, 'Tell me, how's business these days in the undertaking world?'

Cliff said, 'Well, middling, Tamp, not bad.'

'How much are you charging for a coffin these days?'

'Oh nothing special, fourteen guineas,' said Cliff.

'Damn, that's a bit steep. That's a bit expensive. What do you mean, fourteen guineas? I saw one advertised in the paper, twelve pounds ten, and a pleasure to lie in.'

And Cliff Davies came out with the immortal line: 'Well Tamp, take that one if you like. But let me warn you now, pitch pine it'll be, and your arse'll be through it in six months.'

... John Gwilliam, a former Cambridge blue, now a schoolmaster, remained our captain that season. He had strict views on this role and, because his manner was so schoolmasterish, you listened to whatever he said. At that time the Welsh side was an extraordinary combination of labourers, policemen, students and teachers, but he pulled them together as a team. And although his tapping back from the line-out could be a bit of a trial, in other ways he was an effective forward and full of ideas. In March he led us on to Lansdowne Road, so often in the past the graveyard for Welsh hopes of a Triple Crown. But not this time. It staged one of the great games of that era, and for Wales a 14-3 victory and their last Triple Crown until the mid-sixties.

With Rex [Willis] injured, I played outside Roy Burnett's regular partner at Newport, W. A. Williams. He also answered to Billy, but like J. P. R. Williams after him, he was better known by his initials; unless you are blessed with a Christian name like Bleddyn, it's the price you have to pay for being born in a country with no great variety of surnames. After a spell in the selectors' dog-house, Clem Thomas was reinstated in the back row, which sharpened it up a lot. Alun Thomas, who had played against England but not Scotland, was back in place of Bleddyn. Otherwise this was the basic team that Wales had settled on this season, and what's curious is that we played just the same way in Dublin as we had in our other away match at Twickenham. Even down to reproducing that first try against England.

We were on our own line when W. A., not as mercurial as Rex, but a strong, sound player, sent me the sort of fast, flat pass that you need to get out of trouble. As I took it, Jim McCarthy, the Irish back-row forward whose job was to arrive with ball and either nail me or make me hurry my pass, wasn't there. Jack Kyle, too, still one of my great heroes, was going slightly away from me. I came inside him with one little short step, and he missed me by, I suppose, half a yard. Next thing I was tearing up the field towards the Irish line, and on the half-way line I could feel the presence and, out of the corner of my eye, glimpse the red jersey of Ken Jones. Alun Thomas and Malcolm Thomas, our centres, had been baulked, but Ken had run infield from the right wing. And as he came round on my left we did a scissors on their ten-yard line. Phipps, a very fast wing, was in pursuit, but he had no chance against Ken, who just went and went and went until he finally dived over in the corner.

The scissors is a marvellous move when you get it just right, which many British players don't do nowadays. They tend to flick the ball blindly to the other player, and it goes down. We were taught – mainly by Bleddyn, who was a perfectionist – to turn our bodies totally in our scissors, and to see the ball into somebody else's hands. And then, of course, if you didn't let go in a scissors you sold the most effective dummy in the world. You half-turned your body towards the opposing player, you checked for the release of the ball, then you held it and went on in that split second when he wasn't quite sure who had it. The bamboozle was all in the timing of that pass or dummy, and what enabled you to get that right was that you carried the ball in two hands. You didn't have to search for it to pass. Unlike lots of mid-field players as we near the year 2000, who tuck the ball into their bodies not to lose it when they knock people over, we held it out ready to pass or to deceive. Two hands with the ball, that was Bleddyn's teaching, and that season I wasn't the only Welsh back influenced by it.

That try was the second in the match. The first and the last were scored by forwards, Clem Thomas putting Rees Stephens over, then Roy John doing the same for Clem. Ireland's only score was a penalty so, in the end, it was easier than we'd anticipated. Not that we'd thought much about it anyway. I don't believe we had made any tactical preparations for the game, and this really applied for as long as I played rugby. The only thing I remember was some chat about the strengths of the opposition. We'd say, 'Kyle is good, got to be on to him at once. Their back row is very quick off the scrum. Their line-out jumping is pretty hot, would we do better if we threw in short, to number three, say?' But these were very simple tactical things. A scissors movement was something created on the spur of the moment. We didn't plan it, any more than we planned to knock people over in the middle of the field to create second-phase, or third, or fiftieth, possession. There were none of those complications. And while we were aware that they had good line-out forwards, it didn't worry us unduly, because we firmly believed that Rees Stephens and Roy John were even better.

Roy John was phenomenal; he leaped like a salmon coming up out of the river. He seemed to stop in mid-air, catch the ball, and turn and deliver it carefully to the scrum-half as though it was something fragile. Of course, he used to jump into a wedge, that is two other forwards who protected him and blocked any opponent who tried to come through on him, which was legal in those days. Then the laws were changed and the line-out became an unruly mess. I think the game should allow the wedge again. If it's your line-out, it's your advantage, and you should get the ball. We were able to make use of this because we had players who could do things with any clean possession they got, and who were ready to take chances, just as Ken and I had done with that scissors. It was the kind of game the team loved to play and the crowd loved to watch. So that match in Dublin has very happy memories for me, even though, as I discovered later, at a certain point during the play I had broken my leg.

I felt the pain after I had gone through a gap and then turned sharply as I was running. I didn't pay much attention to it on the field. In the tension of the game you can often forget about pain. But back in the dressing room I was in agony. I was lying in the bath when Sammy Walker, former Irish and British Lions captain and now BBC rugby commentator, came in and said his producer, the great Angus McKay, wanted me to go up to the commentary position at the top of the stand and be interviewed by Eamonn Andrews. 'Listen, I can't walk properly,' I said. 'I honestly don't feel like it. There's something wrong with my leg.' He went back and reported to Angus who told him, 'Get someone down there to carry him up.' So that's what they did, and Eamonn asked me about Jack Kyle and about Ken's try in the corner and then what would I remember most about this Triple Crown win over Ireland. I'd been doing a few broadcasts over the last year, and suddenly some advice I'd had from Hywel Davies, head of the BBC in Wales, came to mind: 'Don't be obvious, say something that will surprise them.' So I said to Eamonn: 'My father lost his teeth, and he wasn't even playing.' And it was true; I'd just been talking to him outside the dressing room. I'd given him my one complimentary ticket, and it was an awful seat right up in the corner of the stand next to Mrs John, Roy John's mother. At least it was an awful seat until Ken Jones scored his try in the corner just below them. They saw it perfectly. Dad jumped up and shouted

and spat his top set of teeth fifteen rows in front of him.
He never did get them back.* And that was the story I told.

from *Cliff Morgan: The Autobiography* (1996)
[*The Irish international Tony O'Reilly claimed a man in
Kilkenny was still wearing them ten years later. GW.]

Alun Rees

Cardiff Arms Park

Only to hear some sixty thousand Welshmen
sing natural three-part harmony unrehearsed
while rugby giants battle on the field
is knowing that these men were never English.
The language changes, but the hearts do not.

To see red-jerseyed forwards lift themselves
and drive the startled Englishmen before them
as sixty thousand roar the anthem out
is seeing that this race was never conquered.
The valleys darken, but the fire lives.

To see this, all the same, is to regret
that sixty thousand with this splendid fire
urge fifteen on to drive the English back.
If only they would urge themselves like that.

from *Poetry Wales*, Summer 1966

Lewis Davies

Pre-Match Tension

'Ready then, lads,' announced Glenda from the pinnacle of a bar stool where he had been sitting shuffling team sheets with the secretary and second team captain. Glenda became his nickname after someone had suggested he looked like Glenda Jackson in a Ken Russell film or perhaps it may have been because he had once pulled a bird on tour called Zelda. Anyway the name stuck and in a curious way it suited him.

Glenda led the way through the changing rooms from the bar. Several players were already there in various stages of undress awaiting the arrival of the kit.

'They here yet, Glenda?' asked a voice referring to the opposition.

'Yes, they're here.'

There was a tension in the room, a dull resonating tension that spoke of impending defeat, tired resignation at the end of an unsuccessful season.

Lewis noticed many of the faces who had missed training on Thursday night but he had ceased to care. Liniment singed his nostrils as his team-mates applied various forms of embrocation. Bandages and knee supports, head bands and ankle straps. It was a hard game but some people always over-did it.

The idle nervous chatter of the first few minutes faded into the self-stimulating exhortations to, 'Get your mind on the game, boys.' Lewis allowed it all to pass over him: the team talks, the move explanations, the gentle and not so gentle encouragement. Sounds from the visitors' changing room filtered through and infected the atmosphere, souring thoughts and reminding wandering minds why they huddled together, changing in a cramped sweaty room with fourteen other men on a Saturday afternoon.

A tall figure in a purple jersey entered the room with a self-explanatory, 'Check your studs, boys.'

He moved from foot to foot examining the length, form and roundness of each player's studs. He was more careful than most referees who usually only ran their hands along the bottom of each boot. Instead he examined each pair by eye and even asked one player to change two before warning another of their impending illegality.

He departed announcing, 'Five minutes then, boys.'

Lewis still watched and listened without seeing or hearing anything.

'C'mon in one minute, Lew.'

Lewis joined a huddle of forwards.

'Right then, boys, sit down,' requested Glenda. Most of the team sat down although Daz still struggled to administer his various bandages, supports and dressings which were individually tailored to enable him to survive a game.

Glenda was about to embark on his perambulatory team talk when Dai Fats lumbered out of the changing room reminding everyone as he departed not to forget what he had told them on Thursday night. Lewis looked at his boots willing it to be all over.

Glenda tried again.

'We all know what we've got to do, and we haven't done it this season yet. This is our last chance to do it, or that's it, it's all over and we won't be doing it next season either. You all know you haven't done it. Daz, you haven't done it. Lewis, neither have you, Mike, Buzz, you haven't done it; I haven't done it. But we all know we're going to do it this afternoon because if we don't do it they'll do it to us, because they've been doing it all season. And Lewis, you watch the scrum-half. Right then, a quick one to ten and we're out.'

Lewis stood up to embark on what was collectively known as a psyche-up. The reverberations of the opposition's warm-up invaded their minds as they embarked on theirs. It involved running on the spot, knees pumping high, while shouting the numbers between one and ten in an aggressive manner. How this was supposed to prepare mind and soul for a rugby match was a debatable point. But Lewis enacted the same ritual every Saturday five minutes before kick-off, occasionally he even enjoyed it. He watched the glazed eyes and listened to the shouted numbers while maintaining an acceptable level of participation lest somebody accused him of not taking the whole thing seriously.

'Right then, boys,' shouted Glenda at the finale of the psyche up. He then led the fourteen players out of the changing room: images of Roman gladiators, Christians, lions and Charlton Heston filling his mind as he ran through the polite clapping of interested spectators who fringed the short route to the field.

Lewis ambled out of the changing room near the back of the column of players which followed Glenda onto the pitch. He kept his eyes on the player in front of him, feeling the hard concrete beneath his studs turn to soft mud as he accelerated onto the field.

from *Work, Sex and Rugby* (1993)

John Reason and Carwyn James

Gerald Davies and Barry John in New Zealand, 1971

The Lions had to make use of any ball that New Zealand kicked away. They had to develop the counter-attack and they had to develop the confidence to use it under pressure. The All Blacks and the provincial teams had a tendency to overkick when trying to hoist the ball into the box behind the forwards on the blindside wing, and so the Lions wings had to stand deep so that they were in effect playing as three full-backs. Then they could support each other in their counter-attacks. This had its greatest moment in the match against Hawke's Bay when J. P. R. Williams caught a narrowly missed kick at goal behind his own posts and launched a surging counter-attack which ended with Gerald Davies scoring a try between the posts at the other end of the field.

Davies was then in the blazingly high summer of his powers, and in the match against Hawke's Bay, he gave such a comprehensive demonstration of the range of his skill that it was as if the fates had decreed that he should be given one chance to compress the magic of his career

416

into one afternoon. He took that chance by scoring four tries, three of them as a wing and one of them in his old position as a centre. All were exquisite examples of the most beautiful of the running skills.

For the first five years of his career, Gerald Davies had played as a centre. It was from that position that he scored the most memorable try of the Lions' 1968 tour of South Africa. This was in the Lions' match against Boland, in the Cape Province, and running with the ball from a line-out in his own half, Davies saw that the opposing outside centre had come up too fast in defence. This meant that the Boland defensive line was dog-legged, and Davies made a searing break on the outside before twice sidestepping the cover and running on for seventy yards to score.

Strangely enough, the final try that Davies scored against Hawke's Bay in 1971 was very similar. He had moved into the centre after an injury to Mike Gibson, and when Duncan, in the Hawke's Bay centre, came up too fast in defence from a scrum near his 25, Davies streaked past MacRae on the outside and side-stepped the full-back to score by the posts.

By that stage of Gerald Davies' career, centre-threequarter play had become much more physical and as he was small and lightly-built, he had accepted advice to move out to the right wing. Initially, he was rather reluctant to accept this advice, because he felt he would see much less of the ball. Towards the end of his career, his fears in this respect were fully justified, but at that time, John Dawes was playing in the centre in the Welsh team and he was such an unselfish player and such a supreme passer of the ball that Gerald

Davies was persuaded that there was a whole new world waiting to be conquered on the wing.

The way he conquered that world was one of the supreme satisfactions to be had from watching British Rugby in those few fleeting years when it was at its zenith. Thomas Gerald Reames Davies met all Dave Gallaher's exacting requirements as a back. He had scalding pace and breath-taking acceleration and he had the rare gift of being able to side-step at pace off both feet. Bleddyn Williams insists that very few players have ever been gifted with a true side-step, which is the ability to execute the manoeuvre without perceptible loss of pace, but Gerald Davies was unquestionably one of them.

Being so lightly built, Davies had to develop the instincts of the forest animal. He knew his body was fragile, so he had to depend on speed and alertness and quickness of thought and footwork. Fear is an important element in the make-up of such a player, just as it is in that of the forest animal. It heightens perception, and the adrenalin secreted adds to the surge of acceleration.

Gerald Davies also played the game with his head. He was aware of the possibilities offered by variation in the length of his stride. He learned what paid and what did not pay and he remembered. He learned to stay out in defence and mark his man and to leave the inside man for the cover. He could read the game because he had acute footballing intelligence. His positional work and his assessment of the possibilities of counter-attack were excellent. He was a killing runner-in of tries and yet he knew when he was not going to score and invariably contrived to make the ball available for his support. Mick Molloy, who played in the second row of the pack for Ireland for many years, once said ruefully that he had lost count of the number of games he had played at club and national level in which his own team and all its aspirations had been dashed by one devastating run by Gerald Davies. Wales made nothing like the use of him towards the end of his career that his talents demanded, and for that his opponents all over the world were eternally grateful, but he was that rarity in any sport, a player whom all his rivals acknowledged as the master.

Carwyn James treasured him, as he did all his other gifted backs, but he knew that if those gifted backs were to have the chance to express their skills, the Lions' forwards would have to come to terms with the realities of rescuing every scrap of possession, often from a position of weakness. He knew that on many occasions, the Lions would not be rucking in the ideal situation of going forward. Frequently, they would have to ruck or maul in retreat, and so it was important that they should know how to do it and that they should practise it regularly. That practice alone paid dividends in the first test, when the All Blacks were so much the better side, and yet the Lions got away with a victory.

Finally, the Lions were helped by the fact that there were players in the team who had been to New Zealand and who knew what it was all about. Gareth Edwards and Barry John had toured New Zealand in 1969 and had been rated as nonentities. Their coach was delighted. He knew that two years later, Edwards and John would want to prove themselves, and they did. By the seventh match, when the team played quite beautifully and destroyed Wellington, the Lions felt that they were capable of a genuine roar. Even the brutal match against Canterbury a fortnight later, in which they lost their two test props for the rest of the tour because of injury, did something for the Lions. In one way it was a disaster, the low point of the tour, but after darkness there has to be light, and that match made the Lions more determined than ever to prevail. 'We shall overcome,' they sang. And they did.

... The impact in Britain of the achievements of the 1971 Lions surprised even the players. The phlegmatic British sporting community came as near as it ever will to a ticker-tape welcome, and in Wales, at any rate, the returning heroes went back to their villages in motorcades.

The focal point of this adulation was Barry John, who not only broke the scoring record for a tourist in New Zealand but practically doubled it. Typically, he sensed the type of welcome that would be waiting if he went back to Wales by an orthodox route, so he slipped home unobtrusively and went to ground. Again, no one laid a finger on him.

This was one of the most extraordinary features of his play. He did not have either the scalding pace or the startling acceleration which is almost indispensable to a back, but his running had a ghost-like quality which made him infinitely elusive. He achieved this partly by variation of pace and by the variation of the length of his stride and partly by mesmeric use of the ball, or his hips, or his shoulders, or his feet. One New Zealand flanker confessed ruefully, 'Barry John rolled his eyes, and I fell over'.

Barry John was not a classical passer of the ball, but in the words of Mike Gibson, one of his greatest admirers,

'He got it there'. Barry John also had staggering self-confidence and he was a merciless exploiter of individual weaknesses in the opposition. He was a beautiful kicker, too, and he was left-sided in so many activities that he kicked very well off his left foot. He was fragile in build, and so, like Gerald Davies, he had the same awareness of physical danger as a forest animal. Perhaps this helped him to find as much time and as much space as he did. Certainly he had the rare gift of being almost able to transcend the game in which he was playing and to regard the opposition almost with pity. He had one of Lewis Jones' qualities, too. He could go from third gear to top and then into overdrive and he would surprise an opponent each time. He did it with much less use of energy than Lewis Jones, and he sensed the relative balance of an opponent like that of a dancing partner.

He sometimes did unexpected things in defence. He originated the gentle self-derision about his 'finger-tip tackling' and yet he once stopped Benoit Dauga, the great French lock, five yards from the line at the cost of a broken nose. This saved an international match for Wales against France. In the first test in New Zealand in 1971, he found himself confronted with Colin Meads snorting round the end of a line-out only twenty yards from the Lions' line. The Lions could not go to his assistance and all Barry John could do was get in Colin Meads' way, but he did that, inelegantly but effectively, until help arrived.

He was completely unaware of the organisational technique of Rugby football. He just was not interested. 'Just give me the ball,' he said. He would go to sleep in the team talks when Clive Rowlands was coach of Wales. He got on like a house on fire with the massive intellect of Ray McLoughlin, and every morning tried to remember whether McLoughlin was a loose head donkey or a tight head donkey, but when McLoughlin shared a room with him on tour, and asked him to specify what he would do in certain match situations so that the forwards would know in advance in which direction to run, Barry John asked, his eyes round with wonder, 'How can I tell you? I don't know myself until I get the ball'.

Barry John created his own private world in the dressing room before a match. He shut himself within himself. He did not want a build-up. He created a personal privacy which was so complete that no coach ever thought of intruding. Other players need attention, or reassurance, or motivation. Not Barry John. The only organisation that interested him was soccer. In many ways, he was a much greater student of soccer than Rugby. He knew the strengths of soccer players and could have been a professional himself. He would have enjoyed that. He would have taken to big time soccer like a duck to water.

... He commanded a game from the kick-off. 'Let's see the numbers on their backs first,' he would say. 'Let's see them going backwards.' He could also destroy any opponent who was one-sided, as he did his rivals at outside-half in Wales, and he scored tries with such a complete lack of fuss that opponents rarely touched him. He was the first Rugby player in Britain to be crowned. The Lions called him 'The King'. In Wales, he was all but deified as well, but in the end, he gave it all away, and he did it almost off-handedly.

He played for one more season after the 1971 tour and

then retired. He had been crowned the 'King' not only of Welsh Rugby but of British Rugby too, and it was probably the larger public which felt the keener disappointment at his departure. That public sensed, just as Gareth Edwards sensed, that John and Edwards were on the threshold of a new dimension of half-back play. From Britain's point of view, even more than from the Welsh point of view, it would have been absorbing to see what more they could achieve.

from *The World of Rugby* (1979)

Max Boyce

9-3

Anyone who was at Stradey Park, Llanelli, on that damp October day in 1972, when Llanelli defeated New Zealand's mighty 'All Blacks' by nine points to three will surely never forget the incredible atmosphere at the ground or indeed the scenes that followed that historic win by the 'Scarlets'.

> It was on a dark and dismal day
> In a week that had seen rain,
> When all roads led to Stradey Park
> With the All Blacks here again.
> They poured down from the valleys,
> They came from far and wide;
> There were twenty-thousand in the ground
> And me and Dai outside!

The shops were closed like Sunday,
And the streets were silent still.
And those who chose to stay away
Were either dead or ill.
But those who went to Stradey, boys,
Will remember till they die
How New Zealand were defeated,
And how the pubs ran dry.

Oh, the beer flowed at Stradey
(Piped down from Felinfoel),
And the hands that held the glasses high
Were strong from steel and coal.
And the air was filled with singing,
And I saw a grown man cry.
Not because we'd won
But because the pubs ran dry!

Then dawned the morning after
On empty factories.
But we were still at Stradey –
Bloodshot absentees.
But we all had doctors' papers
And they all said just the same:
That we all had 'Scarlet Fever',
And we caught it at the game!

Now all the little babies
In Llanelli from now on
Will be christened Ray or Carwyn,

Derek, Delme, Phil or John.
And in a hundred years again
They'll sing this song for me.
Of when the scoreboard read 'Llanelli 9,
Seland Newydd 3'.

And when I'm old and my hair turns grey,
And they put me in a chair,
I'll tell my great-grandchildren
That their Datcu was there.
And they'll ask to hear the story
Of that damp October day,
When I went down to Stradey
And I saw the 'Scarlets' play.

from *I Was There* (1979)

Frank Keating

Phil Bennett

For a slight man, Bennett had astonishing power with his right-footed kicking – from the ground but, particularly, with his punts. I can close my eyes now and see that great swingeing follow-through of his – standing upright, but his right boot finishing higher than his Celtic-black smear of hair, like the very best downstage hoofer at the Paris Folies.

He was from Felinfoel, a nondescript scrabble of a large village which brews the watery beer of the same name, and just down the high hill from Barry's Cefneithin on the road which drops on into Llanelli. The choice was 'coal or steel'. Phil's father chose the steelworks – the 'Klondike', they called it. His mother worked at the local car-pressing plant. He was a sickly child, pasty-faced and off-sick and inevitably with a snivelly nose. But mad about sports. And a week's bright-red asterisk was Saturday when Dad, back from his night-shift labours in the furnaces, would have three boiled eggs for breakfast, take off his hobnails and overalls, bath, have a cat-nap... then, refreshed and glad at heart, walk the boy down to Stradey, to The Match. Hand in hand on the 'tanner bank' where, Uncle Thomas-John alongside, they would watch the Scarlets play.

One day, when the boy was nine, they took him down to St Helen's for the crunching death-or-glory annual against Swansea, and many years later, in a marvellously touching memoir he wrote with Martyn Williams, Phil recalled:

'The platform at Llanelli General was a sea of red caps, scarves, mufflers and cloth caps. It was a massive pilgrimage which had left villages and homes deserted of menfolk. St Helen's, I thought, could never accommodate this moving mass of miners, steelworkers, teachers, ministers and boys. They were all good-humoured; the bantering, the jokes, the bets, everything adding to the excitement of the afternoon.

'It was a Derby spectacular, hard, rough and uncompromising. Skirmishes on the field started fights on the terraces; the shouting and the noise was incredible and I kept tight hold of my father's jacket. Swansea were leading by 5-3 in the second half, with precious few minutes to go before the end. Suddenly Carwyn James at outside-half

426

made a half-break and passed to his centre Denis Evans, who gave the ball to Geoff Howells and by that time there was sufficient room for Geoff to round his man in the corner and race for a try underneath the posts. St Helen's went mad! Hats, programmes, bags and newspapers were flung into the air. Some 5,000 Llanelli supporters had witnessed one of those Scarlet miracles'.

The fly-half who had manufactured that winning try for Llanelli was, of course, Carwyn James. If the tot Bennett was nine, it must have been 1958, the year Carwyn was capped for Wales.

So it was fifteen winters later, early in 1973, on a still, and ever will be, celebrated afternoon at Cardiff Arms Park that the names Bennett and James came together in tandem for world consumption (although, by then, Wales – certainly West Wales – knew the pairing of the coach James and the springheeled little fly-half had for some seasons lit dazzling flares for the club at Stradey Park).

Bennett had at once assumed John's mantle for Wales and played in the defeat by New Zealand at the start of the 1972-3 season and in the first match of the Five Nations, when England were well beaten. Bennett's performances in both games did not receive widespread acclamation. Compared to the man he succeeded, Phil was frankly a visible worrypot, much more introverted and obviously insecure about his place. His idolaters at Stradey – the home where he was warm and snug and comfy and, as a result, glistening daring week after week – worried as much as he did whether he could take control in the genuine big time.

A week after the match against England, there was staged the traditional farewell match for the tourists against the flamboyant scratch team, the Barbarians, at the Arms Park. Usually the thing is a fiesta, an exhibition, but this time – especially after a more than grumpy tour by the All Blacks – the Barbarians finale was invested with the title 'Fifth Test Carried Over', meaning that the tourists were looking at it as a 'revenge' game for the singular beating the Lions had given them on their own patch less than eighteen months before. Accordingly, the Barbarians picked up the gauntlet and picked a dozen of those Lions – and also, uniquely for the olde-tyme ethos of the club, allowed Carwyn James to have a hand in the pre-match 'coaching'. Bennett was picked as pivot and playmaker. He was very, very nervous. 'Well, I knew I would be out of it, estranged. It wouldn't have been too bad to be on the wing, but so evidently replacing Barry preyed on my mind. I couldn't even find the ground when we were called for training at Penarth.'

Before the start, James quietly said his 'few words' in the dressing room, particularly singling out the 'self-estranged' Bennett.

The ballads. The hymns. The presentations. The expectations. Of a sudden, the rafter-packed throng is momentarily silent – and then, as Bennett kicks off, it is to a great wall of presumptive sound...

There is that routine first exchange of push and shove, with the ball almost ignored as the two sets of forwards lock horns and flex muscles and spirits... a set scrum, another general affray, then a maul – and the All Blacks have it; the mighty captain, Ian Kirkpatrick, has wrestled it free and is in open ground, blindside going right towards the river end. A decent pass, making space, to his right-wing, the ripping Samoan Bryan Williams, who carves up the touchline, past halfway, then steeples up a perfectly angled diagonal kick towards the Baa-Baas' posts, over the cover defence. It lands, exactly midfield, on the twenty-five-yard line, and daps once, twice, invitingly towards the posts as the New Zealanders greedily pursue it en masse. The Barbarians have to turn, pronto. One minute into the grudge match, and this could be seriously dangerous... Bennett is first to spot the danger, and first to the difficult bobbler, midway between his posts and the twenty-five, knowing this furious wave of adrenalin-charged All Blacks are bearing down on his back, to be sure, can only be yards away...

He gathers the ball, and, as he turns – rather, in the very act of turning – he drives his right foot into the ground fiercely, which causes him to pirouette and face the enemy, one of whom is already there. No, he isn't, he's already done for with that first magical hopscotch step... But here's another... again a mesmerizing right-foot sidestep and then, unbelievably, another... and another.

He is in the clear now, with room to bang the thing into touch and bow low at the wall of applause. But he doesn't. What had Carwyn told him before he went out? So, still inside his twenty-five, he passes to his full-back, the onliest J. P. R. Williams, a yard or two on his left...

And thus Phil Bennett, nervous, shy and presuming

himself to be overawed in such company, announced himself to the wider world. The try which resulted from that voluptuous and bespoke bit of tailoring by Bennett has been reprised and enthused over more, far more, times than any other single incident in all rugby history. It was scored by Gareth Edwards; it co-starred Williams, John Pullin, John Dawes, Tom David and Derek Quinnell; but it was undoubtedly – and the full cast all agree – Conceived, Produced and Directed by Philip Bennett, of Felinfoel, on the Llanelli—Carmarthen road.

It was nice, too, that one Cliff Morgan, of Trebanog and the BBC, was in the television commentary box to relate the facts. This is what he said: '...Kirkpatrick ... to Bryan Williams, this is great stuff... Phil Bennett covering... , chased by Alistair Scown... brilliant..., oh, that's brilliant... John Williams... Pullin... John Dawes, great dummy... David, Tom David, the halfway line... brilliant, by Quinnell... this is Gareth Edwards... a dramatic start... WHAT A SCORE!'

To this day, and typically, Bennett himself plays down his part in that explosively memorable twelve-second passage: 'At the time I was intent only on getting out of trouble. I sensed they were right on top of me. Perhaps the whole beautiful, amazing thing wouldn't have happened if I hadn't heard Alistair Scown's menacing footsteps bearing down on me. As it was, it was a bit of a hospital pass I gave to JPR, wasn't it?'

John Williams chips in: 'Well, certainly I nearly lost my head as Bryan Williams lunged at me. But what utter brilliance by Phil. I remain convinced that the whole thing was really Carwyn James's try. Unique to the Barbarians, who disapproved of coaching, they asked him to give us a talk before the game,

'There was a lot of needle in the game; both us and the All Blacks were treating it as an unofficial fifth Test decider after we [the Lions] had beaten them, coached by Carwyn, eighteen months before. Now, before we went out, Carwyn soothed us, calming and relaxed, told us to enjoy it; and I'll never forget his last words, to insist to Phil, who was full of trepidation, hadn't played long for Wales and certainly not for the Lions, to go out and play just like he did for Llanelli – every Saturday – 'You're not in the shadows any more, Phil bach, go and show the world what Stradey knows'.

Up in the press box, as the applause battered on, sat Carwyn James. He was silent, staring. He took a long, deep, satisfied pull on his Senior Service. He inhaled – and then, as he let the smoke waft out of his nose and mouth, a close observer could notice just a split second snake's-lick of a very private, very contented smile. In his weekly column in the following Friday's *Guardian*, he was to write of the moment, 'rare and unforgettable, when you can play at a level outside the conscious; when everything is instinct, but as clear as a bell because you have practised it so often and, especially, dreamed it – that unique moment when sport, lovely sport, not only achieves, but assumes, an art form.'.

from *The Great Number Tens* (1993)

John Morgan and Gerald Davies

A Rugby Diary, 1984-5

24 February

JM: We drove along the Wye Valley to Monmouth and then across the Usk to Gerald's fortieth birthday party which had been postponed for a fortnight because so many of us were snowed in. His house commands a view of unexpected beauty: this part of Gwent is hardly known to strangers, the hills gentle and green, a territory lost between Pontypool and Usk town...

Barry John arrived, shook his host by the hand and said, 'So glad you could come.' I had met him and Gerald first in South Africa in 1968 when they were playing for the British Lions. Barry impressed me by his achievement in managing to stay throughout the tour, even though he had broken his collar bone in the First Test and did not play another match. A young man, I thought, who could achieve this unique feat, who could so charm the management, would go far. I decided that when they returned to Wales I would try and make a television film for Harlech TV about the pair of dazzling players. It was made and was to contain one of the most remarkable displays by Barry that any sportsman can have offered – certainly for the record.

The Welsh Rugby Union gave us permission for the outside-half to wear a microphone during a match between Cardiff and Swansea at the Arms Park. The audience would thus feel itself part of the game and hear the Cardiff star's chat: he only swore once. The crew and I and the director,

432

Jolyon Wimhurst, stood on the touch-line. From time to time Barry would come and talk, even though this was a serious match between two of the most powerful rival clubs in Britain. What would we like him to do? Not believing that he could be serious, I asked if he would mind scoring a try at the corner flag at the City end of the ground. We positioned ourselves there. Within five minutes he not only had scored a try there, but had wilfully, smiling a little, chosen to jink and glide past seven Swansea players in scoring it. And so it went on. Would we like him to drop a goal? He did. What about kicking a penalty goal? At that time he was not the principal goal kicker for Cardiff or, oddly enough, for Wales. However, he asked his captain if he could have the next kick at goal: certainly. He kicked it. I doubt if anyone else on the field knew what he was doing. Indeed I doubt if the Swansea team would have been best pleased to learn that here was the Cardiff outside-half scoring cheerfully whenever it suited him, for all his opponents' efforts.

His style has not changed. He told us of how in the famous Grand Slam match in Paris in 1971, John Taylor had said to him in the tunnel as they ran on to the field at Stade Colombes: 'Barry, this is a serious match.' What could this mean? 'It means you are tackling today'. Barry ran to the captain, John Dawes, and complained: 'I'm not playing; tackling isn't in my contract.' In that match he broke his nose making a tackle that helped win the Grand Slam and subsequently wondered who it was that had pushed him. He maintains that he never had any mud on any of his Welsh jerseys, and who would dispute it?

Many of that wonderful Welsh side, the best since the turn of the century, remain friends and see much of each other, especially since so many of them are commentators on the game, whether for newspapers or the broadcasting companies. It was a gifted generation. Unlike too many more recent players, they still laugh a lot and did at the party.

29 March

JM: The French press does not read too well about our prospects for the game. There is still bad feeling about John Bevan criticising the French referee after our match at Murrayfield. Hints like fists forecast trouble. We solemnly agreed, in the splendour of the foyer of the Hotel Concorde St. Lazare where we have come to rest, that John Bevan should have given more thought to the welfare of his players when they step out on to the Parc des Princes tomorrow, and then turned our minds to other matters. The Concorde has a mirror in the foyer ceiling, reflecting its baroque and terraced glories. If you are at all unstable it is easy to fall over backwards contemplating the unusual view.

Phil Bennett and Ray Gravell arrive, Ray without his beard, looking younger and more gentle than his ferocious repute on the field might ever suggest. We talk about the native language in Welsh rugby and especially in Llanelli. I remind them that in 1955 fourteen of the Llanelli team spoke Welsh. How many now do? Three it seems, or four if Ray is playing. This does not necessarily mean that the language has suffered so sharp a decline in the Llanelli hinterland as perhaps that more players come to Stradey nowadays from English-speaking districts to the east and west.

We then talked about that wonderful day when Llanelli beat the All Blacks in 1972. I had spent the week before the game with Carwyn James and the team making a film for Harlech TV. Phil Bennett now revealed some detail which had escaped me certainly at the time of that damp, misty triumph, a game as intense in its passion as any I have seen or anyone involved has ever played in. A critical moment in the victory, said Phil Bennett, had been at a dinner in the club house the Saturday before the Tuesday's match. The team had been cast down to hear of the huge New Zealand victory over Western Counties. Carwyn James had been to see that game. He returned to Stradey, stood at the dinner and announced to his team that he was completely confident that Llanelli would beat the All Blacks. His astonished fifteen at once trusted him.

Phil Bennett believes the match was won in the first two minutes. The Llanelli team had been fired in the dressing room both by Carwyn's careful instructions and by Delme Thomas' moving, patriotic address. Carwyn had also arranged another subtle move. When the teams were on the field it was announced over the loudspeakers that the New Zealand national anthem would be played, at which 'God Save the Queen' rang out. The crowd burst into laughter to the mystification of the All Blacks. The key moment, the decisive stroke, in Phil Bennett's view, came when the Llanelli forwards carried out Carwyn's ploy of hitting the All Blacks' formidable forward Kirkpatrick very hard as soon as he received the ball. In my recollection four Llanelli forwards arrived on him together. Phil Bennett says that he looked into the eyes of the All Blacks at that moment and realised that they were beaten. The powerful force of the psychological element in a big game is not always easy to appreciate from the touchline. There can seldom have been a better, more memorable example.

Phil went on to describe the next match Llanelli played after this famous victory – at Richmond. In the intervening three days most of the Llanelli team and indeed most male citizens of the district had been drunk most of the time. The evening and night of the match I had been staying at the Cawdor Hotel at Llandeilo nearby. Although I was the only resident in the bar it was crowded into the small hours. We were waiting for Carwyn to arrive. The barman said he wished to close; a senior policeman present delicately suggested that the licence might not be secure if the bar closed before the great man arrived. It stayed open.

By Saturday the Llanelli team were in poor shape. Carwyn James insisted that most of them play at Richmond. Phil Bennett reports that going on the field he could see forty-five Richmond players; his comrades scarcely knew which of the three-for-every-one they should tackle. Within two minutes the outside-half was required to kick at goal and for the only time in his career hit the corner flag. The defeat was the heaviest Llanelli had ever suffered at Richmond. When Phil Bennett left the field Carwyn put his hand on his shoulder and said: 'Well played, Phil!'

The day was long. I had hoped to steal some secrets from Ieuan Evans who is chairman of the committee reporting on the state of Welsh rugby, but he refused to offer any. Instead we talked of his father's Marxist days in Ammanford, of the anarchists there, of Aneurin Bevan and Jim Griffiths, Arthur

436

Horner and Will Paynter and other heroes of the South Wales miners we had known and of Welsh teams of the past. Men from Ystradgynlais wondered what their chances were of winning the West Wales Championship over Tumble. A group from Bridgend and Aberavon discovering that I was writing a book with Gerald asked if, for a small sum, I would mention their names. Singing broke out, as it will, and early in the morning a group from the Swansea Valley arrived in the hotel having taken three hours to walk the one mile from the Pigalle. They thought they may have lost their way. A party from Aberavon, not feeling too well, were looking for the doctor who had come with them. They discovered he was ill in bed.

from *Sidesteps* (1985)

Alun Richards

Carwyn

He had the most feminine of qualities that were unique in a brash, often combative masculine world and they made him hypersensitive to the feelings of others, a saintly quality which the Italians at once detected. Within a few weeks he was known as the sympathetic one, the man who never raised his voice and slowly, imperceptibly, he began to impress himself upon them. It soon occurred to me that rugby football was a long way away from his essential nature which seemed so far removed from the hurly burly of bruising games, the shouting crowds, the inflamed faces of

437

spectators whose total identification with teams led from one unreason to another. You could not believe that he had played so successfully himself – a will o' the wisp avoiding the maurauding hands of sizeable forwards like his lifelong friend Clem Thomas, or the formidable Pontypool destroyers of half-backs, Alan Forward and Ray Cale, this last a Dostoyevskyan figure, the most frightening forward I have ever seen on a rugby field, yet whom Carwyn always described as 'a perfect gentleman'.

With Carwyn inconsistencies multiplied, contradictions presented themselves at every turn in his life, and while, in describing a friend, it is only too easy to fall into the trap of ascribing to him only the best of qualities, behind that quizzical countenance there was a divine spark that ignited fellow feeling like a reciprocal current in an uncanny way. Being vulnerable and sensitive, he was never a threat in any kind of relationship, but at the same time he had a rare gift that conveyed a special Carwyn empathy so that it sometimes seemed he magically made people grow on the spot. All who wanted to talk to him usually wanted something for themselves for his presence so often enlarged a moment, and on those who mattered to him, he had an instant therapeutic effect in that they so often felt better for having met him. It was this *simpatico* presence which at first astounded the Italians. The constant cigarette smoking, the vicious skin infection, the travelling and ever-growing untidiness were further abrasions in a bourgeois world, but it was as if he rose from the ashes of inconsequential things to point a particular way, to get to the heart of any matter. The chaos was unimportant. When he wanted to, he had the gift of conveying the feeling that you mattered, you alone, and you in particular. It was not charm, and it was certainly not false, but an almost mystical communication of a rare kind from a man often given to long silences whose simple gift of getting the best out of people would never have been achieved without his lifelong habit of listening – an attribute which everyone who knew him well has remarked upon. It was, I discovered, a characteristic he had inherited from his father, a collier, who was also a private man.

Many famous Welshmen are rightly known for rhetoric, the forensic command of language that ignites those bonded in common cause, and in my lifetime I have heard most of them including Aneurin Bevan who had a masterly command of the language and always raised the tempo of the debate. He also had the gift of simplifying an issue with a deadly clarity. He was at his best in attack, his voice and manner combining to wield sentences like scalpels: 'Mr Eden may be sincere, but if he is sincere, he is stupid, more of a fool than a knave, and in either capacity – we don't want him!' But Carwyn was not like this, seldom attacked, perhaps because he was a chapel-goer, never raised his voice and listened far more than he spoke. If there is one phrase to describe him in company, it is his persistent unobtrusiveness. He never pushed, and yet at times he seemed to be everywhere on the rugby scene, always with this charisma that left you with the feeling of uplift which was the hallmark of the most princely of his gifts – friendship. You seldom saw him without the feeling that he was glad to see you, that no matter how unexpected the encounter he had arrived specially to lighten your day.

... Had Carwyn written the story of his own life, there is no doubt what its title would have been, and indeed, he pencilled it several times on the manuscripts which he never completed – A Rugger Man. It was taken from an obscure Welsh short story by W. Aldred Thomas which he knew by heart and sometimes recited aloud.

'I'm a rugger man. You'd just as well have it straight! There may be other games – I suppose there are one or two somewhere, but there's only one man's game – rugger.'

While this drew roars of approval in smoke-filled club rooms, the fact is it represented only the tip of Carwyn's enthusiasm. There is little doubt that he was the most unusual of men and brought to rugby football concepts and passions, and a persona which was uniquely Welsh, all of which reflected his whole attitude to life. In particular, he had his own standards of excellence and a coherent picture of what might be, the artist's glimpse of total possibilities – this an inspirational vision as if, like Shelley, he was aware of the fading coals of creation, of the first moment of seeing which ever after is never quite so bright and the task executed is somehow always paler than the brilliance of the first concept. If it sounds far fetched to apply such a comparison to a mere game, the answer is, of course, that Carwyn never saw rugby football as a mere game. He would reflect, for example, on the careers of such players as the Lions's wing three-quarter Gerald Davies, whose lovely running and daring brought him every honour in the game, and then say, 'His potential has seldom been realised.' It was not that he was unaware of exactly how brilliant Gerald had been, but there was, in Carwyn's mind, more that could have been achieved, aesthetic patterns of

440

play which he had glimpsed and in which the great players might be fully utilised.

It was this vision of what might be which made him the coach of coaches, as if, like an artist, he saw the drama ahead already staged but was waiting for the plot and principal characters to fill it out, all to combine to form an almost theatrical ensemble in which victory played only a part. Victory was important, but not by itself enough, and it was this conception of possibilities which was so fully realised in the kind of rugby football played by his returned Lions in the match of the decade at the Cardiff Arms Park when the Barbarians played New Zealand at the conclusion of the All Black visit in 1973. In many people's minds this was a kind of fifth test match between the 1971 Lions and their old adversaries, even though principal players like Barry John, Gerald and Mervyn Davies were missing. In that game, probably the most widely televised ever, the achievements of previous years were manifested both in the skills shown and the enthusiasms generated, particularly amongst the young. It represented the ultimate in excitement and skill, the excellence which Carwyn revered in the qualities of both teams, two being required to make the bargain. In New Zealand earlier, the battle had, of course, been closer, the touring Lions having seldom been allowed to play with such continuous flair, but the ultimate result, the test victories and unbeaten provincial record represented for Carwyn a high point which – his club successes apart – meant that in rugby football terms his life ever after was an anticlimax.

from *Carwyn: a memoir* (1984)

Alan Watkins

Fan who became a pioneer

Last Wednesday night John Morgan died. He was 59, and had been seriously ill for some three years. He was many things: a television reporter; a writing journalist; both a lover of opera and an opera librettist; an entrepreneur, in a small way of business, having been largely responsible for the setting up of the consortium which inaugurated Harlech Television.

He was also a great Welsh rugby supporter and a pioneering writer on the game. For there can be great supporters, just as there are great players. Though John relished gossip about the misdeeds of rugby's administrators in Wales – the more malicious it was, the better he was pleased – he was the most loyal and romantic of supporters. We were going to win; we always were. I remember, on the evening before the England match in February 1980, casting doubt on Wales's chances. John would have none of it. In fact it was a bad-tempered match, Paul Ringer was sent off and Wales went down 8-9. But as it was two tries to three penalties, this was a moral victory for Wales and for John. 'Alan has always been against the Welsh,' he complained to a friend of ours shortly afterwards.

He was educated at Swansea Grammar School and University College, Swansea. At school he was a promising outside-half and centre, and later played for Morriston. He was close to six feet tall and powerfully built. But, with his sixth-form friend Geoffrey Nicholson, he would often go to see Swansea Town, as it was then called, on Saturday

442

afternoons, during the marvellous days of Ivor Allchurch.

With Nicholson he wrote *Report on Rugby*, 1959. This was an innovative work; for the first time the game was treated as a social phenomenon, particularly in relation to Wales. John possessed much historical imagination, and could sympathetically recapture Imperial South Wales, when its coal kept the Royal Navy afloat and Swansea was the metallurgical capital of the world. Likewise, his rugby reports in *The Observer* in the late 1950s went beyond the game. His account of the train journey to Edinburgh is still remembered as a piece of writing. With the late H. B. Toft, *The Observer*'s, correspondent after the war, he did much to raise the standard of rugby journalism. He also made several memorable television programmes with his friends of the great years, the late Carwyn James, Gerald Davies and Barry John. And he was responsible for the television film of Llanelli's win over New Zealand in 1972.

He was – there is no getting away from it, and no memoir of John would be accurate without mentioning it – something of a romancer. He once claimed to me to have played for Swansea against South Africa in 1951.

'That's funny, John,' I replied. 'I saw that match, and I can't remember you in the Swansea side.'

'I never said I actually played,' he interjected quickly. 'But I was asked to play.'

'Why didn't you, then?'

'Too scared.'

Like most of us, he would have preferred to be a rugby hero rather than the fine writer and even finer talker he actually was.

Almost 20 years after this match at St Helen's, he was to be found at the same ground, demonstrating against the same fixture. The game was called off, amid scenes of some disorder. He never thought that rugby could be separated either from politics or from life. But, as his career demonstrated, he was equally clear that, though rugby could not be separated from life, it was not the whole of life either.

from *The Independent*, 9 December 1988

Dai Smith and Gareth Williams

Gareth Edwards

Gareth Owen Edwards, from a Welsh-speaking mining village perched in the bare north-west plateau of Glamorgan, was to carry the gregarious, chattering vivacity, bred and sheltered in Gwaun-cae-Gurwen, to fields of endeavour far removed from the scatter of streets whose backdrop was the Black Mountain. The talent that accompanied his intensely competitive personality channelled aggression into a rugby theatricality whose virtuosity was honed to perfection by the discipline and expertise of Bill Samuel, P.E. master at Pontardawe Technical School. Gareth Edwards the man was born in 1947, Gareth the rugby international was born in 1964.

'I remember vividly the day at school... when Wales lost... 24-3 in Durban. It had been a typical sporting Saturday for me, with an hour's cricket and a lot of running, I was about to join everyone in the changing room when

444

Samuel, who had told me the Durban score said: "Edwards, where do you think you're going, you haven't finished yet. I want you to do six 220 yards". He suggested some ridiculous time, like twenty-four seconds for each. When he took me home that night I was faint and swaying all over the road and cried when I saw my parents. "He's mad, he's mad", I said.

'Bill Sam' stands in a long line of Welsh schoolteachers, sung and unsung, to whom Welsh rugby owes an unpayable debt. The bill is never presented, only extended. The young Edwards, almost more an athlete than a rugby player, under his guidance and with parental self-sacrifice takes a sporting scholarship to Millfield that is, given his potential, akin to a novitiate's removal from the world before re-entry. The boy who had starred in Welsh Secondary School games is not a mature player when he risks the hurly-burly of Welsh club rugby in 1966 but this college student, and soon Cardiff player, is already formed in attitude. At a trial game for Cardiff's third team even before this, Bill Samuel, his vigilant mentor, had told him when and where a try would materialize, and Edwards scored it. The fact that it was from the blind side of a scrum on the half-way line only delayed, could not prevent, its fashioning. Time would bring the experience for all the rest – seasons of encouraging club and Welsh and British XVs with rolling, devouring kicks that ate up opposition gains and opponents' hearts with their frequency as much as their accuracy; years of combination with the battering ram of Mervyn Davies acting as softener for his spearthrust; games on a wet, greasy November pitch in a Gwent valley or a sun-baked plain half-way round the

445

world; nail-biting games whose outcome hung on Edwards's absorbing punishment at the line-out, as in the first half in each of the two Triple Crown clinching games in Dublin in 1976 and 1978, until his forwards sealed the gaps and his backs were inspired by his courage and composure to assert their own superiority in the second half. On several occasions, it was his sheer indestructibility alone that held Wales together when the storm was at its fiercest, to reveal – and as the Lions tour of 1977, of which he was not a part, confirmed – the hollowness of the convenient cliché that no one is indispensable. In terms of Welsh and British rugby between 1971 and 1978, Gareth Edwards, whose prodigious gifts amounted to nothing less than genius, was wholly indispensable. At the end he was master of everything, even of his weaknesses – the poor, shovelled pass of his early games had become, via spin and power, an extended arm that gave his outside-half a ball for all seasons and a fresh attacking momentum, but he still knew enough to counteract a less reliable left arm with a varied tactic. The last score he registered for Wales was in his last match, against France in 1978, his third drop goal for his country.

Having offered so much in so many facets of play Edwards can be regarded as the best-equipped rugby player of an era intent on a 'total' concept of team and individual play. That would be sufficient to guarantee his niche of fame; the tries he totted up emblazon his name in the game's history. Nothing stopped the conveyor belt of Edwards specials, neither a thickening girth nor an alerted defence, and even less a flicker of doubt that he might not, could not, cross the line. From short distances he became

446

virtually unstoppable. The crowd at Cardiff came to sense when an Edwards charge for the line behind a scrum or round the line-out was 'on' and then, the score achieved, would relapse into a sated stupor that their wishes were at one with this man's capability. Incredibly, throughout his entire career, he never broke a bone, or suffered even a cut that required a stitch; all his injuries were muscular, from which he, like others was always able to make a remarkably rapid recovery thanks to the expert attentions of physiotherapist Gerry Lewis, like his father Ray before him, a magical masseur of national Welsh muscles.

In 1967 the nineteen-year-old tyro international was 5foot 8inches and 11stone 9pounds; in 1978 the thirty-one-year-old veteran carried 13stone 4pounds. He had not grown an inch but his stature was now immense. From 1973 the French, against whom he had made his debut in 1967, simply captioned their programme notes – 'un des grands du rugby mondial'. That was exactly half-way through his international career. Edwards's first try against France had been in 1969, when he ricocheted down the right touch-line like a demented spinning top, breaking at least four tackles and proving in a gyrating, urgent quest for the line, that the determination that came scorching out of his eyes like a double-headed oxyacetylene flame would burn through any human obstacle. Wales drew 8-8 that day but two years later an Edwards try on the left began their downfall. Where Barry John had moved like a self-regulating pendulum, Edwards brought to scrum-half play the pent-up explosive star-burst that Cliff Jones and Cliff Morgan gave to fly-half running, and since Gareth Edwards, knowing the power of his stocky physique, struck for his kingdom from closer in, the coiled inner spring he unwound whiplashed its way to triumph upon glorious triumph.

If he was, through training and education, a back amongst backs, he was, by temperament and shared work, a forward amongst forwards. Edwards often hunted with the foraging Morris whose origins and features echoed his own and the greatest individual try he scored, in a game won crushingly by 35-12 against Scotland, ended not in the elegant touchdown of a graceful three-quarter but in a lunge that covered his face in the anonymity of mud. The uncertainly raised hand to acknowledge the crowd's acclaim – because 'I felt the applause was different' – accepted the common bond and the lack of anonymity that will forever attend a man who scored a seventy-five yard try by breaking round the back of a scrum, handing off a restraining Scot, and running on. It was Cardiff on 5 February 1972 and he had already crashed over from short range, after seemingly being held, still festooned with four Scots; only minutes later, he was to do the impossible. There was no support, for he had broken too quickly and too far out for that; scarcely expecting to broach the first defence but now loose and alone, he raced with Renwick and Steele to dive at the crucially-timed second for the ball before it slithered away to the right-hand touch-in-goal. He lunged, into the mud and onto the red cinder path, beyond the ball that he had, in that final instance of will, touched down....

from *Fields of Praise* (1980)

Raymond Garlick

Cardiff

Passing the Arms Park, hearing
The sixty-odd thousand fling
Their battle chants, bay uproar
For their game of ritual war —
Like that lion-tongued Roman
Crowd, no doubt, when sweating men
Fought in the scorch of Nero's
Eye; passing, the dark thought rose
How, outside the stadium,
So many of these are dumb
For their country – who acclaim
Its crowning in a mere game.

from *A Sense of Time* (1972)

Eddie Butler

Prosser's Pontypool

Pontypool left the 1950s and slid away in the 1960s until
they found themselves approaching the age of the Coach, the
Cup and the general brilliance of the 1970s from the bottom
of a grim pile-up. At the start of the golden decade they were
adrift in that awful, lonely place known as Below Penarth.
That is the moment when Ray Prosser was appointed coach.
Now the age of legend could really begin. And here surely
there was no room whatsoever for any ambiguity.

449

Pross was a single-minded monster, a rock in the second row who had been the one guaranteed supplier of possession for Benny [Jones] and the three-quarter jets in the 1950s. At some stage of his upbringing somebody had inserted railway sleepers where his shoulders should have been. He had played on twenty-two occasions for Wales between 1956 and 1961, a lock converted to prop for international duty. He was hard and crude, skilled and analytical. He was an enforcer and a technician, but only, it seemed, with regard to eight-fifteenths of the side. He professed always to have a fearful mistrust of three-quarters.

He was above all a character. And if much of his colour came from his use of language – Anglo-Saxon at its most effluent, an invective that would draw crowds in their hundreds to the Park on training nights and which could cripple the feeble of spirit at fifty paces – much, too, came from his self-projection as the small-town simpleton. Pross could just about make it five miles up or down the valley, north to Blaenavon Forgeside where he would supervise Sunday morning gallops led by John Perkins high up on the tramways above Big Pit, or south to Cwmbran, but any further than these neighbouring towns in the Eastern Valley and he would fall victim to homesickness. In later years, after his career had progressed from driving a bulldozer to overseeing slag-reclamation at Panteg Steelworks, he would talk of his dislike for the weekly thirty-mile round-trip to Cardiff to pick up the wages.

'Yes, it must be worrying, Pross, having the responsibility for all that money, and you not particularly fond of driving.'

450

'Bollocks to the money,' Pross would say. 'It's just that Cardiff is such a long way away.'

He hated flying even more than driving, he claimed. They once managed to strap him into an aircraft seat for a tour to Washington DC in 1977, but he swore that he would never go into the air again.

And yet... and yet. In summer months his great frame could sometimes be found lying flat out, creating a bow in the warm corrugated-iron roof of his little hut with its stove-pipe chimney among the mountains of slag at the far end of the steelworks. He would be staring straight up into the sky. High above him would be the vapour trails of the flight path to and from the New World, and at their head distant silver specks of flying machines. Pross would know not just every passing plane by its shape – 747, DC10, Concorde, Airbus – but also its specifications and, above all, its safety record. What he feared became the object of serious study.

And as for being a small-town simpleton, it was to some extent true that when he had toured New Zealand with the Lions of 1959, he had pined for home. But it was also true that he spent a large period of the tour in hospital, and that while he was there he dedicated himself once again to serious study, this time of the rugby of the New Zealanders and, in particular, their forwards.

He analysed the New Zealand game from his hospital bed, went home, played on, retired and stepped back for further contemplation. Pontypool went into decline and all the while the coach-to-be stayed away and formulated his coaching philosophy. No doubt, just as he would do with his jet planes, he investigated specifications and performance.

Only this time he was not so concerned about the issue of safety. The giant of post-war rugby in Pontypool crossed his bridge from playing days to coaching career.

It was the start of the 1970s and Welsh rugby was embarking on something gloriously adventurous on the international stage; brilliance and self-confidence were to make the age glitter. Pontypool, typically, were at the rock bottom of the club ladder. Below everyone. Brilliance was for others. Pross started to climb by another route, up a more extreme col. The country was starting to gasp at the exploits of Edwards and John and Gerald and JPR. Pross however needed forwards and he needed backs who would be subservient to his forwards.

From Newport he garnered such backs as centre Ivor Taylor who would become his right-hand man later on the coaching front. But most important of all he welcomed home Terry Cobner after the latter concluded his teachers' training course at Madeley College near Stoke-on-Trent. Cobner of Blaenavon became the on-field inspiration from wing-forward and captain of the new Pontypool.

It seemed that Pross had not had to move outside his self-proclaimed five-mile exclusion zone, although perhaps he extended it to ten miles for that rarer commodity, a back in the county who fitted his bill. Once again, however, it is worth pointing out that while Pontypool truly developed a game that was exclusively theirs – a sort of evolutionary blip, as if they were up some deep-sided valley off-shoot where the sun never shone and that time had forgotten – the reality is that Pontypool never suffered from such acute introspection or even geographic isolation.

452

Travel north from Pontypool towards Abergavenny and to the left rise Mynydd Garnclochty and the Blorenge Mountain, high ridges over which lies Blaenavon, a town of coal and iron. But from right on top of the mountain, at the Keeper's Pond, a reservoir whose waters used to be piped down to the town and the water-balance tower at its forges, the view reveals that this is the first ridge of the industrial valleys of Wales. To the right of the Pontypool-Abergavenny road lies the rolling pasture-land of the Vale of Usk. Pontypool is not confined by twin steep sides. It has always enjoyed flat access to Monmouthshire and the Forest of Dean. There are even in the Eastern Valley accent certain similarities to the drawl of the Forest in terms of quirky grammar, like the use of 'be' for 'is'. The Pontypool voice is obviously Welsh but it is closer to the sounds of Coleford than to the nasal strains of Newport to the south.

It is more than accent. Strong rugby connections exist between the easternmost club in Wales and the clubs of the West Country of England. This story will reveal how relations between the Pooler and many, many clubs grew strained to breaking point, but Gloucester were always strong allies. There were wonderful nights at Kingsholm, of baying crowds and unfettered mischief, of huge confrontation and regular reductions to fourteen players per side. More recently, Bath have been stout supporters of Pontypool's latest drive, in 1998, to climb out of crisis. And closest of all were Berry Hill, from within the boundaries of the royal forest itself, who were like blood brothers, even on the day of the game against the Pontypool second XV, the Athletic, when play was stopped for a search to be conducted in the mud for half an ear. It was a day of brown and crimson hues in the Park.

For the moment, though, at the outset of the Prosser years, isolation referred only to Pontypool's position in the pecking order of Welsh clubs. They were adrift at the bottom. Cobner soon changed all that. Pontypool climbed to eighth in the unofficial championship. The next season they were champions.

There was local talent on tap. Graham Price was playing in the front row as a teenager, a slender, curly-blonde prop on orange squash, who would go home after each game shaking with exhaustion. Ron Floyd, Bill Evans – an outsider from as far away as Abergavenny – and soon John Perkins, another to make the short trip down from Blaenavon, filled the second row.

The message from Pross to his charges was straightforward: utter devotion to the collective cause. In the summer he flogged them up and down the Grotto, a gruelling run from the pitch up to the then ruined Folly Tower – a hilltop landmark rebuilt in recent years, having been destroyed by the army in 1940 to prevent enemy bombers using it as a beacon on their way to the munitions works at Glascoed – and in the winter the forwards themselves flogged other packs at the scrummage.

The anonymous efficiency of the Pontypool pack had its advantages and disadvantages. Ron Floyd was picked to play for Wales B against France B away, a just reward for the big lock's largely unseen contributions at club level. On the eve of the match, as the players of both sides stood awkwardly at some mayoral get-together in the local town-hall, one of the Welsh selectors approached the tall, swarthy man of Gwent and with great deliberation asked him, 'Bonsoir, do you speak English?'

Pontypool were operating at full power. The pack was awesome at the scrummage, fearsome at the line-out, destructive at the ruck. Full-back Robin Williams kicked goals from anywhere inside seventy yards from the opposition posts, equally adept and long-distanced with either left or right foot. Terry Cobner was immense on the charge, hugely strong and with a centre of gravity as low as his boot-laces. But perhaps the power would never have truly been galvanized without the arrival of two players in those rebuilding years of the early 1970s. Two-thirds of the Pontypool front row. They came from the town of Newport via the rugby club of Cross Keys. Yes, Pontypool was transformed for ever when Bobby Windsor and Tony 'Charlie' Faulkner turned up.

Graham Price in those early days was, as suggested, pushing uphill in the grown-up game. He was a local pup, a product of West Mon. school in the town, destined to become one of the Rolls-Royce players of his generation. He was to be a player way ahead of his time, a prop as fast as a back-row with handling skills to match, a tight-head who would win a record number of caps for his position – forty-one between his debut in 1975 at the age of twenty-two and 1983 – and who would play in twelve Lions tests, another record for a prop, on three tours between 1977 and 1983. But three years before his debut for Wales he needed help in the Pontypool front row. It came in the form of a double-act: 'The Duke' at hooker and 'Charlie' on the loose head. Pricey was the quiet one; the other two spiced things up.

They were not that big, although Bobby, when he came home from the Lions tour of 1974, was eighteen stone of world-class athletic venom. Charlie had a strange bottom half to his body, or maybe it just looked slightly spindly compared to his torso from the middle of his back upwards. He was fantastically strong around the shoulders and neck, and if Bobby had an utterly ruthless edge, Charlie had the martial arts of karate. To be fair, he never seemed to use them on the field to hurt people; he preferred to employ more straightforward arts when it came to dishing out pain. Charlie became well-known for his reply to the press when asked about the skills of scrummaging: 'Up, down, inside out – anywhere but backwards.' But he also had another phrase which he would shout out in the club if anyone asked him about his days in the Territorial Army. He would remember nocturnal patrols in Gibraltar: 'Alto. Arriba las manos o disparo'. (Stop. Put your hands up or I'll shoot).

They were certainly not angelic. When I first joined the club in 1976 there was a story going round that the pair of them had been taken in for questioning by the police over some minor misunderstanding. Nothing serious, but it was essential that they synchronized their stories. After the briefest time to prepare, they were led into different rooms and asked to give their accounts separately. Remarkably, every detail of two highly convoluted tales matched perfectly. Except for the moment when a cat had apparently run in front of their car. Bobby said it was black, Charlie said it was white. They were hauled back in for round 2. The colour of the cat was a serious stumbling point. Was it black or was it white? 'Ah, that,' said Charlie. 'Well, you have to remember, it was a very frosty night.'

On the field they could be lethal, although it must be said that they respected the conventions of the battlefield. I once played in a second team game alongside Bobby after we were well past our retirement date, a long time even after the day on tour in Canada in 1985 when he became a grandfather and a father on the same day. Anyway, the Athletic were playing against Tredegar and Bobby simply could not resist giving their scrum-half a little belt. The scrum-half, suitably annoyed, waited and waited until the coast was clear and gave Bob his best shot in return. A neat punch, too. At that moment the referee blew his whistle for the end of the game, and Bob set off after the scrum-half, who not surprisingly had headed for the safety of the tunnel. Suddenly the Pontypool hooker with a trickle of blood coming from his nose was alongside him. The scrum-half turned to run again, but Bob reached out and grabbed him. 'Game's over, Ian,' he said. The scrum-half looked even more worried. 'No, I mean that's it. Whistle's gone, time for a pint, no hard feelings.'

Those hard feelings were reserved for the field of play. There was a time in the mid 1970s when the scrummage was nigh-on uncontrollable, so fast would the front five propel it forward. Oh, in big Cup games the opposition would raise their game and hold firm and Pontypool would be denied yet again a taste of the high life, but in the course of a season's bread-and-butter fixtures, the pack would generate a special quiver, just prior to the put-in by the other team's scrum-half, which meant that the timing of the drive was just right and that somebody had better watch out because rib cartilage was liable to pop. It was the elevation of a humdrum restart activity to some sort of Stalinist collectivist ideal whose goal is the pure joy of destruction...

from *Heart and Soul* (1998)

Siân Nicholas

Jonathan Davies

Jonathan Davies's career revealed the self-assurance of a man who served no ordinary apprenticeship in the game, whose career was not constrained by the game's traditions (traditions that were in themselves fatally weakening), and who as a player sought to control the game rather than let the game control him. His playing style uniquely reflected this attitude. His position, the mythic one of outside-half, brought him both high praise and the highest expectations, but unlike previous players it was not so much the expectations that wore him down as the assumptions, in particular the assumption that an international cap was reward enough in itself. In rugby league he found an environment that was more sympathetic to his character, less dependent on him as the sole matchwinner, and that rewarded his talents openly, not secretly. Once back in 'professional' rugby union, however, he demonstrated how little had changed for the better in the Welsh game in his absence.

After his retirement he finally received the sympathy that he had never courted as a player, as the emotional burden under which he had played his last few seasons became publicly known. But his always uncomfortable relationship with the WRU did not long outlast his retirement, and his media interests now predominate. As an analyst for both rugby union and rugby league on the BBC and for *The Independent on Sunday*, he has attracted respect and something of a following for his unassuming manner and trenchant comments. He has also appeared on the S4C soap *Pobol y Cwm* (as himself) – though the prospect of his following Ray Gravell into an acting career seems unlikely.

What does his career show about Welsh rugby and Welsh society? That Welsh villages could still produce, as if out of nowhere, players with outstanding natural talent, able to adapt to any level – even any code – of rugby at the highest level. That the outside-half position remains, as well as the most glamorous position, also the most thankless, and that not even the best outside-half can – or can be expected to – win games without a pack able to win the ball. That amateurism in rugby union dug its own grave by refusing to acknowledge the world around it: a world where players in all sports seek to be rewarded for their talents with financial security, and where management skills are the first essential, not the last consideration. Finally, that to call Davies an unfulfilled talent reveals the narrowness of a nation's sporting horizons. In a country where rugby league and rugby union had a more equal status, Davies's extraordinary achievement in reaching the heights of both would have received the recognition it merited. But not even the most exciting player of his generation could break the union stranglehold on the Welsh imagination.

What did Jonathan Davies bring to rugby in Wales? The pleasure of instinctive, enterprising running rugby. The frustration that there were not more around him to fashion a team worthy of his, and others', talents. But always, the joy of sheer ability. The last sight of him on the international field, the broad smile amid a sea of defeated Welsh faces on the soon-to-be-demolished National Stadium pitch as he embraced his long-time opposite number Rob Andrew, summed up a career. If one Welsh player of recent times could be said to have exemplified both the most consummate professionalism and the true amateur spirit, Jonathan Davies was that player.

from *Heart and Soul* (1998)

Rupert Moon with David Roach

Moonstruck

I can see the tunnel stretching in front of me and I can hear the noise from the crowd, booming like a tidal wave, sucking me forward onto the pitch. I feel sick. I don't want to go out there but I have to. I'm fighting every instinct in my body, desperate to stay safe in the shadows. Can I leave now? Can I go home? Please, let me go? No. No, this is where I will define myself. A calmness takes over and smothers my anxiety. I want this. I want what's out there waiting for me. My mind jolts, I can't catch my breath, I'm running... someone is shouting, I can hear the studs clattering up the tunnel, scraping, slipping... and suddenly, I'm in daylight and the noise of the howling thousands batters me into submission. I am in the moment. I have over 50,000 reasons to be here. I have a purpose. I have a job to do.

The anthems are over and done with before I know it. I can't hear a thing. Did I sing? I'm sure I sang; I'd put too much effort into understanding the words not to sing, but I can't remember singing. We huddle, I'm shouting, I'm not making any sense but I'm saying all the right things. I'm looking at Emyr Lewis and Ricky Evans, John Davies and Scott Quinnell. What am I saying? They are listening to me with their eyes. I can't hear what I'm saying. Where's Andy Nichol? He's good... sneaky, quick, smart thinking. What's he doing? What's he saying to his pack? No, don't look at them. Don't let them see you, stay hidden, stay secret. Be invisible. Emerge from the forwards like an extra flanker and be big, be bigger and taller, faster and braver than any other player in this arena. My mouth isn't saying what I'm thinking. 'Okay, this is it, boys. I love you, we're off. Let's do them.'

It's wet, the ball is wet. My hands are wet. The ball is too wet. There is water in my eyes. My studs are slipping. There's water in my socks already and we've just started. Where's the ball? Where is it? 'Pegs, where's the ball?' Here's the ball, it's coming now... here it is! Here's the ball. Right, it's mine. Look, pass, where's Jinks? No... he doesn't want it. Where's Nichol? Get it out, just get it out! Go, Ieuan, now. Ball, boot, and kick... yes, solid shot, is that more rain? Stay in play ball, stay in... go, Ieuan, go! Come on, boys, after it... in there...' Ouch. Punches, get in there, take the punch, it doesn't hurt, you can't hurt me, no one can, my body is on the line, show them you can't hurt me.

Hit me again, go on, can't hurt me, hit me! Look at Garin! He's going mad, punching, punching, punching... punching. Whistle. French ref. Shouting... *'Non!'* *'Non!'* I'm in, scragged, someone's flung me on my butt. On the grass... it's so wet! Who did that? Who did that? Logan? 'Logan, you little... was that you, Logan?' He's walking away, smiling. Got me. Get up quick, I look stupid. 'Ref, ref, no, ref... Garin... it's cool, Garin's cool.' Walk away, leave. Don't look, don't think. Breathe, Rupert. Breathe. Breathe.

from *Full Moon* (2003)

Peter Finch

The Stadium

From the hills look south across Cardiff and the chances are your eyes will light on one of two ubiquitous structures. The older is the white, churchlike building that was once Spiller's flour mill, glorious on the flats of the Port. The other is the gleaming, four-towered UFO, landed like a visitor from Andromeda, crouched by the sleek, silver Taff. This second is, of course, the largest retractable-roof public structure in Western Europe, home of rock as much as rugby, the Wales Millennium Stadium. What do we think of this place? Do we like it being there? We do. Do we love it? We do. We do not.

The Stadium is built on the drained, reclaimed land revealed when Brunel realigned the Taff to the west in the mid 1800s. This damp parkland ran from a big house built

462

facing the Castle. This was the Cardiff Arms Hotel, erected on the site of the Red House Inn which had been destroyed by fire in 1770. Bute stayed here, rather than at his Burges-refurbished Castle. The beds were softer. And there was beer. The Cardiff Arms was demolished in 1878 when Castle Street was widened. The Angel Inn, next door, remains. Its original facade can be seen next to the Castle Arcade. The park, the Cardiff Arms Park, given by Bute to the Town, with the caveat that it remain for recreational use, became, in 1848 the first home of Cardiff Cricket Club. As interest in spectator sport increased among the burgeoning industrial-age Cardiff population cricket was joined by football and, in 1874, by rugby. The Wanderers played the Glamorgan 2nd XV. History began. Crowds arrived. Stands went up. The open space, the parkland, became fenced. Charges were levied to walk on Bute's munificence. A focus for Welsh nationhood started to grow. The river flowed.

On a Sunday in 1997 with most of the Arms Park south stand gone and men in hard-hats racing the clock with their tools of demolition the auctioneer begins the bidding. I'm here by accident, walked in from sunny Westgate Street, chasing the fuss. The old Arms Park is being knocked flat to make space for the lottery-funded great white hope, the Millennium Stadium. The memorabilia has to be worth something. The man with the hat and the tannoy is turning it to cash. The content of the changing rooms, the boxes and the bars have already gone. He's taking bids for the seats. There's a crowd of fifty or so. Sunday best: trainers, sweats, jeans, slacks, family groups, hot dogs, cans, valley voices. Someone wants Row G seat 45. That's his. He sat there for thirty years. He's going to get this for his sixtieth. She bids. She wins. She gets G45 and six hard polypropylene red fold-ups either side. Take them home today in the back of a pick-up. A bluff fifty-year-old in a loud check has bought himself twenty-five to put up in the garden round his barbeque. Doesn't matter which twenty-five, so long as they come from here. Local clubs bid for lots of fifty to re-erect in their own tin-shack, wood and roofing-felt stands.

The pitch causes the greatest blood rush. It's being sliced and sold. You can actually buy squares of green sward, the hallowed turf from the holy ground. The bids mount as Welsh clubs battle for their own slivers of green luck, to be trimmed and relayed with care in the centres of their own boot-pocked grounds. Someone gets a piece that will go into the middle of his front lawn. Another wins enough to re-lay a tennis court. Wrong sport but who cares. The magic will travel. This is grail, this is. Glory runs in its wake.

The new Stadium opens in 1999, in time for the Rugby World Cup. Wrangled contracts and bad blood brought it in on cost. Laing, the builders, lost a fortune. The four corner masts that hold the vast sliding roof in perfect steel-heavy suspension gleam white above the City skyline. The Empire Pool and an array of other surrounding landmarks have gone to make space. The pitch runs north-south rather than east-west. The turf comes on pallets. You can take it up, store it in a shed near Bridgend, use the space for shows. There's a wooden walkway suspended alongside the Taff. Neil Jenkins runs on and uses his unerring boot to break the world points record. The crowd of 72,500 scream like they're not going to stop.

On the tour, WRU insignia gleaming, our guide is built like a forward. He's wearing inconspicuous Docs, hard and heavy, good when you are on your feet all day. His line in jokes is soft and easy. He's left his flies undone. Among the twenty-one Germans and twenty assorted locals in our party no one is willing to let him know. We tour the Away teams changing rooms, Graham Henry suspended floors, individual baths in a communal enclosure. Larger than life cuts-outs of the Welsh team stand around for dramatic effect. The tannoy plays a Henry before-game inspiration psyche-up. Punters get snapped standing next to Neil. This is still the Arms Park, our guide tells us, the Wales Millennium Stadium is merely at the Arms Park. When the Millennium Commission's three-year contractual stipulation is over the name will be auctioned. Highest wins. This could well become the Mitsubishi Nippon Arena at the Arms Park. Or the I Don't Believe It's Not Butter Stadium. WRU needs the sponsorship. He smiles. The Germans make notes. Someone takes a photo of the bar staff loading a dozen barrels of lager into the 42-person capacity lift. We move on.

In the open air Harriet the hawk is circling to frighten off the seagulls. There's a crowd-roar tape playing for atmosphere. The kids in the party get a chance to have their photos done holding a replica Rugby World Cup in the Royal Box. I go up the 96 steps to the stadium top. Looking back down gets the vertigo flowing. Try chucking an empty can down from here. Wouldn't reach. 'Brilliant', says the man next to me, a pensioner wearing a red Welsh team shirt. Different every week. Rugby. Soccer. Pop music. Boxing. Wouldn't like to live here. Bloody noise. On match days the city becomes one vast, swirling party. Middle-aged men with painted faces. Kids in fancy dress. Women screaming drunk. Brings the trade. Most of Westgate Street is already wall-to-wall drinkery. Wood and aluminium. Omnipresent plastic glasses. People pissed everywhere. Don't bring your car in. Don't use the station. Don't walk St Mary and certainly don't try to check the history of Quay or Womanby. Good for business. Makes Cardiff the true international centre of our country. A world-class venue in the city with more hotel beds than the rest of Wales put together. We relish the fame but not the effect. For many of us love will be a long time coming.

from *Real Cardiff* (2002)

Dai Smith

All Played Out

Max Boyce, sans bobble hat and leek this time but still the rugby troubadour of less troublesome times, had walked onto the Wembley pitch around 3.30 to sing 'Hymns and Arias' (Old and New) to a crowd expecting more entertainment before the game than triumph in it. That was the Welsh half, anyway, of the near eighty-thousand who had walked up Wembley Way, looked at Sir Owen Williams's Twin Towers of this 1922 stadium, and settled in for their last home-and-away match in the family-friendly oval in north London. Max had delighted his fans: even reminding them that the roof of Cardiff's Millennium Stadium would

466

roll back so that God 'could watch us play'. At Wembley She could just look straight down and smile as a century of Welsh clichés were greeted and applauded with great humour by Welsh supporters now well used to fondling their passions with distancing irony.

'Sing us your song' they gently mocked an English opposition as prophetically stuck on a one-line groove as their groaning team would prove to be two hours later: 'Swing Low, Sweet Chariot' kept doing its circular tour until the wheels came off and the Welsh, gleeful at last, advised something painful about chariots and sphincters. But that was all to come. For now it was the London Welsh Male Voice Choir and 'Cwm Rhondda' and 'Calon Lân' and, to thunderous applause, Tommy Woodward from Treforest in his reincarnation as Tom Jones from Pontypridd and Hollywood about to deliver, in person, Welsh rugby's unofficial hymn 'Delilah'. We had been betrayed so often, why not one more time? The rendering was a magnificent pastiche, a chorus of 'Ha! Ha! Has!' sent ricocheting back to a delighted Tom Jones in a mass *opera bouffe*.

The Royal Regiment of Wales, headed by Shenkyn the goat, strutted onto the pitch in front of the about-to-be-slaughtered Welsh XV while their white-shirted nemesis, Dallaglio's beef-on-the-bone team, all planed cheeks and rooted stance, waited. Then in the bright April sunshine, warm but with sudden hints of colder mistiness, the anthems. Lusty and confident as usual from England, fervent but nervy from Wales, the players looping their arms over each other's shoulders, the New Zealand contingent in the team, full-back Shane Howarth and flanker Brett

Sinkinson, straining for the words of the Land of their Grandfathers. And the crowd, certainly those who had come from Wales that day, singing inside themselves the refrain of the Stereophonics' lead singer, Kelly Jones, who had been popping up on a trail on BBC Wales TV to tell England 'We don't want to be your enemy', but also 'So long as we beat the English we don't care'. It was only half true but as Neil Jenkins kicked off it was a settlement much to be desired and, in the eyes of most good judges, an impossible dream. Yet, in reality, the songs had only just begun as the red caterpillar of the Welsh regiment side-stepped its way off the pitch by going under the posts.

When it was all over the crowd stayed and stayed until the Welsh heroes came out to join the mutual self-congratulation. A conversion of an improbable try in injury-time had brought Wales victory by a single point, 32-31, and the celebrations would not stop until laughter rictus set in. Not since Muhammad Ali had turned his rumble in the jungle with George Foreman into Rope-a-dope had escapology been refined into such a winning sporting tactic. At Wembley, on the streets and outside the pubs, strangers hugged each other, Jacks embraced Turks and anyone wearing red-and-white colours was cheered. For hours the coaches and cars heading home honked at the revellers outside as the revellers inside leaned out of doors, windows and roof hatches. Ecstasy on the move and not a pill in sight. All over Wales on that early Sunday evening telephones rang and people rushed out to find their friends. In Cardiff the capital's usual Sunday-evening calm turned into a bach-on-ale night such as even worldly taxi drivers had never witnessed. And no trouble anywhere. Pedestrianised precincts filled. Pubs let tidal flows of happiness in and out of their doors. Vehicles stalled by the crowds were swept along in a riot of noise and joy which resembled a French general election or a Rio street carnival. Can it possibly mean so much?

The delivery of an expectation beyond any rational belief had, certainly, brought the wider desire to this peak of euphoria. To all intent and purpose, England had won the game they lost. Their dreadnought pack had rumbled and steamed in the loose (though significantly not in the tight where the Welsh front row gripped them for the whole game). They began sensationally when full-back Perry, exploiting missed Welsh tackles after a quickly taken penalty, had broken through, found England's right wing, Dan Luger, on a diagonal run and saw him thrust over at the Welsh posts with less than three minutes gone. The pattern was set. English forward bump and grind, and incisive though not always rewarded running from Catt and his centres, Johnny Wilkinson and the cheekily named 16 stone 6 feet 6 inches giant Barrie-Jon Mather, were followed by penalty goals from Jenkins to keep Wales in touch. Just. For, with the scores at 10-9 to England on twenty minutes, Dallaglio, for the first but not the last time, tells Wilkinson to kick a penalty to find touch in the Welsh 22. England win the line-out, move and drive imperiously right, then left, to put their 19-year-old left wing, Hanley, in almost under the posts. Inexplicably the left-footed Wilkinson misses the conversion so the score remains at 15-9, but if he had taken the earlier penalty as a shot at goal and succeeded it would have been only 13-9 so Dallaglio's confident decision was, at this stage, justified.

Meanwhile, and until the very end, Gibbs was being nutcrackered by the English pincers in the centre, clean Welsh ball was dropped or turned over and England's fanned-out defensive line did not buckle (some thought a Welsh chip kick might have been useful but with the backs playing so flat they would have to turn quickly if it was returned: or, as in their irksome defeats that season at the hands of Scotland and Ireland, charged down with dire consequence). The only consolation was that Jenkins seemed incapable of missing goal from any point or distance on the field and the English propensity to be so up in defence as to be offside gave him the chances he took. The number 10, winning his sixty-fourth cap, had brought Wales to 15-15 with twenty-eight minutes gone, with a straight-on trajectory thump from just ten yards inside the English half. Again Dallaglio spurned two more penalty shots for Wilkinson, who had only missed with one kick after all and had slotted seven against the French at Twickenham only three weeks earlier, before letting the Newcastle youngster stroke one over from in front of the Welsh posts, 18-15. With the English score still first in the mind's eye, for it truly seemed like a home game for them, English voices neighed and bayed around the amphitheatre. In the stands the English coach, Clive Woodward, resplendent in what looked more like an admiral's headgear than a baseball cap, gazed out on victory across the horizon. The Welsh coach, Graham Henry, as inscrutable sartorially in regulation dress of blazer and tie as he was po-faced in expression, arched his eyebrows, more Mephistopheles than messianic – and thought. Half-time approached. His big-hitters, those pedigree Scarlets, the

470

Quinnell brothers, Scott as blond and as bulky as Marlon Brando in *The Young Lions*, Craig as bulky and bald as Telly Savalas in the *Dirty Dozen*, were auditioning like mad but, despite being ably cued-in by the leaping Wyatt and the bullocking Charvis, neither they, nor anyone else, were getting the part they wanted to play. The lines were forgotten completely when Dawson's hanging downfield kick was bumped out of Gareth Thomas's grasp by the oncoming Howarth and seized by Richard Hill for a scrambled but effective flanker's try. Conversion followed and, surely, at 25-15 on half-time, England were moving out of range. Not so. Another huge penalty from Jenks on the stroke of time and Wales went in, battered but not yet beaten, only seven points adrift. At the outset of Graham Henry's reign, Ray Williams, along with other rugby patriots, had wondered about the efficacy of appointing a New Zealander to coach Wales. After all, and no matter how special Henry's record with Auckland in the Super 12 had been, the very nature of Wales would suggest 'a completely different environment' than the one in which he had succeeded. Williams, however, had been both reflective and supportive.

I can predict a culture shock for him when he comes to Wales. But the die has been cast and we need to give Graham Henry our fullest support. I was interested to learn that he had previously been a schoolteacher as had Clive Rowlands, Carwyn James and John Dawes, Wales' most successful coaches by a very wide margin.

This is the profession which has been denigrated from time to time in the correspondence

471

columns of the *Western Mail* with the statement that teachers did not make successful coaches at senior level. But coaching is about communication and motivation, hallmarks of the outstanding teacher...

How the Welsh coach needed those key hallmarks to work for him now. In the dressing-room he told his players they could play much better than that. It was time to start playing. Just as they had sensationally against France five weeks before, when Jenkins firecrackered the entire team with his runs from broken play and tries from Charvis, Ponty's Dafydd James ('There's always so much time playing outside Neil') and Craig Quinnell had bagged the first triumph in Paris since legendary 1975 and the first ever at Stade de France. This was the first time at Wembley against England. Another omen perhaps. Besides, England had been negative, lucky on the bounce of the ball, clumsy in executing a final thrust. They had to be moved wide, pegged back and stretched until their advancing line gaped a hole or two. He had told them after they had narrowly blown a close game against world champions, South Africa, on this same ground and in his first outing in charge of Wales, that he respected them as individuals and as players, but that, cold and pausing before they met Italy, and even with a wobbly win at Stradey Park against powerful Argentina behind them, he did not, yet, respect them as a team. After Italy, all parts firing together, he gave his crooked smile and offered them that too. Now, in the bowels of Wembley, all pre-match joy long dissipated, he told them, again, what to do. It was only the English whose respect they did not have now. Not yet anyway.

The light was becoming greyer as the afternoon advanced and yet, sporadically, more golden and luminous. In the tunnel, out of sight but not out of hearing, workmen began preparing the wooden podium on which Dallaglio would receive the glittering prize for England's record fifth Triple Crown win on the trot in their sixth consecutive win over Wales and their twelfth Grand Slam at the end of the Five Nations Championship forever. Did it mean so much? If the podium became a gallows it would. And two minutes into the second half Wales hinted mercilessly at what would indeed come. Howarth's massive hoof into the England half was knocked on by Neil Back, squinting from under his dove-grey helmet and, tetchily, a liability to his side all afternoon. This time Wales used the penalty to go for a try and, controlling the ball through successive scrimmages and breaks in midfield, they sent Jenkins right across the face of a closing English defence. Superbly, the Pontypridd pivot bulleted a huge pin-point cut-out pass to Howarth who strolled over the line. Jenkins, who converted from the touch-line, had had a split second to make the courageous decision. This was a rugby executive. He simply made it.

Everything about Neil Roger Jenkins looked at odds with what he was achieving. He did not look ice-cool; his shirt flapped loose on the side, his thinning ginger hair was plastered against his scalp, he took his gumshield out to snap and snarl, the perspiration ran down his face and he flicked the sweat from his ears. Wales were hanging on by a fingernail and he knew it. All thought of the cold revenge

473

he had exacted on Thomas Castaignède for the drubbing he and Wales had received (51-0) against France the previous year was no comfort now to the man who, at full-back against England at Twickenham in that doleful 1998, had been part of a record 60-26 defeat at English hands. This was not then or there but it was backs-to-the-wall and Jenkins knew more than anyone about that.

It was as if, in the spirit of this remarkable footballer, somehow things were as defensive and awry as they were in the country itself. In the press conference after the stunning win against France the hacks had quizzed him about his, to them, unexpected dummies and runs. He visibly bridled. He had made breaks before, he told them. In the very first season of the Welsh National League, aged nineteen, he had hit the headlines at Stradey Park when, intercepting a pass and, as his autobiography modestly put it, 'showing a turn of speed' he had helped Pontypridd hold Llanelli to a 'highly improbable 10-10 draw'. Improbable, amongst other reasons, because Ponty had seen their second row Jim Scarlett sent off. It was following that dismissal that Jenkins had chosen to announce his arrival in senior rugby and to recall, in 1998, that the 'minutes which followed Jim's dismissal were probably the most significant in my career. We were looking down the barrel and Llanelli came at us with fresh purpose'. He became a Welsh international in that same season. No one felt the lows, and the occasional highs, of the 1990s more than the unassuming man who had stepped out at Wembley that day already Wales's record points scorer. He ended the game with 767 points scored in all internationals and as the second highest points scorer in international rugby of all time.

It was England who were coming at him, today, 'with fresh purpose'. In 1996, for his beloved Pontypridd, it had been Neath. The favourites, Ponty in their second Cup Final in two years and never a winner (defeated by Swansea 19-12 in 1995), had reeled under the western All Black onslaught to 22-9 down with the clock running out. An inspirational 39-year-old captain, the bearded prop Nigel Bezani, had refused to yield to this arm-wrestle and in the most thrilling Welsh Cup Final Pontypridd ran out winners at 29-22. Jenks had been partnered then, and through the decade, by his childhood friend Paul John, the son of Dennis, the club's inspiring guide since 1991. This was all about family. About connections. On the Sardis Road ground Jenkins kicked his kicks and made his runs, against a backdrop of a colliery winding house (defunct), the unfolding hills of the lower Rhondda (penetrated every twenty minutes by a punctuating train) and a river eponymously named Taff (clear enough now for trout). That was real heritage. Crowds flocked here to see French teams braved (Brive) and English champions (Bath) bested. If there was a symbolic team in Wales for 'the people's game' in the 1990s amongst the ruins of management and philistine commercialism, it was Pontypridd, champions themselves, at last, in 1997. And all the while their catalytic force was judged by outsiders to be a journeyman player and dropped or moved seven times as the Welsh fly-half, or in his case, more accurately, as the half outside. Only Graham Henry had had the immediate courage and insight to put him permanently on the inside straight for Wales.

Graham Henry would proudly talk, later, of the character and guts of his team. He knew that his chosen fly-half personified the relished characteristics. The game, however,

475

was swinging away from the metronomic contribution Jenkins had made, the heartbeat that had, yet again, kept Wales alive. The pendulum moved again. Wilkinson hit over a penalty in direct line of the Welsh goal posts. 28-25. England tightened the noose. Only fifteen minutes into the second period and the Welsh lie offside so Jonny Wilkinson takes England to 31-25. Chariots oscillate close to the ground all over Wembley. The Welsh front row do an all-change but it is the English, balls clutched and then fumbled, who storm on. In an allegedly dangerous passage of play that looks like Shrove Tuesday folk football in Derbyshire, Tim Rodber, the gifted and immense English back-row, is upended and toppled over at a rolling melee. Penalty England. And out of reach, beyond three scores. Except that Dallaglio, with less than five minutes left, supremely and with self-assurance ahead of insurance, tells his young centre to find a touch in the Welsh left-hand-side 22. England attack. Wales, all tension and resolve, escape, clear from under their posts. Back towards the half-way line. Gallant, doughty Wales are sinking to defeat. Consolation prizes are being offered: Jenkins is named man-of-the-match.

Not yet. Not quite. In open play Rodber tackles Colin Charvis's face with his shoulder and fractures the Welshman's cheekbone. The ensuing penalty allows Jenkins to clear to touch upfield for one last effort. Full-time has been played but at a three-man line-out on the right-hand touch-line in the English 22 the bounding Wyatt takes a two-handed catch and throws to Howley who passes to Scott Quinnell standing out to break the line as Wales had attempted before. He shuttles sideways juggling the ball uneasily and so unsettling the drift English defence. And suddenly, coming in fast on a slanting run is Scott Gibbs.

If Jenkins is the beating heart of this team, Gibbs is its mind. The soul thing he will leave to the crowd. He, too, has been in the eye of the storm before. His trick is to pretend, to himself and to others, that it is all about the individual self – on and off the field of play – and that just being a professional is what matters. When in April 1994 he left Swansea for that other St Helens, and rugby league, he was shamefully called a 'rugby prostitute' by the chairman of the club which, at the end of the 1999 season, as another kind of rebel, he will captain to a Welsh Cup victory by a record score against 'loyal' Llanelli. Yet this loner was the clear leader of the Lions in South Africa in 1997. More redolent of this than his ferocious dumping of Os du Randt was his televised exhortation to his gathered team-mates in the crucial Second Test to raise their game, higher and yet higher. They did. Neil Jenkins with whom he had debuted for both the Welsh Youth and the Wales XV had kicked fifteen points, as many as South Africa managed altogether, in the Lions' 18-15 win.

Gibbs and Jenkins were neither a pair of builders nor a firm of solicitors. They were not even alike, physically or socially, except in several vital respects. They were born in the 1970s just as the Welsh world whose apex rugby had seemed to be was disappearing. They grew up on frustration not fulfilment. They had to make their own history if they were not to be the parasites of others' memories. Heritage meant nothing to them. The present was theirs to shape. Scott Gibbs toughened himself mentally against Welsh sentimentality and physically hardened himself in rugby league. He grew in every sense. In the modern era the close, popular appeal that Jenkins epitomized but only found in Pontypridd was the soul put at risk by moneyed, managed, so-called professional Welsh rugby; the heart of the game was none the less, only to be kept alive by a hard-headed understanding that the modern world had altered the stakes and the rest was propaganda. Gibbs could not wait for Welsh rugby to save itself, if ever, by restructuring root and branch. He did it for himself. But, thereby, he was doing it beyond himself, binding the bobble hats and the bourgeoisie in the only possible salvation. For if pits could close and communities shrivel so could clubs shrink and rugby die. How much would that mean? Well, in a populist sense, Wales itself. A National Assembly could be chosen (in 1997 by just 50 per cent of the Welsh population) and elected (in 1999 by rather less than 50 per cent), but if it could not fill the cultural space it inhabited by entering the Welsh imagination it would have no tenable hold on the Welsh future. Gibbs was a patriot beyond politics.

In a slight lull in play just before he scored he had eyed up his Lions colleague, the fourteen-times English captain Lawrence Bruno Nero Dallaglio. The drummer from Pencoed sang out, loudly enough to have Lawrence scratch his head:

I feel good. I feel good tonight... I feel good.

Then we all did.

He took the ball from Quinnell on the burst to brush past a shell-shocked Rodber. The side-step, more baffling than the Rubik cube he resembled, had just begun. Matt Dawson's ankle grab was walked out of; Matt Perry was bamboozled in mid-air by Gibbs's own special re-run of Walt Disney's

478

Fantasia, as a balletic Welsh elephant; and the despairing Hanley was sent one way whilst Gibbs left by the other exit. He even saluted with a triumphantly raised fist as he galumphed his 15 stones over the line. 31-30. To England. The Welsh centre gave the bedraggled Jenkins the ball. 'I had no doubts... he'd kick those over in his sleep, left-footed, wouldn't he?' Gibbs said later. Unlike Jonny without-an-aitch Wilkinson, Neil without-an-aitch Jenkins was a right-footed kicker. So, as it had been an hour or so earlier for his counterpart, it was the wrong side of the pitch for him.

The ritual began. The sandcastle was made. The ball placed at an angle and the foot aligned. Then, five steps, one rather tentatively done as ever, back, before three taken, within an increasing and easy arc to his left side. The foot had been wiped on his calf. Imaginary mud is picked from the sole of the boot. The kicker bows to the ball. He stares at it and up, away to the posts, at it. Eyes down again, and up. It becomes shamanistic. The left hand swiped down the jersey, the right shaken loose, its fingers distended in a paroxysm, all the time the eyes moving from ball to posts, then the object imaginatively ushered in by the back-to-front sweep of an open palm. This eternity of preparation takes hardly any time at all before he runs and, as he says, 'boots it between the sticks'. 32-31. To Wales. We lead for the first and only time in the match. For the last time too. England are played out....

from 'Beyond the Fields of Praise' in *More Heart and Soul* (1999)

FINAL WHISTLE

John Stuart Williams

River Walk, Cardiff

Walking by the river, the morning cold
thick between old trees
dimly spread in parkland ease,
he stops to watch a mess of small
boys, a muddy ruck of all-sorts,
playing at playing rugby, hurts
and triumphs muffled in the turf.
                                        The ball,
kicked true for once, hangs
in the lifting wind, gull without wings,
then drops dead in his unused hands.
The feel of it, the dubbined skin, sends old
signals through his fingers, cold
and clumsy, releases things long forgot,
the smell of wintergreen, the hot roar
of crowds, running in to score,
a snatch of rude song: a scene
that mocks the years in between, fall
of leaf, the cruel quickness of it all.

A clatter of startled rooks breaks
him free: he grins, wryly kicks
the ball back, resumes his steady walk.

from *Dic Penderyn and other poems* (1970)

481

Editor's Afterword

As a teenager I came across Jean Cocteau's obituary to world middleweight champion Marcel Cerdan, and it changed my life in the way that Marcel changed Edith Piaf's. Perhaps that life was already changing. I was still in short trousers when I turned from familiar coral and treasure islands to the muddier, often bloodier fields of sporting endeavour trampled in his autobiography by my hero Trevor Ford, and to the exploits of the 1955 British Lions in South Africa recounted by J. B. G. Thomas. Those two have a lot to answer for. It was only later that a more historically informed perspective enabled me to recognise that sport was and continues to be an integral constituent in the making of modern Wales.

I already knew that the writing on it could be vivid and resonant, and I had long felt the need for an anthology of Welsh sports writing that would reflect the best of it. So when the opportunity came to prepare one for the *Library of Wales,* I leapt at it. I was quite clear my priority would be the quality of the writing rather than the sensational headline, and that my model would be my much-thumbed *Best American Sports Writing* series. A nexus of cultural and historical factors has meant that only until fairly recently have leading Welsh writers embraced sport as a part of their imaginative landscape as creatively as Hemingway, Algren, Mailer, Malamud, Roth and De Lillo, but the more I (re-)read I discovered that in truth the likes of Alun Richards, Ron Berry, Leslie Norris and Dannie Abse can well hold their own. If my favourite opener remains the one written by John Lardner, son of the great Ring, fifty years ago – 'Stanley Ketchel was only twenty-four years of age when he was fatally shot in the back by the common-law husband of the lady who was cooking his breakfast' – there are, I believe, pieces in *this* anthology that seize the reader's attention with comparable urgency. John Morgan's opener 'Punch, Jesus, Punch!' runs Lardner close.

Although deliberately to avoid them would be merely perverse, I have not gone looking for the big games and memorable moments. In general I have been more interested in a scene or an insight within a narrative, a revelatory piece of dialogue like a crucial line from a film or a book that gives both writer and reader a better understanding of the subject. Like the celebrated exchange between Joe DiMaggio and Marilyn Monroe in Gay Talese's piece for *Esquire* magazine in 1966 where Marilyn, just back from entertaining the troops in Korea and being mobbed by crowds of fifty thousand, tells her husband 'Joe, you never heard such cheering' and DiMaggio replies, 'Yes, I have.' The best writing always stands up that way, and I still find reading some of the pieces collected here as exciting as the first time I came across them: Hugh McIlvanney, for instance, has grasped the significance of its boxers to the town of Merthyr so intuitively that we almost feel the quality of the writing justifies the brutality of the sport. Almost.

Researching this anthology therefore has confirmed my long-held conviction that the *best* sports writing is just good writing that happens to be about sport. In the course of compiling it I have incurred several debts, especially to John Jenkins, Andrew Hignell, Emma Lile, Christopher

Meredith, Meic Stephens, Chris Williams, Daniel Williams, Tomos Williams, Colin Thomas, John Tomlinson, and most of all to the *Library of Wales* series editor Dai Smith. Dai's close involvement every step of the way has made this feel almost like another collaboration. Almost.

Gareth Williams

The Authors

Dannie Abse (b.1923) poet, novelist and doctor.
John Arlott (1914-91) writer and quintessential broadcasting voice of English cricket.

Ron Berry (1920-97) Rhondda-born novelist and writer.
Huw Bowen (b.1959) professor of history at the University of Wales, Swansea.
Max Boyce (b.1943) entertainer and troubadour of Welsh rugby.
Richard Burton (1925-84) film star, once described by his fellow Welsh actor Keith Baxter as 'a gifted and enthusiastic rugby player, with a reputation as a fearless and dirty player whose vindictiveness on the field could be boundless.'
Eddie Butler (b.1957) rugby pundit and broadcaster, capped sixteen times for Wales 1980-84.

W .J. T. Collins (1868-1952) journalist and local historian of Newport and Monmouthshire.
Alexander Cordell (1914-97) author of *Rape of the Fair Country* (1959) and other best-selling historical novels about south Wales.
Peter Corrigan (b.1935) sports journalist and historian of Welsh soccer.
Tony Curtis (b.1946) poet, art critic and professor of poetry at the University of Glamorgan.

Gerald Davies (b.1945) writer, journalist and wondrous wing-threequarter for Wales and the British Lions 1966-78.

Idris Davies (1905-53) poet of Rhymney and the inter-war Depression.

Lewis Davies (b.1967) editor, publisher and writer.

Philip Davies (b.1954) Harlech-born former head teacher at Pen-y-fai, Bridgend.

Rhys Davies (1901-78) prolific Rhondda-born novelist and short story writer.

'Draig Glas', the pseudonym of Arthur Tyssilio Johnson (1873-1956) whose satire on the Welsh, *The Perfidious Welshman* (1910), gave the nation apoplexy.

David Eastwood (b.1959) professor of history at the University of Wales, Swansea 1995-2000.

Hywel Teifi Edwards (b.1934) research professor, cultural historian and literary critic.

Wil Jon Edwards (1888-1962) Aberaman coalminer, writer and Glamorgan county councillor.

George Ewart Evans (1909-88) Abercynon-born writer, Welsh Powderhall runner and pioneer oral historian.

David Farmer (b.1929) historian of Swansea's rugby and football clubs, and emeritus professor of Henley, the Management College.

Peter Finch (b.1947) poet and author of the *Real Cardiff* books.

Trevor Ford (1923-2003) forceful centre forward who scored twenty three goals in thirty eight matches for Wales between 1947 and 1957.

Raymond Garlick (b.1926) poet and critic.

Alan Hankinson (b.1926) freelance writer, journalist and mountain climber.

Rowe Harding (1901-91) played rugby for Swansea, Wales (17 caps) and the British Lions between 1923 and 28, later a Circuit Judge.

Carolyn Hitt (b.1968) journalist and broadcaster.

Carwyn James (1929-83) rugby intellectual and inspirational coach of Llanelli and the 1971 British Lions; won two caps for Wales in 1958.

Geraint H. Jenkins (b.1946) historian and director of the University of Wales Centre for Advanced Welsh and Celtic Studies in Aberystwyth.

Martin Johnes (b.1973) lecturer in history at the University of Wales Swansea.

Gareth Elwyn Jones (b.1939) historian and research professor of education at the University of Wales, Swansea.

Jack Jones (1884-1970) Merthyr-born writer who began working underground at 12; author of colourful, sprawling novels of the Welsh coalfield.

R. Merfyn Jones (b.1948) historian of the North Welsh quarrymen, Vice-Chancellor of the University of Wales, Bangor.

Sally Roberts Jones (b.1935) poet and local historian of Port Talbot.

Frank Keating (b.1937) author and *Guardian* sports columnist.

Gwyneth Lewis (b.1959) poet in English and Welsh. The first National Poet of Wales in 2002.

Tony Lewis (b.1938) cricketer, broadcaster and journalist, captain of Glamorgan in championship year 1969 and of England against India and Pakistan 1972-3.

Richard Llewellyn (1906-83) who invented himself and

much else in *How Green was my Valley*, the most famous novel ever to come out of Wales.

Arnold Lunn (1888-1974) mountaineer, Alpinist and skier. The fall in Snowdonia that he describes here permanently shortened his right leg by three inches.

Hugh McIlvanney (b.1933) the award-winning doyen of sports journalists.

Terry McLean (1913-2004) supreme among New Zealand rugby writers, knighted for his sports journalism

J. P. W. Mallalieu (1908-1980) writer, journalist and MP (Labour, Huddersfield 1945-79).

Phil Melling (b.1947) professor of American Studies at the University of Wales, Swansea, and former manager of Welsh and British Students' rugby league teams.

Rupert Moon (b.1968) Rupert St. John Henry Barker Moon played scrumhalf for Llanelli and won twenty-four Welsh caps between 1993 and 2001.

Richard Moore-Colyer (b.1945) professor of agrarian history at the University of Wales, Aberystwyth.

Cliff Morgan (b.1930) played 29 times at outside half for Wales between 1951 and 1958 and helped Cardiff and Wales beat the 1953 All Blacks; a British Lion in 1955; sports broadcaster, producer and commentator.

John Morgan (1928-88) writer and broadcaster on politics, rugby and music.

Kenneth O. Morgan (b.1934) Labour peer, historian, and former Vice Chancellor of the University of Wales, Aberystwyth.

George Owen (1552-1613) prickly squire of Henllys, north Pembrokeshire, historian, genealogist and cartographer.

Siân Nicholas (b.1964) senior lecturer in history at the University of Wales Aberystwyth.

Geoffrey Nicholson (1929-99) Swansea-born writer and sports journalist, passionate about Welsh rugby and French cycling.

Leslie Norris (1921- 2006) Merthyr poet and short story writer who from 1983 taught at Brigham Young University, Utah.

David Parry-Jones (b.1933) writer, broadcaster and rugby commentator.

Jim Perrin (b.1947) rock-climber, essayist, biographer and outdoor writer.

Sheenagh Pugh (b.1950) prize-winning poet who teaches at the University of Glamorgan.

John Reason (1927-2007) for many years the crusty but astute rugby critic of the *Daily Telegraph*.

Charles Redwood (1802-55) an attorney of Boverton near Cowbridge.

Alun Rees (b.1937) Merthyr-born poet and journalist.

Dai Rees (1913-83) professional golfer born at Font-y-gari, Rhoose. Triumphant British Ryder Cup team captain and author of five books on golf.

Alun Richards (1929-2004) Pontypridd-born novelist, short-story writer and playwright.

Huw Richards (b.1959) historian, sports writer and free-lance journalist.

Dai Smith (b.1945) cultural historian and series editor of 'The Library of Wales'.

Peter Stead (b.1943) broadcaster and historian.

Phil Steele (b.1961) schoolteacher and sports commentator.

Dylan Thomas (1914-1953) poet.
Gwyn Thomas (1913-81) writer, school teacher, broadcaster, and humorist.
J. B. G. Thomas (1917-97) chief rugby writer of the *Western Mail,* author of thirty books on what he always referred to as 'the Game'.
Leslie Thomas (b.1931) of Newport, prolific author, including the best-selling *Virgin Soldiers* novels.
John Toshack (b.1949) footballer, coach and poet, scored thirteen goals in forty international appearances for Wales.

H. M .Vaughan (1870-1948) Herbert Millingchamp Vaughan, born in Llangoedmor, Cards., the author of more than a dozen books and one of the south Wales squires he wrote about.

Alan Watkins (b.1933) born in Ammanford, political correspondent and rugby columnist.
Harri Webb (1920-94) librarian, nationalist, poet, pamphleteer and author of topical ballads and patriotic songs.
Gareth Williams (b.1945) historian and broadcaster.
Griffith Williams (d.1977) journalist.
John Stuart Williams (b.1920) poet and teacher.
Raymond Williams (1921-88) novelist and cultural critic.

Foreword by Rhodri Morgan
Rhodri Morgan is First Minister in the National Assembly for Wales, a post he has held since 2000. He was born in Cardiff in 1939 and after university at Oxford and Harvard he worked in economic development in his native city before heading up the European Community's Office in Wales from 1980 to 1987. He was the Labour Member of Parliament for Cardiff West from 1987 to 2001 and was elected as the National Assembly Member for Cardiff West in 1999. His colourful political personality has been characterised by his intellect and his passion whilst his typically Welsh passion for Sport is marked by his conviction of its deep and ongoing significance in the social and cultural life of Wales.

Edited by Gareth Williams
Gareth Williams is Professor of History and Director of the Centre for Modern and Contemporary Wales at the University of Glamorgan. He has written and broadcast extensively on the social history of sport and music, and his books include *Fields of Praise* (with Dai Smith), *1905 And All That*, *George Ewart Evans*, *Heart and Soul*, and *Valleys of Song: Music and Society in Wales 1840-1914*.

Cover photograph by Kiran Ridley
Kiran Ridley is an acclaimed young photographer whose recent work includes subjects as diverse as Cirque de Soleil in Las Vegas to blindness in migrant communities in Ethiopia. He has won a number of awards and his work has appeared worldwide in publications including *The Sunday Times Magazine*, *The Guardian*, and *The Washington Post*. He lives in Cardiff. More information on his work can be found at www.kiranridley.com

With Thanks and Acknowledgements

Parthian would like to thank all the poets, estate holders and publishers for their cooperation in the preparation of this volume. We would also like to thank the editor, Gareth Williams, for his energy and enthusiasm.

The editor and publisher are grateful for the permission to include the selected extracts in this collection.

The publisher would also like to thank Hayley Long for all her work on this publication.

Although every effort has been made to secure permissions prior to printing this has not always been possible. The publisher apologizes for any errors or omissions but if contacted will rectify these at the earliest opportunity.

Further acknowledgements

The publishers would like to thank Mick Felton for assistance in obtaining permission on selected work by Seren Books.

The publishers would like to thank Gomer Press for assistance in obtaining permission on selected work published.

The publishers would like to thank Mainstream for assistance in obtaining permission on selected work published.

All work by Dannie Abse from *New and Collected Poems*, Random House. Reprinted by permission of The Peters Fraser and Dunlop Group Limited on behalf of: Dannie Abse.

Richard Llewelyn *How Green Was My Valley*, Penguin Books, with kind permission.

Poem by Gwyneth Lewis from *Parables and Faxes* by kind permission of Bloodaxe Books

PARTHIAN Library of Wales Trinity College Carmarthen SA31 3EP
email parthianbooks@yahoo.co.uk www.parthianbooks.co.uk

LIBRARY OF WALES

The Library of Wales is a Welsh Assembly Government project designed to ensure that all of the rich and extensive literature of Wales which has been written in English will now be made available to readers in and beyond Wales. Sustaining this wider literary heritage is understood by the Welsh Assembly Government to be a key component in creating and disseminating an ongoing sense of modern Welsh culture and history for the future Wales which is now emerging from contemporary society. Through these texts, until now unavailable or out-of-print or merely forgotten, the Library of Wales will bring back into play the voices and actions of the human experience that has made us, in all our complexity, a Welsh people.

The Library of Wales will include prose as well as poetry, essays as well as fiction, anthologies as well as memoirs, drama as well as journalism. It will complement the names and texts that are already in the public domain and seek to include the best of Welsh writing in English, as well as to showcase what has been unjustly neglected. No boundaries will limit the ambition of the Library of Wales to open up the borders that have denied some of our best writers a presence in a future Wales. The Library of Wales has been created with that Wales in mind: a young country not afraid to remember what it might yet become.

Dai Smith
Raymond Williams Chair in the Cultural History of Wales,
University of Wales, Swansea

LIBRARY OF WALES
FUNDED BY

Llywodraeth Cynulliad Cymru
Welsh Assembly Government

CYNGOR LLYFRAU CYMRU
WELSH BOOKS COUNCIL

LIBRARY OF WALES

LIBRARY OF WALES

WRITING FOR THE WORLD

Dannie ABSE

Ash on a Young Man's Sleeve

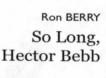

Ron BERRY

So Long, Hector Bebb

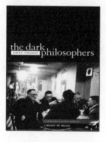

Gwyn THOMAS

The Dark Philosophers

Lewis JONES

Cwmardy & We Live

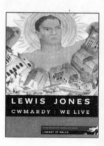

www.libraryofwales.org

Alun LEWIS
In the Green Tree

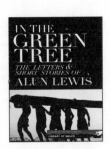

Alun RICHARDS
Home to an Empty House

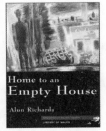

Raymond WILLIAMS
Border Country

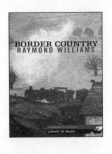

Emyr HUMPHREYS
A Man's Estate

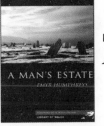

Margiad EVANS
Country Dance

enquiries@libraryofwales.org